A HELL OF A STORM

The BATTLE *for* KANSAS, *the* END *of* COMPROMISE, *and the* COMING *of the* CIVIL WAR

DAVID S. BROWN

SCRIBNER

New York London Toronto Sydney New Delhi

Scribner
An Imprint of Simon & Schuster, LLC
1230 Avenue of the Americas
New York, NY 10020

First Scribner hardcover edition September 2024

Simon & Schuster: Celebrating 100 Years of Publishing in 2024

For information about special discounts for bulk purchases,
please contact Simon & Schuster Special Sales at 1-866-506-1949 or
business@simonandschuster.com.

The Simon & Schuster Speakers Bureau can bring authors to your live event.
For more information, or to book an event, contact the Simon & Schuster Speakers Bureau at
1-866-248-3049 or visit our website at www.simonspeakers.com.

Manufactured in the United States of America

1   3   5   7   9   10   8   6   4   2

Library of Congress Cataloging-in-Publication Data

Names: Brown, David Scott, 1966– author.
Title: A hell of a storm : the battle for Kansas, the end of compromise,
and the coming of the Civil War / David S. Brown.
Other titles: Battle for Kansas, the end of compromise, and the coming of the Civil War
Description: First Scribner hardcover edition. | New York : Scribner, 2024. |
Includes bibliographical references and index.
Identifiers: LCCN 2024018458 (print) | LCCN 2024018459 (ebook) |
ISBN 9781668022818 (hardcover) | ISBN 9781668022832 (ebook)
Subjects: LCSH: United States—Politics and government—1853–1857. | United States.
Kansas-Nebraska Act. | Missouri compromise. | Antislavery movements—
United States—History—19th century. | Slavery—United States—Extension to the
territories. | Slavery—Political aspects—United States—History—19th century.
Classification: LCC E415.7 .B774 2024 (print) | LCC E415.7 (ebook) |
DDC 973.7/113—dc23/eng/20240516
LC record available at https://lccn.loc.gov/2024018458
LC ebook record available at https://lccn.loc.gov/2024018459

ISBN 978-1-6680-2281-8
ISBN 978-1-6680-2283-2 (ebook)

For My Family

We are playing for a mighty stake, if we win we carry slavery to the Pacific Ocean, if we fail we lose ... all the territories, the game must be played boldly.

Missouri senator David Rice Atchison, 1855

Contents

A HELL OF A STORM

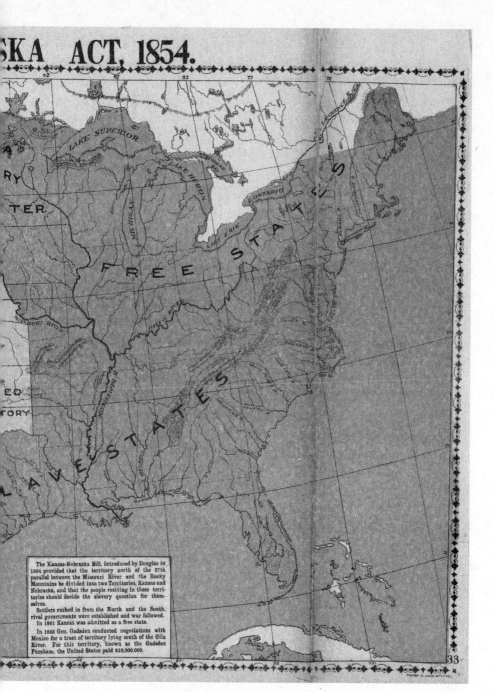

The United States in 1854—the free and slave states are about to engage in a fierce struggle for control of those western territories acquired over the previous half century, by both treaty and war, from France and Mexico.

Introduction:
Right from Wrong

It is wrong . . . letting slavery into Kansas and Nebraska.
Abraham Lincoln, 1854

Among historians, a handful of critical dates are said to convey much of the American experience. In 1800, a little more than a decade after the Constitutional Convention, a southern-seeded Jeffersonianism came to power emphasizing the virtues of planters and plain folk, slavery and states' rights. Parent to an ebbing agrarian order, this once formidable coalition cracked in 1860 as Lincoln's election anticipated the coming crisis of secession and civil war that brought a budding northern industrial regime to the fore. Its congressional protectors, who would be praised in friendly Gilded Age newspapers as the "Grand Old Party," ruled over a growing republic compromised by casual political corruption, coercive labor practices, and enormous concentrations of top-end wealth. In time these mounting ills earned the enmity of reform-minded populists and progressives who challenged its legitimacy, only to see, in the 1896 election of William McKinley, robber baron rule sink into the next century. This long run of capitalist mastery is said to have crashed in 1932 with the coming of a Franklin Roosevelt–led New Deal dedicated, in a flurry of Depression-era legislation, to building a European-style social welfare state. But then came 1968. Cultural upheaval, a widening racial divide, and an unpopular war in Vietnam upended the new liberalism and gave way, finally, to a new conservatism, emblematized in the 1980 rise of Ronald Reagan.

This lengthening bridge of landmark years offers a summarizing if

1

obviously incomplete account of the nation's tumultuous political past. What it offers in concision it surely lacks in precision. A generational approach does have the virtue, however, of helping us to broadly conceptualize distinctions in demography, economic development, sectionalism, and so on. Lincoln's northern-oriented, factory-based, and Republican Party–powered America *was* different from Jefferson's southern-oriented, plantation-based, and Democratic Party–powered America. And, when thinking over the period in which that transition transpired, it seems clear that 1854, even without the prod of a presidential election, proved to be both crux and constellation, a pivotal year of decision that led to immense and enduring change.

This had everything to do with the explosive Kansas-Nebraska Act, almost certainly the most lethal piece of legislation to ever clear Congress. Introduced on Capitol Hill the first week in January, it served as an unintended lightning rod for northern discontent, putting the nation irreparably on the road to civil war. The act opened the way for planters to bring their enslaved peoples to a vast tract extending from the Mississippi River to the Rocky Mountains. This area constituted the core of Jefferson's old Louisiana Purchase (1803) and had been formerly reserved for free labor by the Missouri Compromise (1820). The bill's patron, the squat, broad-shouldered, and shaggy-browed Illinois senator Stephen A. Douglas, a talented if recklessly ambitious politician possessed of a face, one journalist wrote, "clearly expressive of much boldness and power of will," considered himself a champion of national development. As chairman of the upper chamber's Committee on Territories, he anticipated opening these lands to promote the construction of a transcontinental railroad—a nonstarter, he knew, without the sanction of southern support. Though confident that he could manage this dangerous sectional dispute, Douglas appreciated that concerned Yankee constituencies were likely to protest the revered Compromise's sudden repeal—"it will raise a hell of a storm," he had observed at the time. And so it did.[1]

Over the years, historians have recognized the importance of 1854. In his popular eight-volume opus *Ordeal of the Union* (1947–1971), Allan Nevins described the demise of the Missouri pact as "a great catalytic agent" that had "crystalliz[ed] the nation's parties into new forms." James M. McPherson later speculated in his Pulitzer Prize–winning *Battle Cry of Freedom* (1988) that "the Kansas-Nebraska Act . . . may have been the most important single event pushing the nation toward civil war." And more recently, in 2009, noted Lincoln scholar Allen C. Guelzo stated with even greater gravitas: "The Kansas-Nebraska Act of 1854 enjoys the dubious honor of being the only . . . legislation that caused a civil war."[2]

Despite these and other like-minded assertions, there remains a broader tendency to attach the act, without emphasis, to a carefully curated inventory of provocations that led to the collapse of sectional compromise. Time-crunching textbooks in particular have long marched students through a master list of motives. These serial incitements include the Compromise of 1850, "Bleeding Kansas" (1854–1859), the *Dred Scott* decision (1857), the John Brown–led assault on a federal arsenal at Harpers Ferry, Virginia (1859), and Lincoln's crucial 1860 election to the presidency.

On reflection, however, none of these usual suspects seems as essential, as elemental, to the Union's splintering as the opening of free soil to slavery. Much of the country accepted, rather, the Compromise of 1850, which, among other provisions, recognized California's free-state status, outlawed the slave trade in Washington, D.C., and strengthened an existing fugitive slave act by mandating Yankee aid in the return of northern-quartered runaways. Though each of these articles antagonized select constituencies, most Americans seemed eager to set their sectional quarrel aside. Accordingly, both the Democratic and Whig parties endorsed the Compromise in their respective platforms leading up to the 1852 presidential election. The former condemned agitation over slavery as the "efforts of . . . abolitionists . . . [designed] to lead to the most alarming and dangerous consequences," while the latter declared the compact "a final settlement, in principle and in substance." Angling for northern ballots, the Democrats, in a divided Baltimore convention, nominated former New Hampshire senator Franklin—Handsome Frank—Pierce, an unheralded dark horse whose shocked wife, Jane, detesting Washington, fainted at the disagreeable news. Affable if saddled in a grief-attended battle with the bottle (none of his three children lived beyond the age of eleven), Pierce proved satisfactory to southerners for his favorable opinion of the Compromise, which he regarded as a guarantee "that no sectional or fanatical excitement may again threaten the durability of our institutions."[3] Come November he captured the presidency in an Electoral College landslide, defeating the doughty old General Winfield Scott, a Mexican-American War hero born in the 1780s, 254 to 42, and taking twenty-seven of the thirty-one states. Democrats correspondingly increased their majority in the House of Representatives that autumn while retaining control of the Senate.

The saga of "Bleeding Kansas," by contrast, stressed clash over consensus. This mini–civil war on the prairie between pro- and antislavery settlers could hardly have happened, of course, without the enabling legislation in 1854 that first opened the Kansas Territory—and quite possibly neither could Brown's legendary raid. Endeavoring to arm runaway slaves and pursue a violent emancipation down the Appalachians' piney emerald spine, Brown, an elaborately bewhiskered abolitionist warrior in the mold of an Old Testament prophet, had cut his teeth in Kansas.[4] There he engaged in the notorious Pottawatomie Creek massacre, leading a small band on a nighttime raiding party during which these men murdered five ill-starred homesteaders of proslavery persuasion—afterward washing their bloody swords clean in a nearby creek. This studied slaughter, itself a retaliatory raid in recompense for a southern assault on nearby Lawrence, anticipated a series of skirmishes over the next few months in which dozens were killed.

The landmark *Dred Scott* decision, handed down by the Supreme Court in March 1857 and declaring, among other provisions, the Missouri Compromise unconstitutional, might also be read as a reaction to the Kansas-Nebraska Act. In effect the court put a judicial stamp of approval on what Douglas's bill had already accomplished—protecting the property rights of slave owners. Relatedly, its architect, Chief Justice Roger B. Taney of Maryland, seemed particularly if not desperately eager to shut the door on free-soil sloganeering by upholding the plantocracy's place in the western territories. Taney's "growing extremism in the late 1850s," so one scholar notes of this dominant figure on the antebellum bench, was whipped up by "the rise of the Republicans," who continued to proclaim the sanctity of antislavery sentiment in the territories, and "whom he regarded as dangerous fanatics."[5] The Republican Party formed in 1854 to battle Douglas on the very question of slavery's extension.

Finally, Lincoln's path to the presidency also owed something to the Missouri Compromise's repeal, a point the lanky Rail Splitter made public on several occasions. A former one-term Illinois Whig congressman, now five years out of politics and practicing law in the small capital city of Springfield, Lincoln, like many northerners, was astonished when Douglas's bill became law. "I particularly object to the NEW position which the avowed principle of this Nebraska law gives to slavery in the body politic," he said in a speech. "I object to it because it assumes that there CAN be MORAL RIGHT in the enslaving of one man by another." Eager to enter the fight, he hoped to return to Washington, preferably as a U.S. senator; his moral sense having been stirred by the planters' demand to bring their bondsmen and -women west.[6]

If the struggle over the common territories constituted the turning point in Lincoln's political career, it signified further the coming destruction of an older partisan order predicated on a series of imperfect sectional compromises. Only the unforeseen demise of that once sacred system threatened to raise the subject of slavery's insertion in the West to a boiling point. And this is precisely what the Kansas-Nebraska Act carelessly accomplished. Within months of its proposal a "radical" Republican Party emerged, the conservative Whig coalition (winners of two presidential contests) went into a steep swoon from which it never recovered, and the northern wing of the Democratic Party suffered severe electoral losses for its too-blind backing of Douglas. The act more generally operated as a consciousness-raising occasion in the North while southerners, seeing the soured Yankee reaction, began to dig deeper into their own sense of honor, equity, and states' rights. In turn, a cancerous and increasingly sectionalized war of words now made prey upon an ailing body politic. And everything that emanated after, culminating in the unprecedented December 1860 secession ordinance enacted by South Carolina, the first of eleven states to leave the Union, owed something small or large to the decisions made on slavery and territorial development during the fateful Kansas-Nebraska debates—a season of well-poisoning proceedings that produced the greatest miscalculation in American political history.

In 1854 some 26 million people lived in the United States, more than 3 million of whom were enslaved. Most Americans resided above the Mason-Dixon Line; nearly one-third of all inhabitants were New Yorkers, Pennsylvanians, and Ohioans. Of the ten cities with populations exceeding fifty thousand, only two, Baltimore and New Orleans, were southern. A majority in both sections lived on farms, a condition of subsistence they tended to equate, beyond its obvious utilitarian purposes, with independence and personal freedom. Rather than accepting merely being hirelings, they aspired to ownership. "Dependence begets subservience and venality," Jefferson had argued, "while we have land to labour then, let us never wish to see our citizens occupied at a work-bench."[7]

While both Congress and the country skirmished over the Kansas-Nebraska bill, the Boston Public Library opened in a former schoolhouse on Mason Street with a circulation of sixteen thousand volumes; the United States Naval Academy in Annapolis, Maryland, graduated six midshipmen in its inaugural class; and the Kanagawa Treaty between the United States and the Tokugawa shogunate ended Japan's two-century policy of national seclusion. American births that year included the military march master John Philip Sousa, author of "The Stars and Stripes Forever"; George Eastman, founder of the Eastman Kodak Company, whose "roll film" made the motion picture industry possible; and Jennie Jerome, a Brooklyn-born socialite said by one admirer to possess the sable, lithe beauty of a panther, and later known to the world as Lady Randolph, the mother of future British prime minister Winston Churchill, who called her "a fairy princess [whom] . . . I loved . . . dearly—but at a distance."[8]

In the American political arena, a spate of recent deaths foretold the eclipse of a once formidable congressional generation. Between the War of 1812 and midcentury, three statesmen from three sections dominated the country's partisan affairs. Combined, these prominent politicians—Kentucky's slim-limbed Henry Clay, a nationalist known affectionately as "Harry of the West"; Daniel Webster, a powerful (if sometimes alcohol-fueled) orator and unapologetic elitist representing greater Boston's interests; and South Carolina's John Calhoun, the "cast-iron man" whose tenacious defense of states' rights made him the champion of the white South—were widely regarded as the Founding Fathers' successors; some called them "the Great Triumvirate."[9] During their many years in power a number of sectional disputes threatened to upend the expanding Union. These included the oft-embittered deliberations that led to the Missouri Compromise, the nullification crisis of the early 1830s in which the right of states to annul federal law was vigorously debated, and the more recent struggle over slavery's status in territory taken by the United States following the Mexican-American War (1846–1848).

Clay, a westerner who had bid in 1824 to become the first president to hail from beyond the Appalachian Mountains, orbited outside the expectations of northern and southern constituencies and seemed particularly adept at diffusing sectional tensions, winning the warm sobriquet "The Great Compromiser." But he, along with Webster and Calhoun, was mortal after all—and all died between 1850 and 1852. Though lauded for their leadership and sainted in smooth marble statuary, they nevertheless left their political heirs a crushingly difficult situation. In the shadow of a rising Trans-Mississippi West, the time for regional resolutions had wound down; the dispute over slavery's place in the nation's territories neared an inevitable dilemma. A prepresidential Lincoln, finding his footing in a post-triumvirate politics, encapsulated this crisis as clearly as anyone when declaring, paraphrasing the Gospel of Matthew, "A house divided against itself cannot stand. I believe this government cannot endure, permanently half *slave* and half *free*. . . . It will become *all* one thing, or *all* the other."[10]

How this ancestral tug-of-war began to turn decisively toward freedom during the Kansas-Nebraska brawl is the subject of this book. It explores the personalities and the politics, the writings, elections, and ideas, that upended an older America and began to make space for its successor. In 1854 *Uncle Tom's Cabin* author Harriet Beecher Stowe attacked slavery's expansion across the frontier via lectures, letters, and a mass petition campaign, while a sublime Henry David Thoreau published the iconic *Walden*, a deeply felt meditation on the nation's imperfect path to transcendence, independence, and equality. It is the year southern statesmen endeavored to enlarge the boundaries of their cotton sovereignty by purchasing Cuba from Spain, even as the baby-faced Tennessee adventurer William Walker led a ragtag army into the Mexican territory of Baja California, where he audaciously declared slavery legal.

In 1854 a furious Boston convulsed under martial law as thousands of angry protesters faced thousands of armed state and federal troops charged with returning the fugitive Anthony Burns, an enslaved man escaped from Virginia, to servitude; amidst this turmoil, settlers in both sections of the country raced to the newly opened Kansas Territory, setting into motion a violent, protracted confrontation between defenders of free and chattel labor. At a Fourth of July celebration that year the radical abolitionist William Lloyd Garrison, equipped, so one observer insisted, with the brazen "loquacity of a blue-jay," created a stir by burning a copy of the U.S. Constitution, while all through a pulsing summer

scores of "anti-Nebraska" organizations began to form, thus commencing the remarkable process by which the Republican Party would come
to control within a few election cycles the national government.[11]

The incredible year closed at length in a cadence of premonitory
episodes, including Lincoln's autumn campaign-circuit emergence as a
coming political force, the stunning November elections that reduced
the power of the traditional parties, and Harriet Tubman's dramatic
Christmas Day rescue of her three brothers Ben, Henry, and Robert
from enslavement in Maryland's remote Eastern Shore. This last act
illustrated acutely the striking incongruities of a nation unable to remain
much longer in the paralytic practice of "half *slave* and half *free.*"

A ripening awareness of sectional identity informed all these coalescing events. Beyond upending the conventional partisan approach,
the Kansas-Nebraska Act profoundly affected the way that both northerners and southerners saw themselves—and each other. Among an
increasing number of Yankees, the thorny notion arose that a caucus of
planters presumed, by threat or fraud, to reserve the common territories
for their own use. "Where," the Boston-based *Atlantic Monthly* asked,
"Will It End?" Henry Wilson, a Massachusetts Republican and later vice
president in the second Grant administration, argued in a memoir that
"the determined purpose of the Slave Power to make slavery the pre-
dominating national interest was never more clearly revealed than by
the proposed repeal of the Missouri Compromise." After a generation of
concessions, he continued, a deeply shaken North at last refused to allow
the South to have its way: "When . . . Congress had been dragooned
into the adoption of the Kansas-Nebraska Act . . . it was supposed . . .
that it was only a question of time when Kansas should become a slave
State. . . . But [the bill's champions] miscalculated. They did not fully
comprehend the forces which freedom had at command, nor the purposes of Providence concerning the nation."[12]

Southerners construed the territorial crisis much differently, of
course, emphasizing the increasing unwillingness of northerners to
respect the planters' property rights. The *Vicksburg Daily Whig*, for one,
touched upon this familiar refrain when denouncing "The Imperial
North."[13] In writing his own history of these difficult years, former Confederate president Jefferson Davis dismissed a host of so-called causes
of secession before identifying the enigma of expansion, typified in
Kansas-Nebraska, as the true root:

It was not the circulation of incendiary [abolitionist] documents, it was not the raid of John Brown, it was not the operation of unjust and unequal tariff laws, not all combined, that constituted the intolerable grievance, but it was the systematic and persistent struggle to deprive the Southern States of equality in the Union—generally to discriminate in legislation against the interest of their people, culminating in their exclusion from the Territories.[14]

As European nations engaged in a scramble for Africa and Asia, while Britain contested with Russia more narrowly in a Great Game over the Emirate of Afghanistan, so the nineteenth-century United States proposed its own unfurling empire. But far from increasing the country's strength, the western lands coveted by both Wilson and Davis proved to be implacable sources of sectional discord.

This friction began to take on an uncontrollable momentum in the battle for Kansas, whose Appomattox aftermath marked the end of an antique world long the province of Founding Fathers, southern sway, and rickety compromises carried on the tightening back of black bondage. A crowd of mounting and often-clashing concerns, rather—over the deviltry of enslavement, the future of the territories, and the role of states' rights in a people's republic—challenged the existing system until its receding center could no longer hold. With the dismantling of the Missouri Compromise came a great whirlwind from the North, a burst of fear and mistrust, urgency and outcry. The contested frontier filled with Bibles and guns, the nation's congressional conciliation culture came to an end, while new politics and politicians emerged to take its place. Born in an unprecedented era of war and reconstruction, this ringing coda to the antebellum questions of race and regionalism owed much to Douglas's dangerous overreach—a provocation beyond the point of compromise.

The opening chapter of this improbable story starts in a still earlier century. And to trace its recursive roots is to revisit the world and world view of the Founders. These revolutionaries and merchants, planters and politicians occasioned a constitution by turns sound and sage, if nonetheless qualified and constrained by its relationship to human enslavement, which shadowed unsteadily the republic since its inception. This original sin is where we must begin.

Part I

PATHS TO PERDITION

This 1852 print celebrates legislative efforts to preserve the Union by the "Great Triumvirate" of compromise-minded senators John C. Calhoun, Daniel Webster—their hands on the U.S. Constitution—and Henry Clay, sitting beside them in black cloak with walking stick.

1

Original Sin

How is it that we hear the loudest yelps for liberty among the drivers of negroes?

Samuel Johnson, 1775

A thick folio of imperfect agreements, concessions, and codicils antic-ipated the impasse of 1854. The first and most significant of these, the U.S. Constitution, produced a union that, under the latent strains of sec-tionalism, ruptured within three generations. Naturally those caught in the attending collapse wanted to know what had happened. And so, in his eloquent second inaugural address, delivered on a damp and blus-tery March day in 1865 before a mud-speckled crowd of perhaps thirty-five thousand, a gaunt Lincoln, his worn and leathery face deeply lined in an attitude of exhaustion, reflected on the "progress of our arms" before reviewing briefly the reason why such weaponry, so liberally employed, was now moving swiftly under Sherman's command through the prostrate Carolinas and threatening, in the form of Grant's massive Army of the Potomac, to encircle Richmond. He came quickly to the heart of the matter: "One eighth of the whole population were colored slaves, not distributed generally over the Union, but localized in the Southern part of it." These enslaved, he continued, "constituted a pecu-liar and powerful interest. All knew that this interest was, somehow, the cause of the war."[1]

"This interest" predated the Constitution, of course, though the Founders codified in that document the legal principles upon which

13

slavery soon moved beyond its coastal enclaves, penetrated deep into the interior, and eventually attained, under the auspices of a secession-minded planter elite, a fresh destiny, a different ruling regime.

The circumstances that set into motion this pernicious scenario commenced in the late 1780s when a group of nationalists sought to replace the existing form of government, the problematic Articles of Confederation. Put in place during the Revolution by the Second Continental Congress, the Articles reflected patriot concerns of centralized power as read and remembered through the lens of British imperial tyranny. Accordingly, the new government, locked in a reflexive tendency toward state sovereignty, lacked the ability to regulate commerce or to levy and collect taxes. Some of the states, jealously protective of their privileges, fashioned their own navies, bickered over boundaries, and passed tariff laws aimed at other states. One young Founder, Alexander Hamilton, saw early on the need to conceive a more workable framework of federal influence. Born on the Caribbean Island of Nevis, a student at King's College (now Columbia University), and George Washington's precocious chief staff aide during much of the War of Independence, Hamilton possessed an unusual array of experiences. Ambitious, capable, and commanding, he drew the attention of men and women alike. He enjoyed flirtations, was well-mannered (if headstrong) and keen to dance; blue-eyed with auburn hair and rose-tinted cheeks, he exuded a conspicuously healthy, courtly air. Some years after his notorious death in an early morning duel with Aaron Burr, the nation's nimble-triggered vice president, Hamilton received from Massachusetts congressman Fisher Ames a smitten-like tribute worthy of a Grecian god:

> His whole person evinced the utmost symmetry and harmony. . . . His habitual walk was erect and dignified; he was full chested, and his limbs exhibited the most perfect model of beauty. . . . General Hamilton's eyes . . . were of a deep azure, eminently beautiful, without the slightest trace of hardness or severity, and beamed with higher expressions of intelligence and discernment than any others that I ever saw oscillate in the "human face divine."[2]

Coming of age with the fledgling republic, the divine Hamilton determined to see the new Union prevail, prosper, and grow. This required, so he supposed, a sharp reduction in states' rights and the gravitation of influence to a more robust ruling center.

In the late summer of 1780, a bit more than a year before the British defeat at Yorktown ended the military phase of the American Revolution, Hamilton confided to James Duane, a New York patriot, attorney, and fellow nationalist, of his growing disenchantment with the Articles of Confederation. "The fundamental defect," he insisted, "is a want of power in Congress." States, he contended, enjoyed "an excess of the spirit of liberty," while Congress suffered from "a want of sufficient means . . . to answer the public exigencies and of vigor to draw forth those means." Condemning the "confederation itself" as "defective" and "neither fit for war, nor peace," he feared the "idea of an uncontrollable sovereignty in each state," emboldened during the long struggle for independence, "will defeat the other powers given to Congress, and make our union feeble and precarious."[3]

Over the next few years, the Confederation government and its litter of typically forgettable presidents—John Hanson, Elias Boudinot, Cyrus Griffin, et al.—seemed intent on proving Hamilton correct. In early 1783 a cohort of Continental Army soldiers and officers, encamped at Newburgh, New York, mulled over the not-so-small matter of a military coup designed to secure their much-in-arrears pay and promised pensions. "Dangerous combinations in the army," so one Virginia congressman noted at the time, were engaged in "sinister practices." Learning of the proposed conspiracy—"a convulsion of the most dreadful nature and consequence"—a concerned Washington, his own wages long overdue, condemned the scheme in a private meeting with his officers at Newburgh. Standing before them, he attempted to read a letter of reassurance from a member of the Confederation government but suddenly appeared confused and was momentarily unable to proceed. "Gentlemen," he slowly said, "you will permit me to put on my spectacles, for I have not only grown gray but almost blind in the service of my country." Very few had ever seen the aging general in his eyeglasses—demigods being protective of their imperfections. The room grew quiet as the officers, younger men, some now weeping, shrank before the unexpected sight of their commander's sacrifice.[4]

Three years later a self-proclaimed Country Party in Rhode Island, consisting of heavily taxed farmers at odds with the state's ruling regime of urban creditors, managed to come to power and passed a legal tender law allowing for the printing of fantastic sums of paper money that, in aiding defaulters and thus punishing lenders, smacked of class warfare. Not many months after this startling exercise in monetary populism, an armed uprising in western Massachusetts, "Shays's Rebellion" (yet another debt and tax crisis), pitted antigovernment protesters, some of whom had lost land and homes, against Boston's governing elite in a bloody contest that rocked the Bay State and rippled through the rest of the country. Facing forty-four hundred militiamen, some privately funded by frightened merchants and nearly all from the eastern counties of Massachusetts, the Shaysites, more than a few bearing pitchforks and clubs, were easily outgunned. Dozens of them were killed or wounded at the Battle of Springfield in January 1787. Following this rout, the rebellion, led by Daniel Shays, a decorated Revolutionary War veteran presented years earlier with an ornamental sword by the celebrated French military officer the Marquis de Lafayette for distinguished service (having fought at the battles of Bunker Hill, Lexington, and Saratoga), quickly collapsed.

Watching Massachusetts go to war with itself, an anxious James Madison, then serving as a delegate to the Confederation Congress in New York, wrote to a Virginia colleague: "I am sorry to inform you, that it is the belief of people here well informed that this insurrection threatens the most serious consequences." A few months later the compactly assembled Madison, standing barely five feet, four inches and weighing scarcely one hundred pounds, pointedly warned: "Without such a power to suppress insurrections, our liberties might be destroyed by domestic faction."[5]

Amidst these sharpening concerns of internal upheaval, yet another crucial issue confronted the country—slavery. Formerly extant in all the colonies, the institution began during the Revolutionary era to slowly die out in the North, where its numbers were historically smaller than in the staple-crop South. Following a series of legal cases before its Supreme Judicial Court, Massachusetts ended the practice of bondage in 1783, while most of its New England neighbors advanced some form of gradual manumission. The last northern state to abolish slavery, New Jersey, enacted legislation freeing all children of slaves born after July 4, 1804—though these offspring were legally bound to apprenticeships until the ages of twenty-five for males and twenty-one for females. This striking spectacle caused a number of prominent politicians to take note—and hope. Thomas Jefferson, himself the master of Monticello, opined that "the spirit of the master is abating, that of the slave rising from the dust, his condition mollifying, the way . . . preparing, under the auspices of heaven, for a total emancipation." In a similar vein, the New York Founding Father John Jay, soon to serve as first chief justice of the United States Supreme Court, detected a growing readiness among his countrymen to question their formerly reflexive commitment to black bondage, telling members of an English abolition society, "Prior to the late revolution, the great majority, or rather the great body, of our people had been so long accustomed to the practice and convenience of having slaves, that very few among them even doubted the propriety and rectitude of it."[6] But now, Jay suggested, such uncertainties were decidedly in circulation; and this awareness ensured that when the Constitution makers met in Philadelphia in the summer of 1787 the solidly sectional nature of slavery would play a role in shaping their debates.

Madison understood this delicate point quite clearly. In one speech at the convention, he candidly observed "that the States were divided into different interests not by their difference of size, but by other circumstances; the most material of which resulted partly from climate, but principally from their having or not having slaves. These two causes concurred in forming the great division of interests in the U. States. It did not lie between the large & small States: it lay between the Northern & Southern."[7] Another Virginian, George Mason, a planter, politician, and much respected legal mind, no doubt shocked a few of his Dixie brethren when he explicitly condemned slavery in perhaps the convention's most stirring speech. Though blaming Britain for first organizing the North American slave trade and then later averting efforts on the part of some colonies to prohibit this malefic trafficking in Africans, his most telling volleys were aimed at his own people: "Every master of slaves is born a petty tyrant. They bring the judgment of heaven upon a country. As nations cannot be rewarded or punished in the next world they must be in this." He then counseled the convention to create a constitution wholly in favor of free labor—"I hold it essential to every point of view that the General Government have power to prevent the increase of slavery."[8]

Mason further criticized South Carolina and Georgia's tenacious attachment to the slave trade, which, he insisted, both impeded white migration into the Lower South and raised the unwelcome specter of slavery's expansion into those western territories—extending to the Mississippi River—recently won from Britain and recognized in the Treaty of Paris (1783). Though owner of more Fairfax County slaves than anyone not named George Washington, Mason spoke in the liberalizing accent of the American Enlightenment. Other and equally interested voices, however, demanded their say at the Philadelphia convention on this critical issue.

One of these men, South Carolina's Edward Rutledge, the youngest signatory of the Declaration of Independence (a precocious twenty-six), strongly cautioned the Lower South to avoid entering any new framework of government that failed to explicitly protect the plantocracy's interests. On the tetchy question of keeping the slave trade open, he drew a deep and indelible line in the sand: "If the Convention thinks that N. C., S. C. & Georgia will ever agree to the plan, unless their right to import slaves be untouched, the expectation is vain. The people of those States will never be such fools as to give up so important an interest." Rutledge's South Carolina colleague and fellow convention delegate, the Oxford-educated Charles Cotesworth Pinckney, legatee of an aristocratic planter family in Charleston, took an equally assertive stance, insisting, in comments made during the Philadelphia debates, that enslaved labor proved altogether reasonable, humane, and historically defensible. "Slavery . . . is justified by the example of all the world," he confidently claimed, before citing by way of illustration servantry in Greece, Rome, and "other antient States" as well as in England, France, and "other modern States." Cutting to the quick, he observed that, regarding the Atlantic slave trade, "an attempt to take away the right . . . will produce serious objections to the Constitution" that, so Pinckney noted, he otherwise "wished to see adopted."[9]

In a perfectly uneven contest pitting property-rights individualism against Enlightenment liberalism, the former won a decisive victory in Philadelphia. Abolitionist sentiment, only beginning to become a reckoning force in the culture, simply lacked the support at this early date to put slavery on the path to extinction. Still, the distinction between these two positions in the late 1780s anticipated the difficulty in soldering the two sections together. "If we cannot connect with the southern states without giving countenance to blood and carnage, and all kinds of fraud and injustice," so one western Massachusetts man summarized the prospect of uniting with a congeries of planters, "I say let them go."[10]

Though unable to prescribe the peculiar institution's future in the former colonies, slavery's critics looked upon the fate of yet another American region, the emerging West, with far more optimism. While delegates hashed out the Constitution in the Pennsylvania State House (Independence Hall), the Congress of the Confederation, meeting at 26 Wall Street in Lower Manhattan's Federal Hall, correspondingly discussed the future of the rolling lands beyond the Appalachian Mountains—an immensity girdled to the north by the green Great Lakes and corralled to the south by the Ohio River's muddy banks. Ceded by Britain following the American Revolution, the territory quickly attracted white settlement. In July 1787 Congress nearly unanimously adopted the Northwest Ordinance, which, among its several provisions (Article 6), banned slavery "in the said territory." Of vast consequence, this compact yielded, between 1803 and 1848, five free states—Ohio, Michigan, Indiana, Illinois, and Wisconsin. Though more generally, and not without reason, criticized by nationalists like Hamilton and Madison for its lack of power, the Articles, soon to be replaced by a fresh framework of government, implemented in the Ordinance one of the most significant and farsighted acts in the nation's history.

But if slavery was shut out of the Northwest, it had nevertheless begun to extend the perimeter of its southern stronghold. Some seven hundred thousand men, women, and children were captive laborers in the United States in 1787; all of them, except forty thousand, resided below the Mason-Dixon Line.[11] Considering these stark statistics, the Founders obviously faced a difficult challenge. How to consolidate the interests of sections moving spatially, culturally, and economically in different directions? How to address the contradictions of rural agrarianism and a budding urban commercialism? And how, finally, to accommodate the concerns of white southerners for the security of their human property?

On this last point, the Constitution went some great way. In particular, three major items inserted into the document gave southerners enough satisfaction to join the Union. These were the three-fifths clause (counting each enslaved person as three-fifths of a human for purposes of taxation and representation, and thus increasing southern power in both the House of Representatives and the Electoral College), the fugitive slave provision (permitting masters to pursue their runaways in the free states), and keeping the slave trade open for at least twenty more years before Congress could take up the question of its closure. During these decades (1788–1808), Georgia and South Carolina, clearly watching the clock, imported more abducted Africans than in any previous twenty-year period. Without these concessions to white southern sensibilities, the Constitution would never have been ratified.

On the indelicate subject of the slave trade, however, even the South divided. Luther Martin, Maryland's long-standing attorney general, observed that the practice detrimentally affected all the states as the ever-present threat of rebellion, much heightened by the tremorous memory of the twenty thousand black fugitives who had so recently supported Britain during the American Revolution, constituted a national danger. "Slaves weakened one part of the Union," he declared at the Philadelphia convention, "which the other parts were bound to protect: the privilege of importing them was therefore unreasonable." He believed still more generally, so he told his fellow delegates, that creating a republic premised in part on unfree labor "was inconsistent with the principles of the revolution and dishonorable to the American character."[12]

Virginia also hesitated over the provision to keep the slave trade operating for an additional generation. Mason echoed Martin's security concerns, noting that "such importation render[ed] the United States weaker, more vulnerable, and less capable of defence." Possessing by far the largest number of slaves in the country—about 285,000 with South Carolina a faint second at 105,000—the Old Dominion had for years attempted, via prohibitive taxes, to limit shipments of Africans from entering its borders, only, while still in the Empire, to run into Crown opposition. The Revolutionary era's ensuing nonimportation policy against British goods (including those coming from the Royal African Company) allowed Virginia, among other former colonies, to ban the slave trade—only to see it reopened at the postwar behest of both Georgia and South Carolina. Madison, reflecting the concerns of his state, was sorry to see the unwanted question come up. To little effect, he called the trade "dishonorable" and feared it would "produce . . . mischief" in America's new Union.[13]

Delegates from the Deep South disagreed. For several years, planters below the Chesapeake regarded with suspicion efforts by distant Old Dominion statesmen to limit the Atlantic slave trade. In 1784 Jefferson,

for one, had called upon the Continental Congress to pursue its prohibition, to no effect. Now, at the Philadelphia convention, South Carolina's Pinckney argued that the men pushing policy in Richmond merely
wished to line their pockets by increasing through a general scarcity the
value of their bondspeople. "Virginia," he contended, "will gain by stopping the importations. Her slaves will rise in value, & she has more than
she wants. It would be unequal to require S. C. & Georgia to confederate
on such unequal terms."[14]

Like many of the Virginians, Pinckney's views on this subject were
grounded primarily in economic assumptions. During the late military stages of the Revolution, the Lower South and especially South
Carolina experienced astonishingly destructive warfare. In possession
of both Charleston and Savannah, British armies, under such officers
as the notoriously predacious Lieutenant Colonel Banastre Tarleton,
accused of overseeing a massacre in the Waxhaws region of the Carolina
upcountry, marauded repeatedly in the Deep South. Historian Walter
Edgar writes of the general butchery involved:

> As they set about securing what they now considered a conquered
> province, the British and their loyalist allies committed numerous
> atrocities. They took hostages . . . they unlawfully confined civilians;
> they destroyed and willfully damaged institutions dedicated to reli-
> gion; they plundered public and private property. And, against a civil-
> ian population, they committed torture, imprisonment, murder, and
> "other inhumane acts." If these actions had been committed in the
> 1990s instead of the 1780s, [British commander] Lord Cornwallis
> and a number of his subordinates . . . would have been [indicted] by
> the International Tribunal at the Hague as war criminals.[15]

Accounting for the carnage left by the war in the Carolinas, including the loss of thousands of runaway slaves, Pinckney and other concerned men from the region regarded the continuance of the African
trade for another twenty years a crucial factor in their future prosperity.
They would not give it up. Shortly after the convention dispersed, with
the trade's extension safely inserted in the Constitution, Madison wrote
to Jefferson in some frustration: "S. Carolina & Georgia were inflexible
on the point of the slaves."[16]

That winter of 1788, while engaged with Hamilton and John Jay in drafting *The Federalist Papers*, a collection of several dozen articles promoting the Constitution's ratification, Madison offered a more public regret regarding the deadly trade's persistence. He contended in *Federalist* No. 42, published in the *New York Packet* in late January: "It were doubtless to be wished that the power of prohibiting the importation of slaves had not been postponed until the year 1808." Having made this rhetorical concession, he then directed his Knickerbocker audience to consider the Constitution an overall improvement on the importation question: "It ought to be considered as a great point gained in favor of humanity that a period of twenty years may terminate forever, within these States, a traffic which has so long and so loudly upbraided the barbarism of modern policy."[17]

Though controversial, the slave-trade settlement produced a definite dénouement—in 1807 Congress voted 113 to 5 to end the commerce. The two other critical slave-related items imbedded in the Constitution, the three-fifths and fugitive slave clauses, by contrast, reached even deeper into the century; these fixed articles of planter rule were overcome only by civil war. The question of how to count the enslaved arose invariably in the nation's infancy. During congressional debates in 1776 a proposal to raise funds specified that revenue "shall be supplied by the several colonies in proportion to the number of inhabitants of every age, sex, and quality, except Indians not paying taxes." This would have meant taxing slaves. Speaking against the plan, Maryland's Samuel Chase inelegantly insisted "that Negroes in fact should not be considered as members of the state more than cattle & that they have no more interest in it."[18] The idea of a three-fifths ratio originated in 1783 during fresh discussions on determining wealth in the new republic. Land values, rather than population, dictated the apportionment of taxes, but states habitually undervalued their land to lessen their outlays. Most states supported the notion of fractionally counting enslaved people, though the Articles of Confederation required unanimous agreement and both New Hampshire and New York, for reasons unrelated to the apportionment formula, were opposed. The need for reforming the country's policy of taxation—and by connection representation—remained, however, and surfaced again during the constitutional debates.

During these deliberations, South Carolina delegate Pierce Butler reasoned with his colleagues for what he called "equal representation." Madison made note of his speech:

Mr. Butler insisted that the labour of a slave in S. Carola. was as productive & valuable as that of a freeman in Massts., that as wealth was the great means of defence and utility to the Nation they are equally valuable to it with freemen; and that consequently an equal representation ought to be allowed for them in a Government which was instituted principally for the protection of property, and was itself to be supported by property.[19]

Others remained unpersuaded. Massachusetts delegate and future vice president Elbridge Gerry, born into a wealthy Marblehead merchant family, thought "property not the rule of representation." Evoking Chase's old argument for different ends, he denounced the notion that "black . . . property in the South" should have a greater role in affecting elections "than the cattle & horses of the North." Watching this sectionally tinctured debate take shape, Madison recognized that certain concessions would have to be made. "Could it be reasonably expected," he wrote in *Federalist* No. 54, "that the Southern States would concur in a system which considered their slaves in some degree as men when burdens were to be imposed [taxation], but refused to consider them in the same light when advantages were to be conferred [representation]."[20]

"Reasonable" expectation dictated the passage of the three-fifths compromise. Its practical effects proved immediate. In 1790 the first U.S. census found a roughly equal number of free citizens in New Hampshire and South Carolina (140,000), though the latter, with its large number of enslaved, claimed two additional congressional seats. Maryland counted a smaller free population than Connecticut but enjoyed greater representation as well.[21] One could go on. The upshot is that without the compromise Jefferson would not have defeated John Adams for the presidency in 1800, nor is it likely that, as in fact happened, ten of the country's first twelve presidents would, at some point in their lives, have owned slaves.

Near the end of the convention, delegates agreed on placing a fugitive slave clause in the Constitution, thus allowing masters to hunt runaways. It reads: "No Person held to Service or Labour in one State, under the Laws thereof, escaping into another, shall, in Consequence of any Law or Regulation therein, be discharged from such Service or Labour, but shall be delivered up on Claim of the Party to whom such Service or Labour may be due." This provision prevented existing domestic antislavery laws in the North from making a fugitive free upon reaching a free state. It is worth remembering that under the soon-to-be discarded Articles of Confederation, these same states could not be compelled to capture and return fugitives. With sentiment in the North turning slowly against slavery, it appeared imperative to southerners like Butler and Pinckney that a potential safe haven for runaways be closed. During the Revolution, tens of thousands of bondsmen and -women had fled to British lines and from there many made their way to freedom. This wartime exodus constituted, so one historian has argued, "the greatest slave rebellion in American history."[22]

Looking to prevent future rebellions, delegates, particularly in the Deep South, worked in Philadelphia to ensure the protection of their human property. Pinckney, speaking that fall before the South Carolina state convention that eventually ratified the Constitution by a 149–73 count, insisted that he and his southern brethren had fought a strong fight:

By this settlement we have secured an unlimited importation of negroes for twenty years; nor is it declared that the importation shall be then stopped; it may be continued—we have a security that the general government can never emancipate them, for no such authority is granted. . . . We have obtained a right to recover our slaves in whatever part of America they may take refuge, which is a right we had not before. In short, considering all circumstances, we have made the best terms for the security of this species of property it was in our power to make. We would have made better if we could, but on the whole I do not think them bad.[23]

Instead of settling the various questions surrounding slavery, however, the Constitution merely established the legal and linguistic terms upon which a great and increasingly intense argument, spanning several decades, began to bloom. The document's ratification, in fact, prefaced rather than prevented a series of sectional disputes. It served further as a preamble to the combustible events of 1854.

2

Of Crises and Compromises

I know no South, no North, no East, no West to which I owe an
allegiance. . . . My allegiance is to this Union.
                                        Henry Clay, 1850

Though the Constitution created a single nation, the country remained
at many points a republic of regions. Friction emerged almost immediately when the centralization of administrative power in the early
1790s attracted a broad if uniquely southern-led discontent. Under the
energetic stewardship of treasury secretary Alexander Hamilton arose a
governing philosophy—Federalism—that favored industry over agrarianism, deference over democracy, and took a rather dim view of the
"baleful" and "abominable" (so one Federalist newspaper said) doctrine
of states' rights. When faced with growing political opposition from
supporters of Thomas Jefferson and the nascent Democratic-Republican
Party, Federalists in Congress responded by passing the controversial
Alien and Sedition Acts (1798), the former making it more difficult for
new immigrants, who tended to drift into the Jeffersonian camp, to gain
citizenship and vote, the latter criminalizing print criticism of the government. Several anti-Hamilton editors were summarily prosecuted and
convicted. One distraught Republican publisher called the offensive legislation "The *gag law*." Jefferson quickly identified the sectional dimensions of the acts, writing to fellow Virginia planter John Taylor: "It is true
that we are compleatly under the saddle of Massachusets & Connecticut,
and that they ride us very hard, cruelly insulting our feelings as well as

exhausting our strength and substance. Their natural friends, the three other Eastern states, join them from a sort of family pride."[1]

Together, Jefferson and Madison replied to the acts with two anonymously authored protests, the Kentucky and Virginia Resolutions, so named as they were debated and passed by the much-concerned legislatures of those states. Though separately inscribed—Jefferson drafted the Kentucky decree and Madison its Virginia complement—they espoused in common a compact theory of government, describing the Union as little more than a loose and voluntary confederation. Citing the states rather than the people as the Constitution's creators, the Resolutions recognized their authority to determine if the national Congress had overstepped its powers. Should this occur, they claimed, a state reserved the responsibility for protecting its citizenry from federal tyranny.

In collaboration, these documents called for opposition to the Alien and Sedition Acts, though how they did so revealed important temperamental distinctions between their respective authors. A more conservative Madison asserted Virginia's liberties without indicating a remedy should these be breached; he thus carefully elided the language of nullification, the idea that states retained the right to invalidate federal law. The older and more militant Jefferson had no such qualms. His notice opened with a ringing endorsement of localism: "Resolved, that the several states composing the United States of America, are not united on the principle of unlimited submission to their General Government." From there, the document reminded readers of the bound powers invested in the Constitution—"Congress shall make no law . . . abridging the freedom of speech, or of the press"—before finding that the Sedition Act, in targeting Republican publishers, had rather flagrantly infringed upon the rights of the citizens of the several states. In response, the Kentucky Resolutions, reviewing several instances of "violations" connected to the acts, and more broadly noting the constitutional proviso that "the powers not delegated to the United States" by that document "are reserved to the States," declared the Alien and Sedition laws "altogether void and of no force." Thus would Kentucky openly ratify, in Jefferson's words, "a repeal of the . . . unconstitutional and obnoxious act[s]."[2]

Reaction to the Resolutions was quick and, in much of the country, condemnatory. John Marshall, a Virginia nationalist soon to be appointed chief justice of the Supreme Court, thought their adoption "calculated to create unnecessary discontents and jealousies at a time when our very existence, as a nation, may depend on our union." To the north, Massachusetts senator Theodore Sedgwick called the Resolutions "little short of a declaration of war," while the Connecticut Federalist Uriah Tracy appeared eager to hit the barricades. "I had wished," he wrote to a colleague in something of a dark whimsy, "that all the discontented would have made an effort, at this time to overturn the federal Government," thus giving Yankee legions a reason to invade certain southern hot spots. In conquering Richmond, so he surmised, decades before blue-clad Union armies under Ulysses S. Grant conquered Richmond, nationalists would have "establish[ed] the [central state] with more advantage."[3]

Teased by his own martial dreams, Hamilton had also hoped to put the "conspiracy to overturn the government," as he called it, "to the Test." In a February 1799 communication he proposed to Sedgwick a decidedly provocative course: "When a clever force has been collected let them be drawn towards Virginia for which there is an obvious pretext—& then let measures be taken to act upon the laws & put Virginia to the Test of resistance. This plan will . . . enable the Government to triumph with ease." At the time he wrote this astonishing note, Hamilton was serving as the army's inspector general, second in command only to former president Washington, who had been coaxed out of retirement to bolster the U.S. military amidst Federalism's worried response to the French Revolution. Upon Washington's death that December, Hamilton became the army's senior officer. "That man," lamented First Lady Abigail Adams, "Would in my mind become a second Bonaparte if he was possessed of equal power."[4]

Aside from being censured by a number of prominent politicians, the Virginia and Kentucky Resolutions kindled the hostility of several state legislatures. Massachusetts's General Assembly scoffed at the notion that the Alien and Sedition Acts infringed upon individual rights, declaring them "not only constitutional, but expedient and necessary," while the Pennsylvania House of Representatives rebuked the Resolutions for aiming "to excite unwarrantable discontents, and to destroy the very existence of our government." Though some southern voices shared such views, the negative responses were overwhelmingly northern. No fewer than seven Yankee statehouses found fault with the Resolutions, insisting that the nation's Supreme Court ultimately decided on questions of constitutionality. Not a single southern assembly replied in kind.[5]

In 1800, due in degree to the Alien and Sedition Acts, though more generally to concerns over Hamiltonianism's centralizing impulse, the Federalist Party, too patrician to thrive in a democratic age, lost power. "They have attempted to resist the force of current public opinion," the Connecticut lexicographer Noah Webster (of dictionary fame) sighed, "instead of falling into the current with a view to direct it."[6] Jefferson's rise to the presidency, complimented by Democratic-Republican majorities in both congressional chambers, effectively nullified the unpopular acts, whose Sedition and Alien Friends components were allowed to expire respectively in 1800 and 1801. Now ascendant and more secure in office than in opposition, the Jeffersonians began to adopt a frankly nationalistic outlook. Their Federalist rivals, by contrast, turned ever inward—angry, impotent, and improbably promoting the country's first serious secession movement.

The Essex Junto took Federalism's discontent to the extreme. This curious clique consisted of former and current senators George Cabot and Timothy Pickering, the jurist Theophilus Parsons (all from Essex County, Massachusetts), and a smattering of other New England irreconcilables. Discouraged by Jefferson's election, they grew furious when the president approved the Louisiana Purchase. The acquisition, they argued, forever shrank the Northeast's influence, putting the South in virtual control of the continent. "If the middle and Eastern states still retain any thing in the union worth possessing," groused Fisher Ames in a Boston newspaper, "we hold it by a precarious and degrading tenure; not as of right, but by sufferance; not as the guarded treasure of freemen, but as the pittance, which the disdain of conquerors has left to their captives."[7] The Junto thought the Purchase constitutionally dubious and feared a western exodus of slaveholders, thus enlarging the plantocracy's already considerable reach.

Pickering, employing a variation of Jefferson's own compact theory, coolly counseled secession. Having formerly headed both the war and state departments under Washington, he could claim a political reputation perhaps second to no New Englander except John Adams. Disgusted with the three-fifths compromise, which had elevated Jefferson to the executive office, he took to mocking the Virginian as the "Negro President." Boston's *Mercury and New-England Palladium*, among other regional publications, concurred, contending that the

Master of Monticello entered "into the temple of Liberty on the shoulders of slaves."[8]

Writing to Cabot shortly after the United States took possession of Louisiana, Pickering unveiled an elaborate design to dissolve the Union and create a distinct northern confederacy. "The principles of our Revolution," he wrote, "point to the remedy—a separation." He then unpacked a host of questionable assumptions:

> It must begin in Massachusetts. The proposition would be welcomed in Connecticut; and could we doubt of New Hampshire? But New York must be associated; and how is her concurrence to be obtained? She must be made the centre of the confederacy. Vermont and New Jersey would follow of course, and Rhode Island of necessity.[9]

He believed further, and somewhat fantastically, in England's elaborate cooperation: "We suppose the British Provinces in Canada and Nova Scotia, at no remote period, perhaps without delay, and with the assent of Great Britain, may become members of the Northern League." Pickering had little doubt that London hated the Jeffersonians as much as he—"that government can feel only disgust at our present rulers"— and would readily embrace its former Yankee subjects: "A liberal treaty of amity and commerce will form a bond of union between Great Britain and the Northern confederacy." With the Jeffersonians presumably powerless to contest this notional London-Boston buffer, he really saw no reason for an unfriendly divorce. "We wish no ill to the Southern States," he told yet another New England colleague, and thought the prospects of relations between the sections might improve "without the jealousies and enmities which now afflict both, and which peculiarly embitter the condition of that of the North." As Federalism appeared to be "crumbling away," he concluded, "there is no time to be lost."[10]

Accordingly, the humorless, ascetic, and Puritan-like Pickering (if a Charles Willson Peale portrait is to be believed), moved ahead with his ragged plans to form a new union. Along with a number of naïve Yankee Federalists, he supported the outgoing vice president Aaron Burr's bid in 1804 to become the Empire State's next governor. Planted in Albany, Burr, so wrote Connecticut congressman Roger Griswold, "will . . . be considered, and must he not, in fact, become, the head of the Northern interest?"[11] Careful and composed, Burr offered no concrete assurances to the ultras, though, and possibly in some quiet desperation they backed him anyway—but to no avail. Burr lost decisively in the gubernatorial race as his Republican opponent, the Revolutionary War veteran Morgan Lewis, claimed nearly 60 percent of the vote. Jefferson's popularity, the general acceptance of the Louisiana Purchase, and lingering hostility toward Federalism produced this outcome. In sum, New England's hazy secessionary intentions appeared to be convincingly checked, though in fact they merely lay in abeyance.

Jefferson's second term produced increasing discontent in the commercial Northeast. Though initially neutral in the Napoleonic Wars, the United States could do little when the conflict's chief combatants, Britain and France, failed to reply in kind, seizing American merchantmen and their cargos as contrabands of war. To these desperate nations, such state-approved plundering constituted a vital strategy to their survival. This practice of impressment—forcing several thousand U.S. citizens to serve in the Royal Navy—proved particularly offensive, however, as did the outrageous June 1807 confrontation off the coast of Norfolk, Virginia, between the British warship HMS *Leopard* and the American frigate USS *Chesapeake*. Looking for deserters, the *Leopard's* commander, Salusbury Pryce Humphreys, demanded the *Chesapeake* stop to be searched. Rebuffed, Humphreys, following an unheeded warning shot, ordered several broadsides fired into the exposed *Chesapeake*; three of its crew were killed, eighteen were wounded, and the imperious *Leopard* made off with four of its sailors. Overseeing only a very modest military, Jefferson responded by calling for commercial warfare. In December a compliant Congress passed the Embargo Act; the United States would seek to chasten the European powers by refusing to share, sell, or ship its New World bounty across the Atlantic.

The act invariably proved impractical, harming the United States and more especially New England's mercantile economy at least as much as it injured Britain and France. In March 1809, with Madison just days from assuming the presidency and eager to cut loose this inelegant albatross, Congress repealed the act, but over the next year it adopted other trade-restricting measures in the hopes of coercing the European powers to respect American neutrality. These efforts proved elusive. And in 1812 a frustrated Madison administration resolved to go to war with Britain—a controversial decision that stirred not a little hostility in greater Boston. More dependent on London credit and markets than the southern states, pockets of New England condemned the conflict as a war engineered by slaveholders to further reduce northerners' influence in the republic.

By 1814, with its economy in tatters, its coastlines unprotected, and its national political prospects impeded by the three-fifths compromise, a group of anxious Yankees began to push for an assembly of the disaffected. In early October the Massachusetts General Court passed a resolution authorizing Governor Caleb Strong to defend the Commonwealth from British marauders by raising an army of ten thousand. Three days later it approved another motion calling for a convention to gather at Hartford, Connecticut.

Back in Washington, a despondent Madison brooded to fellow southerners over this startling decision to hold a sectional caucus while the war still raged. "He looks miserably shattered and woe-begone," one of them reported. "In short, he looked heart-broken. His mind is full of the New England sedition."[12] Writing to former Virginia senator Wilson Cary Nicholas, Madison deplored the audacity of northern leadership to afford comfort to Britain while "deluding" their citizenry into condemning the conflict:

> You are not mistaken in viewing the conduct of the Eastern States as the source of our greatest difficulties in carrying on the war, as it certainly is the greatest, if not the sole, inducement with the enemy to persevere in it. The greater part of the people in that quarter have been brought by their leaders, aided by their priests, under a delusion scarcely exceeded by that recorded in the period of witchcraft; and the leaders themselves are becoming daily more desperate in the use they make of it. Their object is power.[13]

Most New England states honored the summons to Hartford and sent representatives. The legislatures of Massachusetts, Connecticut, and Rhode Island assigned a combined twenty-three delegates while county conventions elected New Hampshire's two attendees and the citizens of Windham County, Vermont, chose a single deputy. Though not openly calling for secession, the convention caused a nervous federal government considerable concern. Madison ordered Colonel Thomas Sidney Jesup of Virginia to make his way north and report on the proceedings.

If the convention turned radical Jesup planned to move on to Springfield, Massachusetts, and secure its federal arsenal—the object a generation earlier of Shays's farmers' army. The colonel had little doubt of
his duty: "If New England determines on opposition her power should
be instantly crushed: give her time to organize an independent government and she will bid defiance to the power of the Union."[14]

The apocalyptic battle fancied by Jesup never transpired. The delegates, instead, made formal recommendations to end Virginia's long
administrative reign over the American republic. This remonstrating
document called most notably for a repeal of the Constitution's three-
fifths clause in a bid to forestall future "Negro Presidents," and it urged
two-thirds support (rather than a mere majority) in both congressional
chambers for a declaration of war—40 percent of the Senate and 38 percent of the House having voted against the War of 1812. It further proposed limiting the presidency to a single term, while insisting that each
future president hail from a different state than his immediate predeces-
sor. Already three Virginians—Washington, Jefferson, and Madison—
had held office for a total of nearly six terms, while the country's only
other chief executive, flinty John Adams of Massachusetts, had served
for only one.

The Hartford Convention dispersed on January 5 and its proceedings appeared a few days later in the city's *Courant*, still in circulation
to this day and considered the country's oldest continuously published
newspaper. The assembly sought, so the proceedings indicated, "to
strengthen, and if possible to perpetuate, the union of the states, by
removing the grounds of existing jealousies, and providing for a fair
and equal representation and a limitation of powers."[15] These men,
many of them former Hamiltonian nationalists, were now speaking
the language of states' rights. But they came late, disastrously so, to the
table. For on January 8, some fourteen hundred miles to the south, an
American army under General Andrew Jackson of Tennessee defeated
a large British force at the Battle of New Orleans; the following month
the Senate unanimously ratified the Treaty of Ghent (signed on Christmas Eve) and the war ended. Cassandras, which is to say Federalists,
ambled off into a qualified extinction, for though the Essex Junto and
Hartford conventioneers had obviously failed to overturn Jeffersonianism, a palpable post-Federalist discontent remained prominent in the
Northeast. In fact, it began to build.

Indeed, even as the Hartford debates appeared to give the lie to Yankee leverage, Virginia's once firm reign was giving way as rapid population growth in the North invariably shrank the South's political advantage. No one was more surprised by this circumstance than the planters themselves and it almost, on the sensitive issue of admitting Missouri into the Union as a slave state, brought an end to the republic.

The Missouri Crisis commenced in February 1819 when Congress considered enabling legislation designed to bring the Missouri Territory into the Union. Echoing the Essex Junto's opposition to the Louisiana Purchase, some northerners looked askance at limiting free labor's future on the frontier. One of them, Representative James Tallmadge Jr., a New York Jeffersonian, proposed an amendment to the bill that would have banned the further transport of enslaved people (about ten thousand were already there) into the territory. Much of the South resented Tallmadge's bold maneuver and the many months of often-acrimonious congressional debate it provoked. For some Virginians, the right to extend the peculiar institution appeared to be a matter of economic life and death. Owners of more than a quarter of the nation's slaves, the Old Dominion's planter class could no longer count on the state's depleted soil to turn a profit. Selling off this "surplus," however, might yield a pretty income and already a nascent cotton belt had begun to penetrate into the Mississippi Valley. Jefferson seemed sensitive to this consideration when informing his son-in-law in 1820, "A woman who brings a child every two years [is] more valuable than the best man of the farm."[16]

Under such heightened circumstances, the Missouri debates took on an unusual intensity. Southerners claimed that settlers in the territories enjoyed the right to make up their own minds regarding slavery, while their critics countered that the Constitution empowered Congress "to dispose of and make all needful Rules and Regulations respecting the Territory . . . belonging to the United States." As the discussions deepened, the nation's political elite grew anxious. "The Missouri subject," Speaker of the House Henry Clay uneasily observed, "monopolizes all our conversation, all our thoughts and . . . all our time"; a troubled President James Monroe saw secession looming: "I have never known a question so menacing to the tranquility and even the continuance of our Union as the present one," he wrote Jefferson. "All other subjects have given way to it, & appear to be almost forgotten." Jefferson could only agree. "But the Missouri question," he wrote to his old friend John

Adams, "is a breaker on which we lose the Missouri country by revolt, and what more, God only knows."[17]

But no rebellion or revolt attended the western question this time. In the summer of 1819, rather, the Massachusetts legislature allowed its Maine province to leave the Commonwealth and the following year legislation linked Maine and Missouri statehood—thus ensuring an equitable distribution (12 to 12) of free and slave states in the Senate. Wishing to avoid further inflammatory debates, the compact included, as per the suggestion of Illinois senator Jesse B. Thomas, an amendment banning slavery in the rest of the Louisiana Purchase territory north of the 36°30' parallel. Though the compact was called a compromise, the House vote to allow slavery in Missouri barely passed 90 to 87. Clearly many in Congress—and presumably their constituents—opposed this plank. While Secretary of State John Quincy Adams officially favored the arrangement, "believing it," so he confided to his diary, "to be all that could be effected under the present Constitution," he thought a magnificent rupture of the country along sectional lines might nevertheless have brought a real and lasting honor to the North. "This would have produced a new Union of thirteen or fourteen States unpolluted with slavery," he parroted Pickering, "with a great and glorious object to effect, namely, that of rallying to their standard the other States by the universal emancipation of their slaves."[18]

From his home at Monticello, Jefferson looked upon the perils of secession with equally mixed emotions. "This is a reprieve only," he wrote of the Compromise to former Massachusetts congressman John Holmes, "not a final sentence. . . . I regret that I am now to die in the belief, that the useless sacrifice of themselves by the generation of 1776, to acquire self-government and happiness to their country, is to be thrown away by the unwise and unworthy passions of their sons, and that my only consolation is to be, that I live not to weep over it." That Jefferson recognized his own contribution to sectional strife in drafting the Kentucky Resolutions a generation earlier is unclear; though given, as one historian put it, his "psychological dexterity" and ability to live "with massive contradictions," one might reasonably suspect he skated rather smoothly away from making such unpleasant connections.[19] But the idea of nullification, embedded in that provocative document, outlived its author and in the late 1820s became the defining issue in yet another challenge to federal power.

A host of demons bedeviled the larger Atlantic-facing slave states in the early nineteenth century. Uneven economic development, population loss to western migration, and the emergence of abolitionism as a small if evolving feature in public debate made the region brittle. Fears of a Charleston slave uprising in 1822—the alleged Denmark Vesey Plot—alarmed white South Carolinians familiar with the violent Haitian Revolution (1791–1804) that had smashed French colonial rule on the island and created a black republic in the not-so-distant Caribbean. Shaken, the city executed dozens of suspected conspirators including Vesey, a free black carpenter accused of planning the revolt. Nine years later, in 1831, a messianic Nat Turner led one of the largest slave rebellions in U.S. history, resulting in the deaths of some sixty whites in Southampton County, Virginia. A mix of mobs and militias replied by killing approximately 160 of the rebels. Word of the insurrection quickly spread beyond the Old Dominion, seeding the specter of race war throughout the South. That same year, the radical Massachusetts abolitionist William Lloyd Garrison founded *The Liberator*, an antislavery weekly published in Boston. Though circulation never exceeded three thousand, the paper, with a prominent readership, enjoyed a surprising cultural reach.

Contesting this abolitionist agenda informed the response of white South Carolinians to a range of public issues including economic development, policing post offices that disseminated antislavery materials, and limiting political participation to a small planter elite. Not unrelatedly, the Palmetto State claimed the highest percentage of enslaved in the nation (55 percent), while its seafront cities and counties were conspicuously occupied by bondspeople. "In 1830, in the district of Charleston," a scholar has noted, blacks "outnumbered whites three to one; in Colleton the ratio was four to one; in Beaufort, five to one; in Georgetown, eight to one. . . . No other area in the Old South contained such a massive, concentrated" slave community.[20]

Anxious to control this black majority, South Carolina fixated on the federal tariff as the chief source of the state's "decline." The nation's first protective tariff was enacted in 1816 and designed to advance the kind of industrial development that most Americans, survivors of two wars with Britain in two generations, believed necessary for national defense and development. Largely bisectional in its support, the impost passed by a comfortable margin in the House, 88 to 54. Over the next few years, however, as customs duties rose, the slave states began to question what they regarded as an unfair and unequal advantage given to northern manufacturing. John Calhoun, the planter, political theorist, and unbending defender of state power, anonymously drafted in late 1828 a protest against the nation's tariff policy, in effect revisiting Jefferson's controversial claim in the Kentucky Resolutions that the states enjoyed the right to reject federal law.

Four years later Congress enacted yet another protectionist tariff and South Carolina's nullifiers made their move. In October 1832 strict constructionists dominated local elections, soundly defeating the opposing Union Party by capturing strong majorities in both legislative chambers. The following month these men organized a state convention that met in Columbia and demanded a dramatic reduction in the tariff; more provocatively, this gathering also passed (with 83 percent in affirmation) an ordinance declaring the tariffs of 1828 and 1832 unconstitutional. These now "null and void" imposts were, the convention concluded, no longer in force and not to be paid as of February 1.

That winter President Andrew Jackson, who believed the tariff perfectly constitutional, quietly placed federal soldiers in the area of Charleston in case the nullifiers attempted to impede its collection. "I am confidentialy advised," he wrote to an assistant, "that the nullifyers of the south, have corrupted both the Naval officers, and those of the army in Charleston—that the nullies are determined to push matters to extremities, and expect to get possession of the forts &c. . . . Therefore let the [locally recruited] officers & men be relieved by a faithful detachment, and this carried into effect as early as possible."[21] Jackson further shepherded through Congress a Force Bill authorizing the military's use in South Carolina. This proved unnecessary. Unable to garner support from other southern states, the "nullies" now sought to negotiate. Having suspended their self-imposed February 1 deadline, they gave Congress time to conclude yet another compromise—the Tariff of 1833, which lowered the impost over a number of years.

The nullification controversy underscored a growing feeling among southerners that on such vital and interlinking issues as economic development, federal power, and slavery sectional distinctions were increasing rather than diminishing. Though South Carolina's "null and void" solution smacked of extremism to many of her neighbors, these states nevertheless expressed deep concern at the central government's apparent preference for industry. "Any attempt on the part of the Government to force manufacturers into existence, by government bounties," Alabama's assembly warned, "must of necessity operate unequally, and therefore be unjust." North Carolina's legislature pointedly maligned the 1832 tariff as "impolitic, unjust, and oppressive," arguing that "a large majority of the people [of the state] think those acts unconstitutional." Thomas Ritchie, longtime publisher of the *Richmond Enquirer*, one of Virginia's most important papers, observed during the tariff dispute: "The South cannot acquiesce in *such an unjust and unequal system*."[22]

In the wake of this simmering unease, several fresh disputes widened the North-South divide. These included both the (pro-Dixie) "Gag Rule"—a series of resolutions leading to the tabling without discussion of antislavery petitions sent to Congress—and the (pro-Yankee) personal liberty laws that forbade officials in nine northern states from cooperating in the rendition of southern men and women escaping their enslavement. None compared, however, to the sharp debate over slavery's standing in the western territories. In 1846 the United States, looking to both secure its claim to Texas and extend its dominion to the Pacific, invaded Mexico. The American victory in 1848 resulted in the vast Mexican cession, the nation's largest land acquisition except for the purchases of Alaska and the Louisiana Territory, though a new enigma now confronted the country: Would northern capitalism or southern slavery become the dominant economic system in these recently acquired territories?

A small group of Yankee Democrats had attempted to solve this dangerous dispute even before the war's end. In August 1846 one of their number, a young Pennsylvania congressman named David Wilmot, introduced a proviso to an appropriations bill that would have banned slavery in any territory taken from Mexico.[23] The proposal passed through the House 83 to 64, prefacing, against strong southern opposition, the adoption of the entire bill 85 to 80. Two days later President James K. Polk of Tennessee (absentee owner of a nine-hundred-acre northern Mississippi cotton plantation) confided a little irritably to his diary:

> Late in the evening of Saturday the 8th, I learned that after an exciting debate in the House a bill passed that body, but with a mischievous and foolish amendment to the effect that no territory which

might be acquired by treaty from Mexico should ever be a slave-holding country. What connection slavery had with making peace with Mexico it is difficult to conceive.[24]

Others conceived quite easily. Concerned about the planters' expansion into the West, the *Cleveland Plain Dealer* thought "it . . . time that the lovers of freedom should unite in opposing the common enemy [the South, not Mexico] by fixing bounds to their aggression"; the *Cincinnati Gazette* similarly counseled resistance "against . . . any new slave territory . . . and against extending the constitutional inequality in favor of slaveholders [i.e., the three-fifths provision] beyond the states already in the Union."[25] Though defeated in the more conservative Senate, Wilmot's proviso became a rallying cry for advocates of free soil on the unfolding frontier.

The Mexican-American War's conclusion only amplified pressure to settle slavery's fate in the territories. The Treaty of Guadalupe Hidalgo, which went into effect in July 1848, gave the United States not only the Rio Grande boundary it had coveted in Texas but also California and all or much of present-day New Mexico, Nevada, Utah, Wyoming, Colorado, and Arizona. For more than a year a paralyzed Congress stewed over this enormous prize. In January 1850 Clay proposed an elaborate legislative package designed to solve a number of sectionally divisive issues. His compromise included admitting California as a free state; organizing the Utah and New Mexico territories on the basis of popular sovereignty (allowing the territories themselves to decide servitude's status); abolishing the slave trade—but not slavery—in the District of Columbia; and establishing a stronger fugitive slave act to counter the personal liberty laws popping up in the North. These measures, Clay insisted, would produce "an amicable arrangement of all questions in controversy between the free and slave States, growing out of the subject of slavery."[26] Many, from both sections, disagreed.

In Massachusetts a number of men from all parties thought the compromise gave too much to the South and were particularly aghast at the punitive new fugitive slave bill. Charles Sumner, a leading light of the Bay State's Free-Soil coalition and about a year away from claiming a Senate seat, urged his political compeers not to "sacrifice one jot or tittle of our principles." And when, in a sentiment of conciliation, the old Massachusetts senator Daniel Webster delivered a much-anticipated address

President Zachary Taylor precariously straddles the "congressional scales" representing northern and southern sentiment during the fractious debates that led to the Compromise of 1850.

in early March defending Clay's ambitious arrangement, Sumner called The Godlike Daniel, formerly revered for his eloquence, an "archangel ruined" and "traitor to a holy cause."[27]

Mississippi senator Jefferson Davis, by contrast, criticized the omnibus package for an entirely different reason—he wished to see much more of the American West opened to slavery. "In certain climates," he argued, "only the African race are adapted to work in the sun." He proposed that instead of preserving the entirety of California for free labor the old Missouri Compromise line be run to the Pacific; all legislation relating to land and slaves, he struck a deterministic note, is ultimately "written by the hand of Nature upon the surface of the country."[28]

As winter gave way to spring with no resolution to Clay's recommendations in sight, a number of militant southerners decided to air their options should Congress ban slavery in the new territories. Approximately 170 of them, representing nine states, convened on June 3 in Nashville's McKendree United Methodist Church to confederate and perhaps to put the national legislature on notice. Unlike earlier examples of states' rights resistance—the Kentucky and Virginia Resolutions, South Carolina's stand against the federal tariff—a more comprehensive if still somewhat marginal sense of southern nationalism now informed the region. It is worth noting that six slave states, most of them in the Upper South, refused to send representatives to Nashville. As happened at Hartford in 1814, moderates took control of this southern convention and played for time. Rather than traffic in secessionary fantasies, they followed Davis's lead calling for an extension of the Missouri Compromise line, which would have legalized slavery south of Monterey, California. After nine days the assembly adjourned.

A few weeks later radical factions in both sections coalesced to kill Clay's compromise. As the moderate North Carolina Whig David Outlaw put it, the bill's defeat constituted a "triumph of ultras and abolitionists." Beaten, exhausted, and suffering from the tuberculosis that would in two years take his life, Clay left stifling Washington to convalesce in the cool seaside climes of Newport, Rhode Island. At this point, Illinois senator Stephen Douglas assumed responsibility for the proposal. Understanding the difficulty in getting northern and southern congressmen to agree on a single big bill, he shrewdly chopped it into parts and, largely along sectional lines with some crossover appeal among moderates, each individual bill prevailed. By late September Millard Fillmore, the last Whig president, had signed all the measures into law. "I am rejoiced at their passage," he wrote to a colleague in a staggering display of misplaced optimism, "and trust they will restore harmony and peace to our distracted country."[29]

Fillmore's confidence reflected a still broader buoyancy among the nation's political class. Clay, now back in Washington and refreshingly unburdened by the hypocrisy of a false modesty, wrote to his son James: "All our Slavery troubles are now supposed to be adjusted. Every measure which I proposed . . . has substantially passed; and the Country seems to be disposed generally to give me quite as much credit as I deserve." The aging Webster, born in 1782, a year before the Treaty of Paris officially ended the American Revolutionary War, also indulged in various shades of comfortable confusion. "We have gone [through] the most important crisis, which has occurred since the foundation of the Government," he told a colleague that fall and, fumbling upon a familiar cliché, promised that "whatever party may prevail, hereafter, the Union stands firm."[30]

In fact, the time for compromises had come to an end. And in 1854 Americans were forced once again to reckon with slavery's role in the West. The settlements of 1820 and 1850 proved ephemeral, inadequate, and unable to contain the aspirations of competing sectional systems. The unraveling of these incomplete accords began in a fractious winter congressional session that set a divisive tone for a difficult year.

Part II

WILD WEST

Illinois senator Stephen Douglas, "the Little Giant" of late antebellum politics. Thought to be a president-in-waiting, he instead divided the country by advancing an ill-conceived bill to allow slavery into the western territories.

3

Nebraska in the New Year

If I thank God that Massachusetts is not a slave state, how then can I turn round and let Nebraska or Kansas become one by refusing to interpose for their protection?

Robert C. Winthrop, former Massachusetts
senator, 1854

In early January 1854, with the capital city, so the (Washington) *Daily National* noted, "carpeted with snow . . . and the cheerful ceremonies of the season . . . observed by great and small," Stephen Douglas reported a bill before the Senate to organize a mammoth parcel of land called Nebraska—an anglicization of "Ñí Brásge," an Oto Indian word for "flat water," referring to the territory's prominent Platte River. Having to do with the politics of railroad development, the proposal invariably became entangled in the politics of slavery. No one should have been surprised. Whether in Louisiana or Missouri, Texas or the old Mexican southwest, planter potentates had long looked to extend the edge of their elastic cotton kingdom. Seldom did these saber-rattling occasions occur without the accompaniment of secessionary threats either veiled or visible. John Calhoun's 1850 caution to his upper chamber colleagues—"I have . . . believed from the first that the agitation of the subject of slavery would, if not prevented by some timely and effective measure, end in disunion"—is something of an in-character alarum.[1] Few knew the sensitivity of this subject better than Douglas. While shepherding Clay's much-maligned compromise package through a

45

divided Congress nearly four years earlier, he had worked closely with men from all regions of the country, building fragile coalitions and assuaging concerns. Satisfied with his success and armed with an over-weening aplomb, he confidently entered the ring once again.

Considering his restless youth, Douglas appeared to be the ideal pilot of the country's territorial pretentions. Born in Brandon, Vermont, in 1813, and the sixth generation of his family to call New England home, he commenced a succession of migrations to upstate New York, Cleve-land, St. Louis, and finally, at the age of twenty, Jacksonville, Illinois—established in 1825 by a wave of Yankee settlers. Along the way he attended two hardscrabble academies and read law with small-town attorneys. Ambitious and proficient, Douglas received appointment to the Illinois bar in 1834, the year the Whig Party formed to protest the presidency of Andrew Jackson and anti-abolition riots—rooted in the growing pres-ence of free-laboring blacks—ripped for a savage week through segre-gated New York City. Around this time, he wrote to relatives of finding his place on the moving American frontier: "I have become a *Western* man, have imbibed Western feelings principles and interests and have selected Illinois as the favorite place of my adoption."[2]

Douglas's introduction to the lands beyond the Appalachians included more than a passing familiarity with the institution of slavery. Although outlawed in Illinois by the Northwest Ordinance, there was in this region a system of indentured servitude that, throughout the antebellum period, kept perhaps as many as five hundred men, women, and children virtually enslaved. Antiblack laws, moreover, made it dif-ficult for free people of color to enter Illinois; these deeply entrenched mandates lingered on until late in the Civil War. The state's mottled relationship with race and slavery undoubtedly touched upon certain demographic realities not to be easily negotiated. Its white population, around two hundred thousand in the early 1830s and growing quickly, included a significant number of migrants from Dixie who put down roots in its several southern counties, an area known colloquially as "Little Egypt." Much like the nation, this diversely peopled common-wealth admitted to having a host of mixed loyalties.

A coming young man sympathetic to the Jacksonian, which is to say states' rights, perspective, Douglas served as a loyal Democrat in a spate of local and federal positions before, at the strikingly young age of twenty-seven, winning appointment to the Illinois Supreme Court in 1840. In 1843 he was elected to the U.S. House of Representatives, and three years later he ascended to the Senate, which became for this man on the make something of a second home. Washington's rustic, unfinished capital city, torched by the British only a generation earlier in the latter stages of the War of 1812, now lent its refurbished environs to a golden age of speechifying. Constituents, so one French observer wrote,

> take it for granted that their chosen deputy is an orator, that if he can he will speak often, and that in case he is forced to refrain, the few speeches which he does make will show what he can do and include both an examination of all the great affairs of state and a catalog of all their petty grievances. . . . On these terms they promise to vote for him again.[3]

Others questioned the provincial capital's uneven pretensions to a clean-columned eminence. A visiting Charles Dickens, one of the century's more seasoned social critics, sniffed at the ambitious District's unmet prospects with a stinging skepticism: "Spacious avenues, that begin in nothing and lead nowhere; streets, mile-long, that only want houses, roads, and inhabitants; public buildings that need but a public to be complete; and ornaments of great thoroughfares which only lack great thoroughfares to ornament—are its leading features." The British writer Harriet Martineau, typically dry and direct in her measurements, barely more charitably described Washington as a rare mélange of "flippant young belles, 'pious' wives . . . grave judges, saucy travelers, pert newspaper reporters, melancholy Indian chiefs, and timid New England ladies, trembling on the verge of the vortex; all these are mixed up together in daily intercourse like the higher circle of a little village." She found this intensely fluid society "singularly compounded."[4]

In contrast to these distinguished English observers, Douglas delighted in the capital's minor-key cosmopolitanism, even as its budding urbanity drew attention to his green inelegancies. He enjoyed cigars and whiskey, dressed carelessly, and, until he became a more practiced pol, liked to chew (and spew) tobacco. Short, stocky, and lacking in any evident physical grace, he attracted attention with an unusually large head, a thick chest, and palpably stubby legs (some thought the clumsy combination evoked the slapstick strut of a bantam cock). Pocket-sized in appearance but a growing figure in Congress, he soon earned the inevitable sobriquet "the Little Giant." Accounts differ on whether he had blue or gray eyes, though all seemed to agree on his terrific energy and commanding presence. Perhaps to compensate for a lack of stature, Douglas issued a determined enthusiasm that sometimes, in certain familiar company, verged on rowdiness. "His figure would be an unfortunate one," wrote one woman, "were it not for the animation which constantly pervades it."[5]

In the spring of 1847 Douglas married Martha Martin, a native North Carolinian described as "small, hazel-eyed, with fair and graceful features." Compromised by delicate health, she struck some observers as "frail." Offspring of a distinguished political family whose auxiliaries occupied over the years various House and Senate seats, Martha, a dozen years younger than her husband, met Douglas while on a trip to Washington. They wed at her Dan River plantation home thirty miles north of Greensboro. The following year Douglas's father-in-law, Colonel Robert Martin, died and left a twenty-five-hundred-acre Pearl River (Mississippi) plantation and its more than one hundred enslaved people to Martha. His will further directed Douglas to manage the estate and to receive for his efforts 20 percent of its annual profits. In January 1853 Martha died soon after giving birth to the couple's third child; the infant, their only daughter, perished a month later. Moving beyond what a biographer described as "deep despair," Douglas remarried in 1856, taking the tall, chestnut-haired twenty-year-old Adèle Cutts, a Chesapeake beauty from a prominent Maryland family and a great-grandniece of Dolley Madison, as his second wife. Said to enter Washington society "with the air of a queen, with perfect features as if carved in marble, white and smooth as marble, too, with clear liquid eyes and shadowy lashes," Cutts proved to be a rather conspicuous point of spousal pride.[6]

Though the Yankee-born Douglas had married into southern situations, he thought both his political career and the nation's future lay in the West. At one time a limited-government Jacksonian Democrat presumably suspicious of federally sponsored tariffs, banks, and internal improvements, he softened his stance as Jacksonianism receded into the background, and actively promoted railroad development across the advancing borderland. His efforts helped to secure federal grants to build both the Illinois Central and Northern Cross railroads—these serving, so he hoped, as the apprentice pieces to more elaborate paths to the Pacific. An aggressive expansionist, Douglas anticipated a steady Anglo diaspora colonizing the continent. He wanted Texas brought into the Union, the Oregon Territory occupied, and Cuba made an American appendage. He grew particularly infatuated with Nebraska, a colossal enclave extending beyond the western borders of Iowa and Missouri that might serve—when sufficiently peppered with military posts, surveyors, and emigrants—as an artery to the coast. Former president John Quincy Adams, now serving in Congress, informed his diary in December 1844 of the first stirrings on this front: "At the House, Douglas, of Illinois, gave notice that he would, at an early day, move for leave to introduce a bill to establish a new Territory with a strange name."[7]

But what of slavery? The sectional implications of expansion were clear and vigorously debated in the 1840s. Their dangerous repercussions seemed, however, to have little impact on Douglas. He coolly presumed that an uncongenial "desert" climate prevented the peculiar institution's extension in the northern territories, though he seemed indifferent to its sweep across the southwest. He actively supported, moreover, the Gag Rule, denounced antislavery activism—"I have no sympathy for abolitionism," he asserted in 1848—and admonished Britain for its emancipation of its Caribbean empire through the Slavery Abolition Act (1833), denouncing it as an effort to stir up discontent in America "and thus render the Union itself insecure." Embracing the widely held view of racial inferiority, Douglas further objected in a very public and proselytizing fashion to allowing freed blacks to enter free states: "We do not believe in the equality of the negro, socially or politically, with the white man. We mean to preserve the race pure, without any mixture with the negro."[8] Hardly an outlier, Douglas politicked in line with majority race sentiment in Illinois at this time.

His views took on added import in the late 1840s when, following the Mexican cession, governments needed to be established in these newly acquired territories. Along with numerous northern Democrats, Douglas lazily latched on to the convenient principle of popular sovereignty. Advanced by the saggy-jowled, baggy-eyed, and red-tinted-toupeed Michigan senator Lewis Cass, the concept called for the people of a territory—not the federal government—to determine slavery's legality in the public lands. It meant, broadly defined, local self-government, and thus struck a resonant chord with many, though by no means all,

Americans. Some pointed out that the Constitution gave to Congress, not the people, the power to regulate the territories, while others more generally resisted the idea of potentially opening the West to bondage, which they invariably saw as a threat to free labor. Voter reaction, in any case, was mixed and Cass, the pro–popular sovereignty candidate, narrowly lost the 1848 presidential election to the Whig candidate and war hero Zachary Taylor; both men carried fifteen states. In Douglas's hands, however, the principle, as noted earlier, was adroitly employed in the new territories as part of the sweeping Compromise of 1850.

Having solidified his reputation with this spotlight success, Douglas actively sought to protect popular sovereignty. In 1851 Shadrach Minkins, an enslaved Virginia man, was arrested in Boston under the Fugitive Slave Act; the city's Vigilance Committee used force to rescue Minkins from federal marshals and then helped secure his passage to Canada. A sympathetic Boston jury acquitted two men prosecuted for aiding in the escape. Holding court in the Senate, Douglas branded several of his northern colleagues "conspirators" for creating a climate conducive, so he put it, to "evad[ing] the obligations of the Constitution." Glaring angrily and a little theatrically upon four graduated rows of semicircular-seated senators, he arraigned those otherwise unidentified "white men now within the range of my sight responsible for the violation of the law at Boston. It was done under their advice, under their teaching, under their sanction, under the influence of their speeches."[9]

In more reflective moments, Douglas realized that popular sovereignty might now be conveniently applied to those territories still governed under the Compromise of 1820. Certainly, some form of organization needed to be initiated. Several communities in the western parts of Iowa and Missouri were currently pressuring Congress to open the grassy lands just beyond their borders. In 1853 "sooner" groups of settlers and native peoples moved peremptorily into this region and, in July of that year, attempted, without sanction from Washington, to establish a provisional government.[10] As of yet no firm consensus had emerged on how to respond to such sub rosa sodbusters. Douglas's Democratic Party remained divided, largely along sectional lines, on popular sovereignty, though it was now obvious that congressional action could scarcely be delayed much longer. In December Douglas won reappointment as chairman of the Committee on Territories. That same month he received a communication from citizens of Buchanan County, Missouri, all but demanding Nebraska's immediate organization. In a more or less official capacity, he called for them to rally around the principles unveiled in the Compromise of 1850:

> The slavery agitation which followed the acquisition of California and New Mexico . . . had an injurious effect by diverting public attention from the importance of our old territory [the Louisiana Purchase] and concentrating the hopes and anxieties of all upon our new possessions [the Mexican cession]. . . . It is hoped that the necessity and importance of the [popular sovereignty] measure are manifest to the whole country, and that so far as the slavery question is concerned, all will be willing to sanction and affirm the principle established by the Compromise measures of 1850.[11]

The extent to which Douglas actually believed "the slavery question" under control is a matter of conjecture, though by squeezing the Compromise through Congress he perhaps added a little incautious courage to an already ample ego.

Having won reelection to the Senate in 1852 at the age of thirty-nine and considered by many speculating politicos to be a president-in-waiting, Douglas seemed destined for greatness. By now a practiced hand in the capital city's more polished salons, he reached casually for brandy and cognac or even champagne rather than his old spicy rye whiskey with its signature sting; private dinners were served in his quarters on fine French porcelain plates paired with floral damask linen napkins, after which good Havana cigars made the rounds. One might catch about the District a glimpse of the senator draped in flattering "silk and striped Valencia vests and doeskin pants," greeting visitors from Illinois in a "knightly" fashion, so a guest attested, "as if he had been born in the best society."[12] At the peak of his powers, Douglas now moved to organize Nebraska.

He hoped, of course, to stir up as little resistance as possible, even as he endeavored to bring the principle of popular sovereignty to territory currently closed to slavery. Without managing to overturn this taboo, he knew the Senate's imposing line of southern leadership would never go along. Douglas personally believed slavery incompatible with the comparatively arid northern latitude and thought a quiet replacement of "the principle of 1820" (exclusion) with "the principle of 1850" (popular sovereignty) offered the South a merely rhetorical concession that would not lead to the actual removal of enslaved men and women to Nebraska. Accordingly, and on behalf of the territorial committee, he introduced his bill to the Senate on January 4. In calling for Nebraska's settlers to determine the fate of race in the region, it implicitly overturned the 1820 prohibition. Pleased with his work, though underestimating its potential to shatter the unstable sectional peace patched together in 1850, Douglas proudly said of the bill, "It was written by myself, at my own house, with no man present."[13]

One imagines a lone figure, possibly fortified with liberal quantities of tobacco and alcohol, hunched over a candlelit desk, crafting a great state paper—that quickly succumbed to the unexpected pressure of southern disapproval. The bill, this cotton bloc noted, did not explicitly overturn the act of 1820 but rather permitted Nebraska's colonizers, should they wish, to draft a proslavery constitution *when they applied for statehood*. But if slavery were not permitted in Nebraska at the earlier territorial stage, these critics pointed out, then the territory would be de facto filled with free labor. The still-extant Compromise of 1820, after all, excluded slavery in the pre-statehood phase, and the planters now demanded its repeal.

Accordingly, Kentucky's silver-haired Whig senator Archibald Dixon, appointed in December 1852 to serve the remainder of the recently deceased Clay's term, offered an amendment to Douglas's bill on Monday, January 16, rescinding that part of the 1820 act prohibiting slavery. The Missouri Compromise, it read, "shall not be so construed as to apply to the Territory . . . of the United States; but that the citizens of the several States or Territories shall be at liberty to take and hold their slaves within any of the Territories of the United States, or of the States to be formed therefrom, as if the [Missouri] act . . . had never been passed." That evening, elated southern partisans, Dixon's wife, Susan, remembered, crowded "our parlor . . . expressing a delighted surprise." Two days later, in an effort to bridge their differences, Douglas and Dixon took an afternoon carriage ride around the capital, the latter elucidating at length on the need for an amendment that overturned the old Compromise. After some obligatory to-ing and fro-ing, Douglas impetuously, perhaps too hastily—though recognizing all hinged on southern sanction—agreed: "By God, sir, you are right, and I will incorporate it in my bill."[14] Seeing popular sovereignty as a tool to open the West short of, so he believed, literally enlarging slavery's sphere, Douglas presumed his political skills sharp enough to appease both sections, to excise a divisive subject from public debate, and finally to embellish his already considerable reputation. But he overreached.

Over the next few days Douglas's territorial committee introduced two significant changes to the original bill. First, it unambiguously repealed the Missouri Compromise, after which it split the territory in two—calling for the organization of Nebraska and, to its south, of Kansas. This last measure probably had to do with the machinations of railroad development. Proponents of both an "upper" (Nebraska) and a "lower" (Kansas) road might now jointly support legislation to open these territories as their respective routes ostensibly stood equal chance of being selected. But the visible division of the region into northern and southern sections gave to many Americans the unshakable assumption that slavery was to be banned in Nebraska and permitted in Kansas.

Moving forward, Douglas requested the Senate take up the revised bill on the twenty-third, just five days, that is, after he had agreed to Dixon's alterations. He worried, however, about President Franklin Pierce's reaction to the proposed repeal of the Missouri Compromise, which many Americans regarded as a sacred pact. He need not have. Though a Yankee born and raised in New Hampshire, Pierce had the reputation of being a "doughface," a northern man with southern principles. The insult seems to have first appeared in politics during the Missouri debates when the soprano-voiced Virginia representative John Randolph, whose erratic behavior perhaps owed something to opium and alcohol addictions, expressed his distaste for those northerners who voted with the South. "*They were scared at their own dough faces!*" he crowed. "We had *them*, and if we wanted *three* more, we could have had them: yes, and if *these* had failed, we could have three more of these men, *whose conscience, and morality, and religion, extend to 'thirty-six degrees and thirty minutes north latitude'*"—this mocking geographical reference denoting the southern boundary of Missouri, which, apropos the 1820 Compromise, divided prospective free and slave states west of the Mississippi.[15] For a generation now, Democrats above the Mason-Dixon Line hoping to carry presidential contests had to appease their party's minority southern wing. In deferring at times to this truism, the persuasible Pierce—as well as New York's Martin

Van Buren before him and Pennsylvania's James Buchanan after—was occasionally accused of giving too much to the South.

A heavy drinker, Pierce possessed a classic Roman nose, thin lips, and gray eyes; his conventionally good looks exuded, so some said, that ineffable quality of "presidential." While a student at Bowdoin College, he forged an enduring friendship with the writer Nathaniel Hawthorne, who later wrote a slender and slightly ludicrous campaign biography of his classmate—"His speeches, in their muscular texture . . . resembled the brief but pregnant arguments and expositions of the sages of the Continental Congress"—for which the author of *The Scarlet Letter* was appointed to the U.S. consulate in Liverpool: a couple of unpleasant rooms in a dreary building near the city's old docks, though a sinecure for all that.[16] Pierce suffered from depression and self-doubt; he had made his way politically through the increasingly uncertain (given the tumultuous times) arts of conciliation and accommodation, yet even an obliging president could not oblige all.

Before Douglas managed to arrange an audience with Pierce, Lewis Cass had already stolen a march on his Senate colleague, complaining to the president that Dixon's amendment threatened party unity in the North. Secretary of State William Marcy of New York concurred and urged the president to reject efforts to repeal the venerable Compromise. On Sunday the twenty-second, the day before the Senate took up the Kansas-Nebraska bill, Douglas desperately sought an audience with Pierce, though he knew him "rigidly opposed" to conducting business on Sundays.[17] In some haste he went to Secretary of War Jefferson Davis, who, he knew, supported the measure, and asked if he could persuade Pierce to see that very day a small group of congressmen. Davis, close to the Pierce family, did so. The president agreed and Douglas, accompanied by Davis, arrived at the White House with Senators David Rice Atchison of Missouri and Robert M. T. Hunter of Virginia, along with Representatives John C. Breckinridge of Kentucky and Philip Phillips of Alabama. Two of these men would later serve in Davis's Confederate cabinet.

Pierce received this small party in the mansion's second-floor library where, surrounded by southerners including Davis, the only member of his official family present, he soon capitulated. Putting a high-minded spin on this impromptu Sabbath gathering, conspicuous for its absence of Yankee naysayers, Davis later wrote in a memoir that Pierce, having "patiently listened to the reading of the bill and [to his guests'] explanations of it, decided that it rested on sound constitutional principles, and recognized in it only a return to that rule which had been infringed by the compromise of 1820, and the restoration of which had been foreshadowed by the [popular sovereignty] legislation of 1850." Reviewing the episode with more detachment, one recent Pierce biographer concluded that a "great pressure" had been applied to the pliable-as-dough president.[18]

The following day, Douglas brought before the Senate a revised bill containing both Dixon's amendment and the enjoinder to organize two new territories. Considering his undeniable political gifts, it seems fair to ask why Douglas so casually inflicted the Kansas-Nebraska debate upon the nation. Several arguments come to mind. Clearly, he possessed presidential ambitions and understood that only by winning southern support could he one day occupy the White House. Douglas presumed further that a Pacific railroad running to Chicago would secure his political base in Illinois, giving him a comfortable senatorial berth for as long as he wished. More generally, he seems to have sincerely believed in the efficacy of a continent-spanning railroad to promote national growth, trusting that robust economic development might leaven the more evident signs of sectionalism then confronting the country. He knew the plantocracy would never accede to the further opening of the Trans-Mississippi frontier without some hope of bringing its slaves into these territories and he realized further that rapidly growing California, some seventeen hundred miles and a major mountain range (the Rockies) from Kansas City, needed to be more closely integrated into the United States. Underlying all these motives is the element of Douglas's strong personality. Aggressive, ambitious, and determined to fight his way to the front ranks of American statecraft, he saw an opening in the winter of 1854 to tie together, so he supposed, a number of loose ends. Having secured congressional compliance to the Compromise of 1850, he again wagered on his political skills against whatever intrepid opposition might arise.

And that resistance formed quickly. Observing the late January maneuverings in Congress, Chicago's abolitionist newspaper, the *Free West*, liberally singed the Nebraska bill's author for a Judas-like betrayal— "We know of no more fit man to present such an infamous proposition than Senator Douglas, a North Carolina slaveholder [through his

first wife's holdings], who represents the State of Illinois in the Senate."
Two days later the *Alton Telegraph* chimed in, also accusing Douglas of
undue southern sympathies, insisting "his bill, in whatever light it may
be viewed, practically contemplates the introduction of human slavery
into that territory, and proves beyond a peradventure, that the Illinois
Senator, although pretending to represent a free State, is wedded to slavery, and is using his influence for its extension."[19]

These opening volleys, if oscillating between fact and fabrication,
do offer some indication of just how poorly Douglas, though undeniably capable, read northern popular sentiment. Only six years earlier the
Free-Soil Party, dedicated to barring slavery in the territories, took over
10 percent of the popular vote in the 1848 presidential contest (running former president Martin Van Buren), and caused a schism in New
York Democratic politics that may have tipped the state and the contest
to the Whig Zachary Taylor. Four years later, though Pierce claimed
an impressive twenty-seven states in the general election, Whigs and
Free-Soilers polled nearly 49 percent of the popular vote and the shift-
ing of some tens of thousands of ballots in a handful of closely fought
states might have produced a different outcome.

Douglas further turned a tin ear to the moral implications of opening the old Louisiana Purchase lands to enslavers. An advocate of
democracy and local autonomy, he seemed, as noted, to have believed
that a northern majority would predominate in the new territories and
thus the principle of popular sovereignty really gave nothing away to the
South. His antislavery critics clearly saw matters differently. They noted
how the plantocracy, a minority interest in a minority section, had long
managed, through the three-fifths compromise and a controlling influence in the Democratic Party, to play an outsized role in the country's
politics. They argued further that slavery hardly constituted a local
interest but rather put into question the values of an entire nation born
in a struggle against its colonial masters and dedicated to the proposition "that all Men are created equal." If Douglas would neither denounce
slavery by preventing its diffusion nor acknowledge that it contradicted
the country's founding principles, they contended, he could hardly be
trusted to promote the interests of free-laboring men and women.

That January, a growing cluster of Yankees began to look upon the
Kansas-Nebraska bill as evidence of a southern conspiracy. Horace Greeley's *New-York Tribune*, the preeminent Whig periodical in the coun-

try and formerly supposing the South "to be warring on the defensive side," now saw, in Douglas's proposal, a plainly offensive policy. "Slavery is an Ishmael," the paper argued, "it is malevolent. It loves aggression." The Sandusky (Ohio) *Commercial Register* made a similar connection accusing "a weak and imbecile administration" of being pushed by an "ambitious demagogue," who was himself the pawn "of grasping, dishonorable Slaveholders," eager to see ingested "the cup of bitterness which has been pressed to Northern lips so long."[20] Organized opposition became inevitable.

Near the end of January New York's senior senator, William Henry Seward, received an invitation to attend a public meeting in Manhattan "to protest against any repeal or violation of the Missouri Compromise." Seward's antislavery bona fides undoubtedly prompted the solicitation. Nearly four years earlier, late in the debates that produced the Compromise of 1850, he had waved aside southern presumptions that the Constitution promoted slavery's extension, insisting, rather, that the territories were governed by a "higher law" than the mere scribblings of Founders and Framers. The narrow-chested senator, one day to become the chief official in Lincoln's cabinet, commanded respect by the force of his ideas rather than from personal charisma or physical appeal. One contemporary, a grandson of John Quincy Adams, described him as "small, rusty in aspect, dressed in a coat and trousers apparently made twenty years ago and by a bad tailor at that."[21] Seward affected easily a rumpled look complete with disheveled hair and unkempt eyebrows; a beaked nose and large ears accented an unfortunate face. Unable to grace the New York gathering—"My constant attendance here [in Washington] is required"—he nevertheless attached to his regrets a summation of the situation in a transparent if earnest bid to rouse northern public opinion:

> It is . . . evident . . . that Nebraska is not all that is to be saved or lost. If we are driven from this field, there will yet remain Oregon and Minnesota, and we who thought only so lately as 1849 of securing some portion at least of the shore of the Gulf of Mexico and all of the Pacific coast to the institutions of freedom, will be, before 1859, brought to a doubtful struggle to prevent the extension of slavery to the shores of the great lakes, and thence westward to Puget's sound.

On "this great question," Seward assured his readers, "I shall endeavor to do my duty."[22]

A host of other antislavery senators promised to do theirs as well. To the head of this fermenting class emerged Ohio's Salmon Chase, a Free-Soiler, critic of the Compromise of 1850, and now eager to attack the suspect Kansas-Nebraska bill. He promptly began to plan a response, joined by a handful of colleagues equally anxious to beat back popular sovereignty in the West. He seemed especially delighted when at a dinner party a skeptical Thomas Hart Benton, the ancient Missouri senator of large-boned and broad-shouldered build, swore with a flash of the old acid that had once helped him to best Andrew Jackson in a long-ago Nashville brawl—"Douglas [has] committed political suicide."[23]

4

The Battle Begins

Fellow-Citizens . . . it is our duty to warn our constituents whenever imminent danger menaces the freedom of our institutions or
the permanency of our Union. Such danger, as we firmly believe,
now impends.

> "Appeal of the Independent Democrats
> in Congress to the People of the United
> States," January 1854

On January 23 Douglas brought the revised, which is to say the southern-
extolled and Pierce-approved, Kansas-Nebraska bill before the Senate.
A posturing Chase casually, if a little duplicitously, asked for a delay
in order that the amended proposal might more carefully be studied
in its current iteration; Sumner, his confederate in this ruse, suggested
that a week of reflection and rumination would be greatly appreciated.
Douglas cordially agreed to his colleagues' request, oblivious to the
fact that they were planning instead an urgent attack on the proposed
undoing of the Missouri Compromise—to be published the very next
day in the *National Era*, a Washington antislavery weekly. Rather than
flail away at a fait accompli, they wanted to shape a prolonged debate.
"Today the Nebraska Bill was called up, But was postponed till Monday,"
Chase wrote to Edward Hamlin, a former Ohio Whig congressman now
devoted to the free-soil movement. "It is designed to press it through the
Senate for fear of the awakening of popular indignation. . . . I enclose
with this an appeal in the *Era*. The signs all indicate storms ahead."[1]

As innately envious of political success as Douglas, Chase, often pompous and rarely modest, passed for majestic in America's still-primitive capital city. Possessing a towering physique, an unrecumbent carriage, and a cache of fine-cut clothing, he presented a striking phys-ical contrast to the Little Giant. Carl Schurz, a German immigrant who served in both Congress and the cabinets of two presidents, remem-bered Chase with evident regard, calling him

> one of the stateliest figures in the Senate. Tall, broad-shouldered, and proudly erect, his features strong and regular and his forehead broad, high and clear, he was a picture of intelligence, strength, cour-age, and dignity. He looked as you would wish a statesman to look. His speech did not borrow any charm from rhetorical decoration, but was clear and strong in argument, vigorous and determined in tone, elevated in sentiment, and of that frank ingenuousness which commands respect and inspires confidence.[2]

There were others, however, who found Chase's "preening" and "self-righteousness" something less than commendable. An Ohio col-league called him "as ambitious as Julius Caesar," while other epithets—"political vampire," "moral bull-bitch"—touched upon his eagerness to cultivate the growing antislavery crusade for his own ends. Chase, so one student of the era has noted, "was genuinely outraged by Douglas's bill, but he also grasped at the chance to enhance his popularity and strengthen his future political prospects."[3]

As with many midwestern statesmen, Chase could trace his ances-try back to the old Puritan settlers. His family arrived from England in the seventeenth century, eventually, in the generation of Chase's father, Ithamar, making their way to Cornish, New Hampshire. A member of the state legislature and a justice of the peace, Ithamar befriended future Massachusetts senator Daniel Webster and bequeathed to his son a proud (if poor) man's fame. He carried the titles "Honorable before his name," Chase later wrote of his father, who had died when he was only nine, "and Esquire after it." Perhaps with some relief, Ithamar's widow, Janet Ralston Chase, struggling to maintain her brood of ten children, accepted the offer of a clerical relative in the West to care for young Salmon. And so the boy, now turned twelve, was trundled off to rural Worthington, Ohio, to live with an uncle, Philander Chase, the state's lone Episcopal bishop. Two years later Philander assumed the presidency of little Cincinnati College and Salmon followed him there to take coursework. During the 1820s the maturing Queen City's population surged from some ninety-six hundred to nearly twenty-five thousand; strategically situated along the Ohio River, it had already eclipsed Pittsburgh as the largest and most important commercial center in the emerging American West. Home to a thriving hog market, it came to be known colloquially as "Porkopolis," an inelegant if not altogether unfair appellation. Finding the life of the mind circa Cincinnati College insufficient—"It was not a study loving set of boys," Chase once observed with a candid detachment—the junior scholar retreated to the East and graduated from Dartmouth in 1824. He subsequently read law in Washington, D.C., before returning to Cincinnati in 1830 and opening a legal practice.[4]

About this time, in 1831, Chase met Alexis de Tocqueville, the visiting French political theorist then making a deliberate circuit gathering materials for his important work *Democracy in America* (two volumes, 1835/1840). Along with a dizzying cast of pen-and-letter correspondents, Tocqueville confabbed less formally with the country's political class, speaking with former U.S. president John Quincy Adams and future Texas president Sam Houston, as well as numerous judges, congressmen, and the rare Revolutionary era celebrity—including Maryland's Charles Carroll, the last surviving (and sole Catholic) signer of the Declaration of Independence. Interested in the views of a coming western man, he chatted up Chase as well. Shamelessly boosting Cincinnati, the young lawyer told his new French friend "of the rich country around it," bragged of "the ease with which it could be approached," and (conveniently leaving aside his Dartmouth detour) even saw fit to flaunt its "intellectual advantages." He further praised the city's blessed "exemption from the curse of slavery."[5]

Though critical of the peculiar institution, the young Chase engaged more actively in yet another kind of amelioration—temperance. Pious, biased, and a bit preachy, he condemned the many makeshift taverns and whiskey-soaked taprooms that inevitably accompanied incipient Cincinnati's rapid growth. Perhaps in this effort he sought to exert some vicarious cultural influence over the city's German immigrant population, whose proliferating churches, neighborhoods, newspapers, and breweries were arousing interest. Eager, more directly, to see Cincinnati's morals elevated, its commitment to education and the arts exemplified, he, the attenuated offspring of New England's proud Puritan tradition, joined the Young Men's Temperance Society, giving every appearance of being a reformer, an improver, and quite possibly a crusader in some dim quest of a cause.

Though reflexively antislavery, Chase believed that blacks were clearly inferior to whites and, like many other northerners, hoped that abolition, should it come someday, might be efficaciously accompanied by the removal of the formerly enslaved "back to Africa." His early feelings on this rather large subject were informed by essentially pragmatic rather than moral considerations. He never doubted the unjustness of race-based bondage yet thought the practice still more gravely damaged the nation by encumbering economic development in all sections of the country. Not until the summer of 1836 did Chase demonstrate a particular and felt hostility toward slavery, doing so in response to a case that threatened to curtail white freedom of speech. Briefly, mobs in Cincinnati, a city strongly informed by the folkways of Kentucky and Virginia migration, twice that July attacked the printing office of The Philanthropist, an abolitionist newspaper edited by former Upper South slaveholder James G. Birney, an attorney and member of the American Anti-Slavery Society. During the second assault Birney's offending printing press received baptism in the Ohio River. The worked-up crowd, not content with mere property damage, sought Birney himself and throughout a chaotic evening combed the city's black neighborhoods in a fruitless search for the controversial editor. Struck by this blunt violation of civil liberties, Chase later insisted that the episode revealed to an alarming degree the plantocracy's disturbing reach: "From this time on, although not technically an abolitionist, I became a decided opponent of Slavery and the Slave Power: and if any chose to call me an abolitionist on that account, I was at no trouble to disclaim the name."[6]

The following year, Chase intervened for the first time in a fugitive slave case. The affair involved Matilda, a light-toned mulatto woman employed as a maid in the Birney household; Birney and his wife, Agatha, believed her to be white. Matilda, rather, was both the daughter and the property of Larkin Lawrence, a Missouri man; while accompanying Lawrence on a trip several months earlier en route to St. Louis, she had vanished from their docked ship in Cincinnati and taken refuge in the city's black community. Lawrence now demanded her return. Putting up a fight instead, Birney retained Chase, who argued before the Court of Common Pleas that the Fugitive Slave Act of 1793 lacked power in Ohio because the Northwest Ordinance of 1787, which organized the territory, had explicitly outlawed slavery. Chase added for good measure that the enslavement of men and women patently violated the Enlightenment liberalism so proudly "proclaimed by our fathers." Uninterested in debating the nuances of natural rights, the judge, D. K. Este, ruled against Matilda. She boarded a boat bound for New Orleans the following day and was soon after sold at a public auction. The twin tragedies of the Birney and Matilda cases proved decisive for Chase. Formerly a temperance campaigner with an abstract interest in black colonization, he now considered himself, if not quite an abolitionist, then certainly willing to assail the Slave Power by assisting its desperate fugitives.[7]

Socially, Chase's views were validated among Cincinnati's self-appointed literati, a learned fraternity of ameliorators and aesthetes who considered themselves discerningly antislavery. Organized in a membership-by-invitation-only society known as the Semi-Colon Club, these parlor radicals claimed him as an associate—as they did a young Harriet Beecher Stowe, a recent Connecticut transplant. Many of the Semi-Colonites were themselves resettled New Englanders, perhaps eager to mingle among their own in this restless city of pronounced southern sensibilities. Harriet's older sister Catharine, an accomplished educational reformer who wore her hair in girlish ringlets, hoped that such contacts and connections might unite the "intelligent ... sort of folks" and bring a little eastern polish to this frontier pig emporium.[8]

In the early 1840s, Chase, always a hesitant Whig, made his plunge into third-party politics. Unable to secure a state senate nomination and told to drop his interest in "slave-related issues," he dropped Whiggery instead. "No mode will be so effectual in bringing the whole question of slavery before the people," he wrote one colleague, "as Antislavery political action." He hoped to see both the peculiar institution abolished in the nation's capital and the Fugitive Slave Act repealed, though he recognized the right of state law to sanction the practice—and on such private and somewhat qualified terms he joined the Liberty Party.[9] Recently founded in western New York largely on the premise that moral suasion campaigns were politely ineffective, Libertyites stressed the importance of winning elections and securing power. Though never more than a minor faction (Birney, twice its presidential candidate, captured fewer than seventy thousand combined votes in his 1840 and 1844 bids), the party anticipated the emergence of a more widely disseminated anti-planter sentiment energized in the late 1840s by the controversial Mexican-American War and the related question of slavery's future in the western territories. Sensing a gathering momentum, Chase helped to create during these restless years a more potent, pragmatic, and even moderately popular single-issue coalition—the Free-Soil Party. And in 1848 eleven of its members, having captured seats in the Ohio Assembly, held the balance of power in Columbus between larger Whig and Democratic coalitions. Striking a deal, the Free-Soilers agreed to support Democratic control of the legislature in return for the state's next open Senate seat—which went, the following year, to Chase.

Seeking to broaden the appeal of antislavery politics, Chase hoped to poach from the major parties those in their ranks responsive to the siren of Free Soilism. He thought northern Democrats particularly susceptible to abandoning their demanding southern associates. Describing to a colleague his commitment to creating "an Independent Democracy," he argued that such a speckled coalition, "thoroughly organized and appealing alike to liberal Whigs and liberal Democrats to unite in action," would allow the reformers to "do our work best."[10]

Chase's efforts to create a strong national antislavery alliance, one that might facilitate his own political ambitions, ensued amidst a backdrop of some personal tragedy. Between 1835 and 1852 he lost three wives and four of his six children, all daughters. The spouses were felled by a series of familiar nineteenth-century "complications"—of childbirth, vaguely defined illness, and tuberculosis—while the children succumbed to scarlet fever and less specified diseases. "The Lord," Chase grieved to a friend of these sequential deaths, "hath dealt very bitterly with me."[11] The burden of such bereavements narrowed appreciably his domestic commitments, as political life assumed the recess spaces formerly reserved for family life. Now devoted completely to his career, which meant, increasingly, the antislavery crusade, Chase joined with a small coalition of colleagues in January 1854 to attack Douglas's provocative Nebraska bill.

They did so in the "Appeal of the Independent Democrats in Congress to the People of the United States," a pungent seven-page condemnation of the effort to overthrow the Compromise of 1820—and printed, as noted, in the January 24 edition of the *National Era*. The document's origins were likely local, being based on a draft from Ohio congressman Joshua Reed Giddings, a longtime politician residing in the northeastern (called Western Reserve) part of the state, known for its New England settlement and openness to ultra ideas, including abolitionism and women's rights. Perhaps modeled on a response to an earlier sectional controversy—John Quincy Adams's "Appeal Against the Annexation of Texas" (1842)—Giddings's manuscript caught Chase's attention and the senator liberally revised the parchment, while assuming for himself principal authorship. The paper received further if minor editing from both Charles Sumner and New York congressman Gerrit Smith, the latter to financially support (and then plead ignorance of) John Brown's deadly 1859 raid at Harpers Ferry. In all, six men from three northern states—Giddings, Chase, Sumner, and Smith, along with Ohio senator Benjamin Wade and Massachusetts representative Alexander DeWitt—endorsed the document.

That only a half-dozen signatures graced the affidavit might suggest that the "Appeal" lacked strength and influence. And there is no doubt that some critics caught the evident scent of self-interest in its appearance. They regarded Chase and Sumner, both Free-Soilers, as third-party encroachers and Cassandras who were eager to latch on to an issue that might firm up their precarious political futures. Perhaps unsurprisingly, some of their sharpest censures came from the North. Robert C. Winthrop, a prim, dour Boston Brahmin of Whig persuasion, condemned the "Appeal" for presumably scaring off more respectable— that is, less abolitionist—opposition to the bill. Chase and his crew, he complained:

> precipitated themselves into the front ranks of the opposition, in a way to drive off the only persons who could have prevented its consummation. Half-a-dozen of them, under the style of Independent Democrats, got up a flaming manifesto in such hot haste . . . and put it forth, cock-a-hoop, half-signed, to the utter discomfiture of all who hoped to prevent the bill from passing. They usurped a lead which belonged to others, and gave an odor of abolition to the whole movement.[12]

Others, however, thought the odor of the event altogether invigorating. From a front-row Senate seat, Seward wrote his wife, Frances, that

the Kansas-Nebraska bill had coaxed a furious censure from a cross section of constituencies orbiting outside Congress's comfortably draped
and carpeted digs; these reproaches he assured her were "coming down
upon us as if a steady but strong North wind was rattling through
the country."[13] The "Appeal" played an important role in this process,
advancing a critical narrative of slavery, the Constitution, and southern
expansion that both exasperated sectional tensions while giving voice
to long-simmering Yankee concerns. A document equally accusatory
and therapeutic, it would play a role in shaping the terms upon which
Americans addressed slavery's future.

The "Appeal" opened on a gloriously condemnatory note, arraigning
Douglas's proposal as a shameful subversion of the nation's high-minded
promises not merely to itself but to all humanity. Accusations of corruption, duplicity, and conspiracy echoed rather amply through these
early passages. "We arraign this bill," its author's declared, "as a gross
violation of a sacred pledge; as a criminal betrayal of precious rights;
as part and parcel of an atrocious plot to exclude from a vast unoccu-
pied region, immigrants from the Old World and free laborers from our
own States, and convert it into a dreary region of despotism, inhabited
by masters and slaves." The plantocracy and its northern congressional
retainers, they argued, proposed to undermine the evident wishes of the
Founders who, so they claimed, had made plain their desire to contain
slavery by refusing it entry into the Northwest Territory. This vital provision, they emphatically if implausibly argued, constituted "the original settled policy of the United States."[14]

The "Appeal" addressed next the Missouri Compromise, which, of
course, had for a generation banned bondage from the area now designated as Nebraska. The authors noted that in 1820 President Monroe's
cabinet—most of whom were southerners, including John Calhoun—
"gave a written opinion, affirming [the act's] constitutionality." Monroe,
himself a Virginia planter, agreed, and signed the legislation into law.
Northerners only consented to Missouri's entering the Union with slavery, Chase and company claimed, as they were assured that the greater
part of the Louisiana Territory, everything above the southern boundary of Missouri, was explicitly reserved for free labor. "This prohibition"
against bringing enslaved people into the West, Chase and the others
argued, "has been regarded and accepted by the whole country as a sol-

emn compact."¹⁵ These strong if overstated words failed to acknowledge, however, that popular sovereignty, in light of the Compromise of 1850, now enjoyed measured support among many northern Democrats, while a large number of southerners resented any stigmatizing proscription of their property.

Moving from accusation to intrigue, the "Appeal" pointed out that though the bulk of the Louisiana Purchase was presumably reserved for free labor, to date only a single state—Iowa—offered unfettered opportunities for white workers; the admissions of Louisiana, Arkansas, and Missouri into the Union, by contrast, had ensured the security of enslaved labor beyond the Mississippi. That this recent history comprised part of a broader scheme to enlarge the planters' domain seemed self-evident to Chase and his colleagues. They noted that Florida when it was acquired from Spain (1819) "was yielded to slavery without a struggle," and connected it to the later seizure of Mexican soil under the Treaty of Guadalupe Hidalgo (1848). The subsequent employment of the popular sovereignty plank in New Mexico and Utah as part of the Compromise of 1850, the "Appeal" argued, "exposed all the residue of the recently acquired territory to the invasion of slavery."¹⁶

This bleak prospect, it continued, was most assuredly premeditated, a matter of long-standing collusion and conspiracy. Hardly a new thing, the tyranny theme had always played well in America, whose citizens read their history selectively and often as a series of unblest stratagems designed to rob the people of their rights. Britain's King George III was once arraigned for attacking his colonies' liberties ("He has plundered our seas," so the Declaration of Independence waxed extravagantly, "ravaged our Coasts . . . and destroyed the lives of our people"), while in the 1830s a crusading Andrew Jackson had accused the federally authorized Second Bank of the United States (aka the "monster") of undermining through "stock jobbers, brokers and gamblers" the freedom of the country's white working class. In more recent years, fears of a Slave Power had spread with some regularity throughout the North.¹⁷ The "Appeal," picking up on this enemy-within thread, trafficked openly in alarmist language:

> It is a bold scheme against American liberty. . . . The first operation of the proposed permission of slavery in Nebraska, will be to stay the progress of the free States westward, and to cut off the free States of

the Pacific from the free States of the Atlantic. It is hoped, doubtless, by compelling the whole commerce and the whole travel between the east and the west to pass for hundreds of miles through a slave-holding region, in the heart of the continent, and by the influence of a Federal Government controlled by the slave power, to extinguish freedom and establish slavery in the States and Territories of the Pacific, and thus permanently subjugate the whole country to the yoke of a slaveholding despotism.[18]

Summoning Jackson's colorful language, Chase and his colleagues called the effort to recall the Compromise of 1820 "monstrous." "Shall a plot against humanity and democracy," they rhetorically asked their readers, "so dangerous to the interests of liberty throughout the world, be permitted to succeed?"[19]

The document closed with a direct appeal to the people to shun "demagogues"—presumably a host of editorializing southern scare-mongers chattering in their small-fonted weeklies about secession—who rigidly, relentlessly tied the Union's future to slavery's inexorable extension. Americans were to remember, rather, that "ancient law" and "solemn compact"—the golden fruits of the Northwest Ordinance and the Missouri Compromise—dictated a different fate for their country, though one now plainly threatened. Anticipating a sharpening sectional rejection of the Kansas-Nebraska bill, the "Appeal" fairly begged for every means of outcry: "Let all protest, earnestly and emphatically, by correspondence, through the press, by memorials, by resolutions of public meetings and legislative bodies, and in whatever other mode may seem expedient, against this enormous crime."[20]

Though these ringing sentiments suggest, in light of the Civil War, a certain clairvoyance, they hinted at a seer-like control over the situation that Chase never possessed. As a maverick Independent Democrat, he wished to convince northern Democrats (and any Whig-come-latelies) to join in a common resistance to southern control over the territories. At heart a conventional politician accustomed to the existing two-party system, he assumed its persistence, albeit in a manner more responsive to the nation's free-labor majority. Pioneering a successor style of partisanship, one that under the aegis of Lincoln Republicanism would come in 1860 to claim victory as a sectional rather than a national power, was the furthest thing from his mind. But no more than Douglas could he control events. "Without being so intended," Carl Schurz wrote years later, the "Appeal" had radicalized debate on the Nebraska bill, and thus sounded "the first bugle call for the formation of a new party."[21] By arguing that a notional coast-to-coast cotton empire both endangered white workers and thwarted the Founders' presumed efforts to end black bondage, Chase offered a long-marginalized anti-slavery impulse a central place in the nation's history, validated in its resistance to a combination of planters and doughfaces who called con-spiracies "compromises."

This account of the past offered a selective summary that quickly took root and helped, over the coming summer, year, and the next few years, to define the identity of a rising Republican Party. The cause was finding its catechism. Crucially, the shadow Slave Power, as put forth by Chase, became one of the dominant themes leading up to the Civil War. To wit: "The government . . . since this century began, at least," the *Atlantic Monthly* contended in 1857, is "the creature and the tool of the slaveholders"; "I clearly see," Lincoln wrote the following year, "a powerful plot to make slavery universal and perpetual in this nation"; and in January 1861, a few weeks before deputies from seven southern states meeting in Montgomery, Alabama, agreed upon a provisional Confederate constitution, Congressman John B. Alley of Massachu-setts said of the South, "They commenced their aggressions upon the North. . . . Every new triumph of the South and every concession by the North has only whetted their appetite for still more."[22]

Chase's ability to convincingly portray a prolonged planter conspir-acy gave the "Appeal" the confident sheen of a historical text. It remains to this day an iconic antislavery script. In offering its audience of "Fellow-Citizens" a narrative with famous names and familiar dates, it bid to become the authoritative document of the Kansas-Nebraska debate. And yet the congressional manifesto genre from which it emerged had inherent limitations—it smelt of the schoolroom. The "Appeal" is by turns assertive ("we arraign"), pleading ("we entreat you"), and defi-ant ("we shall resist"), though a little bloodless for all of this. It casually slips into legalese, lectures abstractly on the "geographical character" of Douglas's project, and offers a swarm of impregnable proofs as though Americans were ever moved by the cold verities of logic. Put concisely, it failed to present slavery writ large as a human catastrophe, a moral crime, or an existential crisis. It offered, rather, an argument in place of a portrait, settling for statesmanlike instead of stirring. As such, it could only say and do and influence so much.

And thus, when Douglas's bill detonated in the winter of 1854, another literary work—sentimental, shocking, and the best-selling nineteenth-century novel in the United States—more powerfully prodded the culture's reaction to the omnipotent territorial question. All America, it seemed, had become ensnared under the potent spell of *Uncle Tom's Cabin*.

5

About a Book

Why, Sir, look all over the North; look South—look at home—
look abroad—look at the whole civilized world—and what are
all this vast multitude doing at this moment? Why, Sir, they are
reading "Uncle Tom's Cabin."

Frederick Douglass, 1853

In late January, with Chase's "Appeal" suddenly in circulation, a timely
alternate rhyme verse written by Frances E. Watkins, the most significant African American poet since the "elegant . . . genius" (George
Washington's words) of Phillis Wheatley, appeared in *Frederick Douglass's Paper*.[1] Established in 1851, printed in Rochester, New York, and
issued every Friday, the *Paper* (formerly the *North Star*) disseminated
news and announcements, letters and ephemera, related principally to
slavery and emancipation. Watkins's open-letter lyric, "To Mrs. Harriet Beecher Stowe," cordially praised the author of *Uncle Tom's Cabin*,
the remarkably popular abolitionist novel published in book form less
than two years earlier following a wildly successful serialization in the
National Era, the same sheet now disseminating the "Appeal." Watkins
wrote in part:

> I thank thee for the kindly words
> That grac'd thy pen of fire,
> And thrilled upon the living chords
> Of many a heart's deep lyre.

71

For the sisters of our race
Thou'st nobly done thy part;
Though hast won thy self a place
In every human heart.[2]

A writer, feminist, and lecturer, Watkins, so one scholar reminds us, "was the most widely read African American poet before the advent of the Harlem Renaissance." Author of several well-received volumes, she sold over fifty thousand cumulative copies to a devoted biracial audience. Today, by contrast, her staves and stanzas are relegated to the occasional college anthology; their clichéd imagery and mechanical rhyme schemes long out of fashion and bearing silent expression to how an inky ocean of nineteenth-century prosody has disappeared from public memory—consider the virtual cultural extinction of such thrice-named antebellum eminences as William Cullen Bryant, Henry Wadsworth Longfellow, and James Russell Lowell. The few photographs and illustrations we have of Watkins vary greatly and make it difficult to offer a succinct description, though written, if pen-picturesque, testimony offers one avenue. Grace Greenwood, a friend, informed the *Philadelphia Independent* that Watkins possessed "a noble head, the bronze muse; a strong face, with a shadowed glow upon it, indicative of thoughtful fervor, and of a nature most femininely sensitive, but not in the least morbid. Her form is delicate, her hands daintily small." She called Watkins "about as colored as some of the Cuban belles I have met with at Saratoga."[3]

Born in Baltimore in 1825, Watkins lost her mother, a free black woman, at the age of three ("the grave was my robber") and, after being shuffled about various abodes, eventually found a home with an aunt and uncle in the city. While taking classes in a segregated academy, she doubled as a domestic servant in the residence of a local bookseller, where she liberally embellished upon her education and discovered a talent for writing. In time her poetry began to appear in local papers. Leaving Baltimore, Watkins taught briefly (1850) in Pittsburgh before proceeding to Columbus, Ohio, where she offered domestic science instruction (sewing and embroidery) at Union Seminary, an institution affiliated with the African Methodist Episcopal Church. She moved yet again in 1852 to train students in a York, Pennsylvania, AME school, not far from the Mason-Dixon Line. The following year, so Watkins later related, dire news from neighboring Maryland inspired her to become an abolitionist. A sojourning black man, unaware of a recent law emanating from Annapolis barring the settlement of "free people of color from the North" in the state, was arrested, imprisoned, and shortly thereafter sold to a Georgia planter. He reportedly died not long after "from the effects of exposure and suffering." The appalling case, compounded for Watkins by the knowledge that she, a free person of color now living in the North, could never return to her native Maryland, elicited a decisive reply. "Upon that [man's] grave," she wrote a friend, "I pledged myself to the Anti-Slavery cause."[4]

Introduced to the mid-Atlantic region's thriving Underground Railroad community, she soon joined their ranks and, with an obvious facility for words and a charismatic if not comely presence, came to the attention of the Pennsylvania Anti-Slavery Society, which sent her on a series of lecture tours, mainly to white churches along the East Coast. A steady stream of poems—adjuncts of her activism—now appeared in various newspapers and periodicals. And in addressing one of these to Stowe, she inclined to recognize a fellow ally in the antislavery fight. "I thank thee," her address blessed the now hugely famous author of *Uncle Tom's Cabin*, "for thy pleading."[5]

Born in 1811 to Roxana and Lyman Beecher, Stowe grew up in the maelstrom of early nineteenth-century American reform. Her hometown, Litchfield, Connecticut, retained the architectural complexion of a classic Puritan redoubt, complete with a splendidly steepled Congregational church framed in de rigueur white clapboard. Lyman, a distinguished Presbyterian minister with a national reputation, took on the aura cum attitude of a biblical patriarch, fathering thirteen children, several of who would, in the concurrent perfectionist struggles for almshouses and abolition, education and women's suffrage, attempt to scrub a sinful world clean for Christ's return. Doing her part, Harriet, the seventh child, attended one of the nation's first preparatory schools for girls—the Litchfield Female Academy, organized in 1792 by Sarah Pierce, daughter of a Continental Army paymaster, and supporting some 130 students. Highly regarded, the institution, housed in a simple two-story structure capped with a cupola sheltering a clanging brass bell, drew students from several states as well as Canada and the West Indies. Apart from this foundation of formal education, Harriet received an important supplement in the male manner of the family parlor, where any number of ongoing discussions and debates between father and sons dominated domestic life. Possessing an eye for talent, Lyman discerned in his daughter a disciplined and agile mind clearly superior to that of at least one of her brothers. "Harriet is a great genius," he informed a relative. "I would give a hundred dollars if she was a boy & Henry a girl. . . . She is intelligent & studious."[6]

Packed among a household of eccentrics, Harriet inevitably absorbed a sense of mission, looking to advance education and temperance among other accoutrements of uplift. Physically, she struck different chords among different audiences. Some described her as "owlish," others as "beautiful." One memoirist writes that in adulthood she was "a heavy-lidded woman with large cheekbones and full, sensuous lips."[7] Perhaps, as with Eleanor Roosevelt, her strength and complexity eluded surface observation.

The Beechers left New England in 1832 that Lyman might take up the presidency of Cincinnati's Lane Seminary, a recently founded Presbyterian theological college. Dismayed at the large southern German immigration into that city, Lyman determined to make of Lane a stronghold against creeping Catholicism; instead, he nearly lost control of the school. In February 1834, following eighteen days of intense debates presumably on the question of whether freed blacks should be sent to Africa, about fifty junior scholars declared themselves abolitionists. Lane's conservative board of unamused trustees was furious. With Beecher on a fundraising trip in the East, it swiftly banned students from meeting or making public addresses, thus easing out of existence the seminary's fledgling abolition and colonization societies. Upon his return, a torn Beecher, said by a daughter to have "loved the young men as if they were his own sons," went along with the vinegary trustees whose views on abolitionism he happened to share. At this point dozens of the disillusioned "Lane Rebels," declaring in a printed statement "that free discussion . . . is a DUTY, and of course a RIGHT," departed.[8] The embarrassed seminary and its stunned president were vulnerable to the accusation of attacking open speech.

Taking her father's lead, Harriet too spurned the abolitionist label at this time—and for some time to come. She flirted, at least rhetorically, with antislavery sentiment, though the idea of immediate emancipation far outstripped the faculties of her female academy imagination.

Interestingly, the effort to silence James G. Birney during the Cincinnati Riots in 1836, which had drawn Chase into the orbit of antislavery politics, impacted Harriett as well. "For my part," she wrote, "I can easily see how such proceedings may make converts to abolitionism, for already my sympathies are strongly enlisted for Mr. Birney."[9] Whether she conflated the crowd's attack on Birney's free speech—destroying, as it did, his printing press—with the earlier fiasco at Lane Seminary is unclear, though in both instances men defining themselves as emancipationists demanded the right to be heard.

Months before the riots, Harriet had married the widowed Lane professor Calvin Stowe, a rigorous biblical scholar from New England, though given to spectral visions of tormenting devils, winsome fairies, and the occasional zaftig maiden. Reflecting some years later on her husband's academically impressive though otherwise impecunious career, Harriet made light of her load: "I was married when I was twenty-five years old to a man rich in Greek and Hebrew, Latin and Arabic, and, alas! rich in nothing else."[10] Living in the leafy Cincinnati suburb of Walnut Hills, Harriet mixed domestic duties with more professional aspirations; she gave birth to seven children while producing stories for the city's belletristic clubs, placing temperance and other moral tales in various outlets including *Godey's Lady's Book* and the *New-York Evangelist*. This apprenticeship—and the small but much appreciated income it yielded—served her well for several years, offering connections to local writers while leavening some of her starchier New England chauvinisms before the rife multiplicity of religions, races, and opinions circulating though Cincinnati's swelling antebellum boomtown.

In 1850 the Stowes left Ohio. Calvin, exhausted after years of hat-in-hand fundraising for Lane, accepted a position at his alma mater, Bowdoin College, in Brunswick, Maine. Franklin Pierce and Nathaniel Hawthorne, products of the same small Yankee universe, had been his classmates there. For Harriet, the year proved, in more than a migratory sense, to be of particular significance. Caught, as she put it, "with perfect surprise and consternation" by the Fugitive Slave Act passed in September, she presumed that those obliging northern congressmen who supported the bill were variously blind, blinkered, or elsewise oblivious to slavery's cruel and inhumane character. Accordingly, she made plans to acquaint them with its horrors. Delighted that her sister Catharine

despised the new law, Harriet wrote approvingly, "Your last letter was a
real good one, it did my heart good to find somebody in as indignant a
state as I am about this miserable wicked fugitive slave business—Why
I have felt almost choked sometimes with pent up wrath that does no
good." Determined to do good and increasingly confident in her writing,
Harriet knew by the end of 1850 that she was soon to embark on an ambitious literary project. "As long as the baby sleeps with me nights I can't do
much at anything," she wrote that December to a Boston-situated sister-
in-law, "but I will do it at last. I will write that thing if I live."[11]

Considering that *Uncle Tom's Cabin* is elaborately plotted in various southern settings, it is striking how little Stowe understood the
South from personal acquaintance, having only once spent a few days
in northern Kentucky. There, in the small town of Washington, in the
spring of 1833, while visiting one of her students (Harriet taught at the
Western Female Institute in Cincinnati, a school founded by Catharine),
she happened upon a slave auction. That searing experience, along with
other subsequent exchanges—contact with fugitives and writing to the
enslaved husband of her free black servant—proved indelible. In preparing her novel, however, Stowe relied chiefly upon the observations of
others. The narratives of escaped slaves drew her attention, particularly
the published accounts of Josiah Henson (fled Maryland in 1830) and
Henry Bibb (bolted Kentucky in 1842), both of whom passed discreetly
through Cincinnati on their way, respectively, to Upper Canada and
Detroit. Stowe subsequently acknowledged her debt to the testimony of
runaways in a reprinted edition of *Uncle Tom's Cabin*: "Its author had for
many years lived in Ohio on the confines of a slave state, and had thus
been made familiar with facts and occurrences in relation to the institution of American slavery. Some of the most harrowing incidents related
in the story had from time to time come to her knowledge in conversation with former slaves now free in Ohio."[12]

A fair bit of the novel's plot is set in New Orleans and Stowe leaned
principally upon her brother Charles, formerly employed at a cotton
commission house in that city, to provide color and context. These minute observations she supplemented by studying advertisements for fugitives appearing in several newspapers, including the *New Orleans True
Delta*, the *New Orleans Daily Crescent*, and the *Daily Orleanian*.[13] Wanting still more material, she wrote to Frederick Douglass, eager to draft a
credible portrait of enslavement in the Deep South:

In the course of my story the scene will fall upon a cotton plantation. I am very desirous, therefore, to gain information from one
who has been an actual labourer on one, and it occurred to me that
in the circle of your acquaintance there might be one who would
be able to communicate to me such information as I desire. I have
before me an able paper written by a Southern planter, in which the
details and *modus operandi* are given from his point of sight. I am
anxious to have something more from another standpoint. I wish to
be able to make a picture that shall be graphic and true to nature in
its details. Such a person as Henry Bibb, if in the country, might give
me just the kind of information I desire.[14]

Despite Stowe's gesturing to the planter point of view, much of New
Orleans would never forgive her attentive if selective research. Some
years after the Civil War the *Daily Picayune*, upon learning that she had
suffered a serious accident—cuffing her head upon the exposed edge of
a bedstead and then falling back insensibly into a bathtub—saw no reason to mute its well-braided hate at this late hour. "Had the blow simply
gone to her heart," the paper purred, "it would have been painless to her,
and of no hurt to anything except the furniture, as either tin or wood is
apt to be damaged in an encounter with stone."[15]

In March 1851 Stowe, fully embarked on her book, wrote to Gamaliel Bailey, an abolitionist, occasional Lane lecturer, and former *Philanthropist* publisher (succeeding James G. Birney), now in Washington
editing the *National Era*. He faced in the capital, home to some four
thousand enslaved people, the random threat of mob violence against
his paper, having, on more than one occasion, endured assaults on
his offices. Deep into *Uncle Tom's Cabin* and certain of its strengths,
Stowe offered this old Cincinnati acquaintance "a story" of slavery in
America:

I am at present occupied upon a story which will be a much longer
one than any I have ever written, embracing a series of sketches
which give the lights and shadows of the "patriarchal institution,"
written either from observation, incidents which have occurred in
the sphere of my personal knowledge, or in the knowledge of my
friends. I shall show the *best side* of the thing, and something *faintly
approaching the worst*.[16]

Bailey agreed to serialize the work, though he insisted on an uninterrupted run of chapters. The *National Era* appeared on Thursdays in
Washington and he wanted to avoid long editorial delays expended on
endless corrections or anxious authorial second thoughts. It typically
took between two and four days for the manuscripts to find their way
to the capital, and a cooperative Stowe, a full five hundred miles to the
north in Brunswick, resorted to various strategies to meet deadlines;
she sometimes sent the stories from nearby Portland, though an occasional time crunch sent her to Boston and even New York for quicker
deliveries.

By the late winter of 1852 the series neared the end of its run in the
Era, which informed readers of the collection's impending compilation
in a volume to be put out by the Boston house Jewett and Company. John
Punchard Jewett, relatively new to the publishing business, trafficked
mainly in textbooks, though he kept a hand in both antislavery and
fiction writing as well. Catharine Beecher, an author of several studies
relating to women and education, had tried to interest her house, Phillips, Sampson, and Company, in the project, though it passed, apparently concerned about the book's controversial subject and possibly its
author's controversial sex. This rejection must count as one of the more
extravagant mistakes in publishing history. *Uncle Tom's Cabin* appeared
in two volumes on March 20 and retailed in paper binding for $1 (about
$36 in today's currency) as well as cloth ($1.50) and cloth extra gilt
bindings ($2). Its original run of five thousand sold out immediately, a
second printing of five thousand on April 1 sold out several days later.
In July Stowe received from Jewett her first royalty payment—$10,300
(about $375,000 in current dollars).[17] By the end of the year the book
had sold an astounding three hundred thousand copies.

Uncle Tom's Cabin attends to the varying fortunes of two Kentucky
slaves—the kindly Tom and the brave, light-skinned house servant
Eliza; both have families and are devout Christians. Their owner, a
financially strapped Mr. Shelby, well-meaning in Stowe's rendering but
bound to a brutal system for all that, decides, over the objections of his
kindhearted wife, to sell both Tom and Harry, Eliza's young son. Learning of his plans, Eliza flees the Shelby plantation with her boy in tow.
Along their perilous journey to Canada she is reunited with George,
her educated mulatto husband who had earlier run away—"I've paid

for all my keeping a hundred times over," he tells her. "I *won't* bear it." Following a slew of implausible if affecting plot twists, several having to do with evading a gang of relentless slave catchers, Eliza and her family make their way to Canada and from there to France and finally to Liberia. Tom is not so lucky. He is owned for a time by a New Orleans planter of Huguenot descent possessed of "an extreme . . . sensitiveness of character" and respectful of, indeed awed by, Tom's integrity—"I'm not worth the love of one good, honest heart, like yours." But when this man dies and his estate is divided, Tom ends up on the hellish farmstead of Simon Legree, a graceless Yankee pinchpenny come south to make his fortune among the slavocracy. Playing Satan ("I'll *conquer ye, or kill ye!*") to Tom's Christ ("Do the worst you can, my troubles'll be over soon; but, if ye don't repent, yours won't *never* end!"), he determines to break this black messiah, whose impregnable faith sustains him through a saintly martyrdom.[18]

These all too pious extracts pale before the story's most iconic scene—Eliza's remarkable crossing of the ice-occluded Ohio River with Harry pressed against her breast and a posse of slave patrollers at her back. This liberation epic, this wondrous journey over a modern-day river Jordan, enshrined over the years in a cottage industry of stagy Tomitudes including needlework and figurines, illustrations and decorative screens, thrilled readers eager for Eliza to claim her freedom. "With wild cries and desperate energy," Stowe wrote, "she leaped to another and still another cake;—stumbling—leaping—slipping—springing upwards again! Her shoes are gone—her stockings cut from her feet—while blood marked every step; but she saw nothing, felt nothing, till dimly, as in a dream, she saw the Ohio side, and a man helping her up the bank."[19]

The Kentucky farmer who aided Eliza and Henry, himself a transient of sorts, promised not to betray them. His brief soliloquy doubled as Stowe's simmering damnation of the Fugitive Slave Act. "I don't see no kind of 'casion for me to be hunter and catcher for other folks," he tells the exhausted Eliza. A simple, generous man, this Mr. Symmes exhibits an impulsive humanity, which, Stowe suggests, is superior to the surfeit of political compromises that have permitted slavery's unseemly extension into the second half of the century. Though he is but a "poor, heathenish Kentuckian," bereft, she slyly writes, of "instruct[ion] in his constitutional relations," his innate Christian character shines through.[20] He knows, that is, the difference between right and wrong, measured in the urgent river distance separating man's litigation from God's law.

Stowe takes a further swipe at the popular sovereignty vogue introduced by Douglas in the Compromise of 1850. "If all the broad land between the Mississippi and the Pacific becomes one great market for bodies and souls," she omnipotently opines, "and human property retains the locomotive tendencies of this nineteenth century, the trader and catcher may yet be among our aristocracy."[21] In this and other ominous clauses, she gives voice to the terrors, criticisms, and concerns of a painfully divided nation. Expressed only imperfectly by imperfect politicians, these anxieties come alive with a sharp immediacy in the novel, communicating in a heartfelt sense what a conflicted Congress never could.

Such disquieting sentiments are rendered especially effective in Stowe's decision to portray slavery as a shared sin, an ecumenical evil sustained by both sections. In one sharply etched scene a Louisiana planter convincingly accuses a New England cousin of hypocrisy. "You would not have them abused," he says of the enslaved, "but you don't want to have anything to do with them yourselves. You would send them to Africa, out of your sight and smell, and then send a missionary or two to do up all the self-denial of elevating them compendiously." Embroidering this point, Stowe draws out for readers those various northern networks of complicity—merchants and insurers, lawyers and creditors—that keep the business of bondage strong, expansive, and legal. "Shall the whole guilt or obloquy of slavery," she writes, "fall only on the South?" To punctuate this point, she makes the hated Legree, one of the most despicable characters in all of literature, a Vermont expat. Stowe, so one of her sons later noted, "wished to be more than fair to the South. . . . She tried to show that the fault was not with the Southern people, but with the system."[22]

Finding much to praise in this approach, the northern cultural elite took notice. The Transcendentalist Ralph Waldo Emerson called *Uncle Tom's Cabin* the "only book that found readers in the parlor, the nursery, and the kitchen in every household," while New England poet John Greenleaf Whittier told William Lloyd Garrison it was "a glorious work." The Unitarian minister Thomas Wentworth Higginson, bearer of an impressive Hulihee beard and an early male advocate of women's rights, thought the novel unprecedented in its melding of art and social reform: "To have written at once the most powerful of contemporary fiction and the most efficient of anti-slavery tracts is a double triumph in literature and philanthropy," he addressed Stowe directly, "to which this country has heretofore seen no parallel." Sill more succinctly, Frederick Douglass said of the book's opportune appearance, "Nothing could have better suited the moral and humane requirements of the hour."[23]

From the vantage of the early twentieth century, an aged Henry James looked back upon the novel as a benchmark of his remembered youth. "We lived and moved at that time," he wrote, "with great intensity, in Mrs. Stowe's" story. Eliza's journey across the "perilous stream, intrepidly and gracefully performed," remained lodged in his mind, as did the unexpected joy of sharing a cause with numbers untold, caught in "the extraordinary fortune" that reached beyond the passive pleasures of reading toward a "state of vision, of feeling and of consciousness" greater than the individual and larger than any American book that had come before.[24]

The reactions overseas were equally gratifying. A clearly moved Queen Victoria lingered loyally over the novel, unable to shake its oppressive spell, and wrote in her diary: "Found Uncle Tom's Cabin too painful—really terrible. To what can human nature descend. It quite haunts me." Across the Channel the popular French author George Sand described Stowe as a "woman so gentle, so humane, so religious, and full of evangelical unction," while farther to the east the Russian novelist Leo Tolstoy called Uncle Tom's Cabin "one of the greatest productions of the human mind."[25]

Suddenly a star—"Uncle Tomism . . . is now sweeping the Continent" shouted the New-York Tribune—Stowe toured Britain with a small party for several weeks in the spring of 1853, invited by two Glasgow ladies' antislavery societies.[26] Landing in Liverpool, the Americans proceeded to London, pressed immediately into the society of artists and aristocrats. The city's lord mayor arranged a sumptuous dinner in Stowe's honor, held, so the honoree noted, in "a splendid hall." There, and in a pleasant evening of chat, Catherine Dickens and her husband, Charles, appeared to charm the visiting American with their casual bonhomie. At the dining table Stowe observed:

> Directly opposite me was Mr. Dickens, whom I now beheld for
> the first time, and was surprised to see looking so young. . . . We
> rose from the table between eleven and twelve o'clock—that is, we

ladies—and went into the drawing-room, where I was presented
to Mrs. Dickens and several other ladies. Mrs. Dickens is a good
specimen of a truly English woman; tall, large, and well developed,
with fine, healthy color. . . . A friend whispered to me that she was
as observing and fond of humor as her husband. After a while
the gentlemen came back to the drawing-room, and I had a few
moments of very pleasant, friendly conversation with Mr. Dickens.
They are both people that one could not know a little without desiring to know more.[27]

Crossing onto the Continent, Stowe "did" Paris, negotiated the Swiss
Alps, and toured several German cities, making pilgrimages to various
Martin Luther sites. "We breathed where he had breathed," wrote her
obviously enchanted brother Charles. Retreating back to the French
capital and thence to England, Stowe and her troop planned to press
on to Ireland that fall, but Calvin's mewling from the American shore—
"It seems a long, long time to wait till November before seeing you"—
convinced her to cut the journey short.[28]

Back in the United States, the nation's antislavery elite coveted Stowe's
stature and services; she faced the more radical among them with evident trepidation. "I am a constant reader of your paper, and an admirer
of much that is in it," she handed William Lloyd Garrison a bouquet . . .
before politely snatching it back—"At the same time I regard with apprehension and sorrow much that is in it. Were it circulated only among
intelligent, well-balanced minds, able to discriminate between good and
evil, I should not feel so much apprehension. To *me* the paper is decidedly valuable as a fresh and able exposé of the ultra progressive element
in our times. What I fear is, that it will take from poor Uncle Tom his
Bible, and give him nothing in its place. You understand me—do you
not?"[29] Stowe's patronizing attitude in this communication lightly con-
jures the shared condescension of those infantilizing planters and New
England matrons her novel had exposed.

Though predictably demonized in the South, Stowe, in fact, held
views on race more conventional than her critics might have imagined.
Calvin claimed that Lyman Beecher retained "not a little of the old Connecticut prejudice about blacks," while other Stowes recalled Harriet's
fidelity to her father's racial views. When writing *Uncle Tom's Cabin*, two
of them noted, "Mrs. Stowe was not an Abolitionist, nor did she ever

become one after the Garrisonian type. She remembered hearing her
father say about Garrison and [the Boston antislavery crusader] Wendell Phillips that they were like men that would burn their houses down
to get rid of the rats. She was virtually in sympathy with her father on
the subject of slavery, and had unlimited confidence in his judgment."[30]

Such largely private views did nothing to endear Stowe to an affronted
white southern readership. The criticism—and name-calling—came
quickly. George Frederick Holmes of the important *Southern Literary
Messenger*, a Richmond-based paper once an outlet for Edgar Allan Poe,
sniffed that Stowe was "an obscure Yankee school mistress, eaten up
with fanaticism, festering with the malignant virtues of abolitionism . . .
[and] devoted to the assertion of women's rights." Seeing red, a *New
Orleans Crescent* reviewer charged Stowe with "whet[ting] the knife of
domestic murder" by promoting "slavery insurrection," while the popular southern writer William Gilmore Simms (said by Poe to be "the best
novelist which this country has ever yet, upon the whole, produced")
scorned her as a she-devil in disguise: "Mrs. Stowe betrays a malignity
so remarkable that the petticoat lifts of itself, and we see the hoof of the
beast."[31]

Invariably a robust anti-Tom industry cropped up, attacking Stowe's
text but in doing so conceding its power to shape debate. Interestingly,
of the eighteen volumes identified in this genre through 1854, proslavery northerners, several of whom had relocated to the South, wrote
eleven; most of the books were published in New York and Philadelphia.
The titles of these anxious offerings, including Mary Henderson Eastman's *Aunt Phillis's Cabin; or, Southern Life as It Is* (1852) and John W.
Page's *Uncle Robin, in His Cabin in Virginia, and Tom without One in
Boston* (1853), betray every bit of their authors' desire to set the historical and racial records straight. Conceding nothing to her nemesis,
Eastman described abolitionism as "born in fanaticism [and] nurtured
in violence," while finding slavery "authorized by God, permitted by
Jesus Christ, [and] sanctioned by the apostles."[32] These studies in special
pleading might be said to have led straight to the gates of Tara, the fic-
tional plantation in Georgia native Margaret Mitchell's 1936 epic, *Gone
with the Wind*.

Despite provoking such an intense reaction among Dixie's defenders,
Stowe's novel appears to have found a select audience among southern
readers. Advertisements for the book appeared in a handful of news-

papers, while a professor at South Carolina College in Columbia (now
the University of South Carolina) informed a friend of its purchasabil-
ity in the town.[33] Beginning in February 1853 and extending into the
Kansas-Nebraska debates the following year, the Connecticut-born
landscape architect Frederick Law Olmsted, best known for designing Manhattan's urban Eden—Central Park—plied the New York *Daily
Times* with vivid reportage of his fourteen-month circuit of the South.
Some southerners supposed him a spy. He noted, while aboard a steamboat in Louisiana:

> Among the peddlers there were . . . two or three copies of the cheap
> edition (pamphlet) of *Uncle Tom's Cabin*. They did not cry it out as
> they did the other books they had, but held it forth among others,
> so its title could be seen. One of them told me he carried it because
> gentlemen often inquired for it, and he sold a good many: at least
> three copies were sold to passengers on the boat.[34]

The novel's enormous success, prompting a nagging admission from
the *Richmond Enquirer*—"We have . . . produced no romance quite equal
to *Uncle Tom's Cabin*"—made its author a target of some calculated hate.
In one particularly repugnant case the Stowe residence received a package, bearing a southern return address, containing the severed ear of a
black person. More generally, the mails brought from the South a slew
of proslavery censures. "They were so curiously compounded," one relative later recalled, "of blasphemy, cruelty, and obscenity."[35]
    Stowe also received criticism from a small number of northerners
who thought her safely segregationist prescription for the "slave question" in America—voluntary emigration to Africa—abhorrent. Near the
end of *Uncle Tom's Cabin*, she cleanly extricated several of the novel's
characters from the scene, placing them on a boat to Liberia—"On the
shores of Africa," George tells Eliza, "I see a republic." In reply to this
removal fantasy, a cordial but firm Frederick Douglass wrote to Stowe:
"The truth is, dear madam, we are *here*, & here we are likely to remain."
In the more public pages of *The Liberator*, a royal "we"–wielding Garrison, though alive to the undoubted power of Stowe's novel—"we confess
to the . . . trembling of every nerve within us, in the perusal of the incidents and scenes so vividly depicted in her pages"—ended his otherwise
affirming review on a briny note: "The work, towards its conclusion,

contains some objectionable sentiments respecting African colonization, which we regret to see."[36] Despite such caveats Garrison, among
other reviewers, more generally detected in *Uncle Tom's Cabin* evidence
of an older jeremiadic tradition, redolent of Puritan pathos, sensitive to
indices of sin, and committed to a coming day of justice.

In February 1854 Stowe, like much of America, concentrated her attention on the public debate developing over the Kansas-Nebraska bill.
Finding the manifesto style popularized by Chase a comfortable fit, she
penned her own "Appeal to the Women of the Free States" to appear
in the pages of *The Independent*, a reform-minded New York weekly
organized by a trio of Congregationalist ministers. Proclaiming all good
womanhood unwilling "to receive slavery into the free States and territories of the Union," she endorsed a protest of assorted prayers and
petitions designed to direct northern public opinion to the rising crisis
at hand.[37]

Elsewhere that late winter the angular, aquiline-nosed Emerson, a
discerning Stowe admirer of some punditic repute, offered yet another
kind of public prayer against slavery. He spoke for himself, his community, and a restless New England nation, embarrassed by its lapsed status
and eager to slip the short leash of a long slaveholder ascendancy.

6

Emerson in the Arena

This filthy enactment was made in the 19th Century, by people
who could read and write. I will not obey it, by God.

Ralph Waldo Emerson, reacting to the
Fugitive Slave Law, 1851

Like the genteel Stowe, Waldo Emerson came reluctantly to the antislavery crusade. The century's leading booster of "Self-Reliance"—the
title and topic of perhaps his most arresting essay—he emphasized the
person over the party, the self over the swarm. "I have taught one doctrine," he wrote in a journal, "namely, the infinitude of the private man."
The anti-conformity theme is replete in Emerson, a caution against the
dead hand of history, a clarion call to preserve privacy from combinations, organizations, and the blunt force of officialdom. For some years
he accordingly kept away from the brewing politics of social improvement. He refused an invitation to join a utopian experiment in collective living at nearby Brook Farm—"It seems to me a circuitous . . . way
of relieving myself of any irksome circumstances, to put on [a] community the task of my emancipation which I ought to take on myself"—and
maintained a critical distance from abolition coalitions.[1] But then came
the Fugitive Slave Law in 1850.

This all too perfect provocation soon drew Emerson into an open
and ongoing quarrel with the plantocracy. The nation's most respected
public intellectual, he spoke forcefully against the act, most notably in
a well-attended address delivered in Lower Manhattan in March 1854.

With the Kansas-Nebraska debate serving unexpectedly as a blistering backdrop, the lecture, meant to censure a nearly four-year-old evil, suddenly joined that winter's convulsive debate on slavery's bid to break into the West.

Born in 1803 to an old New England family, Emerson blended the region's immemorial emphasis on individual conversion with the rise in his own time of an unprecedented common-man democracy. In each instance the self-reliance theme could variously be gleaned in the imperative power of a single person—to elect salvation or a president. In youth, Emerson appeared to be anything but singular. The astute son of an esteemed Unitarian minister who commanded a prized pulpit at Boston's First Church (est. 1630), he seemed destined, rather, to follow in his well-placed *père*'s occupational path. Educated at Harvard (but of course), he subsequently attended the college's distinguished Divinity School—a staid rectangular brick building in Flemish bond with a hint of brownstone trim—and briefly tried his hand at teaching. Then, for health reasons, he went south. Fearing consumption (two of his younger brothers, Edward and Charles, died of the disease while still in their twenties) and concerned about weight loss, he traveled aboard the "commodious" twenty-five-sailed *Clematis* in late 1826 to Charleston, South Carolina, and, finding its dry winter air "bitter cold," thence to St. Augustine, Florida. There, while attending a Bible Society meeting held inside a simple two-story government building, he caught just outside its walls the unmistakable commotion of a chattel auction. This gross conspiracy of church, state, and enslavement wedged its way into the young man's searching mind. "One ear therefore heard the glad tidings of great joy," he caustically wrote in a daybook, "whilst the other was regaled with 'Going gentlemen, Going!' And almost without changing our position we might aid in sending the scriptures into Africa or bid for 'four children without the mother who had been kidnapped therefrom.'"[2]

In 1829 Emerson made what seemed to be two decisive, life-settling decisions of eros and occupation. In September, after marrying a young, pretty Ellen Louisa Tucker, still in her teens, he received ordination as junior pastor of Boston's historic Second Church (1649–1970) on busy Hanover Street. Fifteen months later, however, a consumptive Ellen died of progressive tuberculosis and Emerson, in the habit of visiting her grave each day, lifting the coffin's lid on at least one occasion, as if to convince himself, appeared quietly lost. Citing, possibly in some cold anger, the perfunctory ceremonies of the church—"dead forms," he thought—he refused to serve communion and soon resigned. Sailing on Christmas Day 1832 for Europe, he wandered about Britain and the Continent, gulping down languages and calling upon a host of literary eminences, among them the Romantic poets Samuel Taylor Coleridge and William Wordsworth as well as the Scottish polymath Thomas Carlyle, before returning home to establish himself as a writer and lecturer. He remarried in 1835.[3]

Emerson's second wife, thirty-two-year-old Lydia Jackson Emerson (called Lidian by her husband), descended from an emotionally austere Plymouth family and had given every prenuptial impression of impending spinsterhood. Reserved, lacking Ellen's easy beauty, but more intellectual, she settled with Emerson in Concord, some dozen miles west of Boston, in a roomy four-square, two-story frame house, now a National Historic Landmark. He remained in the residence the rest of his life, spending hours untold in the bright book-lined first-floor study where, encased in a cushioned rocking chair beside a stained round wood table, he wrote many of his more important works and entertained a gaggle of local luminaries including Henry David Thoreau, Margaret Fuller, and *Little Women* author Louisa May Alcott. The Emersons raised four children in this home; he called her "Queenie"; she called him "Mr. Emerson."[4]

Upon this stable foundation Mr. Emerson produced over the next few years the storied corpus of writings—among them *Nature* (1836), "The American Scholar" (1837), and "The Divinity School Address" (1838)—that secured his reputation as America's high priest of individualism and "self-culture." Rejecting a systemic philosophy of fossilized first principles, Emerson advanced his ideas through poetry, private insight, and occasionally abstruse analogies to nature. Emphasizing a romantic reliance on the self—"trust thyself," "Whoso would be a man, must be a nonconformist," "to be great is to be misunderstood"—he proved undeniably popular and toured America for decades, giving some fifteen hundred public lectures.[5] Tall, long-limbed, and pale-complexioned, Emerson offered discerning observers a tempting target for caricature. One of them, Julian Hawthorne, the only son of the celebrated dark romantic novelist Nathaniel, remembered a physically inelegant man, sober, slightly formal, and "buttoned up":

Emerson was ungainly in build, with narrow, sloping shoulders, large feet and hands, and a projecting carriage of the head, which enhanced the eagle-like expression of his glance and features. His head was small; it was covered ... with light brown hair, fine and straight; he was clean-shaven save for a short whisker; the peaked ends of an uncomfortable collar appeared above the folds of a high, black silk stock. His long-skirted black coat was commonly buttoned up; he wore, on different occasions, a soft felt hat or a high silk one, the latter, from use, having become in a manner humanized. On the street he kept his face up as he walked along, and perceived the approach of an acquaintance afar off, and the wise, slow smile gleamed about his mouth as he drew near.[6]

Emerson's first prominent public venture into the field of social reform occurred in 1838 when he wrote to President Martin Van Buren, condemning the removal of Georgia's Cherokees, the tragic culmination of several forced relocations that decade known collectively as the Trail of Tears. Published in the (Washington) *Daily National Intelligencer*, the open letter accused the United States of lying, stealing, and hoisting a "sham treaty" upon the Indians. Insisting that "a crime is projected" and lamenting "so vast an outrage upon the Cherokee nation," Emerson offered a grim warning should the sham in question be enacted: "You, sir, will bring down that renowned chair in which you sit into infamy if your seal is set to this instrument of perfidy; and the name of this nation ... will stink to the world."[7]

During these years Emerson showed little interest in joining the slowly organizing struggle against slavery. A symbol of self-reliance, he believed that genuine reform could only begin from within. Laws and decrees, precedents and legalese, lacked the capacity to compel moral behavior, which, he promised, emerged only in the quite truths of transcendence. Emerson looked upon organized abolitionism through this same skeptical lens. He believed less in the gyrating stump orator's showy capacity to conjure up an instant conversion than in the power of the whole person to reach higher ground. The uncoupled campaigns of temperance and women's rights, Sabbatarianism and antislavery, that banged about the early nineteenth century thus failed to win Emerson's favor. They struck him as fractional, disjointed, and partial, a sequence of separate assaults that pursued improvement in pieces.

Emerson's journals are consequently littered with sarcastic asides coolly sending up abolitionism. One 1838 entry spoofs reform-minded Concord, where "every third man lectures on slavery" in a feverish bid to "turn the world upside down"; another calls such one-note do-gooders an "odious set . . . the worst of bores and canters," while still another, written in early 1854 as Emerson prepared to deliver his address on the Fugitive Slave Law, questioned both the wisdom and sincerity of the more radical abolitionists: "[Wendell] Phillips, Garrison, & others I have always the feeling that they may wake up some morning & find that they have made a capital mistake, & are not the persons they took themselves for." He dismissed Garrison's uncompromising *Liberator* as "a scold."[8]

These criticisms corresponded to the kind of well-read, well-bred racism that trickled through progressive Boston. "It cannot be maintained by any candid person," Emerson confessed to his journal in 1837, "that the African race have ever occupied or do promise ever to occupy any very high place in the human family. Their present condition is the strongest proof that they cannot." He thought emancipation likely to expose an inability on the part of the formerly enslaved to compete in a dynamic civilization, leaving the "free negro," so he later wrote, "standing as he does in nature below the series of thought, & in the plane of vegetable & animal existence." Surely, he supposed, Africans could have no future in America. "The dark man, the black man declines," he wrote privately in 1854, "the black man is courageous, but the white men are the children of God, said Plato. It will happen by & by, that the black man will only be destined for museums like the [extinct] dodo."[9]

In full, Emerson's racial views embraced both public and personal dimensions that belie a simple assessment. Though doubting the prospects of blacks to succeed in America's competitive capitalist cockpit, he nevertheless insisted upon their right to justice. Contra Stowe and many others in the North, he dismissed entirely the argument that those emancipated should be summarily expelled and displaced to Africa. Rather, and anticipating later calls for reparations, he thought it only fair that formerly enslaved peoples be excused from paying taxes, "on the ground that discrimination denied them the full benefits of citizenship." Such assertions placed Emerson on the progressive side of the race question in antebellum America. His "racism," writes biographer

Lawrence Buell, "was certainly no greater than that of most northern white abolitionists, and far less than the average northern white." Aware of his limitations on this subject, Emerson confessed to Thomas Wentworth Higginson that he had "a mild natural colorphobia, controlled only by moral conviction."[10]

More generally, Julian Hawthorne detected in Emerson an abstract quality that rendered him subtly unadaptable to exercising a condolent pity or rapport. "My father was the shyer and more solitary of the two," he wrote, "and yet persons in need of human sympathy were able to reach a more interior region in him than they could in Emerson. For the latter's thought was concerned with types and classes."[11] Unable to grieve for a race he did not know, Emerson ultimately joined the public outcry against slavery when he recognized the institution as an infringement of *white* freedom. The Fugitive Slave Law's provision that northern citizens engage in the practice of arresting runaways upon the demand of southern masters drew him into this fight. For if the state could compel the people to go against their moral principles then self-reliance meant nothing.

In contrast to other Emersons, Waldo came slowly to abolitionism. His brother Charles, influential aunt Mary Moody, and wife Lidian were all earlier converts to black emancipation. While Emerson looked askance at the antislavery speakers circulating through New England, Lidian found meaning in their message. In September 1837 the prominent Grimké sisters, Sarah and Angelina, born on a large South Carolina plantation but later relocating to Philadelphia (attracted to its Quaker population's broad-minded views on slavery and gender equality), spoke for three restless nights in Concord. "I suppose [you] have heard of the Misses Grimké who [are going] about the country advocating [freedom for] the slave," Lidian wrote with great interest to her sister. "They have passed [this] week in Concord and been well received. They dined & took tea with [me] one day and it was a pleasure to entertain such angel strangers—pure & benevolent spirits are they. I think I shall not turn away my attention from the abolition cause till I have found whether there is not something for me personally to do and bear to forward it."[12] The following month Lidian helped some sixty women—including Henry David Thoreau's sister Helen and his mother, Cynthia—establish the Concord Female Anti-Slavery Society.

Seven years later, in 1844, it was this organization that invited the

organization-averse Emerson to speak at the tenth anniversary of emancipation in the British West Indies. The reasons for his willingness to
offer an address are perhaps varied. Lidian's model and presence no
doubt contributed, as did the nation's increasing focus on Texas, whose
looming annexation promised to buttress the planters' congressional
power and thus, so Emerson wrote privately, "to retard or retrograde
the civilization of ages."[13]

Among his neighbors, a striking number were disinclined to welcome
such a peppery message. Despite a reputation for windmill tilting and
air castle erecting, Concordians viewed with some mixed opinion their
resident savant's speaking on emancipation, and the local churches flatly
refused to house the event. Nathaniel Hawthorne offered up the large
front lawn of the Old Manse, a Georgian box built in 1770 by Emerson's
grandfather and now occupied by the writer and his family, though rain
interrupted this friendly overture. Finally, the principals settled on the
town courthouse. And when a dyspeptic sexton of the First Parish church
balked at ringing its bell, a determined Henry Thoreau raced from door
to door announcing the assembly.

Perhaps predictably, Emerson used this address to cast the abolition
of slavery in the British West Indies as a heroic exercise in transcen-
dental idealism. "On reviewing this history," he said, "I think the whole
transaction reflects infinite honor on the people and parliament of England. It was a stately spectacle, to see the cause of human rights argued
with so much patience and generosity and with such a mass of evidence
before that powerful people." He further described Britain's action as "a
moral revolution" in which London's planters-in-absentia relinquished,
presumably via moral reasoning, their Caribbean slaves. "Other revolu-
tions have been the insurrection of the oppressed; this was the repentance of the tyrant," he claimed. "It was the masters revolting from their
mastery. The slave-holder said, 'I will not hold slaves.' The end was noble
and the means were pure." It was man's "intellect," he contended, that
finally overcame "a love of sugar."[14]

That Emerson seemed not wholly convinced by his performance
might be inferred from a careful communication he wrote a few months
later to Carlyle, a sugar-lord enthusiast. "Though I sometimes accept a
popular call, and preach on Temperance or the Abolition of Slavery,"
he struck a note of contrition, "I am sure to feel, before I have done
with it, what an intrusion it is into another sphere, and so much loss

of virtue in my own."[15] In praising the "purity" of the British planters before a congregation of the converted, he seemed to wonder if he had not finally sold himself to a society. But the times would not let him alone. The admission of Texas, war with Mexico, and Fugitive Slave Law brought black bondage to the vital center of civic debate. The latter of these provocations moved Emerson more closely into the abolitionist camp than he had yet ventured.

That New England's greatest statesman had defended the despised Fugitive Slave Act added yet another wrinkle to its notoriety. As noted, in March 1850 Daniel Webster endorsed the law before a packed Senate gallery. Known as the country's preeminent orator and among its greatest nationalists, he peered at the world with stained, sunken eyes; colloquialized, perhaps not always affectionately, as Black Dan, he exhibited a stern exterior, a sloping nose, and (in youth) jet-black hair. The American writer and Whig politician Samuel Goodrich had met a bevy of important men, ranging from Washington power brokers to King George IV, but thought none Webster's equal: "Not one of these approached Mr. Webster in the commanding power of their personal presence. There was a grandeur in his form, an intelligence in his deep dark eye, a loftiness of his expansive brow, a significance in his arched lip, altogether beyond those of any other human being I ever saw."[16]

Ill, aged, and wedded to a fading vision of the Union, Webster, in an act of evasion for which some never forgave him, presented slavery in his 1850 address as anything other than a moral crisis. He mechanically argued that "the law of nature" kept enslaved peoples out of the West while providing abundant opportunities for the planters in the country's rich cotton-blossoming climes. He further scolded his Yankee brethren for their evident—and legally dubious—aid to runaway slaves. "There has been found at the North, among individuals and among legislators," he said, pointing a thin accusatory finger, "a disinclination to perform, fully, their constitutional duties in regard to the return of persons bound to service who have escaped into the free States." And on this all-important point he averred, "The South is right, and the North wrong." Conscience mattered not at all, except in what it owed the master class: "I put it to all the sober and sound minds at the North as a question of morals. . . . What right have they . . . to endeavor to get round this Constitution, to embarrass the free exercise of the rights secured by the

Constitution to the persons whose slaves escape from them? None at all; none at all."[17]

Though Webster recognized that most northerners had little sympathy for abolitionism, he badly misread the degree to which they would resent a federal law calling for their active cooperation in the rendition of runaways. Criticism came quickly. Massachusetts educational reformer Horace Mann called the senator "a fallen star!," while the Transcendentalist Theodore Parker, a charismatic West Roxbury minister with a strong following, dismissed the speech as "a bid for the Presidency." In something of a representative editorial, the formerly friendly *Boston Atlas* now coldly observed that Webster's "sentiments are not our sentiments"—a conviction confirmed for many that autumn when the state's Whigs convened to condemn the Fugitive Slave Law. Emerson, always drawn to the Great Man motif, counted himself among the disillusioned. Upon Webster's death in 1852 he wrote in a journal: "The sea, the rocks, the woods, gave no sign that America & the world had lost the completest man. Nature had not in our days, or, not since Napoleon, cut out such a masterpiece. . . . But alas! he was the victim of his ambition; to please the South betrayed the North, and was thrown out by both."[18]

Webster's reputation as New England's representative man, heir to the Puritan pulpit, made his fall all the more mortifying. His prosy 1820 Plymouth Bicentennial Address, witnessed by an elderly John Adams, honored the country's Pilgrim foundations ("We have come to this Rock, to record here our homage . . .") and presaged his much-anticipated dedication oration at the Bunker Hill monument five years later. In a famous 1830 Senate debate with South Carolina senator Robert Hayne, a defender of states' rights, Webster brilliantly carried the day declaiming in favor of "Liberty *and* Union, now and for ever, one and inseparable!" Over the years his proud words had penetrated the hearts of two generations of northeasterners; the young memorized his speeches, while the old embraced his ties to the patriot past. But Emerson, who once called Webster "a natural Emperor of men," now rued his former allegiance.[19]

Taking effect in September 1850, the Fugitive Slave Law chased abroad some two thousand free and runaway blacks within a month. In April of the following year Thomas Sims, a captive from a Georgia rice plantation though skilled in masonry, was apprehended in Boston, swiftly returned to the South (following a hasty trial in a courthouse

enchained to keep protesters out), and, after a public whipping, sold to a
Mississippi planter. Inching away from his arch individualism, Emerson
informed his diary that the community's failure to protect Sims "make
us irretrievably ashamed. . . . It is now as disgraceful to be a Bostonian
as it was hitherto a credit."[20]

Less than two weeks after Sims's removal, some thirty-five Concordians signed a letter requesting Emerson to offer a public address
expressing his "opinion upon the Fugitive Slave Law and upon the
aspects of the times." This he did, only a few days later, on May 3. Opening epigrammatically—"the last year has forced us all into politics"—
Emerson attempted to poke and prod his audience. Refusing to bait the
South, he upbraided, rather, this complacent New England assembly,
vain in the virtues won by others in a now-receding Revolutionary past.
"The whole wealth and power of Boston,—200,000 souls, and 180 millions of money,—are thrown," in light of the Sims case, "into the scale of
crime." And in condemning compliance to the Fugitive Slave Act on the
elevated grounds that "if our resistance to this law is not right, there is
no right," he made a case for civil disobedience. Considering the planters' congressional hegemony, courage and conviction now outweighed
whatever statutes or statements emanated out of a captive Washington.
The sole but significant virtue of this otherwise dreadful situation, so
Emerson concluded, is that it "has turned every dinner-table [in Bos-
ton] into a debating club."[21]

And then for nearly three years Emerson, though active on the
fashionable lyceum circuit (adult education and high-mindedness with
the occasional picnic), avoided directly debating slavery. This changed
in late 1853 when he agreed to appear the following spring in a lecture series at the Broadway (Manhattan) Tabernacle sponsored by the
New York Anti-Slavery Society. One of thirteen speakers collectively
described by the series' promoters as "eminent champions of Freedom,"
Emerson would join a strong roster of abolitionists and advocates of
women's rights including Garrison and Phillips, *New-York Tribune* editor Horace Greeley, Massachusetts suffragist Lucy Stone, and Stowe's
mesmerizing brother Henry Ward Beecher, the popular pastor of
Brooklyn's Plymouth Church. The series, commencing in December
and concluding in early March, would present perhaps the most concentrated oratorical attack on slavery in the nation's history. Though
conceived prior to the Nebraska bill's arrival, the lecture cycle took on

added urgency as Douglas's efforts to overturn the Missouri Compromise now dominated public discussion.[22]

Eager to attract large audiences, the series promoters staggered their speakers accordingly. And Emerson, the plumed Transcendentalist, the seer cum sage of American individualism, would take the dais last—significantly, conspicuously on March 7, the fourth anniversary of Webster's infamous speech. Apparently, Emerson had hoped to offer his audience fresh thoughts. Busily engaged, however, on an extensive ("as far as Milwaukee," so he noted) lecture run that winter, he had little time to produce an original address. "I came home near three weeks ago," he wrote to a colleague, "with good hope to write a plea for Freedom addressed *to my set*; which, of course, like a Divinity Collegian's first sermon, was to exhaust the subject & moral science generally." When these good intentions failed to bear fruit, he continued, "[I] had to carry to New York a makeshift instead of an oracle." This improvised effort proved to be yet another attack on the Fugitive Slave Law, though one decidedly enlivened for being given before an audience made restive by the recent upheaval in Congress. "There is nobody in Washington who can explain this Nebraska business to the people," Emerson complained. "It is only done by Douglas & his accomplices by calculation on the brutal ignorance of the people."[23]

The spacious Broadway Tabernacle church, erected in 1836 and located a few blocks below Canal Street on Broadway between Worth Street and Catherine Lane, held some twenty-five hundred. A megachurch of the mid-nineteenth century, its interior featured an impressive central rotunda—to accentuate both stage and speaker—enclosed by six large columns; an orchestra and choir camped out behind the pulpit. The building, its acoustic properties said to be "unusually good," hosted during the antebellum years a crush of discussions and debates intent on soliciting social improvement. "There was no place in the city (with the single exception of Castle Garden) so well suited for popular assemblages," one of the Tabernacle's deacons insisted many years after listening to Emerson's lecture. "And to it the people and strangers from all parts of the country flocked on every occasion. It was a veritable 'Tribune of the people,' and the Cradle of Congregationalism in New York City."[24]

Emerson paraded upon its stage to reenter the four-year debate over the Fugitive Slave Law and to offer his first antislavery lecture outside

Massachusetts. Prevailing again upon Julian Hawthorne, we might collect an impression of this celebrated speaker's appearance before the
Tabernacle faithful:

> On the lecture platform he stood erect and unadorned, his hands
> hanging folded in front, save when he changed the leaf of his man-
> uscript, or emphasized his words with a gesture: his customary one,
> simple but effective, was to clinch his right fist, knuckles upward, the
> arm bent at the elbow, then a downward blow of the forearm, full of
> power bridled. It was accompanied by . . . a glance like the reveille
> of a trumpet.[25]

Emerson's lecture both repeated and deepened positions staked out
in his earlier Concord address. The totemic Black Dan, though now
dead for some seventeen months (suffering at the age of seventy from
cirrhosis of the liver and languidly sustained near the end on soporifics,
morphine, and spoonfuls of sweet brandy), was condemned yet again.
In "the final hour" of an immense struggle between good and evil, liberty and captivity, poor "Mr. Webster decided for Slavery." Still another
well-known knave, the plantocracy, received a predictable thrashing as
well. For the Fugitive Slave Act disclosed, so Emerson aired New England's enveloping unease, "the secret of the new times, that Slavery was
no longer mendicant, but was become aggressive and dangerous."[26]

Hitting his stride and falling upon a favorite theme, he still more
broadly called into question the nation's stress on material over spiritual
well-being. Mere wealth had failed to inspire, after all, the freedom proposed by the Founders or the self-reliance pressed by Emerson himself. A pernicious taste for sugar and tobacco, rather, combined with
the remarkable ascendancy of King Cotton—critical provisioner of the
Boston-based textile revolution in the United States—to make slavery
acceptable, supportable, and even respectable. More than anything,
Emerson argued, the fugitive law "showed that our prosperity had hurt
us, and that we could not be shocked by crime. It showed that the old
religion and the sense of the right had faded and gone out; that while
we reckoned ourselves a highly cultivated nation, our bellies had run
away with our brains, and the principles of culture and progress did not
exist."[27]

Only by embracing emancipation, Emerson continued, might

Americans remain true to something deeper than a republic of mandates and magistrates. Offering a dreary catalog of the controversial accords and divisive legislation that shaped enslavement's history in the United States, he seemed to be making a call to arms. "You relied on the Supreme Court," he told his audience. "But what if unhappily the judges were chosen from the wolves, and give to all the law a wolfish interpretation? You relied on the Missouri Compromise. That is ridden over. You relied on State sovereignty in the Free States to protect their citizens. . . . And now you relied on these dismal guaranties infamously made in 1850. . . . They are no guaranty to the free states." With a hungry wolf pawing at the door, Emerson, reaching for resonance, closed on an equivocal note: "The Fugitive Law did much to unglue the eyes of men, and now the Nebraska Bill leaves us staring."[28]

Reaction to the address in Massachusetts, its bright brick textile mills profiting from a sea of southern cotton, was predictably mixed. The *Boston Bee* called Emerson the leader of "a few hundred ridiculous fools and lazy fellows," a mischief-maker performing before "a parcel of selfish flunkies." A *Boston Transcript* reporter, however, wrote that under the Concordian's command "the old theme" of the terrible Fugitive Slave Law "wears a new beauty when clothed with the graces of his thought."[29]

On March 11, just four days after delivering the Tabernacle address, Emerson pondered uneasily over conditions in the United States, believing that the country was rapidly approaching a point of no return. "American is growing furiously," he wrote his old friend Carlyle, "town & state, new Kansas, new Nebraska looming up in these days, vicious politicians seething a wretched destiny for them already at Washington. . . . The fight of slave & freeman drawing nearer, the question is sharply, whether slavery or whether freedom shall be abolished. Come and see."[30]

Part III

SIDES DIVIDE

Massachusetts senator Charles Sumner, the symbol of New England resistance to the Kansas-Nebraska Act, which, he insisted, "annuls all past compromises with Slavery, and makes any future compromises impossible."

7

Republican Rubicon

One of the earliest, if not the earliest, of the movements that contemplated definite action and the formation of a new party, was made in Ripon, Wisconsin, in the early months of 1854.

Vice President Henry Wilson, 1874

Emerson's ease into "the fight" anticipated a broadening phase in the antislavery campaign. His former reserve, his once discernible distance from more radical expressions of abolitionism had long aligned with the impassive slant of northern public opinion. But this placid stance altered irrevocably over a handful of disillusioning years leading up to the Kansas-Nebraska Bill. And, on March 20, 1854, only days after Emerson's disquieting note to Carlyle on the coming struggle between American freedom and American slavery, a group of townspeople in remote Ripon, Wisconsin, assembled in a small white schoolhouse, eager to organize against both Douglas and the Democrats. The leader of this historic meeting, Alvan Earle Bovay (pronounced "Bovee"), pushed for the creation of a new party to attract those northerners disturbed by the disagreeable string of recent southern successes. At this gathering, and with the general approval of its attendees, he suggested they call themselves "Republicans."

Bovay more broadly wished to put the question of slavery's expansion at the inconvenient center of American politics, something the nation's major coalitions had consistently resisted. But this old order now showed clear signs of exhaustion. Begun in 1828 with the election of the remarkably divisive Andrew Jackson (some saw military hero; others feared military chieftain), it featured sharp increases in suffrage, high degrees of personal party loyalty, and the unshakable supremacy of two parties, the dominant Democrats and their less successful Whig rivals. Efforts to introduce either abolitionism (the Libertyites) or expansion without slavery (the Free-Soilers) were kept at bay by professional politicians who put consensus and compromise above all else. In this emerging electoral landscape of meeting hall and hotel canvassing by way of barbecues and backroom deals, an underlying self-interest in the system itself connected the most powerful parties, who, though they might engage in sporadic mudslinging and campaign fiercely for the presidency, shared a common investment in sweeping disruptive sectional issues from sight. In the fractious Missouri debates' long shadow, one of the budding order's chief architects, a muttonchopped Martin Van Buren, extolled a revived status quo connecting, so he wrote the influential *Richmond Enquirer* editor Thomas Ritchie in 1827, "the planters of the South and the plain Republicans of the north."[1] This bisectional party, made to emulate the old Virginia–New York axis (commonly called Jeffersonianism, 1790–1824), could only survive if slavery appeared restricted to southern climes with no claims to make on the white man's West.

But in the wake of the Mexican-American War the territorial question became predominant, though impacting Whigs more so than Democrats, who were the beneficiaries of an older, populistic, and hero-laded coalition associated indelibly with both Jefferson and Jackson. Whiggery, by contrast, never enjoyed the same kind of cohesion; a conscience wing informed a growing segment of its membership, contrasting with a cotton faction that, up to the early 1850s, had largely directed the party's decisions. Importantly, consensus-building economic issues—centralized banking, internal improvements, and high federal tariffs—formerly a salve to smooth over such tonal differences, inevitably faded from the scene. Sectional tensions, rather, informed by the fraught politics of territorial expansion, edged increasingly toward the political center, causing Whiggery's conscience bloc to chafe at its party's too-apparent southern sympathies.[2] In a notebook entry at this time, Emerson penned an abrasive ballad dedicated "To the Whigs":

These men meant well, but they . . . allowed Texas;
Meant well, but allowed the Mexican War;

Meant well, but allowed the Fugitive Slave Law.
They resisted Nebraska, but it is too late.[3]

In the spring of 1854, a similarly vexed Salmon Chase wrote to the midwestern abolitionist Ichabod Codding of the coming ferment:

In 1850, under the influence of . . . [a] Whig Administration the Compromises were enacted—the fugitive slave bill forced upon the country—and the seeds of all our present troubles sown; and . . . in 1852, in the hope of securing slaveholding support for National Nominees all these abominations were endorsed & sanctioned by a Whig National Convention. Many Whigs now deplore and denounce all this action and think that the time has come for the dissolution of the Old Parties and the formation of a new . . . Party of freedom against the Party of Slavery.[4]

But just what kind of party might take Whiggery's place was as yet unclear.

As early as the summer of 1852 Alvan Bovay had burned to be part of a new political order. Born in rural Jefferson County, New York, in 1818, he attended a series of local schools before graduating from Vermont's Norwich University, the country's oldest private military college. After serving as principal in two upstate New York schools and teaching languages at the Bristol Military Academy in Pennsylvania, Bovay read law in Utica and tiny Brownville (five miles west of Watertown), living in the latter with his grandmother, an apparently prudent soul who encouraged him to learn the cabinetmaking trade as a suitable antebellum plan B. In fact, he won appointment to the Utica bar in 1846, marrying that same year the Connecticut-born Caroline Smith.[5]

By this time, Bovay had joined the National Reform Association (NRA), founded in 1844 by the English expats George Henry Evans and former Chartist (advocate for working-class male suffrage) Thomas Devyr. Believing the West a safety valve certain to produce higher wages and better conditions for labor, they advocated for free public lands and are perhaps best remembered for popularizing the happy maxim "Vote Yourself a Farm." A veteran of assorted efforts to organize toilers and moilers, artisans, and tradesmen, Evans had published a number of union-oriented newspapers up to this time including the *Workingman's Advocate*, *The Radical*, and *The People's Rights*. Though its core involved an urban working-class constituency, the NRA was said, because of its interest in both upstate New York's anti-rent movement and the European-inspired socialist (phalanx) communities advanced by the French philosopher Charles Fourier, to constitute an "agrarian" opposition to unfettered factory capitalism. Karl Marx referred approvingly to the NRA in *The Communist Manifesto* (1848), noting, so he wrote, a clear link between "the relations of the Communists to the existing working-class parties, such as the Chartists in England and the Agrarian Reformers in America."[6]

More than a mere joiner, Bovay actively engaged in NRA operations. He attended an anti-rent convention at St. Paul's Lutheran Church in Berne (Albany County) in January 1845, a forum that broached the breaking up of major estate holdings; a few months later, along with nearly 350 delegates including a young Walt Whitman, he participated in the "World's Convention" at Manhattan's Clinton Hall—a gathering demanding land reform. Bovay subsequently toured a number of upstate and capital-district counties on recruiting trips; rising steadily in the NRA hierarchy, he soon became its national secretary. By 1848 the association had augmented its reform interest to include abolitionism. Standing before a sympathetic convention in Auburn that year, Bovay declared "Negro-Slavery . . . a great, an enormous, and a growing evil."[7] Consequently, the NRA, spurning the dominant Democratic-Whig structure, affiliated with the Free-Soil Party, supporting its presidential candidate in the 1848 election.

Possibly disenchanted with politics, Bovay soon thereafter accompanied a wave of pioneers who pursued solutions to the land question by colonizing in the West. He decided on Wisconsin, joining a phalanx at Ceresco (from "Ceres," Roman goddess of the harvest), a self-sufficient cooperative established in Fond du Lac County in 1844 by followers of Fourier. Organized in the main by Warren Chase, a future state senator in both Wisconsin and later California, it contained at its peak some 180 communitarians who farmed seventeen thousand acres and operated a flour mill; inhabitants lived in a multistory longhouse, which still stands today, remodeled in the 1930s as an apartment building. In common with other phalanxes, Ceresco declined over time, a victim of collective living's inevitable sacrifices (recall Emerson's unwillingness to board at Brook Farm), the beguiling pull of the California gold rush, and expanding opportunities for individual families to own property. The community sold its lands in 1850 and soon after disbanded. Nearby Ripon, founded the year before, absorbed Ceresco in 1853.[8]

In Ripon, Bovay practiced law, helped found Brockway (now Ripon) College, and taught mathematics at the school. "It was natural that the people of a small frontier town should look to a man of Mr. Bovay's training for advice," wrote one historian, "and he was soon recognized as a leader in the political questions of the day."[9] Sensing Whiggery's impending post–Fugitive Slave Law implosion, Bovay began pressing for a new organization to draw together the various strands of northern antislavery opinion.

In June 1852, shortly after the rotund Mexican-American War veteran General Winfield Scott, a bit of a martinet known as "Old Fuss and Feathers," claimed the Whig presidential nomination on the fifty-third ballot, Bovay met the cherubic-faced *New-York Tribune* publisher Horace Greeley at Lovejoy's Hotel on the corner of Park Row and Beekman Street. There, in Lower Manhattan, he complained to Greeley of Scott's selection, which he thought uninspired and symptomatic of Whiggery's persistent failure to make a bold stand for free labor. The Whig platform, rather, offered seven innocuous planks before concluding with an unconvincing plea to stand by the Compromise of 1850 "as a final settlement, in principle and in substance." Hoping to shut the door on critics of both popular sovereignty and the Fugitive Slave Act, it pledged the party to "deprecate all further agitation of the questions thus settled." A distraught Bovay urged Greeley to employ his prominent paper in calling for a new party—christened *Republican*. All to little effect. "I came home to Wisconsin," he later recalled, and "worked hard for Scott, but felt defeat in the air every day. Defeat came—a perfect rout of horse, foot and artillery— and the Whig party had indeed fought its last battle. It never rallied again on the national field. From the hour of that defeat, I thought of nothing and worked at nothing, politically, but the organization of the Republican party. I do not suppose there was one secular day, from the autumn of 1852 until the summer of 1854, that I did not press this matter in conversation with somebody."[10] The sudden intrusion of the Kansas-Nebraska bill into American political life only buttressed Bovay's resolve.

In February 1854, with the Senate anxiously debating Douglas's proposal, Bovay, deep into a frigid midwestern winter, wrote to Greeley, asking again for his aid:

> It seems to me you can no longer doubt, or remain passive. . . .
> The Nebraska bill is sure to become a law. Slavery has been grow-
> ing stronger instead of weaker. . . . Now is the time to organize a
> great party to oppose it. If we wait until the dawn of a presidential
> campaign, that organization can not be successfully effected. . . .
> Your paper is now a power in the land. Advocate calling together in
> every church and school-house in the free States all the opponents
> of the Kansas-Nebraska bill, no matter what their party affiliation.
> Urge them to forget previous political names and organization, and
> to band together under the name I suggested to you at Lovejoy's
> Hotel in 1852, while Scott was being nominated. I mean the name
> *Republican.*[11]

But Greeley, an old Whig and longtime admirer of Henry Clay, continued to hedge, "never fully commit[ting] himself," so Bovay recounted,
"to the dissolution of the Whig organization and the abandonment of
the Whig name; indeed, he had even treated this matter of the name
as rather a small thing, when in fact it is a *great* thing, as it is the visible banner under which the hosts rally." Undeterred by Greeley's hesi-
tancy, Bovay instead moved forward. And in choosing "Republican," he
obviously wished to evoke the grand stature and historical resonance
of the Jeffersonian Republicans, at one time the nation's most popular political dynasty. He further fancied a quick and uncomplicated yet
universal title, insisting that the "name should be single, not double,
like 'Free-Soil.' 'Free-Democrat.' 'Liberty Party,' etc." Finally, Bovay knew
the potential power of immigrant constituencies: "They call themselves
Republicans, *Republicains, Republikaner, Republicanos*—or some mod-
ification of it in all European countries, and this name meets them here
like an old friend." Now all he needed was an organization to make the
appellation real.[12]

Days after writing to Greeley, Bovay, eager to attack Douglas's bill,
summoned a public gathering: "Nebraska: A meeting will be held at
6:30 o'clock this Wednesday evening at the Congregational Church in
the Village of Ripon to remonstrate against the Kansas-Nebraska swindle." Convening on March 1, this small caucus, following the aforesaid

remonstrating, passed a resolution denouncing the "impudent audacity, treachery and meanness" involved in overturning the Missouri Compromise, "a solemn compact held as sacred as the constitution." A further measure promised that should the noxious bill pass the Senate the Riponese there assembled would "throw away old party organizations and form a new party." They did not have long to wait. Only three days later, at the ungodly hour of five in the morning, following an uninterrupted session that had begun at noon the previous day, the Senate saw the bill through. Douglas had managed the drama adeptly, one Massachusetts Whig conceded, dominating the proceedings with an extended speech "able, adroit [and] defiant."[13]

Just days after the Senate vote, on March 7, Bovay received a cautious reply from Greeley, apparently shaken by the upper chamber's acquiescence. "I am a beaten, broken-down, used-up politician," he strained to affect folksy, "and have the soreness of many defeats in my bones. However, I am ready to follow any lead that promises to hasten the day of Northern emancipation. Your plan is all right if *the people* are ripe for it." Uncertain just how primed the people were, he confided to Bovay of suspecting Yankees innumerable—Garrisonians and Emersonians to the contrary—of secretly coveting their own "good plantation and Negroes in Alabama—or even Kansas." To the extent that these ease-dreaming farmers, wage earners, and mechanics could be reached, he continued, "we will try and do what we can. But remember that editors can only follow where the people's heart is already prepared to go."[14] Qualifying, equivocating, and waiting to gauge rather than lead public opinion, Greeley held back, refusing to mention Ripon's resolutions to the *Tribune*'s 150,000 readers.

Pressing on, Bovay and Ripon's disaffected organized a second meeting specifically to form a new party. They gathered at the Little White Schoolhouse—forevermore a GOP shrine—on the southeast corner of Blackburn and Blossom Streets. The building, a simple single-story framed structure with gabled roof and chalky clapboard exterior, opened its doors on the evening of March 20 to dozens of citizens. "I went from house to house and from shop to shop and halted men on the street," Bovay later recalled. Ecumenical in affiliation, the attendees included Whigs, Democrats, and Free-Soilers. "The hour was late and the candles burned low," one participant reported, "it was a cold, windy night at the vernal equinox. But in the end all but two or three gave in and we formed our organization." By vote, the town committees of the Whig and Free-Soil parties were ceremoniously dissolved and a new party—Republican—was fashioned. Its leadership consisted of three former Whigs, a sometime Democrat, and a lapsed Free-Soiler.[15]

Bovay believed, correctly as things turned out, that once the question of slavery's expansion "dominated everything else," American politics would enter a radical phase and upend the old partisan patterns formerly advanced by compromisers like Clay and Webster. "There was one great overshadowing pro-slavery organization, the Democratic party; there must also be one great anti-slavery party to antagonize it," he argued. "The Whig party was not this party, and could not be. . . . It stood there a great, useless, lifeless thing, awaiting some possible political earthquake, which would be violent enough to shake it to pieces." Ripon's Republicans had not, of course, created a new national party, but rather a single body—in doing so, however, they anticipated a score of other groups, factions, and coalitions that coalesced in 1854 into a growing northern movement.[16]

In early June, Bovay wrote to Greeley, again pressing the editor to use the power of his newspaper to popularize "Republican" in the public imagination. On the twenty-fourth Greeley, no longer qualifying, equivocating, or waiting, finally complied in an editorial titled "Party Names and Public Duty." Downplaying nomenclature, his piece proclaimed: "We should not much care whether those thus united were designated 'Whig,' 'Free Democratic,' or something else; though we think some more simple name like 'Republican' would more fitly designate those who had united to restore our union."[17] Greeley's opinion—and his paper—mattered. Just three months earlier, in a letter to Carlyle, an observant (and perhaps mildly jealous) Emerson had wryly noted of the neck-bearded editor's striking influence in the western states:

Greeley of the *New York Tribune* is the right spiritual father of all this region; he prints and disperses one hundred and ten thousand newspapers in one day,—multitudes of them in these [Wisconsin and Michigan] very parts. He had preceded me [on a middle western] lecture tour by a few days, and people had flocked together, coming thirty and forty miles to hear him speak; as was right, for he does all their thinking and theory for them, for two dollars a year.[18]

Many years later, in 1884, Bovay's wife, Caroline, loyally criticized Greeley's failure, in the now-famous June editorial, to credit her husband with coining the new party's name. "I was not at all satisfied with the gingerly way in which it was done," she allowed, "and thought it not worthy of Greeley." Neither did she appreciate his continued silence when, following the Civil War, "Republican" had become the most potent political brand in the land: "I felt aggrieved that Greeley, after the name was accepted and grew famous and strong, never so much as alluded to whence the suggestion came." At least he had the good taste, she granted, not to claim the title as his own invention—"Had he done so, I should have made a fuss."[19]

Greeley, of course, had come late to the game, waiting to make sure, as he had told Bovay, that "*the people* are ripe for it."[20] And while he cautiously paused, other constituencies had moved on. That spring Gamaliel Bailey of the *National Era*, the Washington paper known for serializing Stowe's *Uncle Tom's Cabin* and for printing Chase's "Appeal," joined former New York congressman Preston King in pressing northern House Democrats and Whigs to form a new coalition. Before noon on May 9 about thirty of them did just that, brought together by first-term Maine congressman Israel Washburn and meeting at a Mrs. Cratchett's boardinghouse just east of the Capitol building. There, in two packed rooms, this conclave agreed to call themselves Republicans.[21]

Several weeks later, under a ripening grove of oak trees, an assembly of more than one thousand in Jackson, Michigan, too large to cram into a local hall, became the first state convention to adopt the Republican moniker. Even more clearly than in tiny Ripon did the citizens of Jackson take on the institutional apparatus of partisanship, by nominating officers, organizing committees, and drafting a platform. The latter explained, in martial-like language eerily anticipatory of the desperate war years to come, the crucial name change: "In view of the necessity of battling for the first principles of Republican government and against the schemes of an aristocracy, the most revolting and oppressive with which the earth was ever cursed or man debased, we will co-operate and be known as 'Republicans' until the contest terminated."[22]

More generally a series of antislavery coalitions began to blossom that spring and summer in several northern states including Massachusetts and Vermont, Ohio, Indiana, and Iowa. Some of these assemblies avoided the name "Republican," opting for something less partisan such as "Union," "Independent," and "People's." In the Upper Midwest anti-slavery sentiment proved particularly strong. Wisconsin Republicans, wedded to the Missouri Compromise, demanded slavery's restriction to those states where it currently existed, while Michigan's Republican convention more aggressively called for both the repeal of the Fugitive Slave Law and abolition in the District of Columbia.[23]

In more populated and powerful states such as New York, Pennsylvania, and Massachusetts, however, Whiggery retained a residual following that allowed it, for the time being, to limp along. And Dixie-hugging northern border states such as Ohio, Indiana, and Illinois, though critical of the Kansas-Nebraska bill, still thought of themselves as fundamentally Jeffersonian. Still, the mottled process of turning the section's Whigs, Free-Soilers, and even some Democrats into something other continued throughout the year. The degree of antislavery sentiment among groups and regions mixed invariably with more minute individual allegiances and loyalties to make this process both chaotic and cumbersome. Some wished for nothing more than a restoration of the pre-1854 territorial situation, while an ultraminority wanted to see the end of slavery in their lifetime. Pushed along by the disturbing specter of future Nebraskas, these clashing opinions and preferences gradually began to find common ground.

But it would take time. During this season of uncertainty Abraham Lincoln, still scrupulously Whig, watched the welling Republican movement from the Springfield, Illinois, law office he shared with William H. Herndon. There he read the local and Chicago papers along with Greeley's *Tribune*, which carried news of the new party, congressional debates, and the mounting attacks on Douglas. He may even have sifted through Herndon's scattered copies of the *National Anti-Slavery Standard*. At this point, one scholar notes, with partisan loyalties in play, "it was not clear how Lincoln could make any meaningful intervention."[24] But clarity and the fall elections were coming.

8

Forging a North

The Revolution is accomplished, and Slavery is king! How long shall this monarch reign? This is now the question for the Northern people to answer.

New-York Tribune, May 1854

The fugitive dream of northern nationhood vibrated lightly through the Ripon assembly, as well as those many Yankee-populated political meetings that quickly emanated in its wake. Their intent to create new parties, movements, and pride was by nature regional in its resolve. The Democracy and its Whig other, after all, were national organizations, with offices and supporters stretching from Maine to Mississippi, Shreveport to Chicago. To renounce allegiance to these established entities, to declare defiantly for free labor in the territories with no appetite for quiescence or compromise, could only mean commitment to a partisanship bereft of southern ties. The past pointed suggestively in this direction. The old Essex Junto, averse to planter rule under the Jeffersonians, fancied a confederacy of its own—an ideal not entirely unknown to those disgruntled Hartford conventioneers who, not long after, proposed alterations to the Constitution designed to reduce the Virginia squirearchy's prevailing power. More recently the Liberty and Free-Soil parties advocated causes favorable to thin tiers of northern public opinion. Now fear of slavery's entrance into the nation's frontier sparked a fresh Yankee reply, but, unlike the earlier outbursts, with numbers enough to remake the electoral landscape.

Fueling this fire, a divided Congress waged a bitter war over Douglas's bill through the winter and early spring. The struggle began in the Senate, where five tense weeks of debates took place before attentive audiences and a restive nation. Designed by the British-American neoclassical architect Benjamin Henry Latrobe following the War of 1812, the two-story upper chamber, a semicircular room covered by a sound-bouncing half dome, reeked of Parisian inspiration. Along the eastern wall ran a decorous visitors' balcony, supported by eight mock Grecian marble columns—the stone quarried from the nearby Potomac River. The bowed western wall, added in 1828 and featuring wrought-iron railing, offered a second seating area known informally as the "Ladies' Gallery." A curved table residing on an elevated platform near the center of the room was occupied by the vice president (president of the Senate); an elaborate canopy, crowned by a gilt eagle and shield, covered the dais. The chamber's several skylights were accentuated by a brass chandelier procured from the Philadelphia firm Cornelius and Company, while an 1823 portrait of George Washington by Rembrandt Peale sat high above the east balcony.[1]

This gracious space became, in the winter of 1854, a forum for prickly exchanges, veiled threats, and the random mutual contempt. Having brought his contentious bill before the Senate, Douglas now sought to defend it before a buzzing crowd on January 30. Though giving the appearance of being alone in the arena, he in fact enjoyed certain unassailable advantages—solid southern backing, Pierce's considerable support, and a significant Democratic majority. Entering the fray and eager to face his "Appeal" nemeses, he attacked both Chase and Sumner as rash and irresponsible, exhibiting in these eruptions, so one observer noted, a "defiant tone and pugnacious attitudinization" that released "the terrific tornado raging within him." Chase desperately attempted to cut in, but Douglas—"I will yield the floor to no Abolitionist"—would have none of it. Instead, he defended the principle of popular sovereignty as having already superseded previous agreements. And this form of territorial democracy, he continued, ultimately counted for more than what any Congress could say or do regarding slavery's future. "Let all this quibbling about the Missouri Compromise, about the territory acquired from France, about the Act of 1820, be cast behind you; for the simple question is, will you allow the people to legislate for themselves upon the subject of slavery?"[2] Such an argument served Douglas well. He

Nebraska Bill, in language far less conciliatory than Everett's. He frankly informed the South of its ancillary status in the "eternal struggle between conservatism and progress; between truth and error; between right and wrong." The slave drivers, that is to say, stood—alongside feudalism, the pope, and crazy King George III—on the wrong side of history. Chattel servitude managed to stumble into the nineteenth century, but the institution, an embarrassing heirloom of pharaonic days, failed to match free labor's splendid energy; the size of northern cities, economies, and surpluses attested to this fact and nothing a mere congress might do in regard to a territorial bill affecting a distant spot on a flat map could change that. Adopting a variation of his notorious assertion made during the Compromise of 1850 debates that a "higher law" than the Constitution determined events, Seward now declared, "Man proposes and God disposes. You may legislate and abrogate and abnegate as you will; but there is a superior Power that overrules all your actions, and all your refusals to act; and I fondly hope and trust overrules them to the advancement of the greatness and glory of our country."[8]

These arresting sentiments, informed by an evangelical age's deep impress, pushed Seward miles to the left of Everett, his fellow Whig. But the debate had hardly crested and all of Washington, covered now in a deep winter white, anticipated the speech of a certain Byronic senator. Seward too looked on with great interest. "We are snowed under," he wrote a colleague shortly after delivering his South-baiting address, "the ground is covered with a mantle eighteen inches thick. Mr. Sumner's fame has gathered a bright array of ladies in the gallery; and we are waiting for him to begin."[9]

Making his way before the bright array, Sumner began on the twenty-first. Considering Douglas's bill "already amply refuted by Senators who have preceded me," he felt at liberty to range broadly as the subject, the crowd, and the moment moved him. In short, the Founders, so he said, were protoabolitionists, Douglas ("that human anomaly— *a Northern man with Southern principles*") had betrayed his section, and popular sovereignty broke against the nation's most sacred assumptions. "I am unwilling to admit, Sir," he said, facing the full chamber, "that the prohibition of Slavery in the Territories is in any just sense an infringement of the local sovereignty. Slavery is an infraction of the immutable law of nature, and, as such, cannot be considered a natural incident to any sovereignty, especially in a country which has solemnly declared, in its Declaration of Independence, the inalienable right of all men to life, *liberty*, and the pursuit of Happiness." Appropriating the wrong-side-of-history argument proffered by Seward and others, he declared slavery merely a sectional institution, certain to give way, already giving way, to the irrepressible demands of freedom. "*Nothing*," he closed, "*can be settled which is not right*."[10]

Sumner's speech electrified the Northeast. A print edition circulated by the *Boston Commonwealth* quickly sold out, while separate versions appeared in the *New York Times* and Greeley's *Tribune*. Hirelings in at least one Massachusetts factory were read the address, a paean to free labor, as they worked. Staid Charles Francis Adams, son of John Quincy Adams, informed Sumner of polite Boston's approval of his rhetorical war on the planters: "Since the introduction of this infamous bill into the Senate, your position here has undergone a most sensible change, even those who have been most opposed to you, now acknowledge that you speak the voice of Massachusetts."[11] The conservative Bay State, quite willing to go along with the Fugitive Slave Act in 1850, appeared, in light of slavery's potential extension, willing to go along no longer.

Four days after Sumner's address, the lengthening debate passed over to the Democrats. For a week several men from both sections spoke in favor of Douglas's bill trying, with uneven results, to court consensus. A critical mass of observers, including the distinguished New York lawyer George Templeton Strong, remained wary—"Nebraska or Nebrascal controversy raging," Strong informed his diary on March 2. Beginning late the following evening Douglas, repeatedly stung during the previous month's debate by the slings of Sumner and others, wound up the deliberation by attacking his attackers in a heated three-hour address that spilled over into the following morning. Though the hour grew late, the galleries remained packed with a rapt audience entranced by the unfolding political theater and the rare raw emotions Douglas so liberally displayed. In the course of flaying those senatorial critics of popular sovereignty, he unleashed a slew of "by Gods" and "God damns" that bounced about the august chamber. Turning angrily to Chase and Sumner, he fairly barked, "You degrade your own States," and held them accountable for the bill's many northern critics. "You have stimulated [the people] to these acts," he claimed, and called them "disgraceful to your party, and disgraceful to your cause."[12]

That morning, at 4:55, Douglas's bill passed the Senate by a comfortable if sectionally divided 37–14 margin; the slave states went 23–2 while their northern colleagues split 14–12. In what some undoubtedly took as a weak gesture, Everett, citing illness, avoided the vote. His resignation a few weeks later seemed a portent of moderate politics' declining fortunes in America. More determined partisans, however, regarded the bill's passage as a provocation, and as Chase left the Capitol building with Sumner immediately following the vote, the rumble of distant cannon fire announcing Douglas's triumph to a sleepy city, he turned to his companion and promised a coming struggle: "They celebrate a present victory, but the echoes they awake will never rest till slavery itself shall die."[13]

Now the bill moved on to the House, and with it a sharpening sense of urgency among a growing number of northerners that a crisis loomed. The Latrobe-designed lower chamber (used from 1819 to 1857), the current National Statuary Hall, featured a Greek Revival design that made it look like an amphitheater from antiquity complete with a double-sunk coffered wooden ceiling and fluted marble columns. Members occupied desks organized in tiered, semicircular rows that faced a raised Speaker's podium adorned with a red-draped canopy. As a debating stage, the room proved a beautiful disaster. Noise reverberated, voices echoed, and the acoustics of congressional discretion proved challenging.

Shaken by the fierce battle in the Senate, wary Democratic House managers, possibly hoping to cool emotions, held on to the bill for two weeks before introducing it to their colleagues. But when the lavishly sideburned William Richardson, an Illinois representative, Douglas ally, and chairman of the Committee on Territories, moved on March 21 to proceed, he immediately ran into trouble. Hoping to ensure party unity with a minimum of infighting, he proposed to his colleagues a binding caucus—all to go with the majority. But several northern Democrats, noting the imminent autumn elections and apparently interested in keeping their jobs, wanted the flexibility, should their constituencies show definite signs of discontent, to jump ship and cast career-saving "noes." This raised real questions about the bill's likelihood of success. On paper there seemed to be no doubt of its passage. Democrats enjoyed an immense 158 to 76 advantage in the House, though 92 of these men represented Yankee districts. With anti-Kansas-Nebraska momentum building above the Mason-Dixon Line—Harriet Beecher Stowe, for one, financed a campaign at this time that flooded Congress with the signatures of over three thousand clergymen opposed to the proposal—Richardson realized he faced an unmistakable struggle.[14]

Several of his more vulnerable colleagues demanded a strong statement emphasizing the bill's intent to promote popular sovereignty. Up to this point free-soil sentiment had all too successfully stressed the act's elimination of the Missouri Compromise and its potential benefit to the Slave Power. This endangered those incumbents who wished to engage their respective electorates with a positive narrative of self-government advancing across the frontier. Equally problematic for some representatives was the inclusion of inflammatory language in the bill—the Clayton amendment—which "excluded unnaturalized . . . immigrants from political participation in the organization of the territories." The Democratic Party's northern wing included a conspicuous foreign-born constituency, however, and this proviso struck many of these members as little shy of suicidal.[15]

Accordingly, Douglas's bill (designated S. 22) went not to Richardson's small Committee on Territories, where it was expected to receive fast-track attention, but rather, and following a 110–95 vote dominated by 66 Yankee Democrats, to the Committee of the Whole, meaning the entire House would debate and amend the measure. Moreover, it now lay buried beneath more than fifty other proposals on the cluttered House calendar; an outmaneuvered Richardson worried that it would be "kill[ed] . . . by indirection." This tactic caused a general kerfuffle in the chamber and Francis B. Cutting, a New York Democrat who had made the motion to sink the bill, nearly tumbled into a duel with Kentucky Democrat John C. Breckinridge of Kentucky as a result. The latter, supposing the South deceived, had publicly called Cutting's gambit "the act of a man who throws his arm in apparently friendly embrace around another saying, 'How is it with thee brother?' and at the same time covertly stabs him to the heart." Cutting replied by calling Breckinridge's comments "unbecoming of a Congressman." From there the tenor of the dustup intensified, with both men claiming injury from "personal attack." Cutting finally went a word too far—accusing Breckinridge of "skulking"—and a duel seemed inevitable. Each man considered himself the challenged party and thus took the initiative of choosing weaponry—western rifles for Breckinridge, pistols for Cutting. This farce mercifully collapsed with the judicious aid of friends on both sides, though as a performative exercise it confirmed Yankee suspicions of southern bullying.[16]

Newspapers took great interest in the commotion, of course, with the *Newark Daily Advertiser* roaring at one point: "CUTTING REPORTED KILLED," before more accurately acknowledging (in far smaller font) that it had no evidence of Cutting so much as stubbing his toe. Though no affair of honor had transpired, Cutting received the grateful encomiums of northerners who, so the *Albany Evening Journal* reported, were bone tired of those "fiery braggarts" from the South, "accustomed to swagger in the House." Down in Dixie, the *Richmond Examiner* criticized Breckinridge for playing to type: "Already are the demagogue press of Northern Abolitionism railing out against Southern 'bullyism.' Already are the passions of the populace invoked against Southern *hauteur* and violence. . . . The populace at the North is in danger of being excited to a pitch that will make [their congressional] members more fearful than ever to stand by the South."[17]

Despite Democratic majorities in thirteen northern state delegations, the unprecedented flux in American politics—with Whigs, Free-Soilers, nativists, and growing clusters of anti-Nebraska coalitions in varying degrees of ebb and flow—cast serious doubts on the party's cohesion. All New England along with New York and New Jersey, Ohio and Wisconsin, appeared to be in revolt. While this jockeying ensued, Douglas and the administration worked furiously behind the scenes, applying pressure and patronage to reconcile the irreconcilables in their camp and angle the bill to a vote. With Georgia Whig (and future Confederate vice president) Alexander H. Stephens conducting operations in the lower chamber and Douglas tigerishly managing strategy—"He has every man in the House . . . marked and numbered," noted one correspondent—momentum built for taking up the act. The fifty-some bills impeding its progress were, in a series of roll calls over a fifteen-day period, individually laid aside until, on May 8, it moved to the top of the list.[18]

Debate on the bill began auspiciously in an exhausting thirty-six-hour session on the eleventh that spilled over into the following day. An imperious Douglas offended more than a few congressmen by shouting out orders, browbeating the Speaker, and parading about the House floor as if he were actually a House member. As the deliberations pressed interminably on, some of the parched representatives thought it prudent to fortify themselves with alcohol, which did remarkably little to improve the quality of the debate. A minor fracas, rather, broke out late in the evening of the twelfth when Ohio's Lewis Campbell whetted the frustration of Henry Edmundson, an impatient Virginia Democrat, by conducting a filibuster. Said to be "very drunk and heavily armed," Edmundson attempted to provoke a fight with Campbell. Some men surged to separate the would-be combatants; others stood on their desks to better view the chaos while insults flew about the chamber until the sergeant at arms restored some semblance of order. At that point the House mercifully adjourned.[19]

Over the next few days the nation's papers reported, speculated, and ruminated on the odd rumblings coming out of Congress. "The contest has begun," the *Chicago Tribune* related on the twelfth, "we rejoice to see the spirit and determination with which [Douglas's] opponents enter upon the task of strangling the [popular sovereignty] monster." Three days later the *Richmond Enquirer*, eager to throttle an altogether different kind of beast, counseled a hard push to put down a presumed free-soil minority in Congress. "Extreme cases demand extreme remedies," the paper declared, "and it becomes the duty of the majority, if necessary, to repel violence by violence, and to trample under foot the arbitrary formalities of parliamentary law, rather than suffer them to be converted into an engine in the hands of faction for the overthrow of the government."[20] Such casual encouragement by the cavalier set to squash, elide, or otherwise set aside the practice of "parliamentary law," however, only played to type, and the following day the *Hartford Daily Courant* weighed in, offering a fresh take on the old Slave Power conspiracy:

> A dark spot now arises in the history of our country. The South, having elected a Northern President [Pierce] devoted to their interests . . . have stept over the boundary of the Compromises and insist upon the abrogation of that of 1820, by which a violent contest was pacifically settled. They have obtained their share of the benefits of this Compromise [with Arkansas and Missouri safely in the Union] and now demand of us to relinquish ours. By doing so they have aroused a spirit which will not easily be quieted. This movement has shown that there can be no faith kept by them—and that no terms of contract and no compromise are felt binding upon them when they can be changed by a vote of Congress or bullied out of the North.[21]

Deliberations, often fractious, resumed in Congress until the evening of the twenty-second when, after a few hours of negotiating, Richardson suddenly proposed House bill S. 22 without the noxious Clayton amendment. The way was now clear for northern Democrats to support a vote. This put the opposition in a panic and it tried desperately to adjourn—in each instance beaten back. By 11:00 p.m. the Kansas-Nebraska Act had passed, 113 to 100. Coming out in force, southern Democrats voted 57 to 2 in favor of the bill, while the party's divided northern wing split nearly evenly, 44 to 42. The Whigs evinced an equally stark sectionalism; its slim southern branch voted 12 to 7 for the bill, while all 45 northern Whigs opposed it. Over the coming weeks and months some of these men in the latter camp, and more importantly their constituents, would become Republicans. But Douglas proved deaf to this gathering danger. "Nebraska is through the House," he rejoiced. "I took the reins in my hand, applied whip and spur, and brought the 'wagon' out. . . . Glory enough for one day."[22]

The House version of the bill anticlimactically went to the Senate, which accepted it, complete with the deletion of the Clayton amendment. Pierce then signed the legislation into law. His secretary, Sidney Webster, recognized the extreme degree of administrative purchase it took to see the contentious deed done—"The President is and will be more than heretofore embarrassed," he wrote, "by the inducements held out during the pendency of Nebraska."[23]

Though a great struggle had just concluded, the real fight over popular sovereignty had only begun. Chase saw this clearly and, in the shadow of Douglas's celebration, urged "Freemen and lovers of freedom to stand upon their guard and prepare for the worst events." This fatalistic tone now became vogue. The reliably sober *New York Times*, for one, broke form and called the bill's passage "part of [a] great scheme for extending and perpetuating the supremacy of the Slave Power," while the conservative George Templeton Strong, among many thousands, could sense his once reflexive political allegiances in flux: "I'm resisting awful temptations to avow myself a Free-Soiler. Think I shall come out on the platform at last, a unit in the great Northern party the consummation of this swindle will call into being."[24]

Douglas, by contrast, presumed all to be well. "The storm will soon spend its fury," he wrote to former Georgia governor Howell Cobb that spring, "and the people of the north will sustain the measure when they come to understand it." But as the season and the year wore on just the opposite occurred. Greater acquaintance with the provocative act and its threat to enlarge slavery's domain fostered a fierce reaction. An angry Sumner caught this restive mood when speaking (ironically) to the Senate on the fateful night the House squeezed Douglas's measure through: "Sir, it is the best bill on which Congress ever acted; for it annuls all past compromises with Slavery, and makes any future compromises impossible. Thus it puts Freedom and Slavery face to face, and bids them grapple." Predicting a coming perdition for a political system that, so he argued, had long injured Yankee constituencies, Sumner welcomed the day "when, at last, there will really be a North, and the Slave Power will be broken."[25]

9

Bibles and Guns

Come on, then, gentlemen of the slave states; since there is no
escaping your challenge, I accept it in behalf of freedom. We will
engage in competition for the virgin soil of Kansas, and God give
the victory to the side that is stronger in numbers as it is in right.

William Henry Seward, 1854

In late April, while a divided House fought over the prospect of making the Trans-Mississippi territories safe for slavery, Massachusetts's
Whig governor, Emory Washburn, signed into legislation a bill creating a transportation corporation eager to promote the settlement of
New Englanders in Kansas. This Massachusetts Emigrant Aid Company (EAC), originating under the auspices of the Worcester business-
man and state representative Eli Thayer, obtained a charter to capitalize
stock up to $5 million, "for the purpose of assisting emigrants to set-
tle in the West." The Company, despite what critics later claimed, neither bribed its clientele to make the fourteen-hundred-mile trek from
Boston to Kansas nor bore their traveling expenses. It proposed, rather,
to raise capital, advertise the venture, seek rebates on railroads, and
provide information to assist pioneers. Though primarily a business
enterprise—and dismissive of abolitionism, which, Thayer insisted,
endorsed "disunion"—the Company also publicly embraced free-soil
principles. Accordingly, some southerners, particularly in neighboring
Missouri, saw Thayer's enterprise as an effort to deny them the right to
take their slaves into the nation's commonly held lands. Organizing for

125

"mutual protection," the Missourians, tortured by the thought of a Puritan encirclement, resolved to outpace the Yankee sodbusters in the race for Kansas.[1]

A combination of salesman, promoter, and politician, Thayer had moved quickly to take advantage of the territory's approaching opening. Even before Douglas's bill had cleared Congress—and tracts could be legally acquired from its current Indian occupants—he had convinced both the Massachusetts legislature and a number of important private citizens to support his efforts to, so he later contended, "end the domination of Slavery." Appearing in New York that May to solicit stock subscriptions, he soon realized pledges in excess of $100,000 (about $3.6 million in current dollars); back in Boston, blue-nosed Charles Francis Adams alone anted up $25,000. That same month Frederick Douglass, taking note of a growing Republican response to the Slave Power and the related need to people the West with free labor, wrote an editorial cum advertisement in one antislavery newspaper favorable to Thayer's ambitious venture: "The time for action has come. While a grand political party is forming, let companies of emigrants from the free States be collected together. . . . Let them be sent out to possess the godly land, to which, by a law of Heaven and a law of man, they are justly entitled."[2]

Born poor to a Mendon, Massachusetts, couple in 1819, Thayer liked to assert his ducal descent (seventh generation) from *Mayflower* royalty John and Pricilla Alden, their Plymouth suit and marriage (1621) folklorically commemorated in a popular narrative poem, "The Courtship of Miles Standish," by Henry Wadsworth Longfellow, another descendant. After attending the Worcester County Manual Labor High School, Thayer studied at Brown University, graduating at the age of twenty-six. He then taught for a few years before opening the Oread Collegiate Institute for women. At one time this Worcester school's enrollment exceeded 150 students and it counted a dozen teachers on its staff. Its socially ambitious founder served in several church and civic posts before winning a seat in the Massachusetts legislature at the age of thirty-seven. According to one scholar, Thayer "had made his way entirely by his own efforts, and at the time he projected his Kansas venture he was reputed to have amassed moderate wealth." Ornamented with a thick, bristly beard and dark searching eyes, he flashed, in his conventional black suits and crisp white shirts, a certain intensity that caught the interest of others. Despite his sober dress, so one of his associates later recounted, "He loved notoriety and noise and was a born speculator."[3]

Thayer's plans to make the West more like New England were hardly unique. In 1845 the Bostonian Edward Everett Hale, a Unitarian minister known both as the grandnephew of the Revolutionary War spy Nathan Hale ("I only regret that I have but one life to lose for my country") and as the author of the patriotic short story "The Man without a Country," pushed for Yankee emigration to Texas in a sixteen-page treatise, *How to Conquer Texas before Texas Conquers Us*. "I should have been glad to join any colony which would have tried that adventure," he later remembered. No doubt multiple motives influenced Thayer's own audacious endeavor, though making a shrewd financial investment in land and low-cost transportation certainly ranked near the top. "The enterprise," he candidly acknowledged, "was intended to be a money-making affair as well as a philanthropic undertaking." For this reason, both abolitionists and southerners condemned his efforts as effectively self-serving, a blanket reproach to which Thayer offered no apologies, evenly explaining, "In all my emigration schemes I intended to make the results return a profitable dividend in cash."[4]

It is further plausible that Thayer looked upon the Emigrant Aid Company as an opportunity to break into national politics. That he captured a seat in the U.S. House of Representatives in 1856 largely due to his association with Kansas's colonization is perhaps probable. He served two terms before relinquishing the office in March 1861, a few weeks before the Civil War began. Doubtless a number of incentives prompted Thayer's decision to encourage Yankees to make for Kansas, including the startling implications of Douglas's bill. "During the winter of 1854," he later wrote:

> [I] had felt to some degree the general alarm in anticipation of the repeal of the Missouri Compromise, but not the depression and despondency that so affected others who regarded the cause of liberty as hopelessly lost. As the winter wore away, I began to have a conviction which came to be ever present, that something *must* be done. . . . I felt a personal responsibility, and though I long struggled to evade the question, I found it to be impossible. I pondered upon it by day, and dreamed of it by night. By what plan could this great problem be solved? What force could be effectively opposed

to the power that seemed about to spread itself over the continent? Suddenly, it came upon me like a revelation. It was organized and assisted emigration.[5]

On March 11, in the plain Greek Revival–style Worcester town hall, Thayer addressed a public gathering hostile to the Kansas-Nebraska bill. As the evening's final speaker, he unveiled for the first time the emigration plan—which received, so he said, an "impetuous, spontaneous and enthusiastic response."[6]

Thayer claimed to see colonization as a simple solution, merely a matter of imposing, so he said, "the superiority of a free labor civilization" onto the nation's plains. The eternally active greater Bostonians would bring the institutional pillars of their Christian/commercial way of life— churches and schools, businesses and banks—with them; this New England initiative promised a progressive future, a western suggestion of a broader industrial orientation then beginning to make its way in midcentury America. "We [have] much greater numbers, much greater wealth, greater readiness of organization and better facilities of migration," Thayer heartily tallied up the one-sided sectional score. Under the influence of such obvious energy and initiative, he thought his plan could hardly fail.[7]

In early May, a little more than a week after the April incorporation of the Emigrant Aid Company, Thayer and a select committee of its officers drafted a statement of objectives. These included mapping routes, negotiating low transportation costs, and sending machinery—including grist- and sawmills—to Kansas; they counted on convincing an astounding twenty thousand to resettle. Seeing dollar signs in the guise of a moral crusade, Thayer hoped to franchise the enterprise throughout the West. "There, we should put a cordon of Free States from Minnesota to the Gulf of Mexico," he maintained, "and stop the forming of Slave States. After that we should colonize the northern border Slave States and exterminate Slavery." Despite the combative language, he considered the emigration process itself to be "a peaceful contest," one designed to "convince every poor man from the South of the superiority of free labor."[8] If Thayer harbored an evangelical instinct, in other words, it ran principally in the direction of a righteous capitalism. Yankee profits, not prayers, he argued, would bring about the death of the backward Old South.

Later that month Horace Greeley, already being nudged by Alvan Bovay to declare his influential paper in favor of an emerging Republican Party, took up the Emigrant Aid Company's cause. And in a series of *Tribune* editorials loftily titled "A Plan for Freedom," he endorsed unreservedly the embryonic enterprise. This occurred shortly after a shrewd Thayer showed up in Greeley's disheveled New York office on the twenty-seventh "to secure, if possible, the great influence," as he put it, of the grand man's name. There he found an interested if somewhat occupied patron: "In a very small room, containing two old-fashioned, straight-back chairs, and a very high and very ancient bureau, sat Mr. Greeley, using the latter article for a writing-desk. The top of this bureau, except a very small space at one corner, was covered with papers, both manuscript and printed, in utter confusion." Amid this organized chaos Thayer talked with Greeley for an hour while the latter, though listening carefully, never for a moment stopped writing.[9]

Thayer explained, as if Greeley could not guess, that he wished the *Tribune* to boost the emigration plan, thus convincing or at least cajoling "all the other Whig papers in the North" to follow suit. He left the busy editor a number of Emigrant Aid Company documents and arranged to meet him the following day, a Sunday, for lunch. At this parley Greeley, having perused the materials, proceeded to ask a number of practical questions about funding, prestige of supporters, and likelihood of actually attracting migrants. Convinced by Thayer's detailed replies and long interested in such a scheme, Greeley, whom later generations credited with coining the phrase "Go West, young man," jumped on the bandwagon. Only two days later his *Tribune* declared: "The plan of freedom set forth [by the EAC] . . . has been eagerly seized upon by some of our best and most distinguished citizens. . . . The organization of a powerful association of large capital, in the aid of human freedom, is a step in a new direction of philanthropic effort which may well enlist the sympathies of the unselfish and benevolent, not only for this country, but of all mankind."[10] Thayer now had the press on his side.

His easy enough conquest of Greeley anticipated subsequent appeals to "an influential coterie of Whiggish, unionist, anti-abolitionist industrialists, Free-Soil politicians, philanthropists, and moral reformers." The newly initiated included congressmen, a future vice president (Henry Wilson), and Amos Lawrence—merchant, investor, and heir to a New England textile empire. An Emigrant Aid Company trustee, Lawrence also served as the organization's treasurer until 1857, though far more indispensably as its banker and lifeblood. He virtually financed the enterprise during its first several months and provided necessary funds thereafter when the Company's accounts were inevitably overdrawn. On one occasion he purchased hundreds of shares of its stock, thus pumping some $8,000 (about $280,000 in present-day dollars) into the Company's strained coffers. His support for Kansas's settlement is recognized in both the establishment of the town of Lawrence in 1854 (on former Shawnee Indian land) and his $10,000 gift to the endowment fund that a decade later helped to charter the University of Kansas. His monetary contributions and indelible name were equally critical to the solvency of Thayer's fledgling enterprise.[11]

New England took note of Lawrence's involvement and several of its more princely sons agreed to preside as officers of the Emigrant Aid Company. These included Thomas Wentworth Higginson, John Lowell, and Dr. Samuel Cabot—the latter two descended from impossibly prominent families teasingly immortalized by John Collins Bossidy in a splendid 1910 Holy Cross College alumni dinner toast: "And there is good Old Boston, The home of the bean and the Cod, Where the Lowells talk to the Cabots, And the Cabots talk only to God." A divine of a different kind, Waldo Emerson, also toed the company line, telling an audience in Cambridge, "I know people who are making haste to reduce their expenses and pay their debts, not with a view to new accumulations, but in preparation to save and earn for the benefit of the Kansas emigrants."[12] The Fireside Poet John Greenleaf Whittier committed to verse his support for western free labor in the pounding "Kansas Emigrant Song," which linked present settlers to a glorious pilgrim past:

> We cross the prairie as of old,
> The pilgrims crossed the sea,
> To make the West, as they the East,
> The Homestead of the Free!
>
> We go to rear a wall of men
> On Freedom's Southern line,
> And plant beside the cotton-tree,
> The rugged Northern pine![13]

Some of these incipient pine planters could hardly wait to get started. Isaac Goodnow, a Rhode Island teacher, thrilled to Thayer's inspiring message. "Fully believing that the *rule* of Slavery or Freedom would be settled upon the prairies of Kansas for the whole nation," he later observed, "it occurred to me that every Friend of Freedom should throw himself into the scale."[14]

But exactly where they were to be thrown was as yet undecided. Moving quickly, Thayer and Lawrence employed that June Charles Robinson, a former California Forty-Niner by way of Amherst College, and Charles Branscomb, a Holyoke lawyer educated at Dartmouth, to scout out the southern half of the new territory. The following month these men arrived in a rustic Kansas City (population twenty-five hundred), and from there Robinson journeyed north along the Missouri River to Fort Leavenworth (built in 1827), while Branscomb continued west for 135 miles to Fort Riley (established in 1853). They were tasked with looking into Indian titles, seeking suitable areas of encampment, and more generally getting a feel for the region. While these men trooped about the plains, the Emigrant Aid Company speedily launched its first band of settlers on July 17. Thayer accompanied this inaugural group of twenty-nine men as far as Buffalo; along the way it picked up two more homesteaders in Rochester before crossing Lake Erie to Detroit aboard the steamboat *Plymouth Rock*. The Michigan Central Railroad conveyed the party to Chicago, while another train brought it south to St. Louis. Taking passage on the steamer *Polar Star*, the party then plied the Missouri River all the way to Kansas City. Low water resulted in a higher fare for a more dangerous passage and each settler was charged $12, about $425 in present-day dollars. Hiring oxen teams, the group reached Lawrence on August 1. This advance guard, no doubt exhausted from a difficult two weeks on roads and rivers, hardly paused; it began, rather, to embed and build.[15]

Returning to New England with stops in New York, Thayer continued, as he put it, to "raise colonies and to organize Kansas leagues." These tireless recruiting efforts quickly earned the contempt of an apprehensive South. The (Virginia) *Lynchburg Republican* thought intimidation might beat back a menacing Yankee migration: "We wish them the utmost success their hearts can desire in getting there, for the hardy [southern] pioneers of Kansas will doubtless have tar and feathers prepared in abundance for their reception. Kansas is open for settlement both to the North and the South. Slavery has been kept out of Territories by Congressional enactments, but has never failed to carry the day and firmly establish itself upon new territories when allowed to enter."

The *Charleston Mercury*, by contrast, struck a less certain note, fearing "if the North secures Kansas, the power of the South in Congress will be diminished . . . and the slave population confined to the States east of the Mississippi will become valueless. All depends upon the action of the present moment." More generally, so Thayer later observed, "The editorials of Southern journals in 1854, denounce[d] the Emigrant Aid Company" and called upon their readers to welcome the invading "abolitionists" with "bowie-knives [and] revolvers."[16]

Before southern resistance moved into place, however, the colonizers experienced an altogether different type of challenge—the region itself. Scarcity of lumber, inclement weather, and plow-resistant ground, all proposed to conspire against them. Over the next few months, as successive migration groups arrived, many of their number wondered why they had come at all. "Nearly half of our party became homesick and have gone back," reported one man in Topeka, part of a corps originating from Boston's Fitchburg depot; "some seemed to think they should find farms all fenced, and houses built ready for their reception, every advantage there that they had left behind, and a rich soil, healthy climate, and in short all the luxuries of the [East]." A Salem, Massachusetts, woman dolefully called Kansas "anything but delightful." Fierce gales cutting through the ochre-colored prairie made a vivid impression upon her. "We do not have windy days, such as you have East," she wrote to one correspondent, "but it blows a perfect whirlwind for two or three days and nights, so that I can scarcely stand up when out of doors, and a cloud of dust fills your mouth and eyes." Elijah Porter, a Westfield, Massachusetts, farmer, thought the territory's "baked so hard soil" a deal breaker: "To tell a long story in a few words, I have seen enough to convince me that Kansas is humbug."[17]

Invariably, other settlers found yet other reasons for disappointment. Asa S. White, formerly a New Hampshire carpenter, complained to one New England newspaper that several of his late neighbors had come west with no loftier ambition than to make money: "Most of the settlers here are from the free States, yet many of them do not attend public worship on the Sabbath, they seek only the treasures of earth." This earthly impulse no doubt informed a broad swath of new arrivals—as it did those opportunistic gougers and grifters, sharpers and frontier extortionists, who saw to their primitive material needs. Accordingly, prices in Kansas City for rooms, meals, and horse-keeping skyrocketed.

Hearing of such difficulties, the more prudent arrived with their own rations. "Had we not done so," noted a member of an Osawatomie group flush with a three-month supply of food crammed aboard a two-horse wagon, "we might have starved before this; that is one reason why many are going back, they have no conveniences for traveling, and carry no provisions with them." The exorbitant cost of living, even if a temporary condition, undercut one of Thayer's more attractive goals—giving poor eastern immigrant constituencies the opportunity to better their conditions. Hale had harbored such lofty thoughts as well, writing to his father shortly before the first party went out: "You know how [the Company] has interested me as a means of helping these German and Irish people westward without suffering."[18]

Resistance to the rising Yankee wave began to build early in northwestern Missouri. Over the previous few years, a restless, speculative economy cropped up, accustomed to outfitting men and women passing through to still farther frontiers. Oregon pioneers and California gold rushers had recently transited, dropping dollars on their way, while suppliers of army troops and Indian traders serviced a more stationary exchange. Some border Missourians, even before Douglas introduced his organic act to Congress, had come to Kansas, eager to assert claims on these new lands.

Anxiously assailing the Emigrant Aid Company settlers as abolitionists, concerned Missourians quickly organized to contest this alleged threat. In early June assemblies in Westport and Independence variously called for the creation of vigilante committees "for mutual protection," promised to bring slaves into Kansas, and pledged to "meet and repel the ... fanaticism which threatens to break up our border."[19] On the eleventh of that month a colleague of Missouri's senior senator, David Atchison, received a letter from an associate warning that something akin to the apocalypse now imperiled Kansas:

From certain indications in the North and East, it would seem we are threatened with trouble in this Territory and on the frontier ... by a curse equally at least, in its pestiferous character, the plagues of Egypt, in being made the unwilling receptacle of the filth, scum and offscourings of the East ... to pollute our fair land, to dictate to us a government, to preach Abolitionism and dig underground Rail Roads.[20]

One could fairly see war clouds forming on the flat horizon.

The Missourians assumed neighboring Kansas to be rightfully theirs and looked upon the tent-pitching Yankees as interlopers coming to practice politics rather than farm. Atchison, in a fight to maintain his Senate seat, toured the western border, making provocative speeches designed to focus the fears of his constituents. On September 21, he took the steamer *New Lucy* from Weston and cruised eighteen miles up the Missouri River to the new community of Atchison, Kansas, named obviously in his honor. There he gave a blistering address openly calling for violence against abolitionists,

LIBERTY. THE FAIR MAID OF KANS

In this stylized image of the sections, northern "Liberty, the Fair Maid of Kansas" is at the mercy of heavily armed southern "Border Ruffians," one of whom, a bearded Stephen Douglas who is holding up a fresh scalp, shouts "Victory! Victory! WE WILL SUBDUE THEM YET!"

perhaps remembering his role as a state militia commander when Missouri's Mormon War (1838) resulted in nearly two dozen deaths and the Latter-day Saints' withdrawal east to Illinois. Though sympathetic to the Mormons' right to settle, representing Joseph Smith in land disputes with non-Mormons in Missouri, he eventually backed the military solution that led to their flight.[21] Might the Yankees now be warned off as well?

A sizeable crowd greeted Atchison in Atchison. After feasting on a 50¢ a head picnic lunch of bacon and bread, the senator jumped on a wagon and made the day's main address. In a dispatch sent later that

THE HANDS OF THE "BORDER RUFFIANS".

week to Jefferson Davis, he offered his impressions of what transpired: "I . . . advised in a public speech the squatters in Kansas and the people of Missouri, to give a horse theif, robber, or homicide a fair trial, but to hang a Negro theif [those aiding escaped slaves] or Abolitionist, without Judge or Jury." This call reflected a broader urgency among many Missourians to turn away the northern "horde." Numerous local politicians and publishers encouraged this on-edge attitude throughout the second half of 1854 as the Yankees trickled in. "We have no sympathy for Abolitionism," one *Kickapoo Kansas Pioneer* editorial expressed a commonly held dissent. "Their hearts are as black as the darkest deeds of hell. Away with them; send them back where they belong."[22]

Atchison's fiery rhetoric aligned with the organization that autumn of several secret associations in the border region. These paramilitary bodies—known variously as "Sons of the South," "Social Bands," and "Friendly Societies"—aimed to protect proslavery settlers and intimidate northerners. They enjoyed a pool of important and well-placed support in Washington. As the Kansas situation unfolded, President Pierce publicly criticized the "inflammatory agitation" of the antislavery settlers and thus more generally condemned the free-soil movement from which it came. Assorted newspapers and congressmen—not all southern—openly denounced Thayer's enterprise. Stephen Douglas, for one, complained of his pet popular sovereignty "being struck down

by unholy combinations in New England," while border state senator
J. A. Bayard of Delaware insisted, "Whatever evil, or loss, or suffering or
injury may result to Kansas, or to the United States at large, is attributa-
ble, as a primary cause to the Emigrant Aid Society of Massachusetts."[23]

On the other side of the Kansas divide, Thayer could count several
important congressmen in his corner. Among them, Charles Sumner
attacked the secret southern societies stirring up unrest along the western border—these groups were peopled by mere "hirelings," he supposed in a prickly Senate address, "picked from the drunken spew and
vomit of an uneasy civilization." He had little better to say of Douglas,
describing his Illinois colleague in private correspondence as "a brutal
vulgar man without delicacy or scholarship [who] looks as if he needed
clean linen and should be put under a shower bath."[24]

Though defended by Sumner and other well-placed Yankees, Thayer
ran afoul of slavery's more radical critics, who accused him of pursuing the Emigrant Aid "scheme" merely to make money. Oliver Johnson,
an aide to William Lloyd Garrison, complained that the EAC's "flavor
of craftiness . . . repelled the Abolitionists" by "flatter[ing] its patrons
with hopes of great pecuniary profits." Nearly a year after Thayer sent
his first company to Kansas, *The Liberator* grumbled: "Hardly an abolitionist can be found among all who have emigrated to that country."
Certainly, the demands of those advocating immediate emancipation
grated on the ears of the more conservative Cotton Whigs, some of
whom, as noted, supported Thayer's enterprise but wished to remain
on good terms with their southern suppliers. Thayer himself called the
abolitionists "fanatics" who "could see but one sin in all the world."[25]
Invariably, all sides—Thayer's, the Garrisonians, and the Missourians—
created vivid, dangerous caricatures of their ignoble adversaries.

In 1854 the Emigrant Aid Company sent a half-dozen modest-sized
settler groups to Kansas. Into the following year, and despite Thayer's
extravagant plans, it had managed to transport only 1,240 people. And
yet the first territorial census in 1855 disclosed a population of 8,500,
the bulk of whom, upward of 75 percent, came from Missouri and the
Ohio Valley, about 240 of whom were enslaved men and women. The
1860 census revealed that only 4 percent of colonizers came from New
England. "We are too far off," Lawrence wrote to Charles Robinson,
when this trend became apparent, "we can pay some money and we can
hurrah; but we cannot send you men. . . . The Western States will fur-

nish them, if you have them at all." In November 1855 a *Boston Adver-tiser* editorial reported upon the rather large discrepancy between the public's fanciful notion of a northeastern invasion of the plains and reality. The "very general impression that New England has been drained of a considerable number of her people to settle in Kanzas," it observed, "is entirely false."[26]

The impact of Thayer's much touted and talked-up Emigrant Aid Company, however, extended far beyond the modest numbers it actually sent west. It provided, rather, a model for other colonization associations while, by its mere existence as an outpost of antislavery sentiment, provoking some Missourians into intemperate, even violent action. Just a few months after its formation several other organizations—the Union Emigration Society (Washington, D.C.), the New York Kansas League, and the Kansas Emigration Aid Association of Northern Ohio among them—emerged as well; these were supplemented by more specialized groups aligning with the free-soil theme, including a German society called the Kansas Anseidlungsverein (colonization union) out of Cincinnati and the Vegetarian Settlement Company from Philadelphia. Most pioneers in these and other associations were less motivated by the plight of the nation's enslaved than their own economic self-interest, though when cast against the immediate backdrop of the Kansas-Nebraska Act and the still broader tableau of issues relating to race, bondage, and free labor, the Yankee thrust into the frontier shook planter perception. Thayer's ghost lingered long. In 1859 John Brown, a veteran of the Kansas border war, led, as noted earlier, an assault on a federal arsenal at Harpers Ferry, Virginia, that resulted in more than a dozen deaths. After watching U.S. Marines under the command of Colonel Robert E. Lee take the wounded Brown into custody, a bystander speculated (erroneously) on the radicalization of this arch abolitionist: "Hadn't the Emigrant Aid Society sent him to Kansas?"[27]

The question, loaded with stormy associations, evoked the "Bleeding Kansas" (1854–1859) period of paramilitary guerrilla warfare and gang violence, which resulted in nearly sixty casualties and numerous assaults and raids, along with repeated fraud in territorial elections. This chaos began to show itself already in the autumn of 1854 when disputes over land, cabins, and other forms of property between northerners and Missourians threatened to erupt into violence. Stowe's brother Henry Ward Beecher declared about this time that "Sharps rifle was a truly moral agency, and . . . there was more moral power in one of those instruments, so far as the slaveholders of Kansas was concerned, than in a hundred Bibles." Greeley's *Tribune* echoed this high-strung sentiment, observing that Kansas's Free-Soilers required above all else "the spirit of martyrdom and Sharpe's rifles." And indeed, by the spring of 1855 Robinson was writing to Thayer asking for "200 Sharps rifles as a loan." Desirous of a more immediate response, however, he also sent George W. Deitzler, in the employ of the Company, east to prod his contacts into procuring the desired weapons. "Within an hour after our arrival in Boston," Deitzler recalled in the late 1870s, "the executive commit- tee of the Emigrant Aid Society held a meeting and delivered to me an order for one hundred . . . rifles and I started at once for Hartford, arriv- ing there on Saturday evening. The guns were packed on the following Sunday and I started for home on Monday morning. The boxes were marked 'Books.' "[28]

The question of slavery's contested extension became unrelenting in 1854. And more than merely a Kansas account, it extended beyond the clean tree lines of U.S. territory, enchanting those many sunbaked adven- turers who dreamed of carving out private fiefdoms in distant fields of gold and green. This expansionist impulse invariably became enmeshed in the welter of sectional issues disquieting the country. Its foot soldiers, uninterested in settling on the neighboring plains, set their acquisitive sights elsewhere, peering as odd antebellum pirates to the dusty Sono- ran south, eager for conquest and restless to set out for Mexico.

10

Empires to the South

We know that schemes, open and secret, are . . . set on Mexico.

Putnam's Monthly Magazine, 1854

On May 8, 1854, the day he turned thirty, the American filibusterer William Walker led some three dozen worn, depleted, and defeated men across the Mexico–U.S. border to San Diego. There this uncombed paramilitary—said by one unsympathetic contemporary to consist of "every ruined gambler, outlaw, and used-up person in California"—surrendered to U.S. forces, having failed in its self-anointed mission to assert control over the state of Sonora.[1] An Anglo extract of the Spanish *filibustero*, which itself derives from the Dutch *vrijbuiter* ("freebooter"), the term "filibuster" implied a compulsion to raid, invade, or otherwise claim territory in the New World. Shy, slight, and ascetic, the diminutive Walker hardly looked the part of a privateer or a picaroon. And yet he came in the 1850s to exemplify a certain swashbuckling attitude among a distinct cohort of his countrymen—chiefly a congregation of mirage-minded southerners—to wrest land, islands, and isthmuses from Spanish-speaking peoples. Such banditry appealed to an old impulse; Americans, after all, were long practiced in the dark art of plunder, having penetrated over the last half century deep into the Gulf region, removing tens of thousands of native peoples along the way. Walker's dubious adventures below the border took on a particularly unsettling resonance in light of the broader race, slavery, and expansion triad then challenging the country. They seemed to represent, in some fatal way, the interests of a plantocracy angling to extend its cotton enclave far beyond the reach of abolitionists and emigrant aid companies.

The most notorious filibuster effort in the young United States was almost certainly the Burr Conspiracy (1805–1807). Former vice president Aaron Burr is alleged to have eyed a generous slice of the southern Gulf Coast, including New Orleans and those parts of Madrid-governed Mexico constituting present-day Texas. The mercurial Burr whispered to some that he merely wished to lease land from the Spanish Crown, though in a more belligerent mood he expressed a distinct interest in forcibly detaching a chunk of Spanish territory as a gift to the American republic. But to Anthony Merry, Britain's envoy to the United States, he said something else altogether:

> Mr. Burr . . . has mentioned to me that the inhabitants of Louisiana seem determined to render themselves independent of the United States, and that the execution of their design is only delayed by the difficulty of obtaining previously an assurance of protection and assistance from some foreign Power, and of concerting and connecting their independence with that of the inhabitants of the western parts of the United States, who must always have a command over them by the rivers which communicate with the Mississippi. It is clear that Mr. Burr (although he has not as yet confided to me the exact nature and extent of his plan) means to endeavor to be the instrument of effecting such a connection.[2]

Burr's extravagant project to put New Orleans in his pocket came to naught. Seized in the wilds of Alabama while on the lam—a spooked Jefferson, then president, ordered the arrest—he was taken to Richmond for trial. There the cunning politician won acquittal, though more "official" filibusters soon followed.

During the War of 1812 Jefferson's successor, James Madison, quietly commissioned George Mathews to pursue what became known as the "Patriot War"—an effort by irregular American recruits to launch, with regular U.S. troops lagging not far behind, an insurrection into East Florida. When the unseemly venture became public and threatened the existing peace with Spain, an embarrassed administration disavowed Mathews's unconventional soldiering and ordered the return of the territory it had taken in the Atlantic-facing vicinity of St. Augustine. Not to be outdone, President James Monroe turned an army under Andrew Jackson loose in both Floridas (East and West) in 1818 with orders to pursue border Seminoles marauding—with provocation—in neighboring Georgia. In the process of warring on the natives, Jackson's force illegally seized Spanish citadels and briefly occupied Pensacola, West Florida's capital. Rather than punish the tall, rail-thin, and notoriously aggressive general, already the Hero of New Orleans and perhaps beyond the censure of mere public servants, Monroe stood by Jackson, whose success demonstrated the inability of the Spanish Crown to defend the peninsula. The following year, as part of the Adams-Onís Treaty, Spain ceded all of Florida to the United States.

A generation later, in the 1830s, Americans living in Texas broke away from the Mexican government and established by revolution a new republic. This opened the door to a host of armed conflicts and land acquisitions in the southwest including the annexation of Texas (1845), the Mexican-American War (1846–1848), and the Gadsden Purchase (1854). The latter, negotiated by James Gadsden, a South Carolina–born diplomat disappointed with California's free-state status, anticipated the creation of a railroad connecting New Orleans to the Pacific by bringing yet more Mexican territory—portions of present-day Arizona and New Mexico—to the United States. Combined, the focus on Mexico and overlapping California gold rush sharply reoriented American foreign policy in a southern direction. More, it seemed to give some unstated sanction to filibusterers looking to "liberate" Cuba, or take the mineral-laden Yucatán Peninsula (in the name of saving a white minority from the Mayans), or, à la Walker in 1854, claim the sprawling Mexican state of Sonora. As one student of U.S. imperialism has recently observed, "southern slaveholders," in the hopes of carving out new slave states, "played an outsized part in most of these endeavors."[3]

Along with a distinct Dixie inflection, the midcentury American filibuster profile tilted still more particularly toward the fortune hunter and the freelancer. It included veterans of the Mexican-American War and disappointed gold rushers; it comprised a swarm of drifters and deadbeats, as well as a scattering of crooks and convicts. It appealed further to the adventurous and the penniless, while making a place for the discontented and the grandiose. Most famously, it attracted William Walker. Standing only five feet, five inches tall and weighing perhaps 110 pounds, with fine tawny hair and a thicket of yellow freckles dotting a chaste face, he gave the appearance of being more chaplain than chieftain—boys in school had called him "honey" and "missy."[4] This consummate opportunist, a self-styled "Colonel," exuded some mesmeric charm that enchanted a certain kind of man. In the words of a delighted former recruit, Walker is rendered a surrogate for an older kind of corsair, no longer welcome in an empirical world of contracts, accountants, and time-serving congressmen:

> In the 50's men looked upon life from a more romantic view-point than they do now. There was more sentiment, more singing of songs, and more writing of love verses to sweethearts; . . . the cavalier, with his plumes and ribbons, had not departed, and the music of the troubadour still tinkled amidst the sounds of revelry. Those were days when the ardor for adventure by land and sea was hot in the breasts of men. In the vast regions of the West, the stars shone upon a primeval wilderness, where there was lure of gold, and where hunger and conflict and even death challenged those whose daring and hardihood defied the vicissitudes of fortune in their search for El Dorado. Men had not outgrown the customs of their forefathers . . . they were moved by sincerity, and surrounded by traditions still too potent to cast aside. Such were the men who took service under Walker.[5]

William Walker, the son of a Scottish immigrant and his Kentucky bride, was born in Nashville in 1824. The household leaned toward an abstinent Calvinism and Walker, so contemporaries reported, ate little, smoked not at all, and equitably suffered conspicuously long silences. One friend, the Indiana-born poet, Pony Express rider, and sometime filibusterer Joaquin Miller, best known for his book of western color verses, *Song of the Sierras* (1871), declared "General Walker" to be "the cleanest man in word and deed." Relatives on Walker's maternal Bluegrass side owned enslaved people, though his father abandoned the practice, employing free blacks to whom he paid wages. Steering their son toward the ministry, James and Mary Walker sent young William, all of twelve, to the University of Nashville, aka the "Athens of the South," a respected boys preparatory academy attended by the offspring of the local elite, including the prominent antebellum moderate John Bell, who, running as the Constitutional Union Party's candidate in 1860, captured thirty-nine electoral votes and three states in the presidential election won by Lincoln. Walker studied a clutter of subjects ranging from philosophy, chemistry, and mineralogy to Greek, Latin literature, and political economy.[6] Graduating with honors in only two years, this wunderkind resolved to follow his own lead; dropping the pulpit, he briefly apprenticed under a local Nashville physician, before earning a medical degree at the University of Pennsylvania in 1843. He was still a teenager.

Over the next two years Walker traveled extensively throughout Europe, including the British Isles. While based in Paris he took additional training in the city's hospitals before moving on to the storied University of Heidelberg, founded, upon the prompting of Pope Urban VI, in the fourteenth century and among the Continent's oldest and most distinguished institutions of higher learning; there he attended medical lectures, a regimen he repeated in both London and Edinburgh. Returning to Nashville, he could now claim to be one of the best-trained Americans to ever prepare for a medical career—which only begs the question: Why did he suddenly forsake a medical career? Clearly intellectually curious, he appears to have enjoyed mastering rather than practicing medicine. And given that he would one day invade foreign states with private armies, it's a bit of a stretch to imagine him attending with interest dyspeptic Nashvillians suffering from gout, cholera, or constipation.

Seeking another kind of stimulation, Walker suddenly turned his attention to jurisprudence, reading law for two years and gaining admittance to the Louisiana bar. Along the way he had decamped for New Orleans and, taking his nose out of a mess of textbooks, possibly discovered there a disinclination to strut and preen among the Crescent City's legal eagles. Or perhaps, as with medicine, he had simply satisfied and casually moved on from one transient interest to another. More consequentially, he struck up a friendship during this period with the poshly pedigreed clerk of the U.S. Circuit Court of New Orleans, Edmund Randolph. Tall and attractive, articulate and acclaimed, Randolph, the grandson of George Washington's second secretary of state, may have struck the boyish Walker as a romantic figure, if not a masculine ideal.[7]

Apparently eager to remain in the city, Walker obtained an editorial position on the *Crescent*, a so-called family paper of a miscellaneous

nature. He overlapped slightly on the sheet with an aspiring young poet
from Brooklyn, New York, named Walt Whitman, who, in his capacity
as chief editor, wrote a number of local color reportage pieces including the thirsty-minded "Sketches of the Sidewalks and Levees, with
Glimpses into the New Orleans Bar (Rooms)." The paper's strongly pro-
slavery stance eventuated, after only two months, in Whitman's removal
by its owners. While at the *Crescent*, Walker apparently, and for the only
time in his life, fell in love. The intended, Helen Martin, was a deaf-mute
from birth; her death from cholera in the spring of 1849, Walker histori-
ography has it, put her beau in something of a tailspin, sending him yet
again in pursuit of another situation. "Deeply disturbed," writes scholar
Robert E. May, "he . . . soon emigrated to California."[8]

A throng of fortune seekers, secure or shaken, bereaved or otherwise,
flooded into the propitious vicinity of John Sutter's celebrated Coloma
mill at this time, high tide of the frenzied gold rush. Randolph was
among them, perhaps offering Walker yet another reason to make his
way west. Midcentury San Francisco gave every appearance of being a
booming and vibrant but lawless center of commercial activity. Its rapid
spike in population (from one thousand in 1848 to twenty-five thousand in 1850) exceeded by far the city's capacity to provide adequate
policing, housing, or healthcare. Accordingly, robberies and arson as
well as the odd homicide belied the surface stability implied by the tall-
masted merchant ships milling about the harbor waiting to take gold
plucked in Upper California and the Sierra Nevada to New York broker-
age houses. San Francisco's eclectic and unsettled population, skewing
toward young and male with the occasional deposed Latin American
potentate dropped in, seemed, beyond the lure of mere riches, to attract
a pack of madcap venturers and wanderers of dubious disposition.[9] This
swift influx of people combined with proximity to the sparsely settled
frontier of nearby northern Mexico—a region made restive with the
recent American invasion—to create a situation ripe for banditry. This
was the ramshackle arena William Walker entered in the spring of 1850.

There, and after a few months editing the *San Francisco Herald*, the
print ally of Randolph's political ambitions, Walker returned to law-
yering, forming a partnership in Marysville with Henry P. Watkins, an
attorney eminently susceptible to filibustering's siren song. Predictably, he gradually lost interest in this arrangement. Bored in a profession
whose bread and butter involved the Bartleby-like proofing of deeds and

wills, Walker—and Watkins—left Marysville, sailing in June 1853 for Guaymas presumably to pursue a mining claim and possessed, so they later insisted, with passports issued by the Mexican consulate. Arriving in the sparsely populated seaport town, they were promptly detained and accused of trying to swallow a bit of Mexico for themselves. Parked in Guaymas through the summer, Walker circulated about its arid environs, attracting the attention of both natives and transients. One of the latter, T. Robinson Warner, later recalled the Colonel's perfectly contrary clothing, consisting in the wilting summer heat of an improbably "huge white fur hat" setting atop "a very ill-made, short-waisted blue coat, with gilt buttons, and a pair of grey, strapless pantaloons." Warner thought the swashbuckling lawyer's loose talk leaned extravagantly toward the "insanely confident."[10]

After the U.S. consulate in Guaymas failed to convince Mexican officials—all too familiar with the artful expeditions of filibustering Californians—to permit Walker and Watkins to travel to Hermosillo, the would-be buccaneers returned to San Francisco. But Walker, with only a furtive glimpse, had seen enough. Though confined to tiny Guaymas, he believed, so he later wrote, "that a comparatively small body of Americans might gain a position on the Sonora frontier." He wanted nothing more, so he swore, than to "protect the families on the border from the Indians; and such an act would be one of humanity, no less than of justice, whether sanctioned or not by the Mexican Government." Though obviously self-serving, Walker thought these words might resonate against the backdrop of the Mexican Apache Wars, a generation-long conflict now reaching its particular intensity.[11]

Back in San Francisco, Walker and Watkins engaged in serious planning to invade Sonora. Attuned to the prevailing political winds, they had reason to suppose that the American government might support such banditry. A few months earlier, in his inaugural address, President Franklin Pierce, tone-deaf to the western question dividing the nation's sections, happily chirped that the "apprehensions of dangers from extended territory . . . and multiplied States . . . has proven unfounded." A surprisingly aggressive continentalist, he stated further, "My Administration will not be controlled by any timid forebodings of evil from expansion." Rather, he frankly and a little cantingly called "the acquisition of certain possessions not within our jurisdiction eminently important for our protection." With this presidential imprimatur, the administration pressed Mexico to sell a sliver of land in the southwest, the aforementioned Gadsden Purchase. While these negotiations ensued throughout the summer and fall of 1853, the (San Francisco) *Alta California*, in the manner of the "Manifest Destiny" apologia that came to define an entire era and expression of U.S. foreign policy, announced a new day in the nation's territorial ambitions: "If the acquisitions that may now be looked upon as certain are commenced by negotiations, it will not stop until Young America has secured all her demands, which will prove to be nothing short of the entire scope of territory lying between the Sierra Madre and the Rio Grande, Chihuahua, Sonora, and Lower California, and the reserved right to take more by purchase or force whenever it may be wanted."[12]

In support of their scheme, Walker and Watkins began issuing bonds in an "Independence Loan Fund" with shares going for $500 (about $17,700 in today's currency). The bond entitled the holder to seventy-seven hundred acres of land in Sonora. With the capital they purchased supplies and a store of arms and hired the *Arrow*, a brig proficient in coastal sailing and able to transport two hundred men. Walker advertised his illegal operation to recruits as a humanitarian exercise. The distressed Mexican people, he insisted, were both ill served and ill protected by their government and deserved the same freedoms and security enjoyed by their Anglo neighbors to the north. Those men who mustered under Walker perhaps saw beyond this posturing, likely deciding to join his peculiar army for their own evanescent reasons.

Most of them never left California. Ordered, despite Pierce's aggressive rhetoric, to police the nation's neutrality laws, General Ethan Allen Hitchcock, commander of the U.S. Army's Department of the Pacific, resolved to keep would-be raiders from exiting San Francisco's bustling port. By this time, late September, Walker's plans were nearly complete, but the hum of activity about the *Arrow* drew the local authority's attention and, under the order of the U.S. district attorney, the ship was seized. Undaunted, Walker quickly improvised, chartering the schooner *Caroline* and stuffing it with supplies. Smaller than the *Arrow*, it could only accommodate some fifty passengers, a rather numerically poor corps to conquer Sonora.[13] It slipped quietly out of San Francisco's harbor just after midnight on October 16.

Two weeks and fifteen hundred miles later the *Caroline* reached Cabo San Lucas, the southern point of the Lower (Baja) California peninsula. Unable with his slight army to assault Sonora, Walker planned instead to establish a base in nearby La Paz, Baja's capital, founded in 1535 by an army under the Spanish Conquistador Hernán Cortés, who, in an earlier expedition, had toppled the Aztec Empire. With a population of only fifteen thousand and a small Mexican military presence, Lower California offered Walker an inviting target—he hoped to attract a swift current of recruits from San Francisco. Reaching La Paz in early November, Walker's force promptly arrested Governor Rafael Espinosa and exchanged a Mexican flag on the capital's grounds for that of the "Republic of Lower California"—a white field pennant with two bright red stars signifying Lower California and Sonora. Days later Walker declared himself president and opened La Paz's port to free trade with, so he audaciously announced, "all the world"; he further proclaimed Louisiana's legal code operative in the new republic. This last item suggested to some that he looked to bring slaves into the region, though as a former New Orleans lawyer he knew its laws reasonably well and may have simply reached for something familiar.[14]

Walker's brief three-day deployment in La Paz went awry from the start. The unreceptive La Pazians attacked their liberators, apparently in no mood to be liberated. Walker's force replied in kind, opening fire on the locals in what turned into a ninety-minute skirmish resulting, so a battle report from the American side stated, in the deaths of "six or seven" Mexicans with several more injured. "Our men did not so much as receive a wound," the report summary continued, "except from *cacti*, while pursuing the enemy through the chaparral, in the rear of the town." Too small a force to remain in place, Walker and his men then sailed north to the tiny port city of Ensenada, about sixty miles from the U.S. border; they defiantly called it their new capital. Just up the road a cooperative *San Diego Herald*, bowing before its high-spirited readership, declared that "the capture of La Paz and the establishment of a new order of things [has] excited our American population to the wildest bounds of joy." The hype had a tonic-like effect on the coast. For when word of Walker's supposed exploits trickled into San Francisco, money and recruits began to collect in anticipation for what everyone knew to be this pirate/president's real goal—the conquest of Sonora.[15]

And so in December Watkins organized a second party of filibusterers in the Golden City; numbering about 150, it sailed to Ensenada aboard the British bark *Anita*. Shortly thereafter, the *New York Times* expressed to eastern readers its surprise that "an armed party were thus leaving the . . . Clay Street wharf . . . without the slightest opposition on the part of the authorities." But leave they did. When the craft swung out to sea, so the *Times* reported, "nothing could now restrain the men, and loud and repeated cheers rose from the vessel, which were heartily responded to from the wharf. The [*Anita*] went up the bay to get clear of the shipping, and then, turning, glided past the silent city with the strength of the ebb tide."[16]

While awaiting these men, Walker antagonized Sonoran landowners by confiscating their horses, eating their hogs, and taking hostages; his reckless actions provoked a large posse who skirmished with his army for several days, killing one man and injuring others before dispersing. The *Anita*'s appearance on the twentieth did little to alter Walker's predicament. The ship, enduring rough seas, lost many of its provisions, and food became a concern only desperately met by conducting several raids on nearby communities. As one Mexican witness later stated, "Houses were broken into, families were forced to do the bidding of the invaders, and horses and saddles were taken from passing civilians."[17] By this time Walker's soldiers, eager for a quick victory, were growing discontented. Concerned about both the Mexicans and his own men— as well as the presence of the tri-masted USS *Portsmouth*, a wooden sloop of war anchored abruptly in Ensenada Bay—Walker suddenly moved his makeshift force about fifty miles south to San Vicente. There, on March 1, he ordered its citizens under threat of punishment to take an oath of allegiance to his pretend republic.

About this time the expedition shed some dozen men, deserters eager to flee for San Diego. Though sensing the gravity of his situation, Walker seemed oddly intent to make it graver still. On the twentieth, while a divided Congress in a distant Washington fought over the Kansas-Nebraska Bill, and down to his last one hundred soldiers, he ordered his offbeat army to cross the meandering Colorado River into Sonora. What he hoped to accomplish is something of a mystery. He possessed far too few men to subdue the province (population seventy thousand) and could expect no reinforcements to find him there. More, Sonora lay an exacting two hundred miles away, a ruddy mirage of scorched bronze desert rolling silently below a silky blue sky. Walker later claimed, without a shred of credibility, to be on a mission of mercy: "It was the intention . . . to establish at as early a time as possible a military colony—not necessarily hostile to Mexico—on the frontier of Sonora, with a view of protecting that State from the Apaches."[18] Leaving San Vicente with about one hundred cattle for food, the wavering expedition made its uncertain way north.

Predictably, the punishing march cost Walker both men and much of his herd; two dozen of the livestock were spirited away by trailing Indians. The party, aboard rafts, forged the thin Colorado on April 4; several of their accompanying steers drowned. Even before the crossing, so a group of deserters told a physician at Fort Yuma, Walker's army was "in a most miserable and destitute condition, wearing the same clothing with which they went to the country, and this is in tatters and rags." Recognizing the futility of his venture, Walker quickly retreated across the river only to discover that Antonio María Meléndrez, a practiced bandit whose father's ranch near Ensenada (La Grulla) had lost twenty horses to Walker's marauders four months earlier, was now tracking him, accompanied by eighty men. Both bodies maneuvered carefully, avoiding battle, and the Anglos reached San Vicente on the seventeenth. There Walker discovered that Meléndrez's irregulars had wiped out the skeleton detail he had kept in reserve.[19]

Unable to do anything else, the bedraggled victors of the "Battle of La Paz," down to thirty distressed men, marched north, seeking safety in the United States. Along the way Meléndrez's hired guns shadowed them until they reached the border on May 8, surrendering to a small contingent of awaiting U.S. troops. Nearly four months earlier President Pierce, concerned that American filibustering might kill the still-unratified Gadsden Treaty, had issued a communication informing military and civilian officials to "arrest any violators of the neutrality laws." As a result, Watkins had been tried in San Francisco that March for enlisting recruits and provisioning the *Anita*. Defended by the ubiquitous Randolph and former Mississippi governor Henry S. Foote (who argued that the country's neutrality laws were unconstitutional), he was found guilty by a jury that recommended leniency. The district judge, Ogden Hoffman, a Pierce appointee from New York and filibuster enthusiast, levied a $1,500 fine, which, when Watkins pled poverty, was simply dropped. In 1858 the popular Hoffman captured a seat in the California State Senate.[20]

Seven months later it was Walker's turn to stand trial. Righteously declaring himself "bound on an errand of humanity," he appealed to a sympathetic jury of expansion-minded peers who took less than ten minutes to find him not guilty.[21] Some to the south were disturbed by the trial's predictable outcome. From Mexico City, Manuel Diez de Bonilla, Minister of Foreign Affairs, informed Gadsden in an official capacity of his nation's disgust with the verdict:

> As it is a well known and notorious fact that . . . Walker planned and organized . . . the illegal expedition against Lower California . . . in violation of the laws of neutrality of the United States, of its treaties with Mexico, and of international law . . . [his] acquittal . . . [is] nothing less than a flagrant denial of justice, which clearly shows the protection found in the jurisdictions of some of the authorities of the United States by criminal adventurers who, in defiance of its laws and treaties, have violated the territory of this nation.

De Bonilla feared that in winking at such a brazen violation of its neutrality laws, the U.S. government provided "incitement and inducement" for future Walkers.[22]

If not Walker himself. In May 1855, consumed by the temptations and dangers of filibustering, this restless soul sailed with a few dozen men to an unstable Nicaragua—a conduit for American gold seekers making for California—and violently took tenuous control of the country that fall. Assuming the post of president through a fraudulent election and seeking southern support in Washington, he reinstituted the practice of slavery, it having been outlawed in 1824, and reopened the slave trade; the United States recognized his tottering regime's legitimacy in the spring of 1856, though to no productive end. Defeated by a coalition of neighboring countries fearful for their own security, Walker fled Nicaragua in May 1857. Undaunted, he attempted three years later to establish a government in the Bay Islands off the coast of Honduras. This venture failed completely. Walker was taken into custody in the port city of Trujillo by a force organized under the young British commander Nowell Salmon of the HM sloop of war *Icarus*—in order, so Salmon explained, "to re-establish . . . the authorities commissioned by the existing government of Honduras." Britain, in other words, had its own interests in the region, including ideas of putting an interoceanic canal through Central America, and would brook no freebooting American interference. Walker, though having surrendered and presuming protection under the British flag, was instead turned over to Honduran officials; Salmon, eager, so he said, to end this particular prisoner's "depredations," could have had little doubt of what would happen next. Following a brief trial by court-martial Walker, only thirty-six, was executed before a firing squad.[23]

Walker's delusions of carving out a Lower California empire were not predicated on bringing slavery into the region, though it is easy to imagine that, as in Nicaragua, he would at some point have moved to make it legal. Clearly, he cultivated certain cotton state sympathies and demonstrated, along with millions of his countrymen to be sure, a mechanical belief in black inferiority. "The white man took the negro from his native wastes," so he argued in *The War in Nicaragua*, a self-serving memoir, "and teaching him the arts of life, bestowed on him the ineffable blessings of a true religion." Walker further presumed the enslavement of black peoples sanctioned by the "economy of nature and Providence," a dual approval indicating that "slavery is not abnormal to American society. . . . It must be the rule not the exception."[24]

It is tempting to interpret Walker as sui generis, a rare ruffian out to make himself a Latin king and thus standing outside the more conventional dilemmas facing a Kansas-Nebraska-consumed America. And yet his outré legacy is far more ecumenical. For on the broken road to Sonora he embodied in his frail physique an alarming appetite to pillage below the border, a supreme provocation at the precise moment when the issue of slavery's expansion twisted sectional tensions above the border. This pressure, tremoring unpleasantly through the republic, appeared to be nearing the breaking point in May 1854, the month Walker surrendered to U.S. forces in California, the month the Fugitive Slave Act once again inflamed the nation.

11

Boston Besieged

I have seen that poor slave, Anthony Burns, carried back into slavery!

Martha Russell, 1854

On May 24 Anthony Burns, an enslaved Virginia man lately escaped, was arrested in Boston, and over the next several days the city seethed and shook. If the Kansas-Nebraska Bill infuriated Massachusetts, the pursuit of fugitives in presumably free New England reached even deeper into the state's troubled conscience, provoking a reaction still more visceral and immediate. Men who had formerly thought of Chase and Sumner as political villains, irreparably radical and beyond the two-party consensus, now began to lean their way. Among them, the industrialist Amos Lawrence, de facto banker for the Emigrant Aid Company, though an otherwise proper Brahmin moderate, evocatively recalled the explosive impact of Burns's detainment on staid Boston: "We went to bed one night old-fashioned, conservative, Compromise Union Whigs & waked up stark mad Abolitionists."[1]

For several years the city had quartered a small African American community, whose numbers reached about 2,000 in 1850 compared to 46,000 Irish and nearly 90,000 Anglos. That same year the Fugitive Slave Law sent a shock of fear throughout this and other northern black hamlets. Enforcement of the unpopular act—a response by offended southern sensibilities to the Underground Railroad and a burgeoning network of Yankee safe houses and personal liberty laws—produced a fresh profession of, depending upon one's persuasion, slave catchers or kidnappers.

But what would happen should prevailed-upon citizens refuse to cooperate with the catchers cum kidnappers? On several occasions Bay State residents did just that. Two slaves from Macon, Georgia, Ellen Craft (passing as a white man) and her husband, William (acting as her servant), escaped in 1848; two years later bounty hunters tracked them down in Boston only to be met by a biracial Vigilance Committee that helped the Crafts flee to England. In 1850 the fugitive Shadrach Minkins of Virginia also reached Boston, where he waited tables at Cornhill Coffee House before being arrested by nine U.S. marshals in February of the following year. During legal proceedings, with hundreds of antislavery protesters gathered outside the city's federal courthouse, a group of black men barged into the building and rescued Minkins, taking him to a nearby Beacon Hill hideaway; six days later he crossed the border into Canada. That April, Thomas Sims, a young bricklayer formerly held in bondage by a Georgian rice farmer and now living at a boardinghouse for African American sailors on brothel-filled Ann Street, was also arrested and, unlike the Crafts and Minkins, returned to servitude. His rendition to the South, the first captive to be forcefully removed from Boston under the Fugitive Slave Law, struck many in the state as a sign of the central government's vexing deference to the preferences of enslavers. In relation to this case, a concerned Emerson denounced the "abuse of . . . Federal power," which resulted horribly in "the honor of Massachusetts [being] trailed in the dust."[2] Under such circumstances, it seemed likely that further efforts by planters to pursue their property rights in Yankee courts would be akin to holding trials in tinderboxes.

Born in Stafford County, Virginia, along the Potomac River in about 1834, Burns belonged, as did his mother and perhaps a dozen other men and women, to Charles Suttle, a shopkeeper, sometime deputy sheriff, and colonel in the state militia. Described as possessing "a powerful frame, well filled out, of commanding stature, and a heavy . . . countenance," the colonel, like many Old Dominion masters, owned a surplus of enslaved people and often hired them out. Burns began working at the age of seven for three spinsters and moved on successively to other employers who might purchase his labor for a year or so. At one of these situations, he learned (from the kind wife of a schoolmaster) to read, though, while working for a Yankee couple come south, he acquired a permanent impediment when he badly mangled his right hand in a mill. The damaged bone remained exposed—"a hump an inch high," one contemporary recalled. In January 1854, ritual time of the yearly hiring-out process, Burns was leased to a Richmond druggist named Millspaugh, who, with business slow, proposed that Burns go out each day and sell his labor to the highest bidder. He suggested further that Burns pay for his own upkeep and cumulatively hand over to him, Millspaugh, the sum of $125 (the fee—$4,400 in today's dollars—paid to hire Burns out for the year) and the two would then split what was left over.[3]

Burns agreed, quickly intuiting that his new situation proposed a ready route to freedom. Each day he drifted down to the city's humming docks, attracted not merely to the work but to the sight of sleek northern ships entering and exiting from the wharves, where great quantities of tobacco and flour were stored in rows of fenny-scented brick warehouses. Determined to escape his situation, Burns, having hatched a plan with sympathetic sailors, boarded a ship early one morning near the end of February and waited. A day later the craft left Richmond; its hidden passenger, recumbent in a dark space, hungry and seasick, made his precarious way down the wide James River and up the green-rinsed coast for Boston. Once there, he simply assumed the aspect of a sailor and no one questioned his presence—until he was arrested three months later.[4]

Working variously as a cook and a window washer, Burns had sent a letter disclosing his location to one of his brothers in Alexandria, Virginia, first forwarded to Canada in an effort to promote secrecy. Someone, however, intercepted the missive and gave it to Suttle. The colonel, eager to reclaim Burns, whom he described to a Virginia judge as "a man of dark complexion, about six feet high, with a scar on one of his cheeks, and also a scar on the back of his right hand, and about twenty-three or four years of age," followed up on this lead. Accordingly, on the evening of May 24 Burns, employed by a Brattle Street clothing dealer named Coffin Pitts, suddenly encountered a small company of men on Court Street while walking home. "A hand was put on my shoulder," he later remembered, "and somebody said: 'Stop, stop; you are the fellow who broke into a silversmith's shop the other night.' I assured the man that it was a mistake, but almost before I could speak, I was lifted off my feet by six or seven others, and it was no use to resist."[5]

Burns was quickly hustled off to the Suffolk County courthouse across the street. Earlier that day Edward G. Loring, both a judge and a United States Commissioner—the latter post empowering him to issue warrants for arrest and to make rulings under the Fugitive Slave Act—had authorized Burns's detention; U.S. Marshal Watson Freeman oversaw the men who then grabbed the runaway. Waiting outside the courthouse building, Suttle, eager to establish proof of Anthony's identity, called to him: "How do you do, Mr. Burns?," and made a show of taking his hat off and bowing. "I was brought right to a stand and didn't know what to say," Burns related the following year. "He wanted to know if I remembered the money that he used to give me, and I said, 'Yes, I do recollect that you used to give me twelve and a half cents at the end of every year I worked for you.'"[6] At this point, Burns was taken to an unused jury room—Massachusetts law prohibited confining alleged fugitive slaves in jail cells—where he was shackled and locked up for the night; an iron bar secured the door.

Outside the courthouse, the lawyer Richard Henry Dana, author of *Two Years Before the Mast* (1840), a memoir that bid for better treatment of the nation's sailors, received word while walking to his Court Street law office of Burns's plight. He quickly entered the fray. Though not an abolitionist, he had joined the Boston Vigilance Committee (organized in the early 1840s for the protection of escaped slaves), engaged in free-soil politics, and watched the Minkins and Sims cases with interest. Requesting an audience with Burns, he met the runaway that very night and offered his legal services. The latter, perhaps cowed by the shock of his situation and concerned about further offending Suttle, refused Dana's overture.[7]

It rained for much of the following day as Dana, thus far without Burns's support, began to strategize the fugitive's defense. Others, particularly Boston Vigilance Committee affiliates, mulled over more militant approaches. One of their number, Thomas Wentworth Higginson, lacking confidence in the legal system and eager to initiate a rescue attempt, arranged for a box of axes to be concealed near the courthouse. Loring, the probate judge of Suffolk County, would oversee the case; a Whig and a part-time lecturer at Harvard Law School, he had ordered Thomas Sims returned to slavery in 1851. Two days after Burns's arrest, on the morning of Friday the twenty-sixth, Loring walked into a raucous lecture hall in nearby Cambridge. A group of northern students hissed at his presence while their southern classmates cheered.[8]

That day a great unrest vibrated about Boston. Bristling placards—"A MAN KIDNAPPED"—filled the streets, papers shrieked with indignation, and the city council, presented with a quick petition of important names, agreed to open Faneuil Hall (built in the 1740s by the wealthy colonial slave merchant Peter Faneuil) to a public meeting that evening. It convened at 7:00 p.m., called to order by Samuel Sewall, a lawyer, founding member of the Massachusetts Anti-Slavery Society (1831), and quite auspiciously a descendant of the Puritan judge Samuel Sewall, author, in 1700, of the first abolitionist tract published in New England, *The Selling of Joseph*: "The Numerousness of Slaves at this day in the Province and the Uneasiness of them under their Slavery, have put many upon thinking whether the Foundation of it be firmly and well laid." Standing before an emotional crowd of five thousand, the well-to-do Roxbury merchant and China trader George Russell opened the affair on an anxious note, offering warnings of future filibusters (William Walker was making recent headlines) and daring a napping Yankee nation to stir from its dogmatic slumber. "When we get Cuba and Mexico as slave States—when the foreign slave trade is reestablished with all the appalling horrors of the Middle Passage, and the Atlantic is again filled with the bodies of dead Africans," he thundered, "then we may think it time to waken to our duty!"[9]

Later that evening Wendell Phillips, a well-known figure in Boston's antislavery community and the man who had presented the city council with the petitioners' demand to use the hall, approached the speakers' podium. "His features were cast in the Roman mould, his head was rounded and balanced almost to the ideal standard," reads one contemporary description. "He had an atrabiliar [melancholy] complexion, dark hair, and large, dark eyes that looked forth from behind spectacles with a steady, unwinking gaze." Caught, like everyone in the crowded hall, in the commotion of Douglas's Kansas-Nebraska Bill—it having passed through the House only four days earlier—Phillips linked Boston's fate with that of the western territories: "Nebraska I call knocking a man down, and this is spitting in his face when he is down." He implored the audience to make its presence felt and to further trust that right makes might. "See to it that tomorrow, in the streets of Boston," he appeared open to higher-law justice, "you ratify the verdict of Faneuil Hall, that Anthony Burns has no master but his God."[10]

Following Phillips, Theodore Parker, a plain-faced prophetic religious reformer lacking, so one nineteenth-century source notes, "grace of person" and "charm of expression," though otherwise armed with an "intensity of conviction," provocatively addressed his listeners as "the vassals of Virginia." These proud sons and daughters of Puritans and Revolutionaries had lost their historical patrimony, he argued, ground down in the South's implacable resolve to rule over a planters' republic: "Where are the Rights of Massachusetts?" He exposed for public repudiation the bitter clutch of compromises that made men and women escaping their servitude prisoners on free soil.[11] What further liberties were to be surrendered in the machinery of making bondage a national rather than a local institution—and in seeing the enslavement of people as common and appropriate rather than coarse and peculiar?

Despite such on-high pleas for justice, however, the claims of men like Parker and Phillips assumed an abstract quality, fundamentally removed from Anthony Burns, in whose name they now met. They despaired more evidently, rather, for Massachusetts and for those many whites in danger, be it in Boston or Kansas, of having their civil liberties lost. Though clearly coveting justice for the fugitive in their midst, they wished it for themselves as well and performed that evening a passion play in its name.

Prior to taking the stage, Parker had been apprised of an impending attack on the courthouse planned for that evening. When, in the midst of his talk, the room grew restless and men began to shout about paying "a visit to the slave-catchers," he attempted to defuse the design by telling the audience, "We shall meet at Court Square, at nine o'clock tomorrow morning." For several moments an unsteady peace prevailed, only to buckle before a more immediate impulse to action. The magnetic Phillips, a greater presence than Parker, quickly commanded the podium, at once reasoning with the restless—"the zeal that won't keep till tomorrow will never free a slave"—and assuring them that several of the city's leading power brokers were willing to join them in condemnation of Boston's submission to the South. It looked for an instant as though Phillips had won them over, but suddenly a sharp voice filled a pregnant pause: "Mr. Chairman, I am just informed that a mob of negroes is in Court Square, attempting to rescue Burns! I move we adjourn to Court Square!" In a mad scramble, the historic hall, known as the Cradle of Liberty for giving early American revolutionaries James Otis Jr. and Samuel Adams a forum to air common colonial grievances, emptied.[12]

Racing to the courthouse, the crowd failed to access a fastened door on the structure's east side; this prompted the assembly to move to yet another entry, from which, with the use of axes and a battering ram manned by some dozen protesters, a few managed to break into the building. Higginson, among them, quickly caught a saber in the face, later recalling how "I held my place . . . still hoping against hope that some concerted reinforcement might appear. Meanwhile the deputy marshals retreated to the stairway, over which we could see their pistols pointing." Many of these marshals were moonlighting locals, some of them pressed into service and one of whom, James Batchelder, a twenty-four-year-old Irish immigrant from Charlestown, received a mortal stab wound in the groin—the evening's only fatality. Outside, another kind of pell-mell ensued as stray bricks peppered the courthouse, shouts of, "Rescue him!" rang through the night air, and the city's police force made its inevitable arrival. While a confusion of bells clanged noisily across a galvanized Boston, several arrests were made, officers remained on detail throughout the night, and a tense standoff ensued. Though kept in a makeshift cell, Burns might have wondered at the unusual power of his presence.[13]

The next morning U.S. Marshal Freeman informed President Pierce by wire of both the courthouse assault and his prompt response, which included deploying U.S. troops in the building. "The attack was repulsed by my own guard," he noted, "everything is now quiet." This report met with the president's blessing: "Your conduct is approved. The law must be executed." A few days later the U.S. attorney in Boston, Benjamin Hallett, informed Pierce that he expected more violence and requested that the federal government, in such an event, be prepared to cover military outlays. "Incur any expense deemed necessary by the Marshal and yourself," the president replied firmly, "for the city military or otherwise, to insure the execution of this law." As a result, two artillery companies, a company of marines, and a company of U.S. troops arrived in Boston. That this conspicuous show of strength might prove to be, given the recent courthouse assault and the more general disinclination of New Englanders to aid in the rendition of runaway slaves, an enormous provocation seemed to elude the administration in Washington. "Seldom," a Pierce biographer has written, "was a president so out of touch with popular opinion."[14]

While Boston simmered over a brittle May weekend, Suttle, fearing for his safety, gratefully accepted the escort of a few southern sons of Harvard whenever leaving his upscale Bowdoin Square hotel. On Saturday morning, at the courthouse, Burns's examination resumed; the building—patrolled by marines and militia, its doors chained, and its corridors crowded with fixed bayonets—now resembled an improvised arsenal. Leaving nothing to chance, Suttle's skittish lawyers carried firearms. Burns appeared in court a few minutes after 9:00 a.m., "handcuffed and guarded by five desperate looking fellows," *The Liberator* observed, "all of whom were armed with revolvers, the handles of which protruded from the pockets of their coats."[15]

While the effort to establish Burns's identity ensued inside the courtroom, outside thousands were arriving from all over New England, eager for justice, drawn to the moment, or perhaps simply prompted by sheer curiosity. Some tried to talk their way into the proceedings, others sermonized atop upturned flour barrels, and still others were held—as agitators—under temporary arrest. The *New York Times*, wanting it both ways, expressed a measured opinion sorely out of touch with an era of filibusters, Bleeding Kansas, and electoral fraud: "We have resisted the repeal of the Missouri Compromise and the extension of Slavery. . . . But we feel it incumbent . . . to resist and denounce every attempt at the violent resistance of any law . . . that may be made to substitute popular passion and mob force for the *power of voting*." That evening a small group of Bostonians, including the Reverend Leonard Grimes, a Virginia-born African American abolitionist and pastor of the Twelfth Baptist Church in Boston's Roxbury neighborhood, worked with Hilton Willis, a State Street banker, to raise $1,200 ($42,000 in present-day value) to purchase Burns from Suttle. They met the slaveholder in Justice Loring's office and the colonel, agreeable to cutting short his time in a hostile city, seemed willing to hear them out. But Hallett scotched this. The U.S. Attorney seemed to believe that Washington's money must be well spent and that meant a public enforcement of the Fugitive Act. Possibly he wondered as well at the lenient signal given to future runaways, who might have reason to believe that their own forbidden journeys north might be met, even if captured, with emancipation. Hallett introduced several legal fine points into the conversation and, as the clock crept past midnight, negotiations between the abolitionists and the slaveholder broke down.[16]

This failed effort to free Burns gave way to a tense Sunday in which the streets around the courthouse remained occupied by various military companies, the epithet "Boston slave pen" circulating precariously in their direction. Applying still more pressure, a cluster of neighboring ministers brought Burns's case before their congregations that morning. Taking the dais of the Boston Music Hall on Winter Street (site of an Oscar Wilde lecture some years later), Parker wished to double damn the events of the preceding few days, both the Burns case and the Missouri Compromise's repeal. Determined to identify the enemy within, he singled out the city's complicit Cotton Whigs. "The Nebraska bill has just now been passed. Who passed it?" he asked—and answered: "The fifteen hundred 'gentlemen of property and standing' in Boston who, in 1851, volunteered to carry Thomas Sims into slavery by force of arms. *They* passed the Nebraska bill."[17]

The following day the court's proceedings continued. Dana defended the fugitive while the "slave-catcher lawyer," Seth Thomas, by turns esteemed or condemned for his work in the Sims case, appeared as senior counsel for the claimant. By this time an enormous crowd of perhaps eight thousand milled outside the courthouse area, most, but by no means all, sympathetic to Burns. One contemporary report notes that many, having entrained from nearby villages and suburbs, seemed eager to qualify their daily quotidian with this rare spectacle. These tourists "went up to the Court House, took a good look at its solid walls, its massive doors, and its ponderous pillars; stared at the police who guarded every approach . . . spent a few shillings for dinner, and went home." The examination went on for three days, with little doubt as to its outcome. William Brent, a Virginia merchant, positively identified Burns, whose services he had once purchased, as "the prisoner of the bar," while Dana struggled to produce evidence that his client was anyone other than the fugitive Anthony Burns. Where was he born? Who were his friends? What had he been doing for the past twenty years in the North? Instead, Dana quibbled desperately over the claimant's case, noting that a witness had mistaken the date he last saw Burns in the South and emphasizing an error in Burns's physical description that had arrived from a Virginia tribunal—but to little avail.[18]

Dana did what he could, though the role of fugitive slave crusader seemed an awkward fit. Whiggish, moderate, and conventional, he rejected higher-law politics as clever, if off-key. "I believe that the Constitution requires the . . . rendition of fugitive slaves. I cannot put any other construction upon it," he wrote to Charles Sumner in January

1861, just three months before the Battle of Fort Sumter started the war that made the rendition question eternally obsolete. "I take my oath with a conviction that those rights are to be yielded to slavery."[19]

The day before Burns's trial ended, a number of disparate constituencies were in motion. Dana delivered a powerful four-hour closing argument aimed at the papers ("The eyes of many millions are upon you, Sir," he told the judge. "If you commit a mistake . . . a free man is made a slave forever"), members of the Universalist Reform Society in Massachusetts conferred on the feasibility of their state's leaving the Union, while an anxious Marshal Freeman began to consider with some growing concern the fugitive's route to the wharf, should he be sent south. Late that afternoon he boldly asked Loring his decision, so that he, Freeman, could better anticipate the crowd's response. The evidence is mixed on whether the justice complied. In any case, a tense meeting that evening at the mayor's office included the commanders of the state militia and a marine contingent. Boston's brokers were clearly preparing for the worst.[20]

The following day, June 2, "Bad Friday," began early for Suttle. Possibly anticipating a positive ruling from Loring, if not already in possession of the verdict, he left the Revere House hotel at first light heading toward the Charlestown Navy Yard, where an attending barge took him to the *Morris*, a federal revenue cutter docked in Boston Bay. While the colonel waited in safety, Loring declared court in session at 9:00 a.m. and then promptly announced his finding in favor of the claimant. "Whether the statute is a harsh one or not, it is not for us to determine," he evenly stated. "I think the statute is constitutional, as it remains for me now to apply it to the facts of the case." By this time waves of people were arriving outside the courthouse, met not merely by a wall of soldiers but by a lumbering cannon brought in from the navy yard in near darkness that morning and now sitting with a deliberately menacing air in Court Square. Mayor Jerome V. C. Smith had prepared a proclamation that read: "All well disposed citizens, and other persons, are urgently requested to leave those streets which it may be found necessary to clear temporarily, and under no circumstances to obstruct or molest any officer, civil or military, in the lawful discharge of his duty." Some must have wondered if Boston had just been placed under martial law.[21]

Following Loring's ruling, the authorities moved quickly to transport Burns to the waiting *Morris*. Outside the courthouse troops and cavalry from four states combined with Boston's entire volunteer militia corps (about fifteen hundred) to present a formidable front against any who tried to break their blue ranks. Just before noon these soldiers, their rifles loaded, their glistening bayonets secured, began to clear a path leading down State Street to the Long Wharf. Businesses bordering the route had closed, black crepe adorned many of the buildings (their open windows jammed, their roofs littered with onlookers), and several thousands arrived to clamor, to emote, and to seek release in a deafening chorus. The police and militia stood alongside the sidewalks and cross streets to keep the crowds at bay as a thick knot of soldiers, at approximately 2:00 p.m., began to move Burns, his arms interlocked to an officer on each side, toward the port. Cries of "Kidnappers!" and "Shame!" vied with the sound of pealing church bells, both distant and near. The Boston attorney George Hillard knew something terribly wrong was now happening: "How odious and hateful the whole thing looked! . . . When it was all over, and I was left alone in my office, I put my face in my hands and wept."[22]

Burns acquitted himself well on this grievous day. Originally to be shackled, he blanched at the indignity and talked a deputy marshal into dispensing "with the instruments of disgrace." He now appeared in a fresh suit complete with a frock coat, silk vest, and accenting blue handkerchief—the smart garments provided by his recent keepers perhaps out of respect, though possibly with an eye toward mollifying an angry crowd. The sight of this young captive meeting tragedy with self-possession left an indelible impression. One Bostonian, the son of a hardware store owner, thought Burns appeared "with a face calm and manly, tho' very serious"; Amos Lawrence wrote with admiration that he "held his head up, and marched like a man."[23]

And what he marched through, a confluence of anger and arms converted into street assaults and saber cuts, suddenly brought the city's Revolutionary past to alarming life. For who could miss the school lesson symbolism as the procession moved past the Old State House, site of the Boston Massacre (1770) and with it the patriot death of Crispus Attucks, a dockworker of African and Native American descent? The Bostonian Martha Russell watched the guard moving Burns from the Commonwealth Building, later remembering an overpowering sense of injustice: "Did you ever feel every drop of blood in you boiling and seething, throbbing and burning, until it seemed you should suffocate? Did you ever set your teeth hard together to keep down the spirit that was urging you to do something to cool your indignation that good and wise people would call violence?" From that same Commonwealth Building came a hail of cayenne pepper and a bottle of sulfuric acid aimed at the passing soldiers. One teamster attempted to drive his wagon into a line of police, his horse counting as the only casualty. All the while a pounding din invaded the prisoner's path, enveloping a number of nervous militiamen who sang in their defiance and their fear "Carry Me Back to Ole Virginny," a common minstrel song.[24]

These terrible scenes invariably lived beyond the day. More than a half century later Henry Adams, the grandson of John Quincy Adams and once devoted to the radical Sumner, looked back upon Burns's rendition as Boston's eternal shame. "The sight of Court Square packed with bayonets, and his own friends obliged to line the streets under the arms as State militia, in order to return a negro to slavery," he wrote of himself in 1907, "wrought frenzy in the brain of a fifteen-year-old."[25]

At the wharf Burns was taken aboard the steamer *John Taylor*, which transported him to the *Morris*. At 3:20 p.m. the ship began its slow journey on heavy seas, and it arrived in Norfolk more than a week later on the tenth. With southern honor now presumably satisfied, an earnest negotiation initiated by Grimes commenced. Through an intermediary, he proposed to Suttle that Burns be purchased for the previously offered $1,200. At this point, however, the colonel paused. "I have had much difficulty in my own mind as to the course I ought to pursue about the sale of my man, Anthony Burns, to the North," he replied:

Such a sale is objected to strongly by my friends, and by the people of Virginia generally, upon the ground of its pernicious character, inviting our negroes to attempt their escape under the assurance that, if arrested and remanded, still the money would be raised to purchase their freedom. As a southern man and a slave-owner, I feel the force of this objection and clearly see the mischief that may result from disregarding it.[26]

He nevertheless saw an opportunity to make peace with the situation— and a profit: "Now that the laws have been fully vindicated (although at the point of a bayonet)," his note to Grimes continued, "and Anthony returned to the city of Richmond, from which he escaped; and believing that it would materially strengthen the Federal Officers and facilitate the execution of the laws in any future case which might arise, and influenced by other considerations . . . I have concluded to sell him his freedom for the sum of fifteen hundred dollars." Travel and legal fees, he told Grimes, had extracted "four hundred dollars . . . from my private purse."[27]

The Reverend rejoined that Suttle could have his $1,200, but no more. The colonel let the correspondence drop. Perhaps he worried at the thought of offending southern sensibilities, a not inconsiderable concern seeing that many of the section's whites watched with contempt the late proceedings in Boston. This resentment was openly aired in the celebratory one-hundred-gun salute that met the returning *Morris* in Virginia, and in rhetorical attacks on the Yankee Pierce for supposedly insufficiently supporting the fugitive's return. Richmond's newspapers, rather, stewed in outrage, a studied sulk captured in the *Examiner*'s insistence that the unwillingness of northerners to abide by the Fugitive Slave Act must "awaken the South to a sense of its position and to the necessity of an independent and exclusive policy."[28]

While the papers waxed indignant Burns's journey continued. Arriving in Richmond on the twenty-second, he was kept handcuffed and shackled at the ankles in a large brick building just beyond the city's limits. There he endured in a cramped, unventilated room, eating a punishing diet of corn bread and fetid bacon; he had no lavatory and remained in the same clothing for several months. In November, after receiving medical care, he was auctioned off before a hostile crowd in Richmond. A North Carolina cotton planter named David McDaniel purchased Burns for $905, evidently looking upon the investment as a speculation. For within three months he had reached an agreement with Grimes to sell his famous fugitive for $1,300; he wanted this exchange effected, so he wrote, "without any public excitement." This did not happen. McDaniel and Grimes arranged to meet in Baltimore and, while transporting Burns, McDaniel encountered angry crowds along the way; at one jittery point steaming up the Chesapeake Bay, he thought himself sufficiently imperiled to produce a pistol. Finally, on February 27, in Baltimore's fashionable Barnum's City Hotel, whose guests had or would include presidents John Quincy Adams and Andrew Johnson, the two sides completed the transaction—Anthony Burns was a free man.[29]

His manumission proved but a single of several slights to those southerners angered at Boston's open defiance. The towering expense of returning Burns to slavery, estimated to be as high as $100,000 ($3.5 million in current dollars), all but ensured that no future fugitives were to be returned from that stubborn city, as, in fact, none were. Further, the men who attempted to liberate Burns, an effort that resulted in the destruction of public property and the unfortunate Batchelder's death, avoided prosecution. There were a few indictments, including a contemptuous Higginson who ached, so Emerson reported to Sumner, "to plead guilty," though a pragmatic magistrate quashed these the following spring; no Boston jury, he knew, would ever convict such men. Popular justice, rather, now began to run against Cotton Whig sentiment. Because of his connection to the case, Loring, a convenient and stationary villain, lost his lectureship at Harvard and, in 1858, under the promptings of an antislavery legislature, his judicial position as well.[30]

In 1851 the Sims case hardly provoked genteel Boston, but the Burns rendition, coming on the heels of the Kansas-Nebraska controversy, caused a firestorm of protest on both sides of the sectional divide. Southerners saw the Bostonians as lawless for having made, as one Virginia paper put it, "a mockery and an insult" of the Fugitive Slave Act. One of the mockers, by contrast, a Massachusetts man, wrote Sumner that the twin sins of Burns and Nebraska had worked during that explosive spring "to unite the good men of all parties in a common sentiment of hostility to the encroachments of the slave power."[31] Clear differences on a number of important questions regarding race and republicanism, mandate and morality, now took precedence. These issues had long challenged Americans, though in 1854 they seemed to accelerate with an urgency that showed no signs of slowing.

Anthony Burns, one of the actors of that fateful year, kept moving too. Returning to Boston in 1855, he soon left for Ohio, attending, if intermittently, both Oberlin College and Cincinnati's Fairmont Theological Seminary. He took a pastorship at an Indianapolis church in 1859 but, perhaps due to the state's onerous black laws, soon after made his way to St. Catharines, in Canada's Niagara Region. There, living in a community that included formerly enslaved men and women, twenty-five miles from the American border, he served as a nonordained minister at the Zion Baptist Church. In the summer of 1862, weeks before Lincoln issued the preliminary Emancipation Proclamation, he died of tuberculosis, probably still in his twenties.

Part IV

DEGREES OF FREEDOM

Enraged by efforts to extend slavery into Kansas, the radical abolitionist William Lloyd Garrison called for a "moral nullification" of all compromises with the southern planter class.

12

Independence Day

Where is our Declaration to be proclaimed? Wherever a human being is groaning in bondage! On all the gory plantations of our own land!

William Lloyd Garrison, July 4, 1854

A month after the Burns trial blew up Boston, the United States, in a rite of civic celebration, commemorated the adoption of the Declaration of Independence by delegates representing the thirteen former colonies. Drafted principally by Jefferson, this Enlightenment document protested in a soaring preamble against the old notion of divine right kingships and monarchical privilege in favor of the "self-evident" truths and "unalienable Rights" to be honored in an emerging era of human equality. But how far, soaring preamble aside, were such still-contested rights to be extended? How completely were the promises of "life, liberty, and the Pursuit of Happiness" to be premised? These classic questions, cornerstones of an enduring debate on America's meaning, had acquired added import in the antebellum era, captive, like so much else, to the fiery encroachments of sectional discord. Accordingly, the sacred Fourth, presumably a day of national unity, admitted increasingly to differing loyalties and allegiances among its many celebrators. Abolitionists in particular approached the holiday restive to accentuate the more radical implications of their country's mixed commitment to freedom.

In 1854 this attitude found a clear and critical voice in the Massachusetts Anti-Slavery Society (MASS). Organized by *Liberator* editor

William Lloyd Garrison as the Boston-based New England Anti-Slavery Society in 1832, it stressed immediate abolition and opposed efforts to remove formerly enslaved people to Africa. The following year Garrison and the New York businessman/philanthropist Arthur Tappan, eager to make the association a national force, formed the American Anti-Slavery Society, headquartered in Manhattan. Within five years it counted more than one hundred thousand members. In 1834 remnants of the old New England Society decided to maintain a separate presence in Massachusetts, thus becoming the MASS. The emergence of this and other kinds of organized resistance to bondage grew into an increasingly prominent feature of antebellum public life. In 1829 the black Boston abolitionist David Walker issued *Walker's Appeal*, an unrelenting attack on slavery and racism ("wretchedness and endless miseries . . . poured out upon . . . ourselves . . . by *Christian* Americans"); in January 1831 Garrison began publishing *The Liberator*, and in August of that year the Nat Turner rebellion in Southampton County, Virginia, sent shock waves through the white South (the "horrible slaughter," wrote Jane Randolph, wife of Jefferson's favorite grandson, Thomas).[1] Combined with the rise of the antislavery societies, these indices of opposition suggested a nation beginning to come undone.

At its inception and for several years thereafter, the MASS aided fugitive slaves, subsidized lectures in New England, and endorsed a strategy of moral suasion. By the 1850s, however, these mannerly tactics looked tepid and defensive in contrast to the bold southern surge encapsulated in the Fugitive Slave Law and the Kansas-Nebraska Act. For radicals like Garrison, the Declaration of Independence and the U.S. Constitution, with their strong appeals to the country's property rights tradition—"nor shall private property be taken for public use," the latter noting, "without compensation"—appeared fatally incapable of providing compelling momentum for emancipation. In a February 1854 speech delivered in New York's Broadway Tabernacle, the center of the city's rippling antislavery sentiment and site, as noted, of Emerson's attack (in the same lecture series) on the Fugitive Slave Act, Garrison stressed his divided commitment to such iconic documents. In an artful display of pruning he described himself, rather, as a "believer *in that portion* of the Declaration . . . in which it is set forth, as among self-evident truths, 'that all men are created equal; that they are endowed by their Creator with certain inalienable rights.'"[2] Several months later, on the country's national holiday, this equivocal attitude gave way to a sensational event, a staged provocation on Garrison's part, designed to draw attention to the republic's hardening Mason-Dixon Line divide.

On a blistering hot Fourth of July, under the auspices of the MASS, more than six hundred abolitionists gathered near a sheltering green oak grove in Framingham, about twenty-five miles west of Boston. Shaken by the still-pulsing Burns affair, Garrison and company marshaled a counterprotest contra the usual rounds of rote civic celebration. A screaming placard announced both the event's intent—"NO SLAVERY! FOURTH OF JULY!"—as well as its organizers' aim "to pass the day in no idle glorying in our country's liberties, but in deep humiliation for her Disgrace and Shame, and in resolute purpose . . . to rescue old Massachusetts at least from being bound forever to the car of slavery." On this quasi-contrite note, an echo of Puritan calls for reflection and redress, did droves of attendees arrive, many aboard specially arranged trains from Boston, Milford, and Worcester, as well as various other corners of New England. They collected on benches facing a wooden speakers' platform decorated with briary signs and adages meant to provoke an amalgam of remorse and rage. One, so *The Liberator* reported, blazoned "Virginia" and was festooned "with the ribbons and insignia of Triumph." Another, "hung with the crape of servitude," entreated "Redeem Massachusetts." Two white flags were placed above these contrasting statements of sectional power, bearing the names "Kansas" and "Nebraska." Over the platform dangled an inverted American flag, Union (stars) down and defiantly draped in black.[3]

Following a picnic and petition for donations, the event took on a more formal air when, after a peremptory call to order, Garrison, ignoring the heat and "dressed simply in . . . black frock coat and high stiff collar tied with a plain black cravat," was elected to preside over the affair. Nearly a dozen vice presidents, representing neighboring cities, as well as Connecticut and New Hampshire, were then quickly chosen. Taking the dais, Garrison "read appropriate scripture," which prefaced an antislavery hymn sung by the entire audience. Dr. Henry Orne Stone, a local physician, offered a brief welcome to the assembly and, alluding to the disturbing stage decorations touting Virginia's mastery over Massachusetts, invited "all discontented with the present position of affairs to stand on the anti-slavery platform."[4] He then introduced Garrison, the first speaker.

Returning to the stand, the bald, angular abolitionist, clean-shaven and gazing out from behind a pair of thin wire-rimmed glasses, addressed the crowd confidently with a booming, "Friends of freedom and humanity!" Quoting from the book of Isaiah—"he that departeth from evil maketh himself a prey"—Garrison denounced the "despotic" nature of government, which sought to both isolate and denigrate those intrepid outliers who put conscience first and dared decry their nation's unholy commitment to slavery. "The condition of a true, manly life is persecution," he countered, and held before his audience the proverbial glory of a righteous "martyrdom . . . in some form or other."[5]

Eager to claim both God and the Founders for freedom, Garrison described the Declaration of Independence as a sublime statement of universal truths, invoking without qualification the equality of human- ity. It clearly outlined, he insisted, "the abolition of all caste, the sup- pression of all aristocracy, the extinction of all despotism," while further recognizing the existence of rights belonging to "not one race, but all races." Certainly, many others, including Jefferson himself, had broadly understood the Declaration to address a dawning age of Western liber- alism, though few had applied its sentiments so literally on the volatile subjects of race, slavery, and civil rights. Seeing an opening, Garrison exploited the revered document's language to the fullest, observing that the southern plantocracy denied the Declaration by refusing to respect its intent, and cleaved instead to ancient and less enlightened notions of aristocratic, even arbitrary, rule that contradicted its claims to faith- fully captain the course of republican government. The abolitionists, he continued, were "truer" Americans for embracing the principles, attitudes, and ideologies of the Revolution—though for their fealty, these guardians of freedom were made to feel as outcasts, dominated by a powerful congressional clique of "slaveholders and slave-breeders." Garrison called this a perversion of the nation's past, for what, he asked his audience, "is an abolitionist but a sincere believer in the Declara- tion of '76?"[6]

In effect, Garrison had divided American history in two. Following a glorious beginning came a sure and ruthless assault from slavehold- ers, a determined and cohesive enemy of individual rights. Obviously, the recent success of southern statesmen in leveraging concessions from northern politicians—Webster's capitulation in 1850, Douglas's annul- ment of the Compromise of 1820, and the return of Anthony Burns to slavery—had sparked Garrison's wrath. "The condition required of every man holding office under the government," he spoke in the spirit of a deep sectional shame, "is a ready acquiescence in whatever the Slave Power may dictate." Having watched his country make war on Mexico, respond tepidly to the filibuster schemes of picaroons like William Walker, and push the principle of popular sovereignty into western territories formerly closed to black bondage, he claimed that the U.S. government, under the auspices of cotton state potentates, sought above all else to promote "the security of slave property and the acquisition of slave territory."[7]

And then Garrison, wishing, so he said, to "perform an action" sufficiently indicative of his disdain for "pro-slavery laws and deeds," pulled from his pocket a copy of the Fugitive Slave Law. This he proceeded to burn while exhorting his audience, "And let the people say, *Amen*"—to which the people shouted, "Amen!" He next produced a copy of the Loring decision in the Burns case and, much to the appreciation of his audience, consigned it to ashes as well, before burning for good measure yet another judge's comments to a grand jury considering charges of "constructive treason" against those who had assaulted the courthouse in an effort to free Burns. Lastly, he held up a copy of the U.S. Constitution, which, in giving legitimacy to the other documents just destroyed, had rendered it, so he insisted, "a covenant with death, and an agreement with hell." He then set the paper on fire and once more enjoined the gathering to an emotive, "Amen!," to which some did, though, as *The Liberator* noted, these cries of approval mingled unmistakably "with a few hisses and wrathful exclamations."[8]

This high political theater, meant to evoke Martin Luther's public burning (1520) of the censuring papal bull threatening him with excommunication, sought to shock the audience. Tired of the long-scripted responses to slaveholder ascendency—a formulaic cycle of meetings, prayers, and petitions—Garrison wished to awaken his audience by discarding half-truths and lazy allegiances. The destruction of the copy of the Constitution in particular raised the question of the Founders' role in sanctioning and sustaining slavery's secure berth in the American republic. It suggested further the need to seek a spiritual rather than political solution for the country's current condition. Only in this way, Garrison archly implied, might the nation save its sinking soul.

Charles Remond, a freeborn Massachusetts black and the first African American to testify before that state's legislature (in objection to Boston's segregated railway cars), succeeded Garrison at the podium, offering "an eloquent outburst" before giving way to John Cluer, a Scottish labor radical for several years living in America, who spoke of his recent incarceration for attempting, with others, to rescue Anthony Burns. At this point in the proceedings a one-hour break ensued, "for refreshment and social recreation."[9]

Gathering again at 2:00 p.m., the crowd, somewhat larger than earlier in the day, sang a hymn composed two years earlier by Reverend—and poet—John Pierpont commemorating the rendition of the runaway Thomas Sims:

> For Freedom there ye stood;
> There gave the earth your blood;
> There found your graves;
> That men of every clime,
> Faith, color, tongue, and time,
> Might, through your death sublime,
> Never be slaves.[10]

Then to the stage came Moncure Daniel Conway, only twenty-two and variously a Unitarian, Methodist, and Freethinker, educated at Dickinson College in Carlisle, Pennsylvania, and Harvard's school of divinity. Son of a wealthy Virginia slaveholder and state representative, he touted an impressive southern first-family pedigree, including, most conspicuously, his great-grandfather Thomas Stone, a Maryland planter who had signed the Declaration of Independence. Conway, so one paper reported, "made a very earnest and effective speech," in which he too raised the specter of Anthony Burns and the coercive power of the Fugitive Slave Law: "He said he had been brought up where white men *owned* slaves; now he had come [to the North] where white men *were* slaves."[11]

Next up to the podium strode the abolitionist and women's rights advocate Sojourner Truth, recognized today for an 1851 Akron, Ohio, speech subsequently titled "Ain't I a Woman?" Born Isabella Baumfree, in Dutch-speaking Ulster County, New York, an enslaved woman owned by a succession of men, Truth, with infant daughter Sophia in tow, escaped her servitude in 1826. Years later she took the name

Sojourner, signifying her mission to travel the land, speaking openly of its offenses. Tall (nearly six feet), lean, and dark-skinned, with close-cropped hair, she radiated strength, an arresting virtue in her chosen profession of itinerant preaching. Facing the Framingham audience, she delivered, so *The Liberator* observed, "one of her characteristic speeches, speaking out of her former experience of slavery." Truth pondered further on the wages of race and redemption in America, recognizing with a light touch the people in power's need for pardoning by those they had so long oppressed. "The White people owed the colored race a big debt," she insisted. "And if they paid it all back, they wouldn't have anything left for seed," at which point the audience burst out in laughter. "All they could do was to repent," she closed on a note of contingent hope, "and have the debt forgiven them."[12]

After Truth, the ubiquitous Wendell Phillips, among those irrec-oncilables who had endeavored to free Burns and now faced charges drawn up by a U.S. grand jury, paced the stage. He sought to shame his complicit state—and ensure that those in public office who supported the "Slave Brigade" in both Boston and Washington were duly punished. "I have lost all pride in Massachusetts," he shouted, "till she redeems herself from that second day of June. Let us roll up a petition, a hundred thousand strong, for the removal of Judge Loring." Phillips then stepped aside for the New Hampshire abolitionist Stephen Symonds Foster, who gamely, if not a little seditiously, called for the nullification of the Fugitive Slave Act as a preface to more radical action. "The time is come," he said, "when men should either put a thorough anti-slavery interpretation upon the Constitution, and practically carry out that interpretation, or take a stand with us outside of the Constitution."[13]

The next speaker, the Transcendentalist Henry David Thoreau, had just put the finishing touches on his book *Walden; or, Life in the Woods*. We know from Thoreau's journals that he too brooded over the Burns rendition in the weeks leading up to the Fourth. "What is wanted is men of principle," he wrote in one entry, "who recognize a higher law than the decision of the majority"; another passage revealed a reckless wish that "the State" might "dissolve her union with the slaveholder instantly." Fragments and embellishments of these pungent remarks made their way into his speech. Rising that morning, Thoreau gave scant indication of his impending lecture; "8 A.M.—to Framingham . . . A very hot day," he wrote, before making the fifteen-mile journey south.

Known to his friends as a flaming nonconformist—having notoriously spent a night in a Concord jail cell eight years earlier for failing to pay a poll tax while protesting America's invasion of Mexico (Emerson, who did pay his taxes, thought him "skulking")—he now resolved to engage, at least selectively, in organized opposition to slavery. Like the Garrisonians, he agreed that the crime of human bondage overshadowed comparatively narrow questions of constitutionality—as "men of expediency," so he spat, would have it—and ultimately rested, rather, on moral grounds.[14]

Addressing the crowd at Framingham, Thoreau, "a born protestant," Emerson once remarked, possessed of "a very strong Saxon genius," proceeded to unpack "Slavery in Massachusetts," his incendiary condemnation of injustice. Though all New England had spent the preceding several months following the Kansas-Nebraska debates, Thoreau, always alive to irony, wondered if his sleepy neighbors, thinking themselves gazing on a purely distant sin, realized that "there are perhaps a million slaves in Massachusetts." Recognizing Burns as a citizen, an equal, he insisted on the state's failure to protect the rights of one of its own, and thus doubted its legitimacy. Burns, in fact, was never on trial; rather, "it was really the trial of Massachusetts." The Commonwealth, far from building upon the freedoms established by its celebrated forebears, now seemed morbidly intent, in the name of union, to placate a corrupt plantocracy. "The whole military force of the State," he said, referring to Charles Suttle, "is at the service of . . . a slaveholder from Virginia."[15]

A master aphorist, Thoreau launched a series of sharp and striking lines: "The law will never make men free; it is men who have got to make the law free"; "It occurred to me [after Burns's rendition] that what I had lost was a country"; "I would remind my countrymen that they are to be men first, and Americans only at a late and convenient hour"; "If we would save our lives, we might fight for them"; and perhaps most acidulously, "My thoughts are murder to the State."[16] The power of Thoreau's argument, the vigor of his language, ensured the address an extended life. It appeared in somewhat longer form in both Garrison's *Liberator* (July 21) and Greeley's *New-York Tribune* (August 2). In an editorial appended to the latter, Greeley, already engaged in promoting the interests of both the fledgling Republican Party and the Emigrant Aid Company, now praised Thoreau as a rare and "pure" radical:

No one can read this speech without realizing that the claims of Messrs. Sumner, Seward and Chase to be recognized as Higher-Law champions are of a very questionable validity. Mr. Thoreau is the Simon-Pure article, and his remarks have a racy piquancy and telling *point* which none but a man thoroughly in earnest and regardless of self in his fidelity to a deep conviction ever fully attains.[17]

Introduced to a large audience for the first time, Thoreau commenced on that "very hot day" in Framingham upon a path that led him six years later (1860) to another Independence Day oration in honor of the recently executed John Brown.[18]

The final address that afternoon belonged to the gifted orator, suffragist, and abolitionist Lucy Stone. Massachusetts-bred and Oberlin College–educated, she had for several years delivered speeches in the service of the American Anti-Slavery Society, initially in her native New England, though by the early 1850s including lyceums and churches in Canada, the Midwest, and even some few southern locales. Frederick Douglass called her "one of the most attractive and effective advocates" of the abolitionist crusade, while Thomas Wentworth Higginson described Stone to a colleague as "queen of us all. . . . You have no idea of the eloquence and power which have been developed in her; she is one of the great Providences of History." Melodious and petite, qualities which suggested, despite a commanding stage presence, an underlying innocence, Stone, so one biographer contends, enjoyed a "seductive appeal." The social reformer Mary Livermore thought her "a tiny creature with the prettiest pink color" and Elizabeth Cady Stanton, an organizer six years earlier of the first women's rights convention in the United States (held in a red-bricked Wesleyan church in Seneca Falls, New York), said that Stone's "sweet voice and simple girlish manner made her first appearance on the platform irresistible."[19]

Stone spoke at Framingham of the "low state" of American morality, connecting the corruption of slavery with a still more extensive erosion in social manners. Unfree labor denigrated all industry and made "our young men" slovenly and ill-suited to develop an outstanding national culture. Black bondage, in other words, impeded white progress, worked against the brisk and presumably progressive current of history, and kept America from achieving the freedom-bringing promise of its Revolutionary past. Emancipation thus took on multiple meanings, including a commitment, so Stone concluded, "to arouse the slumbering *soul* of the nation."[20]

After her address, the crowd called for Reverend Pierpont, who reappeared and, in the day's militant spirit, said a few words on the "duty of all men to disregard and disobey all human laws not in harmony with the great and eternal law of God." Garrison next stepped onto the stage and offered concluding remarks, essentially revisiting his earlier speech and calling for a "moral nullification" of all compromises with the planters. The audience then began to gradually disperse, singing "Let All Be Free" as the humid grove emptied.[21]

The Kansas-Nebraska trauma combined with the Burns trial to guide, in the strident higher-law language of the time, the recurrent calls in Framingham for civil resistance. Under the auspices of the Massachusetts Anti-Slavery Society mainly white preachers and speakers, radicals and would-be revolutionaries, were concerned with aiding and shaping this struggle. The following month, however, a group dominated by free blacks and determined to take their futures into their own hands met in a different kind of convention, willing to explore the possibility of removing themselves from America and leaving centuries of race-based oppression behind.

13

No Roads Home

There is little hope for us on this Continent.

Martin Robison Delany, 1854

Framingham's Independence Day protest could be parsed as a variation on a familiar theme in antebellum New England—the ambition
of well-meaning whites to attack planter power. In light of the brewing struggle over Kansas, however, the effectiveness of such efforts
might reasonably be called into question. Politics and petitions, stirring
speeches and Yankee reproofs, seemed defeated by the recent march of
southern momentum. And the notion that a moral crest of Christian
endurance might serve as a strong response, à la the righteous suffering
of Stowe's otherworldly "Uncle Tom," failed to satisfy certain skeptical
constituencies. As a result, and among a number of free northern blacks
in particular, the subject of race-based emigration out of the United
States began to earn a respectable hearing, perhaps reaching its apex in
August 1854 when, amidst the pressures of that pregnant year, a convention of colonizationists met in Cleveland to discuss the practicality
of quitting America. In effect, they proposed an early iteration of what
became known in the succeeding century as black nationalism.

Martin Robison Delany, born in 1812 in Charles Town, Virginia,
to a free black seamstress and an enslaved carpenter, took the midcentury lead in advocating the emigration idea. After living for several
years in the southern Pennsylvania town of Chambersburg, Delany,
while in his late teens, walked 150 miles to Pittsburgh to study both

science and the classics, first at the Cellar School of the African Methodist Episcopal Church and then at Jefferson College, commencing, so he hoped, a career in medicine. A gifted student, he subsequently received admittance to Harvard's medical school, only to be forced into withdrawing upon the protests of several white registrants, who, thinking themselves wronged, hustled up an informal resolution deeming "the admission of blacks at the medical lectures highly detrimental to the interests, and welfare, of the Institution of which we are members, calculated alike to lower its reputation in this and other parts of the country, to lessen the value of a diploma from it, and to diminish the number of its students."[1]

Deeply interested in the race question, Delany devoted several years in the 1840s to running black abolitionist newspapers including *The Mystery* (1843–1847) and, with Frederick Douglass, the *North Star* (1847–1849). The former, a Pittsburgh weekly priced at 2¢, made much of its encyclopedic intent to "aim at the Moral Elevation of the Africo-American and African race, civilly, politically, and religiously [through] the different branches of Literacy Sciences, the Mechanic Arts, Agriculture and the elevation of labor."[2] This rising-people plan, however, barely lasted the decade. Following the Mexican-American War, race-based legislation and mob violence quavered increasingly through northern as well as southern cities, while the argument for extending slavery into the nation's western territories appeared, under the auspices of respected Yankee leaders, to find support in the highest councils of government. Rather than being limited and localized, slavery appeared to be on the cusp of enlarging and nationalizing. And instead of finding a parity of place in the country's dominant economic and political structures, free black people faced segregation or even the possibility of being, like the New York–born Solomon Northup, author of the searing 1853 memoir *Twelve Years a Slave*, kidnapped and bound into bondage. This perfectly daunting backdrop moved men like Delany into taking seriously the question of uprooting in search of black sovereignty.[3]

The emigration idea had for at least two generations teased both white and black minds. In 1816 the American Colonization Society (ACS) was founded under the auspices of Robert Finley, a New Jersey clergyman who envisioned transporting freeborn blacks and emancipated slaves to Africa.[4] Supported mainly by whites, including three-

1.

Recognizing, as he wrote, "that the States were divided into different interests . . . principally from their having or not having slaves," James Madison took a leading role at the Constitutional Convention that formed, as time revealed, an irreconcilable republic of free and unfree labor.

2.

Henry Clay, longtime Kentucky politician, perennial White House hopeful, and Lincoln's favorite statesman, was called "The Great Compromiser" for his efforts to smooth over differences between the sections.

3.

An 1855 map of the newly opened "Nebraska and Kanzas" territory, with projected routes for a railroad to the Pacific.

4.

Ohio senator Salmon Chase helped to organize resistance to the Kansas-Nebraska Act, which, he insisted, threatened to "convert" the west "into a dreary region of despotism, inhabited by masters and slaves."

5.

Author of the nineteenth century's most popular American novel, Harriet Beecher Stowe crafted in *Uncle Tom's Cabin* a protest to the congressional compromise culture that had allowed slavery to grow beyond its colonial-era enclaves.

6.

The Transcendentalist Ralph Waldo Emerson, emblematic of an educated New England elite that had begun in the 1850s to raise critical concerns about slavery's expansion.

7.

In March 1854 a small group, responding to the impending repeal of the Missouri Compromise, assembled in this Ripon, Wisconsin, schoolhouse, threw off their former political allegiances, and fashioned a new coalition: the Republican Party.

8.

Horace Greeley, the inexhaustible editor of the New-York Tribune, the nearest thing to a national newspaper in antebellum America. Greeley's paper had supported the moderate Whigs before backing the "radical" Republican Party.

9.

In a series of illegal invasions, the Tennessean William Walker attempted to root slavery more deeply in the Western Hemisphere by leading private armies into parts of Mexico and Central America.

10.

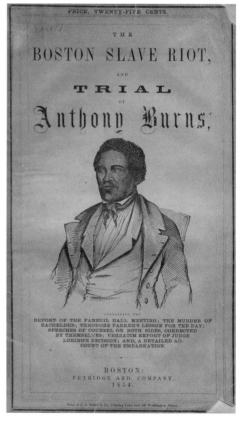

PRICE, TWENTY-FIVE CENTS.

THE

BOSTON SLAVE RIOT,

AND

TRIAL

OF

Anthony Burns;

CONTAINING THE REPORT OF THE FANEUIL HALL MEETING; THE MURDER OF BACHELDER; THEODORE PARKER'S LESSON FOR THE DAY; SPEECHES OF COUNSEL ON BOTH SIDES, CORRECTED BY THEMSELVES; VERBATIM REPORT OF JUDGE LORING'S DECISION; AND, A DETAILED ACCOUNT OF THE EMBARKATION.

BOSTON:
FETRIDGE AND COMPANY.
1854.

Boston erupted in the spring of 1854 when Anthony Burns, a fugitive slave from Virginia, was arrested and, with the aid of militia and federal soldiers, returned to the South, thus turning the city, some said, into a "slave pen" for southern planters.

11.

Born into slavery in New York, Sojourner Truth (née Isabella Baumfree) escaped in the 1820s, becoming an advocate of abolitionism and women's rights. Denouncing efforts to allow enslavers into Kansas, she contended that it was time for "the white people . . . to repent."

12.

MAJOR MARTIN R. DELANY. U. S. A.
PROMOTED ON THE BATTLE FIELD FOR BRAVERY

While the Kansas-Nebraska debate raged, Martin Delany, a free man, advocated in books, newspapers, and conventions for black emigration from the United States, arguing that "negro hate" in America doomed his race. Delany later served as an officer in the Union Army during the Civil War.

13.

Stunned by the return of Anthony Burns from "free soil" to the South, the Transcendentalist Henry David Thoreau delivered a blistering speech, "Slavery in Massachusetts," in which he said, "My thoughts are murder to the State."

14.

WALDEN;

OR,

LIFE IN THE WOODS.

By HENRY D. THOREAU,
AUTHOR OF "A WEEK ON THE CONCORD AND MERRIMACK RIVERS."

I do not propose to write an ode to dejection, but to brag as lustily as chanticleer in the morning, standing on his roost, if only to wake my neighbors up. — Page 92.

BOSTON:
TICKNOR AND FIELDS.
M DCCC LIV.

Completed against the backdrop of a nation in flux, Thoreau's Walden, an experiment in "deliberate" living, questioned the country's unreflective embrace of industrialism, consumerism, and slavery.

15.

Eliza Hamilton, the widow of Alexander Hamilton, died in Washington, D.C., in November 1854 at the age of 97. She was neighbors with Dolley Madison, and the two dowagers, one northern, the other southern, were embraced by a capital city community that could sense an era of sectional compromises coming to an end.

16.

A month after Eliza Hamilton's death, Harriet Tubman, having escaped her enslavement on Maryland's Eastern Shore, returned to the South to rescue three of her brothers. "I was free," she said, "and *they* should be free."

17.

The opening of the Kansas Territory precipitated a border war that brought the militant abolitionist John Brown to the center of a violent struggle against the institution of slavery.

18.

A bird's-eye view of Washington, D.C., in 1852, the still young capital city of a country slowly coming undone.

19.

The neoclassical style Senate chamber in which Stephen Douglas introduced the Kansas-Nebraska Bill and where his nemesis, Charles Sumner, was badly beaten by a cane-wielding southern congressman.

20.

Lincoln's three-hour speech in Peoria in October 1854 condemned efforts to bring slavery into the west. "No man is good enough to govern another man without the other's consent," he argued. "I say this is the leading principle . . . of American republicanism."

21.
An 1857 map of the western territory of the United States ordered by Secretary of War Jefferson Davis for the purpose of planning railroad development. The shaded colors denote the territories of native peoples.

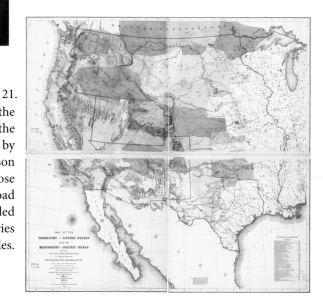

22.

The Exhibition of the Industry of All Nations, the country's first world's fair, was held in New York City in 1853–54 while the Kansas-Nebraska fight unfolded. A supposed symbol of national unity, the exposition, with its emphases on northern industrial goods and southern agricultural products, accurately if unintentionally revealed a divided country.

time presidential nominee Henry Clay and the prominent Maryland lawyer, poet, and author of "The Star-Spangled Banner" Francis Scott Key, the organization proved popular among certain churches, abolitionists, and even some enslavers. And yet, taken on its own terms, it was a failure. In 1821 the Society purchased land in Liberia, and though expatriating some ten thousand black Americans up to the time of the Civil War, the country's enslaved population during this period more than doubled to 3.9 million. Black leaders, it is fair to say, had always been mixed on the question of removal. Some, like Douglass, condemned it as a clumsy effort to assuage panicky white fears while ignoring Africa's now three-centuries-long contributions to the New World.

An unmistakable energy, however, fueled in the late 1840s by the recent acquisition of Mexican lands and the declaration of Liberian independence (making that country a republic rather than an ACS appendage), had built among black emigrationists. A National Negro Convention held in Troy, New York, in 1847 called for the organization of a "company owned and operated by people of African descent" engaged in a commercial enterprise connecting the United States, Jamaica, and Africa.[5] Other possible areas of black expansion were also proposed about this time, including Haiti, Liberia, the British West Indies, Canada, and California.

Delany, an anti-colonizationist when editing *The Mystery*, had moved by the early 1850s into the opposite camp. His and other defections sparked criticism from Douglass, who, in his concern that the country's black cognitive elite might flee, worried for the race's future. "I really fear that some whose presence in this country is necessary to the elevation of the Colored people will leave us," he wrote privately, "while the degraded and worthless will remain behind." Those entertaining the idea of leaving saw matters much differently, of course, and tagged their critics and not themselves as a self-interested elite. The January 1852 *African Repository and Colonial Journal*, a pro-colonization mouthpiece, argued that men like Douglass selfishly rejected resettlement "for the purpose of keeping full churches and school-houses, a plenty of patients, waiters, and other assistants."[6] These black leaders, in other words, a lettered caste of physicians, preachers, and teachers, were said to oppose emigration as it threatened to entice impoverished blacks to move abroad, leaving themselves devoid of their former students and parishes, customers and community power.

Conventions routinely took up the relocation controversy, its delegates typically ending up divided. Between 1849 and 1852 assemblages gathered in Columbus, Baltimore, and Cincinnati, where, in
the latter city, a committee endorsed emigration only to be undercut
by a contrasting minority report. North of the border meetings were
held in Toronto (1851) and Amherstburg (1853) that promised America's free blacks better, less constricted, and more liberated lives. During
this period, Delany authored and self-published *The Condition, Elevation, Emigration, and Destiny of the Colored People of the United States*,
perhaps the era's most concentrated call for a black exodus. Appearing
in April 1852, the book argued that too often "politicians, religionists,
colonizationists, and abolitionists, have each and all, at different times,
presumed to *think* for, dictate to, and *know* better what suited colored
people, than they knew for themselves."[7]

Recognizing in *The Condition* white America's unwillingness to
respect by its own rules the rights of free blacks—"untrue to her trust
and unfaithful to her professed principles"—Delany declared emigration to be the only solution. And so he asked, "Where shall we go?"
Liberia, as noted, had long dominated the imagination of white colonizationists and Delany, eager to assert an independent thread, wished
now to diminish its appeal. Though conceding the Methodist and Baptist churches' presumably edifying footholds in that missionized country and the further presence of no fewer than four colleges dedicated
to the "European principle" of science on the African continent, he
insisted on its ultimate impossibility. Liberia's climate he called "signally
unhealthy" and he thought its much-praised independence "a poor miserable mockery—a burlesque on a government—a pitiful dependency
on the American Colonizationists" in slaveholding Washington, D.C.
He noted further that the country's "heathen population . . . probably
exceeds 300,000," thus swamping the 8,000 or so whom he identified as
making up "the civilized population."[8]

Rejecting Africa, Delany emphasized the virtues of a nearer home.
Reciting a surfeit of familiar platitudes—"freedom always," "liberty
anyplace and ever"—he identified the Western Hemisphere, rather,
as history's focal point for natural rights. Looking north, however, he
quickly dismissed Canada as an option—in light of the recent Mexican cession, he feared its future annexation into the United States. This
left Central and South America, both of which he found attractive for

their "superior" climate, crops, and, more importantly, supposedly liberal relations with their black peoples. "There never have existed in the policy of any of the nations [in this region of the world]," he dubiously speculated, "an inequality of account of race or color." Delany further appreciated the human composition in the Latin countries, noting that from a population of some 25 million, only a mere "one-seventh are whites."[9]

Scattered settlements in the Western Hemisphere, however, promised to do little more than dilute black energy and initiative. And so Delany declared, as though a fleet of ships were at the ready, "We . . . select NICARAGUA . . . and NEW GRENADA." The relatively close proximity of these countries to the United States, their good relations with Great Britain (expected "to protect both . . . from foreign imposition"), and capacity to give "colored people . . . the same chances there, that white people have in the United States" were all practical, if conjectural, reasons. He now bade free blacks to replicate the experiment in pioneer individualism presumably practiced over centuries by Europeans in the Western Hemisphere. Were the descendants of Africans any less intrepid? "Go we must," Delany closed, "and go we will."[10]

Shortly after *The Condition*'s appearance, Garrison and Delany engaged in a spirited correspondence regarding its contents. In something of an understatement, the former detected, so he wrote, a "tone of despondency" in the work, with which Delany agreed entirely: "I must admit, that I have no hopes in this country—no confidence in the American people—with a *few* excellent exceptions [apparently alluding to Garrison and a handful of other white abolitionists]—therefore, I have written as I have done." That same spring Delany assumed a more strident tone with Douglass, who had devoted many pages of his *Paper* to Stowe's recently published *Uncle Tom's Cabin*, a work touting the "settlement of Liberia," while all but ignoring his own *Condition*. "In all due respect and deference to Mrs. Stowe," Delany wrote, "I beg leave to say, that she *knows nothing about us*, 'the Free Colored people of the United States,' neither does any other white person—and, consequently, can contrive no successful scheme for our elevation; it must be done by ourselves."[11]

Publishing Delany's remarks in the *Paper*, Douglas printed his own reply as well in the form of an admonishing editorial comment. After defending the author of *Uncle Tom's Cabin*—"Bro. Delany knows nothing about Mrs. Stowe"—he took up, if only glancingly, *The Condition*. Commencing with a faint accolade, "He has written a book—and we may say that it is, in many respects, an excellent book," he then proceeded to dismiss the work, airy in its abstract assumptions about the Western Hemisphere, for offering free blacks no firm vision of the future: "It leaves us just where it finds us, without chart or compass, and in more doubt and perplexity than before we read it."[12]

Beyond Douglass, others in the free black community observed the mounting pressure applied by pro-emigration assemblies, treatises, and publications with dismay. This constituency wished instead to focus on what could be done in the United States to overcome economic inequality, political disenfranchisement, and social discrimination. In response, a cluster of African American leaders meeting at the "Colored National Convention" in Rochester, New York, over three days in July 1853 proposed to establish a phalanx of black-operated organizations, including a national college, library, trade union, and labor office. In the name of thwarting efforts by emigrationists, in other words, these "stay-at-homes" endorsed an internal kind of black nationalism, predicated on a race-based vision of work, education, and identity.[13]

They affirmed this vision in the Rochester meeting's *Proceedings*, which offered a pointed critique of the emigration position from five black leaders—including Douglass—who declared themselves "charged with the responsibility of inquiring into the general condition of our people, and of devising measures which may, with the blessing of God, tend to our mutual improvement and elevation." Such progress, they insisted, could only come in America, and only by an assertion of the legal rights guaranteed to all Americans. The report emphasized the historical, constitutional, and cultural claims to nationhood that fell upon free blacks. "We address you not as aliens nor as exiles," they wrote, but "as American citizens asserting their rights on their own native soil." The principles of the Declaration of Independence respected this truism, they continued, as did its institutionalization in the country's legal and economic systems, which permitted blacks to own homes, pay taxes, build businesses, and, in select northern cities, vote. The address further quoted from American statesmen acknowledging, in some fashion, black citizenship. Andrew Jackson's proclamation to Louisiana's free black population on the eve on the Battle of New Orleans, for instance, had recognized these "brave citizens" and emphasized their common ties to "Your white fellow-citizens." Douglass and his colleagues were loath to give up this hard-earned ground and clung tenaciously to a careful reading of the past that offered hope for the future.[14]

Soon after the Rochester assembly the would-be colonizers, eager to wrest momentum from the "stay-at-homes," put forth a published summons—"Arguments, Pro and Con, on the Call for a National Emigration Convention"—proposing a meeting of delegates in Cleveland the following August. "We must make an issue," it stated in part, to "create an event, and establish a position for ourselves." Signed by forty-six men representing five states, it pointedly cautioned critics of resettlement, as well as those advocating colonization in Liberia, not to attend.[15]

Douglass promptly attacked this latest effort from the emigrationists in the *Paper*: "We have no sympathy with the call for this convention. We deem it uncalled for, unwise, unfortunate, and premature." Coming on the heels of the Rochester gathering, he thought it signaled to "our enemies" a clear division in the African American community "upon a vital point." He counseled his readers, rather, to continue committing to the United States, by purchasing homes, farms, lots, and property "which looks to permanent residences here."[16]

But this rebuke only stirred up the other side. In reply to Douglass, the African American poet James Monroe Whitfield called for blacks to find their proper place in the Western Hemisphere's southerly latitudes. "I believe it to be the destiny of the negro," he wrote in a piece that Douglass, open to engaging his critics, printed in the *Paper*, "to develop a higher order of civilization and Christianity than the world has yet seen. I also consider it a part of his 'manifest destiny,' to possess all the tropical regions of this continent, with the adjacent islands. That the negro is to be the predominant race in all that region in regard to numbers, is beyond doubt." What a contemporary reader might find striking about this rhetoric, as well as that indulged in by Delany, is the degree to which it traffics in racial tropes commonly advanced by whites. For years discussion of the presumed connections between race and climate—advanced in support of both filibustering and Wasp responsibility for civilization's progress (later embodied in British poet Rudyard Kipling's "The White Man's Burden")—were liberally employed to justify American expansion. William Walker's interest in Nicaragua as a private fiefdom thus finds some strange communion in Delany's own "We . . . select NICARAGUA," while Whitfield's elastic notion of a "predominant race" finds a place in both antebellum manifest destiny mythology and the late-nineteenth-century social Darwinism that followed. The key difference is that the emigrationists were principally interested in self-preservation rather than racial crusading. "A *black patriot* in this country must be [a] fool," Whitfield wrote to a correspondent in late 1853. "[T]he fact is, I have no country, neither have you."[17]

On August 24, 1854, the National Emigration Convention's 106 delegates, among them two dozen women, gathered in the Congregational Church on Cleveland's Prospect Street. Most, including Delany, made the short journey from neighboring Pennsylvania, though representatives from a few states, including Kentucky, Missouri, and Louisiana, arrived as well. Speeches, prayers, and "some highly interesting remarks" were said to have distinguished the convention, though Delany's audience-exhausting several-hours turn at the podium on its second day constituted the event's focal point.[18]

A nineteenth-century biographer once described Delany as "compactly and strongly built, with broad shoulders. . . . His carriage, erect and independent . . . his voice, deep-toned and full . . . with eyes sharp and piercing." Reading his Cleveland keynote address, "Political Destiny of the Colored Race on the American Continent," Delany stressed the connection between freedom and heredity, insisting—just three years before the Supreme Court declared, in the notorious *Dred Scott* case, the Constitution's implicit exclusion of black citizenship—that descendants of Africans would never be recognized as citizens of the United States. Delany drew his audience's attention immediately to this point by addressing them as "Fellow-*Countrymen*" and making the distinction that though citizenship is a "term desired and ever cherished by us," he thought it likely never to come. He offered instead a vision of racial pride absent the many-layered injustices that accompanied the centuries-old systems of organized slavery and segregation. Several ironies accompanied this call, for though Delany made a point of accentuating the separate people theme—"The truth is, we are not identical with the Anglo-Saxon or any other race . . . and the sooner we know and acknowledge this truth, the better for ourselves and posterity"— the words were delivered in a Congregationalist church, at a convention filled with committees, and devoted to exporting, so Delany said, "the highest traits of civilization."[19] One could be excused, if not concentrating especially on the question of race, for considering this Cleveland caucus's work as deeply embedded in the classic panoply of the American political tradition—a godly people, in pursuit of their liberties, and eager to assert a separate destiny.

Delany insisted that the emigrationists asked for nothing unique, merely an opportunity to fulfill their particular pedigree. "The English, French, Irish, German, Italian, Turk, Persian, Greek, Jew, and all other races, have their native or inherent peculiarities," he pointed out, "and why not our race?" Colonization, that is to say, meant multiple kinds of emancipation, cultural as well as political, ethnic as well as economic. Eager to both recognize and assert differences, he invariably surrendered to essentializing. He gave to the "white race" superiority in mathematics, commerce, and architecture, while recognizing a dominant black aptitude in "in languages, oratory, poetry, music . . . ethics . . . theology, and legal jurisprudence." In time, he promised his Cleveland audience, "the black race will yet instruct the world."[20]

As in *The Condition*, he further evaluated the various options for emigration. With "the Yankees from this side of the lakes . . . fast settling in the Canadas" and "infusing" it with "malignity and negro-hate," there could be no northern embrace. Instead, he again enumerated those "generous, sociable, and tractable" Latin peoples as the kind "with whom we desire to unite." Delany thought such a union perfectly equitable, as the émigrés would bring with them "all the improvement of North America" without the racism, invasions, and land grabs so recently on display in the Mexican-American War; the Nicaraguans and New Grenadians could count, rather, on black initiative, improvements, and energy without fear of risking their own rights and liberties. He closed by promising that in a land where "the freest city in America" bends before "southern slave hunters"—a reference to Boston's stunning Burns trial—there is "no hope for us!"[21]

Before concluding, the convention passed a series of resolutions designed to promote black pride. A day of thanksgiving was to be observed "by the Colored People generally of the United States" each fourth Thursday of August; the "terms Negro, African, Black, Colored and Mulatto" were to "ever be held with the same respect" as "Caucasian, White, Anglo-Saxon and Europeans"; free black men would accept full political rights "or accept . . . nothing." And so on. The convention further pledged to take seriously Delany's plan to emigrate and create

a "Negro empire" somewhere in the Western Hemisphere, thus finding "unit[y] . . . as one people, on this continent." In that heady spirit,
a leave-taking reading of Psalm 124—"We have escaped like a bird the
fowler's snare"—filled the emptying hall.[22]

Delany's idle dreams of a retreat southward, always conjectural, inevitably went unrealized. Instead, he moved with his wife and family to
Ontario, Canada, in 1856, practicing medicine and treating "a great portion of those who were refugees from American slavery." In May 1858
he and several others joined John Brown in Chatham, where the group
adopted a Provisional Constitution and Ordinances for the People of
the United States—a proposed new union founded on racial equality.
The following year, setting his old views on colonization in Africa aside,
Delany sailed aboard the bark *Mendi* for Liberia as head of the "Niger
Valley Exploring Party" on what proved to be a futile mission to relo-
cate free blacks from the United States. During this pregnant period he
further authored *Blake; or, The Huts of America*, a novel romanticizing
race insurrection and thus a clear counter to the white pieties found
in Stowe's *Uncle Tom's Cabin*. "I'm not your slave, nor never was," says
Blake, asserting his freedom to the man who claimed to own him, "and
you know it!" With the coming of the Civil War, the seemingly inexhaustible Delany recruited thousands of soldiers for the Union cause.
Following a February 1865 meeting in the White House, Lincoln called
him "this most extraordinary and intelligent black man," and made
Delany a major in the U.S. Army—the country's first African American
field grade officer.[23]

Following the war Delany settled for a few years in South Carolina,
working for the Freedmen's Bureau, engaging in Reconstruction politics (he lost a hotly contested race for lieutenant governor in 1874), and
practicing medicine. He further witnessed the rise of a virulent postwar
racism and once again lingered over the prospects of a black migration
abroad. He sought without success in 1879, the year he turned sixty-
seven, to secure a government sinecure that might have provided him
with the means to go to Africa. Returning to the North, he died in 1885
of tuberculosis in Wilberforce, Ohio, a community named after the
English abolitionist William Wilberforce, where two of his children had
attended college.

Thinking today of Delany's 1854 Cleveland speech, it seems suggestive of the Pan-African visions fostered at different times in the twentieth century by Marcus Garvey, W. E. B. Du Bois, and Malcolm X. Approached within the context of its own era, the address is informed by the looming shadow of an expansive Slave Power. Distrusting his country's narrow conceptions of freedom and reform, Delany sought a Shangri-la abroad, supposing this American republic-of-good-intentions ultimately irredeemable.

Such utopias were popular among prewar perfection seekers, though most of these improvised Edens were on native soil. Among them were the nearly two dozen simple-living Shaker communities largely in the Northeast and Midwest, the free-love Oneida Community of upstate New York (best known as makers of flatware and silverware), and the Harmony Society cooperative community in New Harmony, Indiana. One could also find distinctly less institutionalized searches for sainthood, as in the intensely independent practice of life embraced by Henry David Thoreau.

14

Freedom Defined: Thoreau's *Walden*

I do not propose to write an ode to dejection, but to brag as lustily as chanticleer in the morning, standing on his roost, if only to wake my neighbors up.

Henry David Thoreau, *Walden*, 1854

On August 9, as Delany and other emigrationists made plans to gather in Cleveland, the newly founded Boston publishing house Ticknor and Fields, under whose colophon came a torrent of classic American studies from the likes of Longfellow, Hawthorne, Emerson, and Stowe, released Henry David Thoreau's *Walden; or, Life in the Woods*. Only weeks removed from delivering "Slavery in Massachusetts" before a clamorous audience of abolitionists in nearby Framingham, Thoreau now addressed the republic's precarious relation to freedom and independence in a still deeper and more deliberate manner. The book encapsulated years of observation, writing, and reflection, and while in many respects a highly personal pilgrimage of spiritual discovery, it invariably recalled the vital times from which it so methodically emerged.

In all, Thoreau devoted some nine years to the project, a period encompassing the Mexican-American War, the Compromise of 1850, and the rise of free-soil principles as a force to be reckoned with in American politics. Late in the winter of 1854, as Douglas introduced his Kansas-Nebraska conundrum to Congress, Thoreau mulled over

Walden's eighth and final draft. He confided to a journal on March 1 of having "purified the main body." With his book ripening, he read page proofs in a piecemeal fashion into May. By early August trumpeting notices for the manuscript began to appear—"THE HERMIT BUILDS HIS HUT"—as did the first reviews.[1] Though the product of a profoundly original mind, *Walden* bore both the impress of its author's prolific circle of Concord connections as well as the surfeit of sectional discontent sweeping the country.

That this work selectively ruminated on the race question should come as no surprise. By the 1850s Thoreau could claim acquaintance with several iconic critics of slavery. These included Frederick Douglass, Wendell Phillips, and John Brown, whom he knew as lyceum lecturers, overnight guests at the Thoreau family home, and sometime dining companions. More intimately, his mother, Cynthia, sisters Helen and Sophia, and four aunts had confederated with some several dozen Concord women in 1837 to organize a female antislavery society.[2] The influence of this domestic ménage is evident in Henry's decision, while engaged in writing *Walden*, to assist his family's sheltering of runaways on at least two occasions. His journal entry for October 1, 1851, recorded the first episode:

> 5 P. M.—Just put a fugitive slave, who has taken the name of Henry Williams, into the cars for Canada. He escaped from Stafford County, Virginia to Boston last October; . . . had been corresponding through an agent with his master, who is his father, about buying himself, his master asking $600, but he having been able to raise only $500 . . . [He] fled to Concord last night on foot, bringing a letter to our family from Mr Lovejoy of Cambridge and another which Garrison had formerly given him on another occasion. He lodged with us, and waited in the house till funds were collected with which to forward him.[3]

Thoreau secured a train ticket for Williams and aided his flight to Burlington, Vermont, in passage to Canada.

Two years later, in the summer of 1853, Henry came into contact with another fugitive, whose name is unknown to us. Moncure Conway, the Emerson-inspired, southern-born abolitionist mentioned in chapter 12, recorded the encounter:

[Thoreau] invited me to come next day for a walk, but in the morning I found the Thoreaus agitated by the arrival of a coloured fugitive from Virginia, who had come to their door at daybreak. Thoreau took me to a room where his excellent sister, Sophia, was ministering to the fugitive. . . . I observed the tender and lowly devotion of Thoreau to the African. He now and then drew near to the trembling man, and with a cheerful voice bade him to feel at home, and have no fear that any power should again wrong him. That whole day he mounted guard over the fugitive, for it was a slave-hunting time. But the guard had no weapon, and probably there was no such thing in the house. The next day the fugitive was got off to Canada.[4]

Conway recalled Thoreau that summer as physically resembling his father, John, "French in appearance," and had been struck by the younger man's unusual "mental qualities" and "rare spirit." Emerson, the conduit between Conway and Thoreau, described the latter as "of short stature, firmly built, of light complexion, with strong, serious blue eyes, and a grave aspect. . . . There was a wonderful fitness of body and mind." Years after Henry's death in 1862 another contemporary described him as follows: "light haired, better looking than his portraits, [he] had a healthy complexion with a bright color [though] rather pale for an out-of-doors man; had a strong, prominent nose [said by Emerson to resemble "the prow of a ship"] and good eyes, a face that you would long remember and, though short in stature and inconspicuous in dress, a man you would not fail to notice in the streets as more than ordinary." A practical soul, Thoreau could accurately estimate the weight of farm animals, survey a piece of land, or, after mixing clay with plumbago (graphite), improve upon the quill and ink—replacing products made in his father's profitable pencil factory—John Thoreau and Company. More colorfully, he liked to swim and skate, played a hand-me-down flute, and enjoyed navigating nearby waterways as a boatman. Emerson once said that he "lived for the day."[5]

After *Walden*, Thoreau's most recognized work is probably "Resistance to Civil Government" (more commonly called, though not until after its author's death, "Civil Disobedience"), an 1848 lecture delivered at the Concord Lyceum and published the following year. The essay grew out of the context of New England's mounting antislavery sentiment and, correspondingly, the recent Mexican-American War, which some regarded as an open effort to extend servitude into the southwest. It emerged further from the single night that its author had spent in a Concord jail for refusing to pay his poll tax.

Perhaps in ignoring this civic obligation—a local excise connected to neither the state of Massachusetts nor the federal government—Thoreau sought to assert some psychic, if not economic, distance from the levers of power. The sum in question, $1.50 paid on a yearly basis, comes to about $58 in current dollars. "I was put into jail as I was going to the shoemakers to get a shoe which was mended," Henry recorded of the late July day in 1846 that contributed so much to his legend. The town jailer and resident tax collector, Sam Staples, happened to come across Thoreau and determined, about to retire from the position and eager to put his official affairs in order, to serve him a warrant for non-payment. Staples had arrested Bronson Alcott and Charles Lane three years earlier for the same transgression and had urged Thoreau to pay his delinquent duty. "Oh yes, I'd spoken to him a good many times about his tax," Staples commented years later, "and he said he didn't believe in it and shouldn't pay." Now given the choice between remittance and going to jail, Thoreau, perhaps eager above all other considerations to entertain a fresh experience, chose the latter. "He didn't make any fuss," Staples recalled, "he took it all right."[6]

Conveyed to the Middlesex County Jail in Concord, its three stories built of thick granite blocks, Thoreau shared a cell with a man who had fallen asleep while smoking and inadvertently set fire to a barn. "It was like travelling into a far country," he later wrote of his several-hour incarceration, "such as I had never expected to behold." That evening someone, most likely Thoreau's aunt Maria, came to the Staples residence to pay the prisoner's debt, though Sam, having taken his shoes off and settled in for the evening, refused to return to the jail. "In the morning," Thoreau observed in the manner of a tourist, "our breakfasts were put through the hole in the door, in small oblong-square tin pans, made to fit." He feasted on brown bread and a pint of chocolate.[7]

About a week later, in early August, having returned to his experimental life at Walden, Thoreau hosted in his box by the pond the Concord Female Anti-Slavery Society, gathered to recognize the thirteenth anniversary of the British West Indies emancipation. "I think this the best celebration ever had any where," one attendee declared in Garrison's *Liberator*. The day featured a number of speakers, situated for symmetry in the doorway of Henry's home, who inveighed consecutively before the conclave. "We had seats enough and to spare," a gladdened participant reported, "plenty to eat, and a hogshead of good ice-water to drink."[8]

In company, the unexpected night in jail, the cleansing moral clarity implied at Walden Pond, and the inglorious war against Mexico combined to raise for Thoreau serious concerns about the individual's allegiance to the state. All of which found their way into "Resistance." Embedded in this resonant essay is a philosophy of nonviolent struggle that, long after its publication, attracted through its unwavering ethical concern such seminal figures as Mohandas Gandhi ("Thoreau was . . . one of the greatest and most moral men America has produced"), Martin Luther King Jr. ("I became convinced that what we were preparing to do in Montgomery was related to what Thoreau had expressed."), and Leo Tolstoy, who described "Resistance" in a letter to a colleague as a "beautiful article on the duty of a man not to obey the government," while commending its author for "not wish[ing] to be an abettor and accomplice of a state that legalized slavery."[9]

In effect, Henry put into prose the higher-law ethic then coming into vogue among certain northern antislavery circles. In a series of probing epigrams—"a government in which the majority rule in all cases cannot be based on justice"; "must the citizen . . . resign his conscience to the legislature"; "The mass of men serve the State . . . as machines, with their bodies"—he challenged the notion that ethical individualism must defer to the dictates of blind loyalty. Broadening his view of both humanity and citizenship beyond the dominant culture's narrow code of laws, Thoreau denounced the federal government as a consummate "disgrace" and questioned its moral right to rule. "When a sixth of the population of a nation which has undertaken to be the refuge of liberty are slaves, and a whole country is unjustly overrun and conquered by a foreign army, and subjected to military law," he wrote, "I think that it is not too soon for honest men to rebel and revolutionize."[10]

Like the old Puritan theologian Roger Williams, remembered as an unbending advocate for the separation of church and state, Thoreau feared for the solitary soul should government's coercive powers become too strong and widely spread. No doubt reflecting on his single though clearly significant evening in the Middlesex County Jail, he argued that prison now constituted the "proper place" for Massachusetts's self-thinking free spirits. "It is there that the fugitive slave, and the Mexican prisoner on parole, and the Indian come to plead the wrongs of his race," he wrote, and it is further the only place, in a de facto "slave-state," where "a free man can abide with honor." And should an abundance of high-minded men and women refuse "to pay their tax-bills this year," he continued, then slavery and American imperialism might soon collapse, conjuring a profoundly "peaceable revolution" consistent with the nation's injured but still aspirational founding principles. The integrity of the individual, the fine probity of even a few who refused to be despoiled by the state, could set a listing world aright. "It matters not how small the beginning may seem to be," he concluded, "what is once well done is done for ever."[11]

Often regarded as a companion piece to "Resistance," *Walden* surfaced from a still longer set of aspirations and influences. In 1837, shortly after graduating from Harvard, Thoreau shared a shanty for six weeks with the young Transcendentalist Charles Stearns Wheeler on the shores of nearby Lincoln Pond. A few years later an economizing Wheeler inhabited a primitive shelter for several months on Flint's Pond just outside Concord, undoubtedly offering a model for the kind of deliberate living subsequently celebrated in *Walden*. About this time, in 1841, Thoreau expressed in his journal a desire to emulate Wheeler's example: "I want to go soon and live away by the pond. . . . But my friends ask what I will do when I get there? Will it not be employment enough to watch the progress of the seasons?"[12]

Four years later a more practical purpose finally coaxed Thoreau into encamping at Walden—the desire to write a book about a remarkable 1839 boating trip he took on the Concord and Merrimack Rivers with his now late and much-lamented brother, John. This two-week summer excursion became for Henry an extraordinarily precious memory to be curated with care. In January 1842, eleven days after sustaining a small cut on a finger while stropping his shaving razor, John died in some convulsive agony of lockjaw, resting finally in Henry's helpless arms. Deeply traumatized by his brother's sudden passing, Henry suffered several months of psychosomatic symptoms of the same disease. Wanting to offer a tribute to John and perhaps plumb the depths of his still-unfolding grief, Henry proposed to produce a book on the now-cherished trip.[13] Certain practical circumstances, however, made this difficult. His mother took in boarders and the confluence of clang and bustle made this hum-ming Texas Street house, just a half mile from the town square, an unlikely writer's retreat. And so Thoreau retreated elsewhere.

In doing so, he joined a long train of New England pilgrims and revolutionaries in search of something beyond the casual corruptions brought about by church and state. *Walden* is often read as a sui gen-eris rejection of American values, though it is perhaps more accurate to regard the study as steeped in the rich history, context, and ideals said to have animated the country, at least on its better days. In the book's nega-tion of mere materialism and emphasis on individual freedom, it takes seriously the now-endangered virtues that made the New World, so the French American writer J. Hector St. John de Crèvecœur observed in his classic work, *Letters from an American Farmer* (1782), the bright realm of "a new man, who acts upon new principles."[14] In first occupy-ing his cabin on Independence Day (July 4, 1845), Thoreau seemed des-perately interested in drawing attention to this fledgling experiment in Emersonian self-reliance.

His presence at Walden Pond suggested further a certain rebuke to the well-anointed narrative lazily passed down to generations of Amer-icans. For here an intrepid Concordian occupied a space no more than three miles from the famous North Bridge where, on a clear and chilly April day in 1775, several companies of militia exchanged fire with Brit-ish forces in the maiden military engagement of the Revolutionary War. Presumably Americans had won this long struggle against British tyr-anny, though Thoreau, in rejecting the more dubious fruits of victory—including the continuation of slavery and the fostering of a regimented factory culture that chipped away at private license—questioned his nation's progress. He sought, rather, to revisit the past and to reclaim the promise of those pioneers eager to leave a residual Old World feudalism of manner and mind behind. In evoking the great Puritan migration, in making of Walden a kind of resurgent "city upon a hill," he wished to reset the historical scales. Above all he intensely desired, as the scholar Stanley Cavell once put it, "to live the idea."[15]

Thoreau spotted his Walden home along a sloping bank facing the pond's north shore, some one hundred feet from the water's edge. Squatting on land purchased the previous fall by Emerson (nursing his own designs of a rural getaway), Thoreau wished to be bounded by woods and could see no other dwelling from his own. Hardly an isolate, he lived only a couple miles from Concord and in view of the Fitchburg Railroad, a symbol of the new age's progress made possible due to the efforts of many hundreds of Irish laborers—one of whom, James Collins, sold his old shanty to Thoreau for $4.25 (about $165 in present-day dollars). Having disassembled the small building and brought its bleached boards back to Walden, Henry erected a new structure and began his storied forest life.[16]

His simple if sufficiently furnished cabin included a caned bed, a desk and table, and three chairs—"one for solitude," he endearingly wrote, "two for friendship, three for society."[17] He kept a frying pan and skillet, a cup and dipper, as well as a spoon, two forks, two knives, and three plates. A woodshed and privy were nearby. He sported a battered hat, clomped about in a pair of cowhide boots, and liked to wear "durable and cheap" corduroy; "They have this advantage," he later explained, "that beside being very strong, they will look about as well three months hence as now." He subsisted—when not sharing meals in town with family and friends, or accepting their occasional doorstep alms—on rice, beans, and potatoes, as well as Indian (corn) meal and occasionally salted pork; he drank water. Tea and coffee were cut from his diet, as were milk and butter.[18]

Thoreau continued while at Walden to earn money as a jack-of-all-trades. "For a dollar a day," one biographer has noted, "he built fences, painted houses, did carpentry, bricked up at least one chimney, and performed a host of other odd jobs, often for Emerson." With the coming of cool weather, Thoreau finished his home, shingling its sides, plastering its exposed walls, and erecting a serviceable fireplace. This modest shelter offered its occupant an unusual degree of freedom he thought unavailable to most Americans. The cultural pressures to consume, gain, and display he presumed averse to a more intentional, deeply felt, and better-lived life. Sharpening this point with a stinging metaphor, he coupled in *Walden* what he supposed to be a self-inflicted form of white servitude to the crime of black bondage: "It is hard to have a southern overseer; it is worse to have a northern one; but worst of all when you are the slave-driver of yourself." He further noted in the book the dangerous relationship between luxuries (in which he included the aforesaid tea and coffee, as well as "meat every day") and the ready expenditure of state power and violence to maintain their ubiquity. The price paid by the individual, he argued, involved his very soul. For the upkeep of such appetites required a certain coercion "to compel you to sustain the slavery and war and other superfluous expenses which directly and indirectly result from the use of such things."[19]

Moving from the general to the particular, *Walden* gives a human face to slavery in a late chapter, "Former Inhabitants." In these illuminating pages Henry assays the biographies of several outcast Concordians who, like himself—if more conclusively and convincingly—lived apart from the nearby villagers. These vicarious neighbors included Zilpah White (1738–1820), an enslaved woman who gained her freedom about the time of the Revolution. Rather than find employment as a live-in laborer, she dwelt for forty years in a one-room house near the pond, about a half mile east from Thoreau's own abode; one might note the Zilpah-like manner of his experiment. She earned a meager but independent existence keeping chickens, spinning flax into linen fiber, and making mats and baskets, brooms, and perhaps pottery.[20] Thoreau discovered unburied bricks from White's chimney in what became his bean field; her lingering presence, the occasional topic of local gossip and guessing, interested him greatly:

> Here, by the very corner of my field, still nearer to town, Zilpha [*sic*], a colored woman, had her little house, where she spun linen for the townsfolk, making the Walden Woods ring with her shrill singing, for she had a loud and notable voice. At length, in the war of 1812, her dwelling was set on fire [by arsonists] . . . when she was away, and her cat and dog and hens were all burned up together. She led a hard life, and somewhat inhumane. One old frequenter of these woods remembers, that as he passed her house one noon he heard her muttering to herself over her gurgling pot,—Ye are all bones, bones![21]

Thoreau's interest in Zilpah White's "hard life" is evident, though so too is his lazy inclination to make her into a kind of Walden witch, whispering cryptic incantations over a frothing cauldron—the "bones" comment may have reflected her appetitive difficulty obtaining meat, a commodity Henry himself considered a luxury. In this particular strain of stereotyping, the well-fed Thoreau, regarded by many of his contemporaries as uncommonly inner driven, shared a fairly common tendency to make something exotic of an elderly black hermitess.[22]

Concord's hidden black heritage also included Brister Freeman (1744–1822), another former slave who found, as his name asserts, freedom. Zilpah's younger brother, he was given as a wedding gift to Colonel John Cuming, a wealthy landowner and country doctor much esteemed in Concord. Brister enlisted to fight in the Revolution under the name Brister Cuming, serving a three-year term and identifying himself as "Freeman" on his last enlistment. Following the war, he purchased a one-acre plot known as the "Old Field" in Walden Woods. There he and his wife, Fenda, raised three children in a modest house; they survived by keeping pigs, planting an orchard, and, so Thoreau claimed of Fenda's especial contribution, telling "fortunes, yet pleasantly." Anticipating Henry's minor-by-comparison tariff trouble, Brister failed for several years to pay his poll taxes and in 1791 Concord officials insisted he sign over his house. He was still able to live in the residence but lost his right to partake in town meetings—perhaps, after all, the suit's true intent? Intrigued by Freeman's biography, Thoreau included him in *Walden*, calling him "a handy Negro" and noting that his legacy persisted in the "large old trees" he had planted not far from the glossy pond—"their fruit still wild and ciderish to my taste."[23]

Thoreau further commemorates, if lightly, the life of Cato Ingraham (1751–1805), said to be an African-born "Guinea Negro" who, though formerly enslaved to a Concord lawyer, lived out his last decades as a free man with his wife, Phyllis, on a sandy lot in Walden Woods, not far from Zilpah's house. Possibly ruminating on the underlying injustice of race relations, even in free Massachusetts, Thoreau wrote of Cato: "There are a few who remember his little patch among the walnuts, which he let grow up till he should be old and need them; but a younger and whiter speculator got them at last." As with Zilpah's ghostly exposed bricks and the "ciderish" legacy left by Brister, Cato too drew Thoreau into searching for evidence of this former neighbor's lingering presence, which the Transcendentalist eventually located in a "half-obliterated cellar hole" not far from his cabin.[24]

That none of these former Waldenites, their children, or their extended kin remained in the area suggested to Thoreau an essential resistance in liberal Concord to their presence. Mired in poverty and relegated to segregated spaces, they defied, by their mere existence, the industrializing, gentrifying spirit emanating out of Boston and penetrating its surrounding satellites. Perhaps Thoreau saw some connection between his own removal to Walden Pond and the lives of the wood's "former inhabitants." Here, amidst the orchards and shore, the fields and hills, once dwelt formerly enslaved people, outcasts even in their freedom who nevertheless endured, raising children, tending animals, claiming new names, and standing in some vital sense as symbols for the kind of liberty their white neighbors asserted by birthright. All that remained of these cottagers were resonances and relics, the taste and texture of the blooming fruit, and the crumbling structures they left behind. "With such reminiscences," Henry wrote, counting himself something of an aloof legatee in their small circle, "I repeopled the woods."[25]

Thoreau first shared his experiences of living at the pond while still billeting on its banks, delivering an evening address, "A History of Myself," for the Concord Lyceum in the town's classic white-framed Unitarian Church in February 1847. Fragments of the text subsequently appeared in "Economy," *Walden*'s opening and longest chapter. The talk went well and Thoreau reprised the performance the following week. "Henry repeated his lecture to a very full house," wrote one observer, "it was an uncommonly excellent lecture—tho, of course few would adopt his notions—I mean as they are shown forth in his life." Emerson informed Margaret Fuller, the Transcendentalist, journalist, and women's rights advocate, that "members of the opposition came down the other night to hear Henry's account of his housekeeping at Walden Pond, which he read as a lecture, and were charmed with the witty wisdom which ran through it all."[26]

Later that year, in September, Thoreau returned to Concord, completing a two-year, two-month, two-day experiment in, so he said, "deliberate" living. Over the next several years, amidst a host of other writings and wanderings, he labored on several drafts of *Walden*. His most intense effort, in the winter of 1853–54, overlapped the period in which the nation debated the Missouri Compromise's repeal. During these charged months Henry added more than a hundred manuscript pages and arranged the chapters into their final form. The book, selling for $1, was released in early August.[27]

Reviews were generally positive (the *Providence Journal*, for one, thought its author "shrewd and eccentric" and his book "worth reading"), though several were unsympathetic, if not cutting. "It is a sorrowful surprise," sniffed the *Boston Atlas*, "that a constant community with so much beauty and beneficence was not able to kindle one spark of genial warmth in this would-be savage." A particularly strong notice appeared in the *National Anti-Slavery Standard*, which enthusiastically embraced Thoreau's philosophy: "If men were to follow in Mr. Thoreau's steps, by being more obedient to their loftiest instincts, there would, indeed, be a falling off in the splendor of our houses, in the richness of our furniture and dress, in the luxury of our tables, but how poor are these things in comparison with new grandeur and beauty which would appear in the souls of men."[28]

An equally positive if more discerning appraisal of the book appeared in the January 1856 *Westminster Review*—its author, the British novelist Mary Ann Evans (subsequently to publish, as George Eliot, such classics as *Adam Bede*, *Silas Marner*, and *Middlemarch*), thought Thoreau exhibited a striking environmental sensitivity, the product of a rare artistic intelligence. "His observations of natural phenomena," she wrote, "are not only made by a keen eye, but have their interest enhanced by passing through the medium of a deep poetic sensibility; and, indeed, we feel throughout the book the presence of a refined as well as a hardy mind." These penetrating, warmly put words could not, however, make *Walden* a financial success. Though it outperformed its underperforming precursor, *A Week on the Concord and Merrimack Rivers* (1849), it took five years to retail the two thousand copies produced in 1854. A second printing was not issued until March 1862, two months before its author died of tuberculosis at the age of forty-four. "Now comes good sailing," he said near the end.[29]

On August 8, the day before *Walden*'s publication, Thoreau informed a colleague of his recent literary labors with some affected regret: "Methinks I have spent a rather unprofitable summer thus far. I have been too much with the world, as the poet might say." And certainly the season's essential effort—the searing "Slavery in Massachusetts"—had kept its author engaged in the abolitionist mission. But despite yielding a piece of his prized independence, Henry seemed willing to risk the timely association. On the eleventh he wrote to his publisher requesting that gratis copies of *Walden* find their way to Charles Sumner and Horace Greeley, two of the leading figures in the herculean efforts that year to take on the Slave Power. The following day Daniel Ricketson, a Massachusetts Quaker, and evidently one of *Walden*'s first readers, thanked Thoreau for including in his fecund study attention to black bondage. "I feel that you are a kindred spirit," he wrote. "I was pleased to find a kind word or two in your book for the poor down trodden slave."[30]

Inevitably a product of its portentous times, *Walden* raised both questions and doubts about the depths of America's commitment to its founding principles. Though in certain respects an idiosyncratic text— one can scarcely imagine Emerson, the sage of self-reliance, trooping off to live in a pinched hut—it nevertheless captured in a unique tapestry of satire and self-discovery a broader cultural conversation on individualism and nonconformity. These contested principles took on a particular intensity in 1854, the year of Burns, Bovay, and Nebraska. But they did not go unchallenged. Thoreau wrote in relation to a rich New England jeremiadic tradition honed inescapably in generations of song and sermon. Regional in its resolve, it touched but a single strand of the antebellum omnibus, and before the summer's end the appearance of an extended southern statement challenged several of *Walden*'s strongest assertions.

15

Freedom Denied: Fitzhugh's *Sociology for the South*

The South . . . has, up to this time, been condemned without
a hearing.

George Fitzhugh, 1854

In September the prominent *Richmond Examiner* offered the first commentary on a newly published compendium of proslavery thought—
Sociology for the South; or, The Failure of Free Society—authored by
the largely self-taught Virginia theorist George Fitzhugh. The anony-
mous reviewer believed the book a welcome departure from the "half-
way, namby-pamby defence of slavery" that southerners, so he insisted,
customarily offered up to their critics. The study's explicit defense of
the peculiar institution as paternal and benign combined with its cate-
gorical denunciation of northern industrialization to offer a backward-
looking riposte to growing Yankee economic and demographic sway.
Though attentive in its provocative pages to new influences in the
emerging social sciences, Fitzhugh selectively engaged these insights in
the name of defending a vanishing agrarian order giving way to a rising regime of liberalism, individualism, and free trade. Supposing this
new system fundamentally debasing in its unapologetic materialism, he
denied its right to lecture the South. For in the North, he wrote, "what
makes money, and what costs money, are alone desired. . . . The intense
struggle to better . . . one's pecuniary condition, the rivalries, the jeal-

ousies, the hostilities which it begets, leave neither time nor inclination to cultivate the heart or the head."[1]

Fitzhugh's defense of Dixie runs, in some sense, counter to the main trends of early American intellectual history. For ideas one customarily looked to ecclesiastically steeped New England with its crush of Puritans and Congregationalists, Unitarians and Transcendentalists. In the decades leading up to the Civil War, however, as both black bondage and white factory labor made increasingly indelible marks on the public mind, a notable circle of southern sages—including John Calhoun and the luxuriantly maned Virginia agriculturalist Edmund Ruffin (who would die, following Lee's surrender, by his own hand while swathed in a Confederate flag)—formed a competing school. Rejecting capitalism's encroachments, it advanced a fine-tuned cavalier lament: free trade degraded and exploited workers; bourgeois society undermined church and family; the strong always looked to exploit the weak. Upholding a planter ethos imbued, so they argued, with an appreciation of grace, leisure, and continuity, they claimed the South superior to a numerically larger and wealthier North. On certain subjects, say materialism's mounting prevalence in American life, they might even have found a soupçon of common ground with men like Thoreau.[2] But their self-serving vindication of slavery put their ideas beyond the pale of northern reformers. Presumably driven by an objective search to dissect such seminal problems as class and race, labor and hierarchy, they more generally approached the study of human society with an underlying end to endorse their increasingly vilified section.

Fitzhugh traced his southern bona fides to the 1671 arrival of William Fitzhugh, a distinguished Bedfordshire lawyer and "fair classical scholar" who, upon arriving as a land agent for Lord Fairfax, settled along the Potomac River in King George County near present-day Fredericksburg. A fortunate marriage to one Sarah Tucker in 1674 brought to William, upon the death of her father, grants of nearly one hundred thousand acres in Virginia's Northern Neck, a collecting ground of affluent planters whose precarious tobacco fortunes were made on the backs of enslaved blacks. The Fitzhughs remained a socially prominent if fading Old Dominion family over several generations leading up to George's birth in 1806. His father, an army surgeon and small plantation owner, died in 1825; the surgeon's indebted estate was sold off four years later. Sporadically practicing law, George married Mary Brockenbrough of Port Royal about this time and thus by dowry came into possession of several hundred acres of tired peninsula soil along with a few slaves and a shabby bat-infested mansion described by one contemporary in classic Southern Gothic–ese as "rickety old" and "situated on the fag-end of a once noble estate." Possessed of little formal education, Fitzhugh rejoiced in his rural isolation, rarely leaving the Northern Neck. "We are no regular built scholar," he once allowed. "We have by observation and desultory reading, picked up our information by the wayside, and endeavored to arrange, generalize, and digest it for ourselves."[3] He feasted on the *Southern Quarterly Review*, the *Southern Literary Messenger*, and *De Bow's Review*, a fair sampling of cavalier literary culture in whose aspirational pages one might find an eclectic commingling of statistical data, literary criticism, and economic analysis. He further perused the older agrarian writings of fellow Virginian John Taylor (1753–1824, an exemplar of the country gentleman ideal), and the more contemporary offerings of the British social critic (and Emerson's longtime correspondent) Thomas Carlyle, absorbing in the aggregate an education partial to the planter perspective.

The ramshackle nature of Fitzhugh's estate found its hexed compliment in King George County's steadily declining population. The 1790 federal census showed some seventy-four hundred citizens, though by 1850 the number had dipped below six thousand. There, indifferently ensconced as an esquire, Fitzhugh read, casually researched family genealogy, and more energetically engaged in a sustained defense of slavery, by which he might yet vindicate the long experiment in aristocratic living conducted by generations of Tidewater Virginians. His quixotic assault on the Yankee industrial establishment, replete with historical, scriptural, and economic arguments favoring bondage, emerged from an unstructured but active mind. Finding the plantocracy indicted, so he said, "without a hearing," this peculiar Port Royal lawyer sought in *Sociology for the South* to absolve both state and section.[4]

Hardly a new project, the origins of proslavery thought go deep into the past. The Greeks and Romans had voluminously justified enslavement (Plato and Aristotle regarded so-called barbarian and unreasoning peoples as ripe for bondage), as did prominent medieval thinkers, including Thomas Aquinas, who argued that a natural chain of order, evident even in heaven where some angels ruled over others, guided mankind. Later such Enlightenment-era intellectual eminences as the

British philosopher David Hume ("I am apt to suspect the Negroes . . . to be naturally inferior to the whites") and the German thinker Immanuel Kant ("this fellow was quite black from head to toe, a clear proof that what he said was stupid") presumed connections between race and intelligence.[5] Men like Fitzhugh trailed in their considerable cultural wake.

In colonial America the Bible offered slavery's defenders a ready reply to critics. A 1701 treatise by John Saffin, a wealthy New England merchant with commercial ties to Virginia, cited arguments in Leviticus (Israel's divine right to hold slaves) and First Corinthians (Saint Paul's hierarchy of humanity) as definitive. "God," Saffin wrote, "hath Ordained different degrees and orders of men, some to be High and Honourable, some to be Low and Despicable; some to be Monarchs, Kings, Princes and Governours, Masters and Commanders, others to be Subjects, and . . . yea some to be born Slaves, and so to remain during their lives." A few years later the distinguished Puritan divine Cotton Mather produced "Essays to Do Good" (1710), a sort of primer for Christian living in a sinful world. On the questions of gradation, station, and obligation he wrote: "Masters, yea, and mistresses too must . . . do good unto their servants," God, he continued, having "put them into your hands."[6] Considering the long link between scripture and slavery, perhaps it is only apt that masters occasionally recorded the births and deaths of their slaves in family Bibles.

Ecclesiastical defenses of servitude, however, became less compelling over the decades. These were unfashionably at odds with the natural rights philosophy emanating from both the Enlightenment and the American Revolution. In 1764 the Boston lawyer James Otis Jr., known for the maxim "Taxation without Representation is tyranny," observed in a treatise asserting the rights of Britain's overseas subjects that "the Colonists are by the law of nature free born, as indeed all men are, white or black. . . . Does it follow that 'tis right to enslave a man because he is black?" That same year the Virginian Arthur Lee, later to serve in the Continental Congress, wrote: "It is evident, that the bondage we have imposed on the Africans, is absolutely repugnant to justice." And in 1776 Jefferson attempted to indict the British Crown for inflicting, so he argued, slavery upon his colonial subjects. In a passage edited out of the Declaration of Independence (Congress knowing these same subjects had eagerly enough cultivated the trade) Jefferson arraigned King George III for having "waged cruel war against human nature itself, violating its most sacred rights of life and liberty in the persons of a distant people who never offended him, captivating and carrying them into slavery in another hemisphere, or to incur miserable death in their transportation thither."[7]

Despite such rhetorical assaults on slavery, the institution, though declining in the North, otherwise expanded dramatically in the years following the Revolution. In consequence, the sublime Jeffersonian assertion that liberty was a self-evident truth, a right not to be removed, was abandoned. Among its critics, the Virginia statesman John Randolph, squire of a Charlotte County plantation, insisted in 1826, "If there is an animal on earth to which [the notion of equality at birth] does not apply . . . it is man—he is born in a state of the most abject want, and a state of perfect helplessness and ignorance."[8] Such highbrow sleight of hand invited a veritable industry among certain theorists, eager to quash the problematic incantations of freedom embedded in the nation's founding documents. Thus the Declaration was deemed abstract, obscure, and abstruse, a kind of air-castle acclamation not meant to be taken plainly. In any case, the Founders never sought in such calculated pomposity, these elucidators alleged, to make universal claims on human equality.

In the decades following the War of 1812, slavery was paradoxically becoming both more diffused and more reviled. The Missouri debates, emergence of radical abolitionism, and discussions of emancipation followed by colonization made the plantocracy defensive. Eager to acquit an uncoiling cotton belt, its scholarly and congressional retainers built upon the positive-good argument. Calhoun popularized the phrase in an 1837 Senate address—"the relation now existing in the slaveholding States . . . is instead of an evil, a good—a positive good"—though the idea that the enslaved profited from proximity to a superior culture had been floating about for some time. Thomas Cooper, an Anglo-American political philosopher and president of South Carolina College (now the University of South Carolina), advanced such a view when claiming in one 1826 pro-planter pamphlet: "Slavery has ever been the step-ladder by which civilized countries have passed from barbarism to civilization. History, both ancient and modern, fully confirms this position." An impressed Jefferson had referred to Cooper in correspondence as "one of the ablest men in America."[9]

Invariably, the dropping of natural rights dogma led a number of southern thinkers to embrace fashionable scientific arguments for enslavement. These were rooted in the assumption that races sprang from different origins (polygenesis) and thus explained black "inferiority." Josiah C. Nott, an Alabama surgeon trained at the University of Pennsylvania, studied skulls and declared Africans to be an entirely different species, somewhere between *Homo sapiens* and orangutans. The eclectic Jefferson, a great source of southern scientific opinion, had once made a glancingly similar supposition, writing crudely in his 1785 study *Notes on the State of Virginia* of "the preference of the Oranootan for the black women over those of his own species."[10]

Employing a raft of dubious statistics, impressions, and observations, proslavery scientists maintained that black peoples were idle and inattentive, listless and lazy; but these same scholars also found them to be ideally suited, because of their dark skins and "colder nature" as one report put it, for laboring efficiently under the hot southern sun. Those held in bondage were said to be genetically inclined to crime, disease, and poverty; they were further thought incapable of producing scientists, authors, or artists and thus suited to be servants, fitted to take orders and to imitate but not create. In response to abolitionist claims that the enslaved were debased by their servitude (nurture over nature), proslavery thinkers sought to demonstrate physical difference between races or, as some would have it, species. In his *Crania Americana* (1839) Samuel George Morton, an eminent professor of anatomy who took an advanced degree from the University of Edinburgh and taught in Philadelphia, asserted that while whites were large brained, blacks lacked cognitive aptitude. "Up to the present time," he wrote, "instances of superior mental powers have been of extremely rare occurrence."[11]

Despite such tortured exercises of the crania mania kind, the scientific school's influence proved to be of a limited and not altogether satisfying value to the planter class. For though the biological argument catered to ready-made rationalizations for slavery, it did little to assuage southern concerns of an ascendant Yankee leviathan. Free society, in other words, also needed to be scrutinized, possibly minimized, and very probably demonized. This is where George Fitzhugh made his mark. Conversant with census results, government committee reports, and sundry Atlantic World reviews, he proposed to go beyond biblical and scientific justifications for slavery in developing a grand sociological interpretation that upheld southern mores, censured industrialization, and invariably called into question the liberal, democratic progress of the past two centuries.

All to say, one might read Fitzhugh—empirical airs aside—as a data-driven whisperer of moonlight-and-magnolia mythology. He could hardly have hoped to convince northern readers, nor could his arguments offer white southerners anything more than elaborate synopses of their relative decline, with no apparent prescription to stem the slide. Despite appearing to engage in a hard and sharp science of society, *Sociology for the South* trades, rather, along the softer shores of a carefully combed sentimentality. Competitive capitalism, urbanization, and frontier democracy are all dismissed as antithetical to a paternal planter ethic tied to older agrarian inheritances that were once the young republic's bread and butter.[12] Efforts to create a chimerical equality were bound to result, dangerously so, in confusion, chaos, and violence. At heart Fitzhugh's is a Port Royal perspective, one that yearned for an imagined past that made of slavery the solid rock of better days gone by.

To register the belletristic versatility of agrarian nostalgia, one might further consult Fitzhugh's midcentury contemporary the South Carolina scholar William J. Grayson, author of "The Hireling and the Slave" (1854). This epic poem offered an idyllic expression of southern labor juxtaposed against the sad state of the new industrial hireling class, "free but in name—the slaves of endless toil." Casting the plantocracy's enemies as either political opportunists ("There supple Sumner, with the negro cause; Wins the sly game for office and applause") or, as with Stowe, irresponsible defamers ("Careless . . . whether truth she tells; And anxious only how the libel sells"), Grayson liberally indulged in therapeutic rebuttal. A product of the bucolic Sea Islands ("A shelving beach that sandy hillocks bound; With clumps of palm and fragrant myrtle crowned"), he feared the fast-approaching industrial future with its attendant factories and poorhouses.[13]

That Grayson and Fitzhugh invariably overlap in their respective indictments of northern civilization speaks to a general dispersal of planter apologia among the last antebellum generation. *Sociology for the South* is replete with warmed-over complaints, including the by now compulsory critique of workshop culture, the perfunctory dismissal of Enlightenment liberalism, and the casting of races into rigid biological hierarchies. Individualism and free markets are attacked; agrarianism and tradition are extolled; servitude is regarded as the natural order of humanity, while Yankee efforts to advance equality have resulted, so Fitzhugh contended, in a misguided misery.

More original and interesting, however, is his argument that liberal capitalism pits all against all, inevitably creating a vast class of powerless workers ripe to be exploited by those holding large concentrations of wealth. He maintained that the distinguished Scottish economist Adam Smith, author of *The Wealth of Nations* (1776), had radically miscalculated the fruits of private enterprise, seeing its likely and beneficial impact as trending universal rather than appearing in select pockets, thinking that its reach included farmers and mechanics as well as bankers and bosses. "He was absent, secluded and unobservant," Fitzhugh said of Smith. "He saw only that prosperous and progressive portion of society whom liberty or free competition benefitted, and mistook its effects on them for its effects on the world."[14]

Within just a few decades such analyses would impact the nation's philosophical response to the Gilded Age. In this Progressive Era (1890–1920) an entire class of activists and officials, including Theodore Roosevelt (who called "the capitalist . . . an unworthy citizen" in a memoir), advanced state-centered political and economic reform to rein in railroad oligarchs and Wall Street money lords. More broadly, since the onset of the Industrial Revolution, economic disruptions and dislocations had given rise to a population of discontents so immense that several anti-capitalist ideologies, including Marxism, socialism, syndicalism, and anarchism, emerged in its churned-up wake. Americans often regarded these responses as foreign and exotic, yet Fitzhugh offered an early and native critique that questioned the free-market dynamo. He thought of socialism, a word that appears repeatedly in *Sociology for the South*, as a humane response to the "disintegration of society, which liberty and free competition occasion . . . [among] the poorer class."[15] Eager to advance a more feudal, hierarchical, and ordered theory of cultural development, he portrayed the South as an organic, paternalistic society, protected from a harsh caveat emptor code employed by the strong to prey upon the weak.

Fitzhugh placed *Sociology for the South* within a fresh school of studies responding to the "disease" of free labor under industrialization. He identified the utopian socialism of the Welsh manufacturer Robert

Owen and the French philosopher Charles Fourier as compatible with his own opinions. All seemed aware, he argued in the book, that "liberty and equality have not conduced to enhance the comfort or the happiness of the people." They have made materialism, rather, the ultimate arbiter of what is permissible, appropriate, and worthy. "The moral effect of free society," he wrote, "is to banish Christian virtue"—and in this absence of ethics honor is invariably assessed in dollars, thus making individualism a veil for selfishness. In full, Fitzhugh offered a southern-spiced indictment of Benjamin Franklin's America. The shrewd purveyor as "Poor Richard" of honeyed capitalist homilies—"Early to bed and early to rise, makes a man healthy, wealthy and wise"; "A Penny saved is two pence dear"; "God helps them that help themselves"—Franklin enshrined the principle of moneymaking into a carnal catechism. Fitzhugh turned this dubious achievement on its head arguing, rather: "Temperance, frugality, thrift, attention to business, industry, and skill in making bargains are virtues in high repute, because they enable us to supplant others and increase our own wealth."[16]

Considering Fitzhugh's lavish attention to Yankee ways, he might just as easily have titled his book *Sociology for the North*. For if the enslaved are well fed, the "wage-slave" is undernourished, and if the productive field hand enjoys heat in the wintertime, the unemployed factory hand shivers in the cold. "At the slaveholding South," he wrote, ignoring the systemic violence, deeply rooted racism, and long-standing fears of black insurrection that haunted the region, "all is peace, quiet, plenty and contentment. We have no mobs, no trades unions, no strikes for higher wages, no armed resistance to the law, but little jealousy of the rich by the poor. We have but few in our jails, and fewer in our poor houses." Years of perusing southern periodicals offered Fitzhugh a fugitive knowledge of industrialization's discontents and this he used to qualify northern claims to liberty and equality. These rote, unreflective convictions he thought were mere constructs, made to make condemned men feel free in their servitude. Yankee bondage he deemed inferior to southern bondage, however, for northern masters were hard rulers, brought up to look down upon those without fortune and, having been weaned on thrifty Poor Richard's "Drive thy business or it will drive thee" creed, lacking a parental, protective instinct. "The men of property," he insisted, "are masters of the poor; masters, with none of the feelings, interest or sympathies of masters."[17]

Wishing to have their abundance blessed in a suitably progressive philosophy, a rising manufacturing elite, Fitzhugh wrote, made an idol of "unfettered talent, genius, industry and capital." Embracing Smith's classical economic theories, they thought of markets as essentially self-regulating systems operating best without state oversight. Individual success, these satisfied men smiled, made nations richer, put more people to work, and promoted prosperity. But this roseate vision merely ministered to the needs of the anointed, Fitzhugh continued, leaving out "the unemployed poor, the weak in mind or body, the simple and unsuspicious." Thinking globally, he pointed out that the British Empire was "daily growing richer," though her decidedly less industrious colonies, including a cluster of Caribbean sugar islands, the African Gold Coast, and much of India, suffered as a result of their conscripted connection, becoming "poorer, weaker and more ignorant."[18]

In Fitzhugh, present-day readers might hear an unexpected echo of the sharp debates on economic inequality that currently draw our attention. He laments the lack of guaranteed employment and medical care for workers, is critical that a woman is "reduced to the necessity of getting less than half price for her work," and reflects uneasily on the commercial exploitation of developing countries, treated essentially as dependencies. His observation, moreover, that free trade in the United States' western territories threatened to cheat the region's workers "of the profits of their labor," also bears consideration. The emergence of a robust Populist Party centered in the impoverished plains states—its great champion, William Jennings Bryan, claimed 46 percent of the popular vote in the 1896 presidential election—later produced a prolonged critique of America's rising robber baron republic along lines not altogether unfamiliar to previous generations of southern censors.[19]

Ultimately, however, Fitzhugh's socialism is less about the iniquities of factories than the perfections of plantations. His blatant racism (the enslaved cotton hand "is but a grown up child"), uncritical assumption that the master class served virtuously as "parent or guardian," and insistence that any hierarchal relationship amounted to slavery of a similar depth and degree—"Three-fourths of free society are slaves, no better treated, when their wants and capacities are estimated, than negro slaves"—could only have persuaded the already persuaded. After reading Fitzhugh closely, the twentieth-century literary critic Edmund Wilson found him annoyingly "inconsecutive and repetitious,

often self-contradictory and full of extreme statements, condemnatory or eulogistic, which ring out with the full intonations of expansive
after-dinner drinking over the generous Virginia board."[20]

That somewhere beyond the bluster and cant Fitzhugh knew black
bondage to be a corruption is evident from a communication to a colleague written in 1855: "I assure you, sir, I see great evils in slavery, but
in a controversial work I ought not to admit them." He sought in *Sociology for the South*, rather, to confess nothing other than the immense
errancy of a northern industrial regime that created, so he claimed, an
overeducated elite of "quacks, visionaries and agitators." For generations, he knew, white southerners had suffered the moral preachings of
their prim Yankee neighbors—and now the southerners wished to be
heard.[21]

A few months after the book appeared, Fitzhugh received an invitation to speak on slavery at a New Haven lyceum, after which Wendell
Phillips would offer a reply, thus making the event a de facto debate.
With the support of his section—the *Fredericksburg News* thought
Fitzhugh eminently able "to acquit himself in a manner worthy of the
subject and himself"—and the need to pay off a looming $530 debt (the
Yankees were offering a stipend), he headed north. New Haven proved
surprisingly congenial. It respected free speech, housed a thriving local
carriage industry that did a brisk business in the South, and contained
few blacks.[22]

In Brewster's Hall, Fitzhugh spoke on "The Failure of Free Society"
before a large audience. "It was often applauded," he later wrote, "and listened to politely throughout." Essentially, he had summarized *Sociology
for the South* to an affable gathering, some of whom hobnobbed with the
visiting scholar during his short stay. Fitzhugh mingled with Yale fac-
ulty, met a sister of Harriet Beecher Stowe, and received a personal tour
of the town by Stowe's uncle Samuel Foote, who, in an attitude of cordial rebuke, pointedly drew the southerner's attention to the tidy homes
and clean cottages occupied by local laborers. The day after Fitzhugh
spoke, Phillips took the podium and, after briefly defending the free-
trade principle, more controversially criticized northern churches for
their silence on slavery. Fitzhugh dismissed the lecture as "an eloquent
tirade against Church and State, Law and Religion" that veered dangerously toward "flat treason and blasphemy." He thought little more of
New Haven's comparatively secular tone, convinced that only southern

institutions could sustain the virtues of "order, subordination, law, and government" in America.[23]

In the 1880s, many years after the Civil War, William Herndon, Lincoln's third and last law partner, remembered, "I had a Southern work called *Sociology* by Fitzhugh, I think. It defended slavery in every way. This aroused the ire of Lincoln more than most pro-slavery books." Fitzhugh, whose Port Royal house was shelled during the war while he served the Confederate Treasury Department in Richmond, perhaps and unexpectedly succeeded in raising the northern conscience as much as the southern. It is with this consequence in mind that *Sociology for the South's* last sentence takes on an ironic, premonitory power: "Let us now . . . act on the offensive, transfer the seat of war, and invade the enemy's territory."[24]

In this aggressive key, as sides divided in Kansas and the off-year elections loomed, a Dixie-driven agenda presumed to extend America's cotton kingdom beyond its native shores. Its champions hoped to make Cuba, one of the last lingering outposts of Caribbean enslavement, the thirty-second state.

Part V

PREMONITIONS

A former single-term congressman, lately a prairie lawyer, Abraham Lincoln reengaged with politics by opposing the Kansas-Nebraska Act, which unexpectedly put him on the path to the presidency.

16

The Ostend Fiasco

The portentous question now is connected with Cuba. To secure
that island money to any amount will be lavished, and war will
be braved. This Administration is a cross between the pirate and
the scorpion.

Charles Sumner, 1854

For several decades a winding parade of expansion-minded Americans
had openly coveted Cuba, the bright pink Pearl of the Antilles. Some
nationalists regarded the island, about a hundred tempting miles from
the warm Florida coast and one of the last outposts of New Spain, as strategically important to the United States, while southern opinion came
over time to regard the near-at-hand enclave, with its many thousands of
slaves, as an ideal addendum to the Union. Tobacco and molasses, sugar
and rum, were its economic staples, drawing, invariably, the attention
of planter presidents. "I have ever looked upon Cuba," Jefferson wrote
James Monroe in 1823, "as the most interesting addition which could
ever be made to our system of States"; and in 1848 James Polk (under
whose stewardship ensued the annexation of Texas and the massive Mexican cession) unsuccessfully proposed $100 million, about $3.8 billion in
present-day dollars, for the island. Beyond official overtures, bravos like
William Walker, enticed by persistent instability in Central and South
America, pursued quasi-private empires in the region. Cuba, with a population of 1.2 million in 1850, became a plaything for such men.[1]

Narciso López (1797–1851), a dapper, dark-eyed Venezuelan-born

Spanish army general cum soldier of fortune, stood out among their sort. The product of an affluent merchant family of Basque ancestry, he fought against the Republican forces that finally, in 1823, claimed victory in the Spanish American wars of independence. An adroit horseman, he subsequently participated in the First Carlist War (1833–1840, a struggle for the Spanish throne) before moving on to Cuba as an assistant to higher-placed officers. In 1843, following the posting of a new governor, López lost his position. Perhaps in response, and following a series of failed economic ventures, he drifted into the camp of Cuba's independence-seeking revolutionaries. By 1848 Spanish authorities were arresting such opportunists and López bolted for America.[2]

There he quickly cultivated men eager to help him return to—invade—Cuba; these included John L. O'Sullivan, a bespectacled and thickly mustached New York editor who had recently popularized the phrase "manifest destiny" when braying for U.S. expansion in Texas and Oregon. López managed, while based in Manhattan, to recruit some eight hundred men, largely a mix of Cuban exiles and American volunteers, who convened on a small island in the Mississippi Sound in the summer of 1849, preparing to take three chartered transport steamer ships to Cuba. These craft, however, along with one thousand muskets and numerous swords, were seized by a careful Zachary Taylor administration, which, in observing the nation's neutrality laws, denounced such illegal efforts to enlarge the nation's borders. Undaunted, though recognizing the need for greater support, López carefully courted southern interest in Cuba. He established himself in New Orleans and, in a bid for quick credibility, sought the assistance of Mexican-American War veterans including Senator Jefferson Davis (who was promised $100,000 "for the use of Mrs. Davis") and Major Robert E. Lee—both of whom, though apparently intrigued, turned him down; Lee, who would one day accept a place in the army of a foreign power, the Confederate States of America, considered it at this time "wrong to accept a place in the army of a foreign power."[3]

López did find an ally, however, in Mississippi governor John Quitman as well as some lesser-placed politicos and a few bit-chomping newspaper editors. Having managed to raise another army of several hundred, López with his irregulars actually invaded Cuba in May 1850, briefly taking control of Cárdenas before the threat of advancing Spanish soldiers—and a lack of support from the locals—sent them, under musket fire, back to the sea. Defeated, López's men withdrew to Key West. Quitman, implicated though by no means repentant, was compelled to resign his gubernatorial seat, though neither López nor his bedraggled legion, indicted for violating the nation's neutrality laws, were convicted. Instead, López, possibly filled with what turned out to be an errant sense of immunity—much of the South regarding him as a hero—planned yet another invasion.

This assault, sustained by only four hundred men including a smattering of immigrant Germans and Hungarians, was carried out in August of the following year. Again, López failed to receive critical support from the Cuban people, though he now paid supremely for the miscalculation. Captured in the highlands, he was subsequently brought to a plaza in Havana Harbor near Morro Castle. There, on September 1, having ascended a wooden tower, his wrists tied in front and elbows bound from behind, he told an assembled audience, "My intention was good, and my hope is in God." He then settled into an iron garrote chair while his legs and throat were secured, the latter in a metal collar. Barely had López time to kiss a small cross before an executioner maneuvered a screw that tightened the metal neckband and strangled the prisoner.[4]

López's doomed efforts seemed to capture the contradictions of American foreign policy in this period. While presidential administrations often inveighed against the filibusters, strong sentiment in parts of the country enthusiastically supported such efforts. "We have a destiny to perform," the respectable *De Bow's Review* declared about this time, "a 'manifest destiny' over all Mexico, over South America, over the West Indies."[5] By the early 1850s such piratical impulses—prompting the question of slavery's extension—invariably became entangled with the broader free-soil struggle as played out in the Kansas-Nebraska drama.

A number of important government officials, including President Pierce and Davis, now secretary of war, coveted a Caribbean presence. "I want Cuba," the latter proclaimed, "and I know that sooner or later we must have it."[6] Two of the country's more important diplomats, the financier August Belmont, minister to the Netherlands, and James Buchanan, minister to the Court of St. James's in London, hoped to cajole Spanish bondholders in Europe to apply pressure on Spain to sell off the island. More generally, the Pierce administration sympathized with the Young America movement, an expansionist-minded informal society boosted by men like O'Sullivan and finding some casual political support within

the Democratic Party. Among the less casual of their faith, no one advocated for empire quite like the nimble Quitman.

A New Yorker by birth, leonine with a thick, bristling beard and
bushy gray hair, the picaresque Quitman taught school in the North
before journeying to Natchez, a center of Mississippi River trade, to
practice law. There he discovered something altogether more visceral
than a mere vocation; "He soon became," a biographer notes, "a southerner." In 1824 Quitman married above his meager station and this for-
tuitous union financed his entry into politics at the state level; assuming
the prerogatives of the master class, he further invested in slaves (own-
ing some 150 people) and purchased or acquired, through his wife,
four plantations of varying sugar, cotton, and molasses cultivation in
assorted states. At the age of thirty-six he served briefly as Mississippi's
governor, and a decade later he was a Brigadier General of Volunteers
in the Mexican-American War, where he participated in the pivotal
battles of Monterrey and Chapultepec, as well as the siege of Veracruz.
Champion of a rising Anglo southwest predicated on enslaved labor, he
acquired a vast forty-thousand-acre domain in eastern Texas.[7]

Concerned about California's recent free-state admission into the
Union, Quitman conceived of Cuba as a suitable quid pro quo and began
to make connections with "free Cuba" confederates in America, including López's former supporters. This went on for some time with the well-
connected Quitman negotiating the terms upon which he would lead a
filibuster; he thought a million dollars at his disposal a suitable inducement, though finally agreed to $800,000, and in the spring of 1854 bonds
were being sold to raise this considerable sum. Quitman curried support
from Cuban exiles in the United States by promising the island's liberation, though he really sought its annexation, perhaps noting how, in 1830s
Texas, an independence movement had opened the way for another slave
state. With this recent history in mind, he determined to occupy Cuba
rather than risk its purchase. The latter strategy suggested a drawn-out
affair and might result in the emancipation, by Spanish officials, of the
island's enslaved population. Abolitionist sentiment in the North, moreover, would certainly resist the prospect of yet another planter-dominated
appendage entering the Union—better to present these critics with a fait
accompli.[8]

While the selling of bonds openly advertised the Cuban adventure, Quitman went about recruiting his improvised army. As might be

expected, a batch of Mexican-American War veterans showed interest, as did men who had formerly rallied around the defeated López; a smattering of students at southern military colleges, boyishly eager to capture their portion of glory, also took note. Of course, many of these spoils seekers hoped to roll quickly into high rank, prettily beribboned and festooned. Other and more prominent backers of this lawless enterprise also came to the fore, including Alabama governor John Winston, former Mississippi congressman John Francis Hamtramck Claiborne, and current Georgia congressman Alexander H. Stephens. The latter, in an 1854 communication to a colleague, expressed unequivocal support for Quitman's irregular crew: "As for myself I am for Cuba, and I think if our citizens see fit to go and rescue the Island from Spanish misrule and English abolition policy they ought not to be *punished* by us for so doing. . . . I am against Cuba's becoming a *negroe state.*" Several Mississippi newspapers and legislators responded positively to the emerging momentum for a filibuster; their backing, along with that of other peripheral parties, included a mixture of money, speeches, and advertising.[9]

Northern interest in a Cuban invasion proved tepid, though a few enterprising Yankees made inquiries; Quitman, possibly preferring a clear field for southern aspirations, seems to have ignored these solicitations. Other Dixie filibuster enthusiasts took a similar sectional line. One central Mississippian described as "almost unanimous among Southern men in this part of the State [the] desire that Cuba should be acquired as a Southern conquest"; another loyalist believed that Cuba's subjugation represented "the only hope of the South."[10] To such madcaps, eager to see a golden circle of Caribbean slavery, the moment to strike seemed at hand.

Spain could hardly fail to take note of Quitman's gathering plans and, in September 1853, countered by appointing the Peruvian-born Captain General Juan M. de la Pezuela—abolitionist by sentiment— Captain-General of Cuba. Formerly governor of Puerto Rico, Pezuela quickly put in motion a controversial program designed to align the island's black population with his regime; most palpably he enacted laws to curtail the slave trade and declared that enslaved peoples brought to Cuba after 1820 were to be freed—in effect, considering the large numbers involved, a de facto emancipation proclamation. He additionally welcomed these and other blacks into the militia, while simultaneously banning whites from bearing arms. Stunned critics in America—the Cuban junta—called this agenda "Africanization."[11]

That winter, in late February 1854, Pezuela sent yet another unmistakable message to an American government he thought only too eager to abet filibusters—he seized, on a technicality involving a ship's manifest, the *Black Warrior*, a coastal steamer stopping, as it had done many times before, in Havana Harbor on its way to New York with a load of Alabama cotton. President Pierce condemned the action while Louisiana's legislature demanded "decisive and energetic measures." Some congressional southerners called for the repeal of the nation's neutrality laws, while at least one cabinet member, Attorney General Caleb Cushing of Massachusetts, pushed for a blockade of Cuba. Others pushed back. Ohio congressman Joshua Giddings, having the previous month attached his name to the "Appeal of the Independent Democrats" in protest of Douglas's Kansas-Nebraska Bill, now protested again. "We are to have war with Cuba," he fumed, "not on account of the seizure of . . . [the] Black Warrior, but to forestall emancipation, to stay the progress of liberty there."[12]

Giddings's reference to slavery stressed the danger that Pierce now faced. Already confronted with the Kansas question, he hardly needed an only slightly less explosive Cuba question to further burden his administration. Northern and southern opinion alike looked now to see what he would do. In May 1853, amidst rumors that Spain might emancipate the island's enslaved population in an effort to court Britain's and France's good favor, Pierce sent a special envoy, former justice Alexander Clayton, occupant of a large Mississippi plantation, to ferret out the truth. As Secretary of State William Marcy put the matter in his official orders, Clayton was to find out if Spain leaned toward "Africaniz[ing] Cuba if England and France would guarantee her control of the island" against mounting U.S. pressure.[13] That late autumn Clayton reported finding no evidence to support this contention.

Perhaps that is why Pierce took a soft line toward Madrid in his annual December message to Congress. "Independently of our valuable trade with Spain," he observed, "we have important political relations with her growing out of our neighborhood to the islands of Cuba and Porto Rico." He further warned against any Walkeresque undertakings in the Caribbean: "I am happy to announce that since the last Congress no attempts have been made by unauthorized expeditions with the United States against [Spain's] colonies. Should any movement be manifested within our limits, all the means at my command will be vigorously exerted to repress it." But Pierce also appeared to be playing for time. Rumors of an impending British-backed emancipation in Cuba continued to tease the fretting president throughout the winter. In March, with the *Black Warrior* affair still unresolved, he sent a second envoy, Charles Davis, to Havana. In his orders to Davis, Secretary Marcy emphasized that the freedom of Cuba's slaves "would disturb the repose of the Union. The President is resolved that . . . [this] shall not occur, so far as it is in his power to prevent it." He closed on a provocative note: "The attitude of Spain towards the United States is beginning to assume an aspect threatening to the peace of the two countries."[14]

Two months later, in May, Louisiana senator John Slidell introduced a motion to suspend the country's neutrality laws. A handful of southern senators supported this act of political theater and a few newspapers lined up as well. "At all events," the *Natchez Daily Courier* commented on June 3, "our filibusters will be enabled without hindrance to carry out their own plans until Congress can be dragooned into the measure."[15]

In the midst of this uncertainty, an improbable personality, Pierre Soulé, the U.S. minister to Spain, brought his erratic temperament to bear on the brewing Cuban crisis. A French native and son of a prominent justice of the peace, Soulé, an anti-Royalist, had fled Europe in the late 1820s and settled as an attorney for cotton planters in New Orleans. A Democrat, he won a Senate seat in 1849, which he resigned four years later to take the post of U.S. minister to Spain. Only two months into that situation he managed to wound a French diplomat, the Marquis de Turgo, in a duel. Apparently de Turgo had failed to curb a rude guest at a party; the Duke of Alba, having eyed Soulé's attractive creole wife, Henrietta, is said to have made comment on her generous décolletage. Soulé's son, Nelvil, overhearing the remark, challenged the discourteous duke to a duel—which they performed, ceremoniously swinging heavy swords at each other, without injury. Seeking a bit of honor of his own, Pierre (the "French Yankee") then insisted on an apology from the evening's host, de Turgo, who refused, saying, "Such a demand could be replied to only at the point of a pistol." And so out came the pistols—the marquis receiving a wound to his right leg on the second round.[16]

Soulé made himself additionally obnoxious in Madrid by rhetorically supporting (and possibly subsidizing) Spanish republicans determined to overthrow the monarchy. These men somewhat dubiously promised the minister that once in power they would surely part with Cuba—for the princely sum of $300,000. Now, in early 1854, Soulé received from Marcy a communication indicating increasing State Department impatience for Spain's "disturbances in regard to Cuba" and, referencing the *Black Warrior* affair, "a causeless aggression upon our commerce and national rights." The secretary, no doubt taking his tone from Pierce, seemed to be flirting with the idea of war. But like so many questions facing the country at this time, Cuba's future could not be discussed without stirring up sectional tensions. Slidell, having already called for a suspension of the neutrality laws, argued in yet another blustering Senate speech that Quitman's filibusterers were on the right side of history. "One thing is certain," he seemed to evoke the U.S.'s own colonial revolt against a European power, "that in despite of all your statutes, your collectors, your marshals, your Army and Navy, if the revolutionary standard be once hoisted in Cuba, and maintained for a few short weeks, no Administration can prevent our citizens rushing to the rescue in such numbers as will secure its triumph—a Democratic President would not desire to do it."[17]

In response, Slidell's Senate colleague Salmon Chase pointedly stated that should Britain and France play a part in emancipating Cuba's slaves, he would offer them nothing but his "best wishes." Slidell might have hoped for a northern Democrat to rise in reply, though he surely understood that such an effort, in the exercise of extending slavery, was most unlikely. Debate persisted into May with a few southern senators shrieking about Africanization and the dire need for American intervention, but to no avail. The dangerous divisions in Congress convinced Pierce that Cuba could only be acquired through diplomatic means. Accordingly, he applied pressure on Spain over the confiscation of the *Black Warrior*, which it had released two months earlier after receiving payment of a $6,000 fine. A calculating Marcy wrote to Soulé in Madrid: "The damages to the owners of the Black Warrior and her cargo are estimated at three hundred thousand dollars, and this amount you will demand as the indemnity to the injured parties claimed for them by this government." He then proceeded to rattle the American saber:

> This outrage is of such a marked character, that this government would be justified in demanding immediate satisfaction of the

wrong-doers [in] Havana, and, in case of their refusal, of taking redress into its own hands; but the President, anxious to preserve peaceful relations with Spain, has determined to bring the case to Her Catholic Majesty's notice.

Soulé was directed to avoid "any further discussion" of the matter with the Spanish government, but rather wait for an answer "to your demand."[18]

That answer arrived later that spring—the *Black Warrior*'s $6,000 fine was remitted, though the note said nothing about a $300,000 reparation. It seemed that Madrid had called the wobbly American bluff. The Pierce administration understood that wide support for war did not exist, and yet, even hemmed in, the president's Cuba fever persisted. Taking an altogether different tack, Marcy thus wrote to Soulé with orders to buy the island. "The domination of Spain over Cuba," he opened, "subjects our citizens to frequent acts of annoyance and injury, interrupts our commerce and invades our national rights." Though acknowledging "this will be a delicate and difficult negotiation," he stressed "the natural connection" that presumably bound Cuba with the United States. Pierce, so Marcy continued, thought $100 million "a liberal price," though he held the prize "so very desirable" that he agreed to go as high as $130 million.[19]

Under different circumstances, Pierce may have struck a more belligerent pose. But as Marcy wrote in late May to John Mason, the moon-faced American minister to France, "The Nebraska question has sadly shattered our party in all the free states and deprived it of the strength which was needed & could have been much more profitably used for the acquisition of Cuba." Instead, the president maneuvered for a diplomatic solution. He thus refused to back Slidell's attempts to overturn the neutrality laws but issued instead a proclamation on May 31, one day after signing the Kansas-Nebraska Act, announcing his determination to prosecute men making illegal expeditions abroad. It identified, no doubt with Quitman in mind, "sundry persons, citizens of the United States . . . engaged in organizing and fitting out a military expedition for the invasion of Cuba." Pointing out that such an undertaking contradicted "the spirit and express stipulations of treaties" between the United States and Spain, it promised the government's resolve "to prosecute with due energy all those who, unmindful of their own and their country's fame, presume thus to disregard the laws of the land and our treaty obligations."[20]

Committed to acquiring Cuba via diplomatic channels, Pierce subsequently asked Congress in August for a $10 million appropriation to provision an American mission to Madrid. The sum struck a number of politicians as unduly large and they found Pierce evasive on its allocation. The Senate Committee on Foreign Relations, entrusted to offer an opinion on the request and perhaps mindful of the sharp divisions brought about by the territorial debates, suggested discussion be put off until the new legislative session in December. Congress having distanced itself from Cuba, Pierce, hoping to claim his island after all, adopted still another strategy—using American diplomats in Europe to work in concert to convince Spain to sell. These men, presumably to convene in London or Paris, were Soulé, Mason, and James Buchanan, the latter openly disenchanted with the plan. "I can not for myself discover what benefit will result from a meeting," he candidly wrote Pierce in September, "every object which you have in view can, in my opinion, be accomplished by correspondence."[21]

But Pierce got his way and the ministers, seeking, so Buchanan said, an inconspicuous site as "all . . . eyes would be upon us," met at Ostend, a fashionable coastal city in the Flemish region of Belgium convenienced with a transit harbor to England. After only three days, however, the party, supposing itself under surveillance, moved 150 miles east to Aix-la-Chapelle in Prussia (present-day Aachen, Germany). A former Roman spa town, it counted among its amenities one of Europe's oldest cathedrals, in which the medieval emperor Charlemagne received burial in 814. Though hesitant to gather on the Continent with his colleagues, Buchanan sensed their potential to shake up a crumbling colonial status quo. The conference, he supposed to one relative, would "probably make noise enough in the world."[22]

On October 18 the ministers fashioned and signed a dispatch forever to be known as the Ostend Manifesto. A clumsy, quarrelsome document, it bore evidence of America's underlying foreign policy confusion in a time of sectional tension; whereas only a few months earlier, amidst the *Black Warrior* affair, Pierce seemed willing to go to war, now, with the country divided over Kansas, his administration seized upon a less aggressive line. But Soulé, possessing unhelpfully ambiguous orders from Marcy, assumed the men in Ostend were charged with drafting a bold and decisive statement—and thus they denounced Cuba's colonial rulers for fostering "tyranny and oppression . . . which may result in direful consequences to . . . America." In any revolutionary struggle, they warned, "it is vain to expect that the sympathies of the people of the United States will not be warmly enlisted in favor of their oppressed neighbors." And one neighbor, in particular, drew the ministers' predacious interest:

> After we shall have offered Spain a price for Cuba, far beyond its present value, and this shall have been refused, it will then be time to consider the question, does Cuba in the possession of Spain seriously endanger our internal peace and the existence of our cherished Union. Should this question be answered in the affirmative, then, by every law human and Divine, we shall be justified in wresting it from Spain, if we possess the power.

As though the preservation of their nation were not enough, the Manifesto's authors brazenly offered still another and altogether piratical proof for adventuring in Cuba: "Besides, the present is an age of adventure in which restless and daring spirits abound in every portion of the world."[23]

The American ministers thereupon scrambled for the high ground, seeking in their dispatch to strike a humanitarian note by balancing belligerency with benevolence. They promised to stamp out the African slave trade to Cuba and stressed the end of Spain's "wretched financial condition" with a quick infusion of American dollars. "Should Spain reject the present golden opportunity for developing her resources and removing her financial embarrassments," they contended, gracelessly engaging in an elaborate confidence game, "it may never again return."[24] They offered to go as high as $120 million.

Two days later, on the twentieth, Soulé wrote to Marcy from London, clearly unaware of the secretary's desire for some type of *diplomatic* maneuver (or miracle) to pry Cuba from Spain. Armed aggression had for months been off the table. But Soulé, noting that England and France were currently allied with the Ottoman Empire and Sardinia in a prolonged conflict to keep Russia out of the Middle East—the Crimean War (1853–1856)—thought the timing perfect to pressure Madrid. "Let it be now," he argued, "while the great powers of this continent are engaged in that stupendous struggle which cannot but engage all their strength and tax all their energies." The Pierce administration, however, though willing to give its diplomatic corps broad discretion, could not advocate the kind of naked aggression, for the entire world to see, couched in the audacious Manifesto. The *Times* of London, for one, denounced "the habitual pursuit of dishonorable objects by clandestine means" carried out by the American ministers; another critique called the Ostend statement a "highwayman's plea."[25]

After seeing the (embarrassing) diplomatic correspondence published, the Pierce administration repudiated the ham-handed Manifesto largely by ignoring it and Cuba remained in Spanish hands—until 1898, when another controversy regarding another American ship, the USS *Maine*, helped to ignite the kind of American response that Soulé and Quitman had called for in 1854.

With hindsight we know that the fumbling efforts of the Americans at Aix-la-Chapelle capped a prolonged period of antebellum expansion that had brought the Louisiana Purchase, Florida, and Texas, along with the

James Buchanan is robbed by four toughs who are mimicking the Ostend Manifesto, which proposed that the U.S., if refused the opportunity to purchase Cuba, take the island from Spain. Quoting from that document, one of the men demands the "immediate acquisition" of Buchanan's hat.

vast Mexican cession lands, to the United States. But these acquisitions became entangled ultimately in sectional concerns. It seems fair to say that this transitional phase in American diplomacy prefaced as well the passing of the men who had once so conspicuously coveted Cuba. Soulé, the driving force behind the Ostend Manifesto, resigned in 1855 and never held another government appointment; Mason served in Paris

until his death in 1859, and Buchanan, fortuitously out of the country during the toxic Kansas-Nebraska debates, captured the presidency in 1856 only to serve a disastrous single term that culminated in the secession of several southern states from the Union. The man who replaced Buchanan, Abraham Lincoln, embodied in midwestern farm, factory, and railroad republicanism the dominant political/economic direction of the century's second half. But in October 1854 he was only beginning to find his way.

17

Lincoln Arrives

This . . . *real* zeal for the spread of slavery, I can not but hate. I hate it because of the monstrous injustice of slavery itself. I hate it because it deprives our republican example of its just influence in the world.

Abraham Lincoln, 1854

Abraham Lincoln turned forty-five the year of the Kansas-Nebraska Act, ostensibly a statesman-in-waiting no more. Despite a respectable start, representing Sangamon County in the Illinois General Assembly before serving a single term in the United States Congress, a host of antebellum inconveniences appeared to bar his further ascent into the starry American political heavens. Illinois trended Democratic, though Lincoln identified as a Whig; southern slaveholders or their Yankee doughfaces all but owned the presidency; and no candidate hailing from west of the Ohio Valley had ever won the White House. Lincoln's accumulated handicaps might thus be shortlisted as a thrice-cursed case of wrong party, section, and state. But the canceling of the Missouri Compromise altered this archaic calculus, sweeping away old heroes, parties, and platforms. In its considerable commotion, few benefitted from the chaos quite like Lincoln.

Though a reluctant Republican, he helped to inaugurate a fresh regional dynamic—a rising Midwest—that ruled the nation's political roost for decades. Following Lincoln's death, Ohio-born candidates captured seven of the next nine presidential contests; during this period

(1868–1900) not a single southerner so much as sniffed a major party nomination. Lincoln's own Bluegrass roots give a certain poignancy to this story. Born in a one-room log cabin near Hodgenville, Kentucky, in 1809, he moved at the age of seven with his family to the Indiana Territory—"partly on account of slavery," he later observed. In 1830 the Lincolns relocated once again, this time to central Illinois; the following year Lincoln left on his own for New Salem, a spartan hamlet sitting on a sloping bluff above a milldam. Finally, in the spring of 1837, he settled in Springfield (formerly called "Calhoun" until the South Carolina senator's disputed views on states' rights became widely known) a city of twenty-five hundred and designated only months earlier as the state's next—succeeding Vandalia—capital. There the young country-bred lawyer languished in a rather awkward anonymity. "This thing of living in Springfield," he confided to a correspondent, "is rather a dull business. . . . I am quite as lonesome here as [I] ever was anywhere in my life. I have been spoken to by one woman since I've been here, and should not have been by her, if she could have avoided it. I've never been to church yet, nor probably shall not be soon. I stay away because I am conscious I should not know how to behave myself."[1]

Slowly these insecurities gave way and in 1839 Lincoln met his future wife, twenty-one-year-old Mary Todd, then visiting a sister in Springfield. The proud daughter of a well-to-do Lexington, Kentucky, banker said by a relative to be "generous and refined . . . and known throughout the State for his hospitality," Mary aspired to a certain genteel ideal.[2] She received a boarding school education and could speak French; the family, keepers of house slaves, lived in a fine two-story structure (formerly an inn and tavern) on Lexington's Main Street.

Comely and petite, quick if often precipitous, Mary attracted immediate attention in Springfield, playing the part of an urbane belle among a swarm of upstart farmers and merchants. Emily Todd Helm, a half sister, drew a memorable portrait of Mary's pleasing appearance as well as her sometimes stormy personality:

She had a plump, round figure, and was rather short in stature. Her features were not regularly beautiful, but she was certainly very pretty, with her lovely complexion, soft brown hair, and clear blue eyes, and intelligent bright face. . . . She was singularly sensitive. She was also impulsive, and made no attempt to conceal her feelings;

indeed it would have been an impossibility had she desired to do so, for her face was an index to every passing emotion. Without desiring to wound she occasionally indulged in sarcastic, witty remarks, that cut like a damascus blade; but there was no malice behind them.[3]

Mary and her long-limbed beau were wed in 1842; their contrasting regional loyalties remained forever a part of the turbulent marriage they made for themselves, never more so than during the Civil War when eight of Todd's thirteen adult full and half siblings supported the Confederacy. Of these, one succumbed to friendly fire near Baton Rouge, another died in Tennessee at the Battle of Shiloh, while yet another received a wound during the siege of Vicksburg along the heights of the Mississippi River. A brother-in-law, General Benjamin Helm, the son of a former Kentucky governor, was killed by a sharpshooter at Chickamauga in the autumn of 1863, having earlier spurned Lincoln's offer to serve as a Union Army paymaster.

These several casualties resulted from the collapse of the sectional compromises once common to American statecraft. Lincoln played a late and somewhat oppositional role in this process, taking, as a freshman member, a humble back row seat in the nation's 30th Congress during the closing stages of the Mexican-American War. In January 1848 he joined a slender 85 to 81 House majority—all Whigs, including an aged John Quincy Adams, who died just weeks later—in declaring that President Polk had precipitated the fighting by ordering U.S. forces onto Mexican territory without congressional approval. The clause called the war "unnecessarily and unconstitutionally begun." These few words attacked still more broadly the unsettled spirit of manifest destiny. "I will stake my life," Lincoln wrote the following month to his law partner and fellow Kentucky native William Herndon, "that if you had been in my place, you would have voted as I did. . . . That soil was not ours."[4]

Shortly after the resolution passed, Lincoln delivered a sharp attack on Polk in Congress. "I more than suspect already," he told his peers, "that he is deeply conscious of being in the wrong—that he feels the blood of this war, like the blood of Abel, is crying to Heaven against him." Back in Illinois, home of more Mexican-American War volunteers than any other state except Missouri, one Democratic gathering denounced the address as "treasonable." Along with other Whigs, Lincoln walked a fine partisan line in 1848. Though condemning the president, he praised

Zachary Taylor as a war hero, recognizing the popular general's political appeal. In late April he wrote to an Illinois colleague: "In my judgment, we can elect nobody but Gen. Taylor," who in fact received the Whig nomination in June. Lincoln, who had preferred Henry Clay, campaigned for the victor of Buena Vista (and a southern slaveholder) that summer, making a well-received speaking tour in New England. Assuring audiences that northern Whigs considered slavery "an evil," he won the respectful attention of northern Whig papers—the *Boston Daily Advertiser*, for one, thanked this callow midwestern congressman for delivering "one of the best speeches ever heard in Worcester."[5]

But best or otherwise, it could not keep Lincoln's seat warm in Washington. His district harbored several young Whig aspirants and as a condition for their support he had pledged not to run for reelection. Thus, when his congressional term ended in March 1849, he hoped to be appointed Commissioner of the General Land Office by a grateful Taylor, but that post went to another candidate and the new president offered Lincoln instead the governorship of the far-off Oregon Territory. Thinking this an unpalatable assignment, though officially pleading Mary's veto, he declined. Lincoln was now a private citizen, his barely realized political ambitions blocked, his future uncertain.

And so, for the next five years, until the Kansas-Nebraska Bill exploded, Lincoln, though engaged in a growing Springfield law practice, elsewise struck an attitude of abeyance. True, he gave a few stump speeches in 1852 for the lavishly bemedaled General Winfield Scott, whom Whigs hoped voters might conflate with earlier epaulette-wearing/sword-bearing executives of the Washington-Jackson-Taylor type, though his landslide loss to Pierce seemed to betoken Lincoln's own place on the losing side of the antebellum political divide. Watching both time and the cycle of elections pass him by, he wrote to a relative in the early 1850s: "I can no longer claim to be a young man myself."[6]

Deep demographic trends, however, were beginning to work in his favor. Illinois's population doubled in the 1850s to over 1.7 million, putting it behind only New York, Pennsylvania, and Ohio, while relegating vaunted Virginia, looking increasingly like a fading eighteenth-century power, to a distant fifth. Much of Illinois's growth occurred in the state's northern counties, where Whig and antislavery sentiment were strongest. The percentage of Illinois citizens of southern extraction, by contrast, dropped appreciably through the decade, from 17 to about 10 percent.

At the same time the number of immigrants increased from 13 to 19 percent; Irish arrivals tended to become Democrats while large numbers of Germans and Scandinavians found their way into Republican ranks. The state further took off as an economic force, becoming the country's largest grain producer and investing heavily in railroads. The Illinois Central, opening in 1856 and extending five hundred miles down the state from Galena to Cairo (its marshy lands described as "desolate" and "dismal" by a sojourning Charles Dickens), was for a time the world's longest railway. Men like Lincoln, argued historian Don E. Fehrenbacher, offered to this new enterprise "professional service as attorneys, lobbyists, and publicists. The railroads needed the friendship of public men and openly courted it with judicious distribution of their legal business, printing contracts, and other patronage. . . . Lincoln, although not a railroad promoter or investor, acted as counsel for a number of companies in the 1850s and was on a regular retainer basis with the Illinois Central during much of the decade."[7]

Illinois's emergence converged in 1854 with Douglas's efforts to legislate popular sovereignty into the western territories. Until that pivotal moment arrived Lincoln, so he later insisted to a biographer, "practiced law more assiduously than ever before" and, though "always a Whig," appeared to have turned his attention to more private concerns: "I was losing interest in politics." But then, he recounted, "the repeal of the Missouri Compromise aroused me again." In Illinois a Democratic-controlled legislature passed, over rising criticism, resolutions endorsing this contentious act. As a consequence, the bill's in-state opponents begin to collect into the kind of anti-Nebraska coalitions—à la Ripon and elsewhere—soon to cohere into a formal Republican resistance. Sensing the importance of the moment, "Appeal of the Independent Democrats" signatories Joshua Giddings and Salmon Chase, anxious to weaken Douglas's popularity at home, toured Illinois, speaking in the small Springfield courthouse among other sites.[8]

That September Douglas himself returned from Washington, confident he could weather the welling storm. Prior to giving a homecoming speech in Chicago before a hostile audience of some five thousand, he complained to a colleague, "They threaten a mob," adding unmindfully, "I have no fears. All will be right." Instead, protesters in the crowd, reserving "right" for themselves, unleashed a thick screen of hisses, slurs, and shouts that drowned out an occasionally foot-stomping, fist-shaking Douglas. Various objects were thrown at the speaker's platform, which precipitated several arrests and Douglas's angry retreat. The *Chicago Tribune* exulted, predicting that the city's indelicate handling of a former favorite son now sinner would "carry joy and strength to the hearts of the lovers of freedom, and dismay and panic into the ranks of the slaveocracy." Other postmortems were less sanguine. Greeley's *New-York Tribune* worried that mob violence threatened to snuff out free speech, while the *New York Herald* thought the "mob" hypocritical: "here we find the members of a party which has inscribed on its banners the motto, 'free speech—free labor—free men,' uniting to put down the exercise of a right guaranteed by the constitution."[9] Determined to meet this challenge head on, Douglas canvassed for the state's Democrats throughout the fall of 1854 with something more than his usual concentration. In a difficult year grown yet more demanding, the Little Giant now sought vindication through the political process. Here, on the campaign trail, he would encounter Lincoln.

On September 3, just two days after Douglas received Chicago's rude welcome, a Springfield Whig named Dr. William Jayne put an announcement in the *Illinois Journal* declaring Lincoln a candidate for the state legislature. On the road campaigning for incumbent national congressman Richard Yates, Lincoln could hardly register a protest at this time, but Mary, knowing her husband's disinterest in a mere state office, immediately sought Jayne out to acquaint him with this fact. Jayne listened but bided his time. And when Lincoln returned to the couple's comfortable five-room cottage at the corner of Eighth and Jackson Streets (enlarged two years later into a two-story Greek Revival), the doctor came calling to make a personal plea, insisting on the boon to Yates's candidacy should Lincoln's name also appear on the ballot. The presumptive candidate hesitated. He knew in this unusual year that an anti-Kansas-Nebraska nominee stood a real chance of winning a Senate seat, a post Lincoln coveted. He also realized, however, that he might be blamed should Yates fall to a Douglas Democrat and Whigs more generally fare poorly in Sangamon County. Cornered, he pragmatically if unenthusiastically agreed to make the state race.[10]

Now directly invested in the upcoming elections, Lincoln displayed a gravitas formerly lacking in his first political life. This resolution gave added strength and stature to his words that fall. Some years later John Nicolay and John Hay, both of whom served Lincoln in the White

House, though already at this time known to him through work or relations, remembered his progress in 1854:

> Men were surprised to find him imbued with an unwonted seriousness. They heard from his lips fewer anecdotes and more history. Careless listeners who came to laugh at his jokes were held by the strong current of his reasoning and the flashes of his earnest eloquence, and were lifted up by the range and tenor of his argument into a fresher and purer political atmosphere. The new discussion was fraught with deeper questions than the improvement of the Sangamon [River], protective tariffs, or the origin of the Mexican War.... [Rather, the Kansas-Nebraska Bill] furnished material for the inborn gifts of the speaker, his intuitive logic, his impulsive patriotism, his pure and poetical conception of legal and moral justice.[11]

Disturbed by Douglas's casual overturning of the Missouri Compromise and no doubt eager to enter again the political arena, Lincoln came to the fall campaign impatient to make his case.

Audiences in central Illinois encountered a tall, lean figure with tanned and toughened skin who, though only in his forties, evoked already in whispered tones the sobriquet "Old Abe." "He was not a pretty man by any means," Herndon recalled, and described his law partner as "homely ... careless of his looks, plain-looking and plain-acting." One noticed immediately upon encountering an upright Lincoln the striking length of his legs. "In sitting down on a common chair he was no taller than ordinary men," Herndon continued. "His legs and arms were abnormally, unnaturally long, and in undue proportion to the reminder of his body. It was only when he stood up that he loomed above other men." Lincoln weighed 180 pounds and stood six feet, four inches—about nine inches taller than the average mid-nineteenth-century American male. An 1854 daguerreotype taken in Chicago shows him with a mess of clipped if unkempt dark hair, cadaverous cheekbones, and a strong, protrusive chin. His eyes are sunken and shadowy; the large nose "a little awry toward the right eye," so Herndon insisted, gave some surface symmetry to the protruding ears and thick lower lip that resided above a conspicuously bobbing Adam's apple. A prominent mole graced the right cheek. Nearly a decade later Walt Whitman, working as a volunteer nurse in Civil War Washington's army hospitals, lovingly described

Lincoln as having "a face like a Hoosier Michael Angelo, so awful ugly it becomes beautiful, with its strange mouth, its deep cut, criss-cross lines, and its doughnut complexion."[12]

All through the late summer and an active autumn, Lincoln honed his attack on Douglas. Following a speech in Winchester at a Scott County Whig meeting, the *Illinois Journal* said he "exhibited the great wrong and injustice of the repeal of the Missouri Compromise" in a manner "replete with unanswerable arguments, which must and will effectually *tell* at the coming election." Days later Lincoln again hammered away at the popular sovereignty platform, this time in a two-hour speech in Carrollton, and followed that up with correspondence and editorials on the same subject. In a September 7 letter to John McAuley Palmer, an anti-Nebraska Democratic state senator from nearby Macoupin County, he struck a note of conciliation in what he supposed to be a shared skirmish: "You know how anxious I am that this Nebraska measure shall be rebuked and condemned every where. . . . You are, and always have been, *honestly*, and *sincerely* a democrat; and I know how painful it must be to an honest sincere man, to be urged by his party to the support of a measure, which on his conscience he believes to be wrong." He then suggested that Palmer put "his conscience" before party: "You have had a severe struggle with yourself, and you have determined *not* to swallow the *wrong*. Is it not just to yourself that you should, in a few public speeches, state your reasons, and thus justify yourself? I wish you would."[13]

Four days later, on the eleventh, a Lincoln opinion piece excoriating the Kansas-Nebraska Act ("this outrage") appeared in the *Illinois Journal*, and over the next three weeks its author gave speeches in Bloomington and Springfield following Douglas addresses in these same cities, the senator refusing to debate a mere candidate for state office. "This is my meeting," Douglas said of the Bloomington appearance. "The people came here to hear me."[14] These performances prefaced Lincoln's famous Peoria talk, delivered on October 16. Subsequently transcribed by Lincoln—hence its value, we have his words unmediated by editorial go-betweens—and published over several installments in the *Illinois Journal*, it elevated his stature considerably, contributing to his eventual notice as a national figure.

The state's second-largest city, with a population approaching ten thousand, Peoria hugged the left bank of the Illinois River, seventy miles north of Springfield. Lincoln knew it well, having transacted in this coming county seat a great deal of legal business over the previous two decades. In 1840 he delivered there his first campaign speech, for the victorious Whig William Henry Harrison.

Lincoln's emergence in 1854 benefitted considerably from a rivalrous in-state association with the nationally known Douglas, presumably on his way to the presidency. Their differences begged for attention. Newspaper editors printed the two men's clashing views of the western territories; illustrators sported with the corporeal contrast in a towering Lincoln hovering above an elfin Douglas; and Illinois voters grew accustomed to seeing their names conjoined in a fierce struggle bedeviling the country. Peoria proved so consequential for Lincoln largely because Douglas had spoken there earlier in the day. Reduced by weeks of canvassing to a raspy delivery and aware of Lincoln's telling shots on the campaign trail, the senator dreaded a long series of sharp exchanges with, so he told a colleague, "the most difficult and dangerous opponent that I have ever met."[15] Not wishing to be accused of ducking Lincoln, however, Douglas agreed that his critic might speak after his own address. Thus Peoria received in a single long afternoon (and part of a night) one of the more intense tutorials on the subject of slavery and the territories delivered that year.

Both Lincoln and Douglas probably lodged at the Peoria House, a sturdy four-story building reputed to be the largest hotel in Illinois. The next day they met at the courthouse on Adams Street, a Greek Revival brick and stone structure erected eight years earlier. The debate took place on the steps of this building, which faced an adjoining lawn accommodating some two thousand attendees. Hoping to minimize Lincoln's effectiveness, Douglas spoke for over three hours, concluding a bit after five o'clock and thus, he supposed, leaving little time for a rebuttal before a restive audience, desiring its dinner, drifted off. A seasoned orator, he adeptly defended popular sovereignty as a democratic agent "to allow the people of the territory to decide domestic questions for themselves," all the while rejecting on climatic grounds the notion that slavery might actually gain a foothold in the presumably arid West. He thought his critics susceptible, moreover, to the wheedling of dangerous abolitionists. Effusive cheers and the outburst of an attendant band greeted the conclusion of Douglas's speech; the crowd now called for Lincoln, who shrewdly suggested a break of an hour or so that the audience might stretch and sup before regathering. He planned to speak for as long as Douglas.[16]

At seven o'clock, his gaunt visage lit by candles and lanterns, Lincoln turned to the crowd. Speaking in shirtsleeves, a concession to an unusually warm evening, he proceeded in a slightly shrill and halting cadence, searching for an internal rhythm. In a matter of moments, he began to sweat, and his dark matted hair looked askew. Herndon, who had witnessed Lincoln on many occasions in court, noted that when he began a speech "his body inclined forward to a slight degree. At first he was very awkward, and it seemed a real labor to adjust himself to his surroundings." Soon, however, "he became somewhat animated," bobbing his head, and "as he moved along in his speech he became freer and less uneasy in his movements; to that extent he was graceful. He had a perfect naturalness, a strong individuality; and to that extent he was dignified."[17]

Lincoln opened his address on an ironic note. Declaring Thomas Jefferson "perhaps . . . the most distinguished politician of our history," he asked his audience to remember that this Virginia planter called for slavery's restriction in the Northwest Territory, an area encompassing much of the Midwest including, of course, present-day Illinois. This region, Lincoln argued, "is now what Jefferson foresaw and intended—the happy home of teeming millions of free, white, prosperous people, and no slave among them." The men and women he now faced, in other words, were the lucky sons and daughters of a free-soil theory suddenly under threat.[18]

Lincoln next referred to Douglas directly, quoting from an 1849 speech in which the senator had lavishly praised the Compromise as a sacred pledge deserving of "the sanction and approbation of men of all parties in every section of the Union." It had, Douglas observed in words that could now only mock his new emphasis on popular sovereignty, "allayed all sectional jealousies and irritations" related to slavery. Disinclined to South-bait, Lincoln hastened to add that the peculiar institution challenged the humanity of all Americans. "The Southern people . . . are just what we would be in their situation," he said. "My first impulse would be to free all the slaves, and send them to Liberia," he continued, though recognizing the practical impossibility of such a plan. He next raised the prospect of "mak[ing] them politically and socially our equals" but found this equally impractical. "My own feelings will not admit of this, and if mine would, we well know that those of the great mass of whites will not." Instead, he clung to the hope of gradual emancipation, though acknowledging even in this instance, "I will not undertake to judge our brethren of the South."[19]

He would, however, judge Douglas. And in a lawyerly, forensic fashion he proceeded to demolish the senator's insistence that a harsh, inhospitable climate prevented slavery from expanding beyond its Deep South stronghold. Such a notion, Lincoln said, laughing, "is a palliation, a lullaby." He pointed out, rather, that no fewer than five slave states—Maryland, Virginia, Delaware, Kentucky, and Missouri—were north of the Missouri Compromise line; and the census of 1850 showed that nearly a quarter of all the nation's slaves toiled in these border areas. Lincoln further picked apart Douglas's claim that popular sovereignty involved only a *local* population's right to rule. Rather, he maintained, "The whole nation is interested that the best use shall be made of these Territories." For more than two centuries, Europeans had come to the New World in search of a new start, and "free states," he argued, "are the places for poor people to go to, and better their condition." An expansive plantocracy, in other words, endeavored to shut off areas for free labor, and thus threatened the white working class with a different kind of servitude.[20]

At bottom, Lincoln thought slavery inarguably injurious to the nation. It corrupted the idea of property rights, pitted northern abolitionists against southern fire-eaters, and threatened to enflame a real shooting war in Kansas. Morally, he found the institution indefensible. "No man is good enough to govern another man without the other's consent," he flatly stated. "I say this is the leading principle, the sheet-anchor of American republicanism."[21] Straining to close on a consensual key, he claimed a shared destiny for the sections—if not the world:

> Let North and South—let all Americans—let all lovers of liberty everywhere join in the great and good work. If we do this, we shall not only have saved the Union, but we shall have saved it [so] . . . that the succeeding millions of free happy people, the world over, shall rise up and call us blessed to the latest generation.[22]

Some years later, in December 1862, with the country locked in a deadly fraternal war, Lincoln reprised these words in his annual message to Congress: "Fellow-citizens, *we* cannot escape history. . . . In *giving* freedom to the *slave*, we *assure* freedom to the *free*—honorable alike in what we give, and what we preserve. We shall nobly save, or meanly lose, the last best, hope of earth."[23]

Horace White, a young journalist on the *Chicago Evening Journal*, had followed Lincoln for several weeks on the autumn campaign trail. He later described the Peoria speech as "the first public occasion that laid a strong hold upon [Lincoln's] conscience and stirred the depths of his nature." It further, so he claimed, reduced Douglas's popular sovereignty panacea to "a heap of ruins." Lincoln embellished his Peoria laurels with speeches in Chicago and Quincy, catching the attention, so one reporter said, of "all men, of all parties."[24]

The country's first Republican president, Lincoln might be considered the ultimate beneficiary of this upheaval, though he personally desired nothing more in 1854 than to retain the existing Democratic-Whig concert. Terribly impressed by the sequence of sectional compromises conducted by Henry Clay ("my beau ideal of a statesman"), Lincoln lingered over the notion that Clay's party might yet frame another settlement—he wanted above all to restore the Missouri Compromise.[25] But the time for such conciliations had run out, and Whiggery proved to be among its greatest casualties.

Though a dying concern, Clay's old party remained in 1854 perhaps the only viable political home for Lincoln, who kept a careful distance from the abolitionists and could not as yet gage the strength of the Independent Democrats. Budding Republicanism, moreover, had yet to concentrate anti-Kansas-Nebraska sentiment into a single association. And so Lincoln remained a Whig. He declined to attend a Republican convention in Springfield that October and refused an invitation the following month to appear at a Republican State Central Committee meeting in Chicago. "I suppose my opposition to the principle of slavery is as strong as that of any member of the Republican party," he wrote the abolitionist Ichabod Codding, "but I had also supposed that the extent to which I feel authorized to carry that opposition, practically, was not at all satisfactory to that party."[26]

By this time, the November elections had upended Illinois. Anti-Nebraska candidates captured five of the state's nine congressional House seats while the state legislature swung decisively in their direction as well, 59 to 41. Naming a new senator constituted this incoming body's first order of business, and if these fusionists could join together, they would control the selection. Lincoln, elected to the legislature, quickly resigned and angled openly for the Senate seat. "It has come round that a whig may, by possibility, be elected to the U.S. Senate; and I want the chance of being that man," he wrote to Thomas Henderson, a member of the Illinois House. "You are a member of the Legislature, and have a vote to give. Think it over, and see whether you can do better than to go for me."[27]

But therein lay Lincoln's difficulty. For though his speaking tour had energized Illinois politics, more established men were also crafting their upper chamber cases. The incumbent, James Shields, an Irish immigrant and Democrat, is perhaps dimly remembered by a sliver of scholars as the only senator in the nation's history to represent three different states—and for once challenging Lincoln to a duel. More than a decade earlier the future president, then a young Springfield lawyer, had publicly impugned Shields, a state auditor at the time, for declaring paper currency issued from the recently closed State Bank of Illinois unacceptable for payment of taxes. A defender of the bank's interests before the legislature, Lincoln, adopting the nom de plume "Rebecca," raised the possibility in a local gazette that hard-money Democrats like Shields (advocates of gold and silver currency) had falsely proclaimed a financial crunch in Illinois that they might now attack the bank's paper-money policy, and by association the pro-paper Whig Party. Thus Shields's decree constituted, so "Rebecca" insisted, nothing less than "a lie, and not a well told one at that. It grins out like a copper dollar. Shields is a fool as well as a liar. With him truth is out of the question."[28] This low satire was not one of Lincoln's better moments.

With a little editing from Mary Todd and her friend Julia Jayne (the good doctor's wife), the letter appeared in the September 2 *Sangamon Journal*. On learning shortly thereafter that an angry Shields considered seeking satisfaction, the two women imprudently, though with a certain coltish hilarity, proceeded to egg on the controversy by drafting their own note as "Aunt Rebecca." "Let him only come here," they wrote, "and he may squeeze my hand. . . . If that ain't personal satisfaction, I can only say that he is the fust man that was not satisfied with squeezing my hand." Decidedly unsatisfied, Shields wrote Lincoln on the seventeenth, desiring "a full, positive and absolute retraction of all offensive allusions used by you in these communications." After a bit of toing and froing, the two men actually agreed to a duel. As the challenged party Lincoln had pick of weaponry and, with a considerable height and reach advantage, poked at the situation's absurdity by choosing cavalry broadswords. "I did not intend to hurt Shields unless I did so clearly in self-defense," he later stated. "If it had been necessary I could have split him from the crown of his head to the end of his backbone."[29]

Dueling in Illinois constituted a crime, and so the aggrieved parties agreed to meet across the Mississippi in Missouri. But there, with the aid of handlers and presumably a healthy fund of common sense, they ended up shaking hands having spilt no blood. Now, more than a decade later, Lincoln faced Shields in a much different kind of contest—though a number of other contenders also blocked his return to Washington.

On February 8, 1855, following a prodigious snowstorm, the Illinois legislature met in the Hall of Representatives to select a senator. "Every inch of space on the floor and lobby was occupied by members and their political friends, and the gallery was adorned by well-dressed women, including Mrs. Lincoln," one observer remembered. "The excitement was intense."[30] Lincoln held a slim lead over Shields on the first ballot 45 to 41, with the anti-Kansas-Nebraska Democrat Lyman Trumbull a distant third and Democratic governor Joel Matteson even further behind. After six rounds it became clear that Shields, tainted by his support for the Missouri Compromise's repeal, could not win and his backing moved to Matteson.

By the ninth ballot Lincoln had dipped to only 15 votes, while Trumbull stood at a tenuous 35 and Matteson surged to 47, only 3 shy of victory. Choosing the lesser of two evils—an anti-Douglas Democrat over a Douglas Democrat—Lincoln directed his diehards to support Trumbull—who then, on the next canvass, claimed the prize. The following day Lincoln, putting on a brave face, wrote to a colleague: "I regret my defeat moderately." Trumbull's defection and election by Whig and fusion votes, he knew, had humbled the Illinois Democrats. "It is a great consolation," he quipped, "to see them worse whipped than I am."[31]

The autumn electoral season more broadly produced similar revelatory results throughout the North. In consequence, the nation's ailing majority party, its ties going back to Jefferson and the eighteenth-century planter South, faced the unwelcome prospect of becoming a minority party. If this trend continued, the character of antebellum partisanship, along with its undercurrent of questionable compromises, would never be the same.

18

Electoral Upheaval

We consider the Whig Party a thing of the past.
New-York Tribune, October 1854

In the crucial 1854 congressional elections, a hodgepodge of parties battled the Democrats. Considering that within two years the Republicans emerged as the dominant northern partisan voice and would soon after capture the first of six consecutive presidential elections, a feat equaled in our history only by the Democratic-Republican triumvirate of Jefferson, Madison, and Monroe (1800–1820), one might be excused for assuming its easy ascendancy.[1] But this was not the case. Many Americans, rather, cleaved tenaciously to both the Whigs and the Democrats as established national networks engaged in the struggle to ease sectional disputes. Republicans, by contrast, were regarded by these traditionalists as dangerously radical and the epithets "Abolition party" and "Black Republicans" received fairly wide circulation. If overstated, these attacks nevertheless drew attention to a growing element of Yankee opposition to the peculiar institution and its planter chieftains. "He, who believes slavery to be a great wrong and desires to promote its abolition by political action," wrote Salmon Chase about this time, "is a political abolitionist."[2]

Republicans entered the autumn contest a coalition of contradictions. These moving pieces included an antislavery wing, as well as a larger body of free-laboring farmers and wage earners, and a third cluster of merchants and manufacturers concerned, noting the hardening degree of southern obstinacy, with the Union's future. Many disgruntled northern (former) Democrats also filed in line. Only a major crisis could bring these disparate constituencies together, and that impasse arrived in the guise of the Kansas-Nebraska Act. With great clusters of northern opinion already exasperated by the Mexican-American War and the Fugitive Slave Law, Douglas's ill-considered bill opened a Pandora's box for more far-reaching opposition to the Slave Power than the Whig Party, a national organization with a southern wing, could have ever accomplished.

Weeks before the fall elections, Charles Sumner, already a Republican, in contrast to more circumspect men like Lincoln and Seward, delivered an address at Worcester Commons designed to lift the new party's profile. This prominent spot, site, in 1776, of the Declaration of Independence's first public reading in New England, fairly begged for a Revolutionary-era association. Calling Sumner "the most conspicuously representative man" in the state "since the death of John Quincy Adams," the chairman of the committee in charge of the event, John A. Andrew, declaimed in his invitation that all "are . . . anxious to greet you." These ripe words were more than mere flattery. As one nineteenth-century historian has written of the event, "Never did a public man receive a heartier and more enthusiastic welcome. . . . Never had [Sumner] been so near the heart of Massachusetts as then." The audience rose as one, unleashing a series of powerful cheers that purled through the air to receive the senator. His fiery speech, "Duties of Massachusetts at This Crisis," prefaced a conference of candidate nominations for the coming in-state canvass, though it stands in a still broader sense as a critique of the nation's ailing governing system. Assured of a friendly hearing, Sumner spoke for an hour and a half, his more telling points punctuated "by loud and prolonged applause." Linking the Kansas-Nebraska crisis with Anthony Burns's humiliating rendition via "a prostituted militia," he called for a new partisan approach to replace the old Democratic-Whig consensus in the free states. The section must bravely rally "as Republicans," he insisted, "to encounter the Oligarchs of Slavery."[3]

Not everyone agreed, of course. Several Massachusetts Whigs were at pains to point out, rather, that the northern wing of their party had voted en masse against the Kansas-Nebraska Act—and that Republicans, radical or otherwise, could hardly have done more. Tainted by association with their southern Whig brethren, some swore off any future cooperation in that questionable quarter—but this admission only posed the problem of whether a *national* two-party system could then be sustained. And if not, then what distinguished, at least in the northern states, Whigs from Republicans? The former seemed incapable and the latter unwilling to forge yet another so-called compromise. In either case, a continuation of the old ways of conciliation looked to be a thing of a now and not so fondly remembered past. Still, the residue (if not inertia) of partisanship remained strong and Massachusetts Republicans fought an uphill battle in 1854. "I can do my duty more efficiently and sincerely," the conservative Bay State congressman Thomas Dawes Eliot wrote to Sumner in something of a representative statement shortly after the Worcester speech, "as a Whig than in any other way."[4]

By which, Eliot meant, rejecting not one but *two* new parties. For in Massachusetts, as well as in other electorally large states such as New York and Illinois, attempts to create dominant Republican organizations were countered by the sudden emergence of a growing nativist movement. To many northerners, in other words, their section faced both the power of the plantocracy and the growing political influence of immigrants. One student of the subject notes the astonishing spike in late antebellum European crossings that provoked a fierce nativist backlash:

> Decade after decade, the pace of immigration quickened, peaking in 1854 when more than 400,000 Europeans settled in America. From 1845 to 1854, some 2,900,000 immigrants landed in the United States, more than had come in the seven previous decades combined. As a percentage of the nation's total population, the influx of immigrants from 1845 to 1854, amounting to 14.5 percent of the 1845 population, has never been surpassed.[5]

Possibly as many as 1 million Irish (out of a pre-famine population of 8 million) came to the United States during this period, part of a larger exodus fleeing a potato blight that occasioned unrest across the Continent. Almost as many Germans migrated as well, including political exiles, displaced artisans unable to compete in an increasingly industrialized economy, and those more generally escaping poverty, unemployment, and rising food prices—the Hungry Forties having touched a number of European nations and empires. Immigrants, many lacking work skills, tended to congregate in America's cities, which made them conspicuous while also slowing assimilation. Aside from a few notable Catholic enclaves—New Orleans and Baltimore, Louisville and St. Louis—the recent arrivals tended to avoid the South, where slavery both depressed employment for white workers and undermined the dignity of labor.[6]

Historically, fears of "popery" had long teased the Anglo imagination on both sides of the Atlantic, conjuring up feverish images of the 130-ship Spanish Armada anchored off Calais (1588) and the Gunpowder Plot to blow up Parliament (1605); it further gave sanction to the Glorious Revolution's overthrow of England's last Catholic monarch, King James II, in 1688. Beginning in the 1830s, anti-Catholic riots and violence had emerged as unwelcome facets of life in various American cities; convents and churches were especially targeted for destruction.[7]

In 1849 Charles B. Allen of Manhattan organized the Order of the Star Spangled Banner, an oath-bound society whose members pledged to limit the political power of both immigrants and the parties—mainly Democratic—they joined. The Order constituted at this time but one of the country's many nativist organizations; several Ohio cities, for example, including Youngstown, Cleveland, and Cincinnati fielded such clubs. By the spring of 1854 the semi-secretive Order had come to be more generally identified as the Know-Nothings for their supporters' coached reticence to oblige news reporters' queries. It briefly emerged as a major faction in the shake-up brought about by the Kansas-Nebraska Act.

The movement drew a broad cross section of Anglo adherents including, beyond a de rigueur anti-Catholicism, critics of slavery and proponents of temperance. The party openly trafficked in bigotry and not a little paranoia. Broadly speaking, it feared a popish plot bent on overturning America's "Protestant liberties" of democracy and property rights. As a result of this and other scapegoating fever dreams it called for restrictions on immigration, a permanent ban on office holding for the foreign born, and a remarkably long residency requirement—twenty-one years—for citizenship.

The clinging power of anti-Catholicism in America might be realized by recalling that more than a century later, in the waning summer of 1960, then–presidential candidate John F. Kennedy met with a group of Protestant ministers in Houston. Addressing what he called "the so-called religious issue," Kennedy argued that "the real issues in this campaign have been obscured" by those who sought to disparage his faith.[8] He further referenced Jefferson—architect of Virginia's Revolutionary era establishment of religious freedom—for promoting toleration of all creeds in an ecumenical republic. That he felt the need to take up the indelicate subject testified to its lingering purchase, perhaps having crested in 1854.

It is telling, considering Know-Nothingism's short shelf life, that it found a sudden popularity at the precise moment that the country's prevailing partisan system began to implode. Only when sectional issues relating to slavery became, in the wake of the Mexican-American War, too large for politics-as-usual to handle did a politics-of-the-unusual come into play. This, perhaps as much as any foreigner phobia, is what attracted as many as 1.5 million Americans to join the Know-Nothings, and what further explains the rapid mobilization in just a few months in 1854 of a rising Republican opposition. Both coalitions were inimical to the Democrats, whose northern wing pocketed immigrant votes while pandering to the Slave Power. These concerns coalesced in the argument that Irish Catholics provided decisive support for Democrats on critical issues, including the right to extend slavery into the western territories. Some nativists thought they detected this noxious entente in the narrowly fought Kansas-Nebraska Act, as well as in Pierce's appointment the previous year of new postmaster general James Campbell, the country's first Catholic cabinet officer. The much-followed U.S. tour (June 1853–February 1854) of Archbishop Gaetano Bendini, an envoy of Pope Pius IX tasked to "observe the state of religion" in America, also raised certain suspicions.[9]

In their efforts to contain Catholicism, Know-Nothings pushed for moral reform, including liquor laws and temperance mandates as a hedge against the evils of "Rum and Romanism." Along such overlapping lines, some conservative Whigs, themselves parlor patrons of moderation and sobriety, consorted with nativists. These men further recognized in the anti-immigrant crusade a possible diversion from the slavery question then moving like a wrecking ball through American politics. With their own party in eclipse, many of them chose to align with Know-Nothingism. No doubt some wishfully conceived of this awkward alliance as the foundation for a great unionist faction that might replace Whiggery, edge aside radical "black" Republicanism, and, when called upon, repeat the past to craft the occasional sectional compromise.[10]

Northern Know-Nothings, however, were more opposed to the westerly course of bondage than many Whigs suspected. In Boston, a Brahmin stronghold of intense anti-Irish sentiment, the city's *Evening Telegraph* argued: "Slavery and Catholicism are essentially one"; Mason Tappan, the New Hampshire nativist formerly a Free-Soiler, noted that his new political affiliation "says nothing about ignoring the slavery question"; and Washington's *National Era*, though critical of the Know-Nothings, nevertheless acknowledged that "many Anti-Slavery men . . . have joined the new party."[11] Given the volatile times, it is clear that Yankee voters were searching for a fresh political framework to assert their concerns. Nativism's broadening appeal in 1854 thus rested on its opposition to both the urban boss and the southern enslaver. Each took advantage, the argument ran, of a constitutional system that, through the three-fifths compromise and the marshaling of ethnic votes, provided two minority special interests with power that could be used to bypass the concerns of white, Protestant, free-laboring constituencies.

In November the second American party system suffered a near-fatal blow. Of the forty-four northern House Democrats who had supported the Kansas-Nebraska bill, only seven survived. As a result, Democratic representation above the Mason-Dixon Line shrank from 91 seats to a shocking 25. This contraction ensured that the party's southern wing, the branch most dedicated to slavery's extension, though constituting only a modest bloc of all Democrats in the country, could now decree party policy. But to what end? In the previous (33rd) Congress, Democrats and Whigs held a combined 228 of the 234 House seats; now they claimed only about 135 (affiliation uncertain in a handful of cases).[12] In the more aristocratic Senate, and with only a third of its body facing voters, no such implosion occurred, though the seating of a half-dozen Republicans, Free-Soilers, and Know-Nothings gave an indication of the prevailing political mood.

The degree of anti-Kansas-Nebraska sentiment in the northern states is striking. Of New York's thirty-one incoming congressmen, all but two condemned Douglas's bill—the same can be said of nearly the entire slate of successful lower-house candidates in Pennsylvania, Indiana, and Ohio.[13] In Massachusetts, a hub of Irish immigration, this anti-Democrat alignment contributed to a strong Know-Nothing majority. Many Anglos resented the economic movement in recent decades toward an enveloping industrial system based in greater Boston and took their frustrations out at the polls. The fading agrarian tradition, with its arcadian connections to craft, skilled, and artisanal labor, gave way now to the raw redundancy of factory labor. And though exploited in depressing sweatshops and pinched uncomfortably in blighted North End neighborhoods, the Irish were made in some sense to stand as the symbols of this deep and uncertain change in New England life.

As a result, the Know-Nothings, joined by a strong contingent of Free-Soilers who believed, so the *Boston Commonwealth* reported, that the city's "Catholic press upholds the slave power," captured all eleven Bay State congressional contests. They also claimed the copper-domed statehouse and elected the opportunistic convert Henry J. Gardner—a wool merchant and former Whig now occupied in full-throated denouncements of immigrants, slavery, and alcohol—governor over the incumbent Whig, Emory Washburn. Gardner captured an astonishing 63 percent of the vote. Prior to the polling, a Worcester man told a reporter for Greeley's *Tribune* that nativists "will form an overwhelming majority in all our cities and large towns—in Boston, Salem . . . Springfield, New Bedford, etc.—and will be found numerous even in the smaller towns. They expect to cast 50,000 votes this fall." In fact, they exceeded 80,000, some 60 percent of tallied ballots, dwarfing the combined 48,000 earned by Whigs, Democrats, and Republicans.[14]

The rest of New England gave congressional majorities to both Know-Nothings (in New Hampshire, Connecticut, and Rhode Island) and a fusion of anti-Kansas-Nebraska coalitions (in Maine and Vermont). In common, these states combined with Massachusetts to radically reduce Democratic representation in the region. Only a single Democratic congressman (from Maine, formerly a Jacksonian stronghold) survived.

In the western states, the cradle of the embryonic Republican Party, Know-Nothingism counted for considerably less. As in New England, immigration strongly impacted the region (peaking in Wisconsin's 33 percent foreign-born population), though these largely Protestant and northern European people—principally Germans and Scandinavians—

sparked comparatively fewer tensions. Regarded as diligent, productive, and industrious, they got on well with their native-born neighbors.
"Our German settlers," so one Illinois newspaper observed, "are valuable acquisitions to the state and are doing good service in opening
up its waste places to the hand of cultivation. . . . It is seldom, indeed,
that we hear of one being in the poor house or under the care of a pau-
per committee."[15] With this relative restraint of ethno-cultural tensions,
Know-Nothings failed to capture even a single congressional seat in the
region; Republican-led opposition tickets, rather, claimed majorities in
five of these states, while Iowa split.

Elections were held over a number of days and a frustrated Douglas
suffered a prolonged agony. A political colleague wrote to him shortly
before Illinois balloted that "the disasters in Penn., Ohio and Indiana
have driven from us every doubtful vote" and predicted that Illinois
itself "is lost at least for a time." In late October Senator James Shields,
soon, as noted in the previous chapter, to surrender his seat, confided
to the editor of the *Illinois State Register*, "The Anti Nebraska feeling
is too deep—more than I thought it was." Douglas himself recognized
only belatedly the coming electoral crisis, though in its wake he spurned
responsibility, blaming, in a rattling fashion, fusion's success on anything but the Kansas-Nebraska Act. After the votes were counted and
the Democratic Party's defeat seemed complete, he huffed that the Missouri Compromise's repeal meant very little compared to the "cruci-
ble into which poured Abolitionism, Maine liquor law-ism, and . . . the
Protestant feeling against the Catholic."[16]

Taking the opposite view, Greeley's *Tribune*, exulting in its timely
support of the Republican Party, pinned the election results on Yankee doughfaces. Under the late leadership of Daniel Webster and President Millard Fillmore (assuming office as an accidental executive upon
Zachary Taylor's death in 1850), northern Whigs, so a series of *Tribune* editorials argued, disastrously defended the Fugitive Slave Act and
thus unwittingly cut the party's throat. This "successful attempt" to place
the party "on a pro-slavery platform" anticipated, so the paper said, the
betrayal of the Kansas-Nebraska Act and led to Whiggery's well-earned
defeat in 1854.[17] A little hyperbole aside, these print prognostications
got it right, for the elections demonstrated, if anything, the failure of an
antediluvian system to deal effectively with the deepening sectional crisis. As the emblems of an older order, northern Whigs and Democrats

were now paying the high price for the sequence of altercations and legislation—the Burns case, the brewing war in Kansas, the failed popular sovereignty panacea—that they helped set in motion. Events were now beginning to move beyond their control.

In degrees of resentment and confusion they struggled, in their post-election postmortems, to understand why. An angry Illinois editor, ignoring Douglas's disastrous bill, complained in a hit-and-miss manner, "The Democratic banner has gone down before the torrent of abolitionism, Whigism, freesoilism, religious bigotry and intolerance." A Whig paper in Buffalo could offer little more than a bleak obituary: "We are utterly wrecked. It is altogether idle to think of a reconstruction of the Whig Party. It is past all surgery, past all medicine." Salmon Chase, however, much cheered by the stunning snub of old guardism, noted with particular relish the results in his native Ohio. Here, he assured one correspondent in late December, a genuine "People's movement" arose "for the purpose of . . . rebuking the proslavery action of the Administration Party."[18] Having months earlier launched, with a small group of renegade Independent Democrats, the anti-Kansas-Nebraska movement in Congress, Chase might have thought himself author, in some sense, of this most extraordinary election cycle.

Because of the unusual volatility in the recent campaign, the country's political future remained for the moment unclear. And considering the results in New England, nativism looked to many at least as likely as Republicanism to become the North's dominant antislavery shield. But this posed certain problems, for Know-Nothingism contained a fairly significant southern presence—that region sending more American Party candidates to Congress in 1854 than the Midwest. In their fear of foreign influence, these Dixie nativists could see the specter of radicalism and social breakdown, an echo of the dystopic scenario of overcrowded Yankee cities advanced in George Fitzhugh's *Sociology for the South*. Further, and perhaps more importantly, these men anticipated in Know-Nothingism a probable replacement for Whiggery and its still-resonant strain of southern unionism.

But Dixie's Know-Nothings firmly backed the extension of slavery in the territories and thus shattered any hopes of making their party a national presence. A few months after the elections, at a national council meeting in Philadelphia, northern nativists from several states walked out when their southern compeers, along with certain consensus-seeking allies, incautiously passed a platform favoring the Kansas-Nebraska Act. The party had failed, so North Carolina nativist Kenneth Raynor wrote, to avoid "that dangerous rock of slavery." In the North, the fusion of Republicans and Know-Nothings ultimately favored the former, as the cause of free labor proved more compelling to more people than that of nativism. The preservation of the Union eclipsed concerns of foreign influence and convinced a growing number of Yankees to cast their lot with the Republicans, who cooperated by calling for internal improvements and protective tariffs—platform-expanding issues dear to many old and ex-Whigs. Their efforts were altogether successful. As the historian David M. Potter wrote some years ago, "The nativist-antislavery alliance had been made to work with a minimum of nativism and a maximum of antislavery."[19]

This union, if somewhat one-sided, seems appropriate considering the significant affinities connecting Republicans and northern Know-Nothings. Aside from condemning slavery's extension, both camps appealed to similar Protestant constituencies while drawing membership from the same social classes. They further incorporated a common and occasionally conspiratorial suspicion of elites into their respective world views, be they distant southern power brokers seeking to close off the West to white settlement, or the almighty Church of Rome, armed with the potent weight of superstition and a legion of black-clad Jesuits plotting to overturn republican government. Critics of these much-bruited-about villains often pointed out their salacious sides, commenting at length upon the sexual exploits of the parish priest and the incestuous planter, whose fields were worked by his own dark-skinned children. The regional overlap in the two movements is also worth noting. Know-Nothing and antislavery sentiment were strongest in New England, thus suggesting the common threads, platforms, and prejudices that linked these Yankee reformers in coalescing crusades.[20]

In reducing Whiggery to a near nullity, nativism achieved its greatest impact. For this allowed thousands of former Whigs—men like Lincoln and Seward, soon to be the first great leaders of the Republican Party—to gracefully extricate themselves from perishing partisan loyalties. As Ohio congressman Joshua Giddings smartly put it, Know-Nothingism offered a "screen . . . behind which members of old political organizations could escape unseen from party shackles." Another Ohioan, Roeliff Brinkerhoff, editor of the *Mansfield Herald* and formerly a tutor to

Andrew Jackson's adopted son, remembered the success of nativist candidates in 1854 as "simply a stepping-stone to what followed. It enabled disaffected Whigs or Democrats to act together in secret, and prepared them for open co-operation in the . . . Republican Party."[21]

Though Whiggery briefly tottered on, even holding a presidential nominating convention in Baltimore in 1856 where a rump remnant of Silver Gray Whigs nominated former president Fillmore to run under the nativist banner, the party never recovered. "I take it to be well settled," Giddings correctly intuited about this time, "that the Whigs will never again rally under their own name."[22] Some, like Seward, had hoped they might survive principally as a northern party, but, with Republicanism's growing strength, that proved impossible.

Whiggery's demise raises the question of why the Democratic Party, vulnerable to the same stresses and North-South tensions, survived. Several reasons are suggestive. The Democracy, the party of Jefferson and Jackson, was older, more victorious, and far better established in the context of American electoral politics. Blessed with a populist reputation in a people's republic, it had, since 1800, carried eleven of fourteen presidential contests, built up a formidable national political machine, and come internally to some unstated sectional truce that long encouraged cohesion. Hence the expectation among southern Democrats that Douglas would, if pressured, agree to repeal the Missouri Compromise. During the party's early history Virginians (Jefferson, Madison, and Monroe) occupied the executive office, while their New York ballot mates (Aaron Burr, George Clinton, and Daniel Tompkins) made do with the vice presidency. By the late antebellum period the preponderance of northern power had made this arrangement untenable, and a new tradition took hold in which Yankee Democrats (Van Buren, Pierce, and Buchanan) secured the White House, while their running mates (Richard Mentor Johnson, William R. King, and John C. Breckinridge) hailed from Dixie. If the past had held form, the "Compromise of 1854" would have propelled Douglas into the presidency in 1860.

Interestingly, Whiggery's extinction helped to bring about its greatest goal, making the Democratic Party the nation's minority party. Resistance to the Kansas-Nebraska Act from antislavery Democrats, some of whom would become Republicans, put into play a fundamentally altered electoral landscape.[23] For unlike the Whigs, Republicans, with no southern wing to satisfy, could resist the pressure of planter power. Indeed, their success at the polls depended on defying efforts to expand the peculiar institution. Any attempt to revive the imperfect era of compromise politics could only do them harm.

Perhaps above all, the elections of 1854 legitimized in Yankeedom a broadening embrace of an emerging industrial labor system soon to dominate the rest of the century. In contrast to both the xenophobic Know-Nothings and the divided Democrats, the Republican Party offered at its inception a forward-looking vision dedicated to the advancement of the white working class. Its insistence on excluding slavery in the western territories while respecting the planters' property rights in southern states struck many northerners as essentially correct. Hardly abolitionists, most Republicans defined themselves, rather, as nonextensionists. It was this issue, after all, illuminated in a year of radical upheaval, that had brought them into existence.

19

Endings and Beginnings

She was ninety-two years of age at this time ... [a] tiny dot of
a woman. . . . She kept me by her side, holding me by the hand,
telling me . . . how she knew Washington and Lafayette.

Julia F. Miller on Eliza Hamilton, widow
of Alexander Hamilton, 1902

On November 9, 1854, as arriving election returns began to confirm
a paradigm shift in American politics, Eliza Hamilton, the widow of
former treasury secretary Alexander Hamilton, died in her shrine-
like Washington home at the age of ninety-seven. Her final days happened to overlap the delightfully eclectic Exhibition of the Industry of
All Nations, a world's fair held in New York City. These two seemingly
unconnected events presented illuminating contrasts for anyone willing
to notice. Eliza's passing emphasized the end of a chapter in the nation's
history, while the fair pointed to a future based increasingly on factories
and free labor, materialism and mobility. These contrasts might more
especially be said to have mirrored the plenty of tensions separating
the sections, as older notions of economy (agrarianism), power (states'
rights), and politics (deference) lost purchase. In their erratic wake, the
country moved forward, its identity a thing in flux.

It seems somehow fitting that Eliza's demise corresponded with
Whiggery's collapse. For in these convergences the nation's first
(1792–1824) and second (1828–1854) party systems might be said to
have met in a shared extinction. Hamilton, in youth a colonial subject,

though now a grande dame of the old republic and widowed a full half century since the death of her husband in a notorious duel with Aaron Burr on a humid July morning in Weehawken, New Jersey, constituted the last remaining human connection to George Washington's first cabinet. Among its officers Jefferson lived longest, succumbing to intestinal and urinary disorders in 1826; except Eliza, none of their wives survived beyond 1810, the year Elizabeth Nicholas Randolph, wife of Attorney General Edmund Jennings Randolph, died. Eliza outlived not only this governing group but also many who belonged to its succeeding antebellum cohort, including the Great Triumvirate of Clay, Webster, and Calhoun. With her passing, the celebrated Republican Court of the 1790s became a thing of memory.

The second daughter of Continental Army general Philip Schuyler and Catherine Van Rensselaer Schuyler, legatee of a Dutch patroon fortune, Eliza was born in Albany in 1757. At the age of twenty-two she met Hamilton, then Washington's indispensable aide-de-camp; they wed the following year. Their union produced in its casual turbulence eight children, a little money trouble, and the random scandal—rumors of financial impropriety and a messy extramarital affair. Aside from Eliza's aristocratic birth, a pleasing appearance perhaps drew Hamilton, himself the out-of-wedlock issue of a married (but abandoned) woman and a Scottish merchant, to his future wife. While courting, he called her "unmercifully handsome" and yet agreeably free "of those . . . affectations which are the prerogatives of beauty." Her excellent qualities included, he continued, "good sense . . . affability and vivacity," which together made her a model of the "virtues and graces of her sex." Quiet and retiring, Eliza, so one relative noted, capably assisted her mother in "the management of the house," which included overseeing a number of enslaved people.[1]

Widowed at the age of forty-seven with an uncooperative income and several dependent children (the youngest only two), Eliza survived on her wits, her inheritance, and the considerable generosity of loyal friends. From a clandestine subscription organized by Gouverneur Morris, author of the U.S. Constitution's Preamble ("We the People of the United States . . ."), came about $80,000—something north of $1 million in today's currency. Waiting out the presidencies of her late husband's chief political rivals, Jefferson and Madison, she succeeded in winning from Congress another $10,000 in recognition of Hamilton's military service in the Revolution. In 1837 Congress awarded her an additional $30,000 for the pension his death in a duel had prevented.[2]

Finding her footing, Eliza devoted considerable time during the second half of her life to charitable organizations, including orphanages in both New York and Washington. She also enjoyed traveling, including sojourns beyond the rote eastern city circuits. In the late winter of 1837, shortly before turning eighty, she described Pittsburgh as "a considerable town" blessed with "good Buildings" though "gloomy from the use of coal." Two months later, in transit from Cincinnati to St. Louis, she called the shallow Mississippi "very spacious, but very difficult of navigation."[3]

Perhaps unsurprisingly, considering her gilded heritage, this aging matron grew intensely interested in having the historical record her way. In the summer of 1840, "desirous," so she wrote, "that my children should be fully acquainted with the services rendered by their Father to our country," she prepared a statement attesting to her husband's drafting of George Washington's farewell address. This iconic document warned Americans against "the baneful effects of the spirit of party," cautioned them (amidst the wars of the French Revolution) to "steer clear of permanent alliances," and urged a relinquishment of states' rights: "Your Union ought to be considered as a main prop of your Liberty." Hamilton had worked on the text, Eliza observed, "principally at such times as his office was seldom frequented by his [law] clients and visitors, and during the absence of his students to avoid interruption; at which times he was in the habit of calling me to sit with him, that he might read to me as he wrote, in order, so he said, to discover how it sounded upon the ear." Eliza further maintained an active correspondence among a thinning family of old Federalists who could assist her efforts to both burnish Hamilton's reputation and see his heirs benefit financially for his considerable contributions. "Most of the[se] contemporaries," she soberly noticed one day, "have . . . passed away."[4]

In 1848 Eliza moved to Washington with her youngest daughter, Eliza Hamilton Holly, the childless widow of a New York merchant. There she succeeded in selling her late husband's papers to the government for $20,000. Now in her nineties and increasingly frail, Eliza maintained the home habits and sartorial style she had adopted decades earlier. Prayers were said on bent and brittle knees; black silk bombazine dresses (asso-

ciated with mourning wear) were favored; ruffled linen bonnets evoking
the colonial era adorned her dressing room, while a soft shawl warmed
her slender shoulders. Eliza brought to her rented multistory H Street
(NW) house near Lafayette Square a prized Gilbert Stuart half-length
portrait of Washington, French china, and a sleek marble bust of her
husband carved more than fifty years earlier by Giuseppe Ceracchi and
resting conspicuously on a mantel. A shiny silver wine cooler, given by
Washington himself, quickly caught the eye.[5]

Despite her age, Eliza remained active in the capital. She walked several blocks with the aid of a cane to a favorite florist, wove mats on a
tiny-pinned frame, and liked to ply visitors with stories of her long and
interesting life. "When I was young," she explained of her preference for
backgammon, "Mr. Franklin taught me to play. He visited my father's
when I was a girl, and was very kind to me." One caller remembered
her relating a story "of a great gathering of the Indians of eastern New
York at Saratoga," which she attended at the age of thirteen; there "all
the chiefs and greatest warriors of the Six Nations" arrived to negotiate
trade "with a small group of whites."[6]

In antebellum Washington, power invariably took notice of her quiet
if conspicuous presence. In the late winter of 1846, while still a resident
of New York and only visiting the capital city, she received an invitation from President James Polk to a forty-person dinner party, including cabinet members and their wives. "Mrs. Gen'l Alexander Hamilton,
upon whom I waited at table," the president wrote in a diary, "is a very
remarkable person. She retains her intellect & memory perfectly, and
my conversation with her was highly interesting."[7] The invitations only
increased once Eliza and her daughter settled into H Street. Presidents
Fillmore and Pierce summoned her to state dinners and receptions, she
attended New Year's Day and Fourth of July celebrations, and she more
generally won the attention of well-wishers, gossips, and the merely
curious, all eager to be near "history."

Next door to Eliza's rented address, the country's most celebrated
soldier, General Winfield Scott, kept a fashionable residence. And not
far away, in a modest gray house on Lafayette Square, lived former First
Lady Dolley Madison. The two dowagers, one a northerner, the other a
southerner, and widows of the two men who wrote most of *The Federalist Papers* before breaking over ideological differences of the nationalism
versus states' rights kind, were now regarded as symbols of sociability in

a Washington increasingly rife with conflicting sectional fidelities. Their husbands had helped to draft the Constitution, championed its ratification, and then worked mightily to launch the precarious experiment in republican government. Perhaps in the presence of these two remarkable women did a new generation, one nearing the precipice of civil war, cleave to the remnants of a receding founding era. This gesture seemed to be of paramount importance when both were invited to attend the cornerstone laying of the Washington Monument on July 4, 1848. With a vivid memory of the old general, Eliza embraced the occasion, writing to the chairman of the Committee of Arrangements: "The ceremony in which I am invited to participate calls back recollections so deeply interesting to me, from my early and intimate association with the illustrious man to whom this tribute of a nation's gratitude is so justly due, that I cannot deny myself the great satisfaction of witnessing it."[8] Joining both her and Madison at the event was an obscure single-term congressman from central Illinois named Abraham Lincoln.

Six years later, as Lincoln attacked the Kansas-Nebraska Act and made a bid for a Senate seat, Eliza died following a brief illness. Her remains were taken north to Manhattan and laid in Trinity Churchyard; a simple white marble slab in the "Daughter of . . ." and "Widow of . . ." mode rests next to her husband's more elaborate grave.[9] As far as monuments went, it struck a quiet note of grace. Farther up the island, by contrast, by coincidence, the celebrated Exhibition of the Industry of All Nations demanded to be noticed. An arresting symbol of midcentury mechanical development, it made a case for young America's place on the world's expanding stage.

The Gotham fair aimed quite openly to second the success of the Great Exhibition (1851), housed in London's posh Hyde Park. Attracting artists and aristocrats, commoners and the acclaimed, a staggering 6 million people, among them Queen Victoria, Karl Marx, and Charlotte Brontë, toured its thirteen thousand exhibits from dozens of countries. These meant-to-impress items resided in the massive Crystal Palace, a glorified greenhouse of the glass pane, iron frame kind. Most of the displays were unapologetically native and meant to point up Britain's role as the world's leading industrial power. Its seemingly endless aisles of engines and presses, adding machines and velocipedes (an early bicycle), suggested that any nation wishing to be considered modern, vogue, or à la mode, must embrace the improbable innovations coming out of England—master makers of "tomorrow."[10]

Certainly, numerous itinerate Americans took notice. About six thousand traipsed through the Crystal Palace—"the most marvelous edifice," so the *Brooklyn Eagle* gushed, "in the world"—eager to gaze over a trove of motorized treasures. Their own nation, by contrast, exhibiting at the fair an abundance of underwhelming farm and garden items, seemed uncomfortably provincial by comparison. This calculated overflow of Yankee fruits, meats, starches, and soaps appeared to have erred on the side of cornucopia, failing to impress those many patrons entranced by the Palace's preference for mechanical automations. To be sure, the Americans could take pride in exhibitions featuring Samuel Morse's electric telegraph, Cyrus McCormick's revolutionary grain-harvesting reaper, and the self-taught chemist Charles Goodyear's vulcanized rubber, though these paled beside the casual glut of European genius on display—"every conceivable invention," so the queen enthused. *Tribune* editor Horace Greeley, seemingly at every important event of the 1850s, trooped about the Crystal Palace with a slight burn of inferiority, acknowledging, "Our Manufacturers are in many departments deficient."[11] Might they make a better show of things in a future fair? And do so on their own soil?

Such busy thoughts bounced about the designing minds of certain New Yorkers. Motivated by a mix of pride and profitability (the London affair financially blessed its sponsors), these investors, by the summer of 1852, sought to construct a competitor crystal palace in Manhattan as the centerpiece for what they would regally call the Exhibition of the Industry of All Nations. A number of movers and shakers, many with Wall Street ties, combined with a scattering of the city's old gentry, including Eliza's son Alexander Hamilton Jr., to create a corporation that issued $300,000 (over $10 million today) in stock.

The American fair resided on a then-uptown "four-acre site along Sixth Avenue between 40th and 42nd streets" that is now Bryant Park. Situated beside the high granite-walled Croton water reservoir, the beggarly location could hardly be called elegant. Its rapid development that decade did, however, play to type. For Manhattan was in the midst of a great population surge—from 700,000 in 1850 to 1.2 million just ten years later—that remade the city's booming built environment. These additions included dozens of hotels on Broadway, along with several theaters, marketplaces, and museums, all capable of catering to generous concentrations of tourists.[12]

The exhibition's crystal palace, a minor-key paraphrase of the London structure and erected under the guidance of two immigrant architects, Karl Gildemeister of Germany and Georg Carstensen of Denmark, featured fifteen thousand translucent glass panes capped by a massive dome. Nearly as striking, an iron-braced wooden observation tower capable of accommodating two thousand and erected by "a local inventor/hustler" named Waring Latting, offered panoramic views of the city and its surrounding satellites. Rising 350 feet into the sky—"the ascent is a little fatiguing," so a *New York Times* reporter wrote, "but it improves the digestion"—the hastily built spire, its base crammed with shops and a popular ice-cream saloon, was suddenly the tallest man-made structure on the continent. Though one nineteenth-century source damned the design for being "built without regard to beauty of form and for a purely commercial purpose," others were obviously enchanted, including a certain French civil engineer named Gustave Eiffel, who later acknowledged "that the original idea of the [Eiffel] tower was borrowed" from this American antecedent.[13]

Like Latting, a number of entrepreneurs looked upon the exhibition as a golden opportunity to cash in. George "Gaslight" Foster, a journalist said to know the city intimately by both daylight and gas lamp, observed, when nearing the fair's gates, that one unexpectedly encountered an "accumulation of coffee houses, grog shops, [and] peep shows" featuring the latest animal oddities, including alligators and the occasional three-headed calf. These zoological curiosities were paired inside the grounds with curiosities of a different kind, including President Pierce, who formally opened the exposition on July 14, 1853. Cohesion seemed to be the American theme, a wishful reflex edging uncomfortably against a hardening line of North-South discontent. Flour from Ohio and Indian corn from New York nestled near Kentucky hemp, Louisiana sugar, and several varieties of cotton. Among industrial artifacts, one could find a number of tall muskets and shorter-barreled musketoons brought up from the small federal arsenal at Harpers Ferry.[14]

Straining amidst the guns and butter for a bit of culture, the exhibition featured a slew of pretty pianofortes backed by a cache of more common keyboards, woodwinds, and brasses. Into this aesthetic space were stationed a surprising number of bare-bottomed Joves, naked

Venuses, and undraped Dianas along with, so *Putnam's Magazine* put it, "hosts of pretty little, naughty cupids." The American neoclassical sculptor Hiram Powers, for years living abroad in a genial Florence, contributed his famous marble statue *The Greek Slave* ("so undressed," sighed a smitten Henry James, "yet so refined"), which gave pious fair-goers permission to gaze without shame on a beautiful young woman adorned only in chains and a small cross and locket, about to be sold by the iniquitous Turks. Some abolitionists, perhaps aching for vicarious atonement, thought this stylized statue of a light-skinned European bore a distinct parallel to the miseries of American slavery.[15]

More conventionally, the fair exhibited the practical fruits of industrial development. Threshing machines from Canada, steam engines from France, and tons of British textiles littered the exhibition halls. As a point of departure, Eli Whitney's original 1793 hand-crank cotton gin earned a place among the displays as a curio of the mechanical past. Mass production, rather, now stood poised to claim the future, a new self-evident truth displayed in queues of curtains, coffeepots, and carpeting amidst a rapacious consumer paradise of scarfs, hats, hosiery, books, bonnets, ribbons, watches, and so on.

While its gates remained opened—from July 1853 to November 1854— the fair, with an admission price of 50¢ ($16 in contemporary currency), attracted some six thousand visitors each day. Among them roamed a much-impressed seventeen-year-old Sam Clemens, a russet-haired itinerant printer with a hawkish nose still a decade away from styling himself "Mark Twain." He reveled in the exhibition's various delights, alive to their intoxicating color and wonder. "'Tis a perfect fairy palace," he wrote his eldest sister, Pamela, in St. Louis of the crystal contraption; "beautiful beyond description. . . . the flags of the different countries represented, the lofty dome, glittering jewelry, gaudy tapestry, etc. . . . it would take more than a week to examine everything on exhibition."[16]

Walt Whitman, working as a house builder in nearby Brooklyn and sauntering over several months ("days and nights") through the fair in the fine company of temporary companions, described an earthier experience than Clemens. He recalled "Bill," possessed of a "thoughtless, strong, generous animal nature, fond of direct pleasures, eating, drinking, women, fun, etc."; as well as "Peter," a "large, strong-boned young fellow . . . of strong self-will, powerful course feelings and appetites"; and finally "George," a "Yankee boy" with a "fine nature" pleasantly possessed with "sensitive feelings" that made him "a natural gentleman." *Leaves of Grass*, Whitman's American epic, includes "Song of the Exposition," which strikes an attractively democratic note when recognizing that the fair's chief virtue involved the fraternal uniting of "all the workmen of the world here to be represented."[17]

One of those workmen, of a kind, Henry David Thoreau, fresh off the triumph of *Walden*, journeyed to New York at Greeley's behest to take in the crystal palace, remarking in his journal of its fine "specimens of coal . . . sculptures and paintings." He found time, as well, to wander about Barnum's American Museum on the corner of Broadway and Ann Street, a stage for strange and educational attractions, in which the earnest Transcendentalist "saw the camelopards [giraffes]" and pondered over the deep mystery of their ornamental horns.

A showman Maximus in the annals of nineteenth-century American promotions, Phineas Taylor Barnum became directly involved with the exposition in the late winter of 1854. Its governing board, meeting at the Metropolitan Hotel, deduced that the fair's receipts, despite its drawing more than a million attendees, ran to a dispiriting red. The stockholders rebelled and demanded a new Board of Directors—who then chose the legendary Barnum (his shows, these status-conscious Americans noted, having won over European royalty) to assume the association's presidency. Knowing his penchant for chicanery—he had given credulous audiences George Washington's wet nurse, passed off a mummified monkey as a Fijian mermaid, and introduced the world to a cigar-smoking seven-year-old known as "General Tom Thumb"—a few irreconcilables thought the dignity of the exhibition (and apparently its trove of "naughty cupids") imperiled.[18]

But the commanding Barnum, tall and charismatic with piercing blue eyes, brought both cash and connections to the fair and this made stockholders eager to give this "Prince of Humbugs" or "Greatest Showman on Earth," depending upon preference, an opportunity. He conscripted new exhibitors, negotiated with railroads and steamboat companies for reduced transportation rates, and cut the exhibition's price of admission. All to limited avail—"it was up-hill work," he conceded. With the exhibition slated to end that fall, little time was left to entice customers beyond the already fair-saturated region and receipts continued to decline. "I was an ass," Barnum wrote one colleague, "for having anything to do with the Crystal Palace."[19]

Closing its doors that November, the exhibition suggested in its promise of material prosperity a better future, one very nearly at hand. And yet another generation would pass before the country once again considered itself so united, flourishing, and fortunate. In between, of course, the Union cracked in two, giving way to years of bitter civil war followed by imperfect efforts to move forward on issues of race and reconciliation. Such tensions were evident even at the Sixth Avenue shebang, presumably an ecumenical space of American advancement. Eager to condemn this alien enterprise to the North, the *Richmond Inquirer* called the fair a "contemptible" display of Yankee hustling, cheating, and dollar chasing. Southerners, the paper swore, were getting squeezed: "We have been caught. Thousands of inquisitive people from the South have traveled to New York through dust and heat; have suffered the torments of an over-crossed city; had their pockets picked, their persons searched, their toes mutilated, and for what?"[20]

More charitably, the fair might be said to have accurately (if unintentionally) conveyed the contradictory character of America in 1854. Rather than promote a false sense of the country's unity, it accentuated its dangerously widening divisions. So many of the laborsaving devices on display hinted at slavery's encroaching obsolescence before a growing industrialism. And thus as a marker of transition the exposition seemed of a piece with the approaching power of the Midwest and its ascendant political persuasion—Republicanism. Change, in an era of telegraph technology, took on new speed as, apropos Eliza Hamilton, the last remnants of the Revolutionary generation faded from the scene. Fresh leaders, parties, and promises came to the fore, though unable in their turn to create an abiding consensus. The promoters of the crystal palace, eager to tout the nation's technological advances, cultural achievements, and patriotic past, ignored these differences, something a growing number of Americans found increasingly difficult to do.

20

The Ship of Zion

I had crossed the line. I was *free*; but ... I was a stranger in a strange land; and my hope, after all, was down in Maryland; because my father, my mother, my brothers, and sisters, and friends were there. But I was free, and *they* should be free.

Harriet Tubman, 1869

Eliza Hamilton's passing, followed closely by the end of America's first world's fair, gave confirmation to a fateful year's volatile nature. Informed by unprecedented political change, the fallout from the Nebraska bill had brought actors both old and new before a restless public. In the patent contrasts between, say, Burns and Buchanan, or Douglas and Delany, the country, a three-generation concern, came to recognize how little it understood itself. Thus, while questions of freedom took on a new intensity in the homespun Yankee verities of a Stowe or a Thoreau, they drew from the skeptical Fitzhugh a sociology of profound doubt. In more immediate terms, this struggle over liberty imposed itself most intensely on those bereft of citizenship and rights. And in December 1854 Harriet Tubman, a runaway enslaved woman, secretly returned to the South on a mission of emancipation, engaged in a single act of rebellion, rooted in an indestructible idea.

Tubman's place in the American story is secure. John Brown called her "one of the best and bravest persons on this continent," while William Henry Seward said to a colleague after the Civil War, "I have known her long, and a nobler, higher spirit, or a truer, seldom dwells in the human form."[1] Frederick Douglass expressed his admiration in a generous private "Dear Harriet" communication:

> The difference between us is very marked. Most that I have done and suffered in the service of our cause has been in public, and I have received much encouragement at every stop of the way. You on the other hand have labored in a private way. I have wrought in the day—you in the night. I have had the applause of the crowd . . . while the most that you have done has been witnessed by a few trembling, scarred, and foot-sore bondmen and women.[2]

These tributes came in the wake of several risky expeditions by Tubman to rescue dozens of enslaved people. Draped, as Brown said, in bravery, the raids gave her a role and reputation that only grew with time. Like Lincoln she began, in the year of the Kansas-Nebraska Act, to find her way, to make a name, and to leave a legend.

Tubman lived her early life on Maryland's rural Eastern Shore. This marshy terrain housed a hodgepodge of planters and slaves amidst a significant population of free blacks and impoverished whites. Here in the late 1780s Harriet's mother, Harriet ("Rit") Green, was born, enslaved to Atthow Pattison, a Revolutionary War veteran. At that time, after winning their independence, northern states were adopting both immediate and gradual forms of abolition; manumissions in nearby Maryland, then moving toward less labor-intensive crops, were also on the rise. But this momentum gave way within a generation to a new economic reality. Between 1812 and 1819 Louisiana, Mississippi, and Alabama all entered the Union. And in these Gulf Coast states emerged thriving cotton and sugar plantations that, in connection with the ending of the slave trade in 1808 and subsequent removal of the region's native peoples, increased the price of unfree labor. Maryland and Virginia in consequence became what some called breeder states. Professional slave traders (colloquially called Georgia Traders on the Eastern Shore) began to inundate the area, making the notorious coffle—a train of dark-skinned adults and children chained together—a fearsome sight.[3]

Tubman, born Araminta Ross in about 1822 and perhaps on the large Thompson plantation near the Blackwater River in Dorchester County, grew up in this Eastern Shore norm of cash-strapped masters selling off their slaves. Maryland's papers were filled with notices that invariably told the story of ebbing estates and the breaking up of black families. This last eventuality touched Tubman directly when, probably in the 1830s, her sisters Linah and Soph were sold. Tubman's parents, Rit and Ben Ross, were in bondage though living within close proximity— she as a cook for Edward Brodess (whose mother was Mary Pattison Brodess, Atthow's granddaughter), he for the neighboring Thompsons (Anthony Thompson was Mary's second husband and thus Edward's stepfather). Rit and Ben's long union, extending beyond the Civil War, produced nine children. Franklin Sanborn, a journalist, Transcendentalist, and early Tubman biographer, called her "the grand-daughter of a slave imported from Africa" and said she "has not a drop of white blood in her veins."[4]

Tubman, née Araminta and called "Minty," spent her early childhood on the Brodess plantation. About the age of six, she began to be hired out to local whites. In the early 1860s the *Boston Commonwealth*, rooting into the life of this by-now-famous emancipator, recorded an early effort to train her as a weaver—an undertaking she took some pains to impair. "She would not learn," the paper observed, "for she hated her mistress, and did not want to live at [the mistress's] home, as she would have done as a weaver, for it was the custom then to weave the cloth for the family, or a part of it, in the house." This anxious early history of negotiating masters and hirers, along with the various uncertainties and cruelties the circumstances imposed, no doubt left an indelible mark on Tubman. The sales of Linah and Soph, moreover, along with the multiple Eastern Shore estates that held hostage parents and children, cousins and companions, gave some pernicious perspective to Tubman's own itinerant situation. As an adult, possibly seeking an antecedent to her unconventional career, she identified Rit as a maternal protector willing to employ violence to shelter her vulnerable kin. Tubman insisted that Brodess had once contemplated selling one of Rit's boys, only to be put off by an ironclad command: "The first man that comes into my house, I will split his head open."[5] The sale apparently never transpired.

Tubman's uneven domestic apprenticeship ended before her teen years. Self-willed and perhaps temperamentally unsuited to living and working in close quarters with masters (reportedly biting one on the knee), she was taken, at the age of twelve, out to the fields. There she cut wood, drove oxen, and plowed fields. Such arduous labors—and the respect they earned from overseers who conceded she "did all the work of a man"—seemed to bring her confidence in the rare store of her physical strength.[6]

About this time, between ages twelve and fourteen, Tubman received a violent blow on the head that nearly killed her and, so one source reported decades later, continued to afflict her into adulthood. During harvest season an enslaved man owned by a farmer named Barrett and working late in the evening, perhaps husking corn or harvesting wheat, left his labors without permission and went to the village store. Cornering him in the cramped building, which stands to this day, an exasperated overseer called upon Tubman, in attendance, to help him tie the man up to be whipped. She refused and, when the truant broke for the door, lingered in the path of his pursuer; blocked, the overseer picked up a two-pound iron weight off a counter and, though aiming it at the fleeing man, struck instead Tubman on the head, leaving a permanent scar above her left temple. "They carried me to the house all bleeding and fainting," she recalled. "I had no bed, no place to lie down on at all, and they lay me on the seat of the loom, and I stayed there all day and the next." The assault "left her subject to a sort of stupor or lethargy at times," a nineteenth-century source reported, "coming upon her in the midst of conversation, or whatever she may be doing, and throwing her into a deep slumber, from which she will presently rouse herself, and go on with her conversation or work." She might today be diagnosed as suffering from periodic epileptic seizures.[7]

After rising from her sickbed, Tubman was hired out to John Stewart, the son of a prominent shipbuilder who kept a 250-acre wheat and corn plantation idling along the Choptank River in Dorchester County. She performed a variety of jobs for Stewart, beginning with domestic work but also hauling milled grain and transporting goods to market; she perhaps swept out Stewart's small mercantile store. After having completed her assignments for the day Tubman often aided her father (freed in 1840), who, as a timber inspector, secured lumber for Baltimore's insatiable shipyards. In all, she put money in Stewart's pockets for six years.

In 1844 Minty married John Tubman, a free black man—they lived on one of the Thompson plantations. John got his name from the Tubmans, an old seventeenth-century Eastern Shore Catholic family of slaveholders, the residue of which now occupied a plantation, Lockerman's Manor, near Cambridge and extending to the Choptank.[8]

For John, the marriage meant a lessening of his spousal rights, as any children the couple might have belonged to Harriet's owner, Edward Brodess; nor could John prevent the sale of his wife, or their offspring. It was Tubman's master, rather, who would decide where she lived and worked.

Not long after marrying, Minty hired a lawyer to investigate her mother's legal status, which, considering that she inherited Rit's condition, meant her own as well. Possibly the examples of John and her emancipated father, combined with suspicions of broken promises from previous masters, prompted this decision. She paid the attorney $5 to inspect the will of Atthow Pattison, who had died decades earlier. He discovered that upon being bequeathed to Mary, Rit was to remain her mistress's property until the age of forty-five. This implied emancipation, though the language was imprecise, not explicitly confirming her freedom but simply stating that she no longer belonged to Mary. For Tubman this confusion suggested several sins—from her aging mother's continued enslavement, to the possibility that some of Rit's children were born into freedom but mistakenly held in bondage, to the duplicity of those in the Pattison family familiar with the contents of Atthow's will. Possibly this sobering episode, laced in betrayal, began the momentum that led Tubman to escape.

Positioned on slavery's northern rim, Maryland recorded an unusually high number of runaways. According to the 1850 census, 259 bondsmen and -women had fled "in the past year," a sum exceeding all other southern states.[9] This figure included only those chattels reported missing, of course, and the actual number must have been even higher. The feasibility for flight, far more difficult in the country's expanding southerly cotton belt, seemed to a growing number of enslaved people in the Chesapeake an eventuating possibility, many knowing of friends or family members either self- or otherwise emancipated. The region produced, moreover, the country's most famous fugitive, Frederick Douglass, who, while living in Talbot County, just north of Tubman's Dorchester, had in the late 1830s escaped from his bondage. In 1850 Maryland had fewer slaves than in 1790 and in Baltimore free blacks numbered twenty-five thousand, dwarfing the fewer than three thousand enslaved persons in the city. Tubman, so near to freedom on the neighboring Eastern Shore, might for some time have calculated her chances for flight.

In the late winter of 1849, five years into her marriage, Minty, think-ing her master, Edward Brodess, an immoral man, commenced a pro-tracted prayer vigil to redeem his endangered soul. She hoped that his conversion might attend to an attitude of repentance leading to the emancipation of her kin, kept, she believed, in defiance of Atthow Patti-son's will. While engaged in this prolonged appeal, she came to believe that Brodess, "bringing people to look at me," intended to improve his financial position by selling her and her brothers and sisters. "[I] changed my prayer," she later recalled, "and said 'Lord, if you ain't never going to change that man's heart, *kill him*, Lord, and take him out of the way, so he won't do no more mischief.'" Tubman almost certainly embroidered her legend in such after-the-fact remarks, for the forty-seven-year-old Brodess died at nearby Bucktown on March 7—apparently of a lingering illness, having instructed a lawyer only a day or two prior to his passing to make out a will. Tubman swore to being astonished and thought to implore the Lord once more "to bring that poor soul back," only to dis-cover that she had no charity left for the man she blamed for her con-tinued bondage.[10]

With Brodess's passing, Tubman's greatest fears now came to the fore. That July, Gourney Crow Pattison, Brodess's uncle, filed suit against Brodess's wife, Eliza, claiming ownership of Rit and several of her offspring. Again, the vagueness of Atthow Pattison's will left room for interpretation, and Gourney maintained that Brodess retained a right to Rit's labor only until the age of forty-five; at that point, he con-tinued, she and her children belonged to the Pattison estate. In early August Gourney lost his suit, though he appealed, and a lengthy legal tussle looked about to break. During that summer Eliza, upset over her husband's death, the Pattison imbroglio, and mounting debts, decided to sell some of the people in her possession, including, so rumor had it, Minty. Considering herself freed via the Pattison will and unwilling any longer to abide by her precarious condition as a plantation append-age, to be bought and sold like livestock, she resolved to escape. "I had reasoned this out in my mind," she later recalled, "there was one of two things I had a *right* to, liberty, or death; if I could not have one, I would have the other."[11]

On September 17 Tubman, along with her brothers Ben and Henry, took off, intending to reach the North. Early the following month Eliza, accustomed to her husband's hiring-out policy and perhaps initially unconcerned by the occasional extended absences of his slaves, now placed a notice in the *Cambridge Democrat*, quite typical for its time:

THE HUNDRED DOLLARS REWARD

Ranaway from the subscriber on Monday the 17th ult., three negroes, names as follows: HARRY, aged about 19 years, has on one side of his neck a wen, just under the ear, he is of a dark chestnut color, about 5 feet 8 or 9 inches height; BEN, aged . . . about 25 years, is very quick to speak when spoken to, he is of a chestnut color, about six feet high; MINTY, aged about 27 years, is of a chestnut color, fine looking, and about 5 feet high. One hundred dollars reward [about $3,900 in present-day dollars] will be given for each of the above named negroes, if taken out of the State, and $50 each if taken in the State. They must be lodged in Baltimore, Easton or Cambridge Jail, in Maryland.[12]

The notice failed to recover the runaways—the runaways, rather, returned themselves. The brothers appeared to have grown concerned on the open road, fearing capture and punishment as prelude to a retributive sale to some distant Deep South cotton complex. Tubman wished to press on, but "in spite of her remonstrances" the men "dragged her with them."[13]

So she decided to go it alone. Just days after returning and without telling a soul, Tubman left her cabin on the Thompson property and, under the cover of darkness and using the North Star as a guide, made her way up the peninsula along the Choptank, probably following the river into Delaware and finally to Philadelphia—a distance of some 130 miles. Along the way she benefitted from the assistance of Eastern Shore Quakers, other well-wishers, and abolitionists who offered a sequence of safe houses over this particular Underground Railroad route. "There was such a glory over everything," she recalled, "and I felt like I was in Heaven . . . when I found I had crossed that *line*."[14]

With numerous black churches and charities, Philadelphia, the nation's fourth-largest city (population 120,000), offered Tubman—now calling herself Harriet, perhaps to honor Rit while signifying her new self and status as a free woman—a certain ease of anonymity. Though slave catchers circulated in the region, it appears that no one knew of Tubman's exploits; Eliza apparently never pursued her capture. Free but alone, Tubman proposed to liberate her family from bondage and quickly began, through a series of domestic jobs in both Philadelphia and Cape May, New Jersey, to earn money toward this end. Courage, a capacity for hard work, and an unyielding sense of justice, always evident in her makeup, now came to more fully inform her decisions.

And so Minty became Harriet who in turn became Moses. In December 1850, after working in the North for a little more than a year, she managed her first mission, rescuing her niece Kessiah and "Kizzy's" two young children, all soon, it was presumed, to be otherwise sold. Details are sketchy, though it appears that Kizzy's husband, a free black named John Bowley, rowed his family across the Chesapeake Bay to Baltimore. There Tubman met them, and after several days she took the fugitives to Philadelphia.[15] A few months later she returned to Baltimore and conveyed a brother and two other men to freedom.

Over the next several months Tubman worked, setting aside money for another raid into Maryland, this time to Dorchester County itself, where she hoped to reunite with her husband. This did not happen. Nearing Cambridge she sent word of her arrival, though John, who had refused the previous year to go with his wife, refused again, having taken in her absence another companion, named Caroline, a free woman, later to bear his children. John declined even to see Harriet. Though stunned, she determined to make something of this mission and guided a small party of perhaps four or five fugitives to Philadelphia.[16]

Later that year, in December, Harriet conducted still another group to freedom, this time to Canada, beyond the menacing reach of the recently passed Fugitive Slave Act. "I wouldn't trust Uncle Sam with my people any longer," she insisted. Returning to the United States the following spring, she found employment in hotels as a cook to build up the capital and the connections that allowed her to make additional trips south. Sensitive to danger, alive to premonitions, and able to evade those who sought her capture, she took with each success increased courage, confident in her abilities to, as she once put it, fly "like a bird . . . over fields and towns, and rivers and mountains."[17]

Hardly a lone liberator, Tubman received assistance from white patrons including Lucretia Mott, a New England Quaker, abolitionist, and women's rights activist then living in Philadelphia, and benefitted further from the support of numerous black churches and benefit aid societies. Gaining experience, she developed in the early 1850s a set of strategies that ensured safe passage to the South and back. She typically started out with runaways on winter Saturday evenings, the hours of additional darkness and unlikelihood of notices going up on a Sunday aiding the effort. Only infrequently did Tubman set foot on plantations, preferring, rather, to connect from a distance with her party. Engaged in a dangerous enterprise, she carried a pistol and is said, when confronted with the occasional frightened fugitive who suddenly wished to return, to have offered the recalcitrant a simple choice: "You go on or die!"[18]

Faith appears to have played an important role in Tubman's rescues. Conversant with Bible stories from youth, she meshed these recitations with a sense of personal mission that gave, beyond mere inspiration, a blessed meaning to the convulsions she sometimes suffered from her old injury. As the historian Kate Clifford Larson notes, "Her seizures continued . . . and the religious visions accompanying them often comforted her. . . . While the seizures were disquieting to those who [attended] her on her rescue missions, Tubman's accepting attitude about them bespoke her overall confidence in God's will and reassured those around her." One contemporary, R. C. Smedley, a Chester County, Pennsylvania, physician and abolitionist, recalled that Tubman "had faith in God; always asked Him what to do, and to direct her, 'which,' she said, 'he always did.' She would talk about 'consulting God,' or 'asking of Him.' Just as one would consult a friend upon matters of business; and she said, 'He never deceived [me].'"[19]

By 1854 Tubman had made several trips south and conveyed about thirty runaways to freedom. In the spring of that year, she attempted without success to rescue her brothers Robert, Ben, and Henry—though managing to leave Maryland with a twenty-seven-year-old enslaved man named Winnibar Johnson. Filled with portents and concerns for her brothers' well-being, Tubman resolved over the next few months to redeem these men and again returned to the Eastern Shore. In preparation, and in concession to her illiteracy, she dictated a coded letter written out by a Philadelphia friend and sent to Jacob Jackson, a free black in Dorchester County. Though the historical record is unclear, Jackson apparently had some connection to Tubman, one she now prevailed upon. She knew he had an adopted son and the note affected to come from him. After a series of perfunctory remarks, it more germanely read: "Tell my brothers to be always *watching unto prayer*, and when the *good old ship of Zion comes along, to be ready to step aboard.*"[20]

Soon after, in late December, Tubman once again slipped below the Mason-Dixon Line, perhaps taking a train to Baltimore and then crossing the Chesapeake to Cambridge. Reaching her brothers on Saturday the twenty-third, she, along with Ben and Harry, began that evening a forty-mile journey to their parents' cabin. As they neared their destination, Robert, having told his wife, Mary, he intended to hire himself out, joined his siblings. Though several years had passed since Tubman last saw her mother, she and her brothers, concerned that Rit might in the excitement of a reunion endanger their escape, dealt only with their father, staying hidden during a long Christmas Day—along with several other Cambridge-area men and a woman accompanying them—in a nearby corn crib. Reprovisioned, they set out again that night, reaching Wilmington, Delaware, in three days, where they briefly lodged with Thomas Garrett, an affluent merchant well versed in piloting runaways north; he had incurred a $1,500 fine six years earlier for such practices, Supreme Court Justice Roger B. Taney, later to be known for his leading role in the *Dred Scott* decision, served as one of the presiding judges. "We made arrangements last night, and sent Harriet Tubman, with six men and one woman to Allen Agnew's [in Chester County], to be forwarded across the country to the city [Philadelphia]," Garrett wrote directly after aiding the party. "Harriet, and one of the men had worn their shoes off their feet, and I gave them two dollars to help fit them out, and directed a carriage to be hired at my expense, to take them out."[21]

The fugitives were likely dispatched to Manhattan, and from there journeyed upstate to Albany and finally to St. Catharines, Ontario. They became part of Tubman's improbable march into the history books, one of perhaps thirteen raids she made in the South between 1850 and 1860, freeing some seventy enslaved people.[22] She was only hitting her stride. During the Civil War Tubman aided runaways in South Carolina's occupied Hilton Head district; she further nursed soldiers in Port Royal and, following Lincoln's Emancipation Proclamation, became the first woman to plan and carry out an armed assault on the Confederacy, advising Colonel James Montgomery on a campaign against numerous plantations along the Combahee River in South Carolina's southern Lowcountry. The operation included the liberating of several hundred people.[23]

But before the war, in the shadow of 1854, Tubman's missions into Maryland called into question both the old blueprint of bondage and the rheumatic political compromises that had long sustained it. Her remarkable efforts conformed to a broader pattern of resistance only gaining intensity in the year of the Kansas-Nebraska Act, the rendition of Anthony Burns, and the birth of the Republican Party. Each instance built on what came before, cohering in an ascending momentum that led just six years later to the separation of the sections. In this brief span, conditioned by the struggle over slavery's uncertain future, time was running out.

Frederick Douglass insisted after the Civil War that the great "effect of this Kansas battle . . . [was] how it made abolitionists of people before they themselves became aware of it."

Coda: Meanings

Public sentiment in this country is in a transition state. . . . Old parties, old names, old issues, and old organizations are passing away. A day of new things, new issues, new leaders, and new organizations is at hand.

> Alexander Stephens, future vice president
> of the Confederate States of America,
> December 31, 1854

Harriet Tubman's brave Christmas raid ended the astonishing year on an equivocal note. It might be said to portend increasing pressure on the institution of slavery, though it could also be regarded as a case of isolated courage before the immense consequence of the Missouri Compromise's recent repeal. The nation's political class entered December similarly divided. "Action against slavery," a combative Salmon Chase wrote a colleague on the fifteenth," is the *best means* of bringing the country to a correct understanding of its true character"; while just three days later an exhausted Stephen Douglas countered with an errant optimism: "The Nebraska fight is over."[1] Weaned on the uneven conciliation politics of the past, the Little Giant clung desperately to the slowly sinking Whig-Democratic ship, even as the recent elections gave its likely survival the lie.

Tied to this graceless arrangement, the executive office could hardly escape the year uninjured; the sequent afflictions of 1854, rather, played a decisive role in cankering two presidencies and destroying the prospects of yet another. Pierce, under the prodding of several southern senators and key cabinet members, lined up behind the Kansas-Nebraska Bill to appalling results. When he entered office only two years earlier

281

with strong partisan majorities in both the House and Senate, his success looked assured. And even today it seems striking that he should be the only Democratic president between Martin Van Buren (1836) and Franklin Roosevelt (1932) to win office with a popular vote majority. Pierce's backing of Douglas's measure, however, proved disastrous. Many in the North regarded him as a southern sycophant, hostile to the coming power of free-soil sentiment. Despite wanting a second term ("All his cabinet agreed to it," one insider reported), Pierce was not renominated, the party's more prudent members wishing their candidate to be without a direct link to the brewing fight on the frontier.[2]

An 1856 broadside in which a group of northern Democrats, including Pierce, Buchanan, and Douglas, all loyal to a "Democratic Platform" that appeased their southern brethren, are forcing the North to swallow slavery in Kansas.

This opened the door in 1856 for the silky gray–haired Buchanan, a long-serving warhorse largely bereft of wit or imagination, who, on the seventeenth ballot of a fractious Cincinnati convention, captured the nomination. But when he—and the party's platform—endorsed the divisive "Douglas-Pierce policies," a swarm of free-soil Democrats bolted, believing this elder statesman just another doughface. One of the disenchanted, Maine senator Hannibal Hamlin (later to serve as Lincoln's first vice president), insisted after Cincinnati, "The old Dem. party is now the party of slavery. It has no other issue in fact and this is the standard on which it measures every thing and every man." This exo-

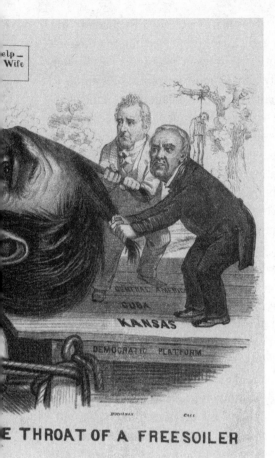

E THROAT OF A FREESOILER

dus of irreconcilables proved telling. For though Buchanan managed to win the election, he carried just five northern states; only four years earlier Pierce had taken all but two.[3]

Barely had Buchanan settled into Pennsylvania Avenue when Bleeding Kansas, the bitter fruit of 1854, proceeded to wreck both his administration and Douglas's own scarcely hidden White House ambitions. Concerned about southern threats of secession, Buchanan anxiously hoped to see Kansas become a slave state, and, through electoral fraud, phony voting, and intimidation at the polls by bushwhackers and border ruffians, this nearly happened. A constitution drafted in the tiny county seat of Lecompton guaranteed planters the right to bring their slaves into the territory and was submitted to the president, who crowed before Congress, "Kansas is . . . at this moment as much a slave state as Georgia and South Carolina." Douglas's unwillingness, however, to shepherd the corrupt constitution through the Senate, a charter opposed by the territory's antislavery majority and certain to kill him politically in Illinois, caused an irreparable rift in his relationship with southern Democrats. "Mr. Douglas," Buchanan reportedly said to the senator during this clash, "I desire you to remember that no Democrat ever yet differed from an administration of his own choice without being crushed."[4]

This fraternal war marked a real dividing line in the party's history. For generations Democrats had frequently followed one another—Jefferson handed the presidential baton off to Madison, who gave it to Monroe;

Van Buren succeeded Jackson, while Pierce preceded Buchanan.[5] But after the Kansas-Nebraska Act nearly a century passed before Roosevelt and Harry Truman won consecutive elections in 1944 and 1948. Though in Truman's case—and Kennedy heir Lyndon Johnson's—elevation to the office occurred because of a chief executive's death. Thus, if the question is posed, who was the last Democratic president to succeed a *living* Democratic president?, the improbable answer is Buchanan.

Under the circumstances it is fair to ask what Democrats gained in 1854. The answer is devastating. In return for granting southerners a rather empty right—neither Kansas nor Nebraska became slave states—Douglas's bill more dearly stirred up a hornet's nest of northern suspicion and distrust. "The battle . . . in Kansas, for the compulsory establishment of Slavery . . . by the interposition of the Federal arm," the *Atlantic Monthly* warned, "will be renewed in every Territory as it is ripening into a State."[6] Determined to contest this appalling prospect, a mess of anti-Nebraska coalitions congealed into a powerful Republican opposition. Beginning in 1860 and extending into the 1920s, it defeated the Democrats in every national election except four.

Viewed through a long lens, it is possible to see the events of 1854 as linked to a broader dynamic of Yankee discontent. During the Jeffersonian era Massachusetts senator Timothy Pickering, advising a group of restive New England elites, denounced the slaveholders' ascendancy. Distraught, he counseled secession. "Without a separation," he wrote, "can those [northern] States ever rid themselves of negro Presidents and negro Congresses, and regain their just weight in the political balance?"[7]

In 1820 dozens of congressional Yankees balked at bringing Missouri into the Union with enslaved labor. Then–Secretary of State John Quincy Adams quietly arraigned the Framers in a diary for leaving their heirs to wrestle with this profoundly difficult dilemma: "And so it is that a law perpetuating slavery in Missouri . . . has been smuggled through both Houses of Congress. I have been convinced from the first starting of this question that it could not end otherwise. The fault is in the Constitution of the United States, which has sanctioned a dishonorable compromise with slavery." In the 1830s and 1840s this resistance resurfaced, challenging Texas's annexation and the aftermath of the Mexican-American War. Daniel Webster brought before Congress at this time a resolution from the people of Massachusetts declaring their opposition to "any new territory to this Union, in which the institution of slavery is to be tolerated."[8] The fight over the futures of Kansas and Nebraska, in other words, might with reason be regarded as both one of the last southern victories and the first fully concentrated northern opposition to the planter class.

Underlying this vivid history is the sudden consciousness-raising the struggle provoked. "The important point to me, as one desiring to see the slave power . . . abolished," wrote Frederick Douglass after the Civil War, "was the effect of this Kansas battle upon the moral sentiment of the North: how it made abolitionists of people before they themselves became aware of it." Certainly, as this study notes, the "moral sentiment" of such as Emerson and Tubman, Burns and Chase, Garrison and Greeley, all converged, despite contrasting backgrounds, beliefs, and expectations, to make the case for their nation's rethinking of its relationship to both slavery and the statutory system that sustained it. Farther to the west, a puzzled Lincoln, eager to reach the Senate but for the moment tied to a dying party, could feel the political ground moving beneath him. His 1855 confession to a friend "I think I am a Whig; but others say there are no Whigs, and that I am an Abolitionist" coheres to Douglass's claim that many Americans had begun to adopt new positions on old questions before "they themselves became aware of it."[9]

For generations, careful accommodations on slavery had moved the republic erratically along. But this compromise culture broke before a crush of moral and economic contradictions that had evolved inexorably over time. Demographic change and industrial development increased northern potency and power, while the rise of Christian evangelicalism, legacies of eighteenth-century Enlightenment liberalism, and persistent pressures of enslaved people to challenge a system that injured them contributed as well. Emerson, the avatar of American progress, took note. "In human society," he argued, "the enterprise, the very muscular vigor of this nation, are inconsistent with slavery."[10]

That contradiction, always apparent, took on an added intensity in the quest for Kansas. Stephen Douglas presumed a victory in the arid West for free labor, though free labor, observing slavery's relentless extension into the nation's shared territories, thought—and feared—otherwise. And so it organized. This occurred in 1854, the year that seeded the Republican Party, promoted a growing sense of northern nationalism, and paved Lincoln's return to public life; these signal months further undermined a once tenacious confidence in compromise, blew up the existing political system, and threatened a small shooting war in the West. Over the next six years the country, weakened by self-inflicted wounds and torn by distrust, angled inescapably toward Armageddon.

During this pregnant period, a host of post-Kansas provocations had piled on, all connected in some sense to Douglas's original bill. On a late May day in 1856 Charles Sumner, unlimbering a lengthy Senate address on "The Crime against Kansas," described a colleague, South Carolina's pompadour-haired Andrew Butler, as having "chosen a mistress to whom he has made his vows, and who, though ugly to others, is always lovely to him . . . the harlot, Slavery." Two days later South Carolina representative Preston Brooks, tall, trim, and thirty-six years old, entered the Senate chamber looking for Sumner. Butler's first cousin once removed, he believed his adversary's address to be slanderous. Disdaining legal action, he resolved to defend both family and section by resorting to the southern code duello—though without informing Sumner, whom he thought likely to report him to the police. Determined to thrash an inferior, Brooks's options were a cane or a horsewhip—he chose the former, a thick gutta-percha with a gold head. Standing before a sitting Sumner, Brooks opened with, "It is a libel on South Carolina, and Mr. Butler, who is a relative of mine . . . ," as a preface to raining down a series of blows on his pinioned victim.[11] Badly beaten, the senator, suffering from head trauma and post-traumatic stress disorder, spent three years convalescing—"Bleeding Sumner" now a grim compliment to "Bleeding Kansas."

The following year, the Supreme Court struck down the Missouri Compromise in the *Dred Scott* case, thus adding a judicial imprimatur to what Douglas had earlier accomplished. This meant, according to the 7–2 majority, that not only could Congress not exclude slavery from a territory, but neither could a territorial government created by Congress. In effect, the entire West was now open to enslavers. Intent on contesting this sequence of southern victories—the caning of Sumner, Buchanan's election to the presidency, the Taney court's judicial activism—John Brown, a product of the Kansas wars, raided a U.S. arsenal at Harpers Ferry, Virginia, eager to initiate a slave revolt. Though it failed, leading to Brown's hanging forty-seven days after the attack on charges of murder, inciting slave insurrection, and treason against the Commonwealth of Virginia, the assault more broadly demonstrated to a furious planter class the increasing unwillingness of northerners to comply with the conditions of living in a republic undergirded by enslavement.

Perhaps this is why a handful of southern agricultural conventions in the late 1850s pursued the elusive goal of reopening the African slave trade, closed by act of Congress in 1808. This monstrosity had absolutely no chance of success, though it might have served a therapeutic purpose for a jittery section that could feel its control of the country giving way. South Carolina fire-eater Leonidas Spratt tied the barbaric trade to the western question when complaining in late 1859 that "ten thousand masters have failed to take Kansas, but so would not have failed ten thousand slaves. Ten thousand of the rudest Africans . . . would have swept the free soil party from the land."[12]

In fact, much the opposite occurred. Lincoln captured the presidency the following autumn, precipitating the secession winter crisis in which several deep southern states left the Union. And in between the withdrawals of Georgia (January 21, 1861) and Texas (February 1), a Republican-controlled Congress brought a free Kansas into the Union. The southern goal to expand slavery into the nation's shared territories, seemingly so near, had now and forever collapsed.

But not before a civil war made the fruits of 1854, along with a cast of congressmen, abolitionists, transcendentalists, and southern theorists, permanent fixtures of history. Chase and Seward joined Lincoln's cabinet respectively as secretaries of the Treasury and State Department; the former later replacing the deceased Taney as chief justice of the Supreme Court. More than inheriting an office, this succeeding of a proslavery southerner with an antislavery Ohioan pointed to the trajectory of a nation tilting free-soil and on the cusp of locating much of its political and economic power in a rising Midwest.

In teeming Concord, Emerson continued on the path of self-reliance, publishing a popular book of essays, *The Conduct of Life*, in 1860 and insisting, once fighting had broken out, on the immediate emancipation of the enslaved. Thoreau, hailed by subsequent generations as an apostle of nonviolence, championed John Brown's deadly attack on black bondage. In three flaming essays—"A Plea for Captain John Brown," "Martyrdom of John Brown," and "The Last Days of John Brown"—he made the case for this border warrior's sainthood. After all, he reasoned in one of the sketches, "It was through his agency, far more than any others, that Kansas was made free."[13]

Elsewhere, William Lloyd Garrison regarded Lincoln's Emancipation Proclamation as the fulfillment of his long-standing hopes. The last edition of *The Liberator* appeared, along with the ratification of the Thirteenth Amendment, in December 1865 and Garrison spent his final years supporting women's rights. Harriet Beecher Stowe remained a busy author, churning out novels, poetry, stories, and articles prior to her death in 1896. During the Civil War she met Lincoln in the White House for what her daughter Hattie, also present, insisted to a correspondent was "a very droll time. . . . I will only say now that it was all very funny." Stowe's son Charles later spread the apocryphal story that the president had said to the author of *Uncle Tom's Cabin*, "So you are the little woman who wrote the book that started this great war!"—a polite fiction that perhaps captures after all a certain veracity of sentiment.[14]

On the other side of the North-South divide, Missouri senator David Atchison lost his seat in 1855, favored secession when the war came, and served as a major general in the pro-Confederate Missouri State Guard, to whose ranks a skeptical Sam Clemens briefly belonged. Equipped with a "shabby old shot-gun" and astride, so he said, "a very small mule," Clemens discovered that "nobody would cook" in his company and exited this irregular army after two fitful weeks, at which point he left for the Nevada Territory, wrote for several newspapers, and by the war's end had published a small piece on a jumping frog in Calaveras County, California, that some people thought funny.[15]

Harriet Tubman, working with Union forces in South Carolina, survived the war, dying in her early nineties in 1913, six days after the inauguration of the Virginia-born Woodrow Wilson, the first southerner elected to the presidency since Zachary Taylor in 1848. Frederick Douglass remained an advocate for black rights deep into the century, giving countless speeches, serving as the United States Marshal for the District of Columbia, and publishing successive editions of his autobiography *The Life and Times of Frederick Douglass*. In 1877, from Baltimore, he boarded the steamer *Matilda*, crossed the Chesapeake to the Eastern Shore, the place of his enslavement, and docked at St. Michaels, where, eager to pin down his patrimony and birth year— and possibly come to some private reckoning with the past—he met for twenty minutes in a crumbling brick house with an ailing Thomas Auld, "my old master," the man, Douglass noted, who once "made property to my body and soul." Perhaps to his surprise, Douglass discovered inside himself an unexpected peace: "Here we were after four decades once more face to face—he on his bed, aged and tremulous, drawing near the sunset of life, and I, his former slave . . . holding his hand and in friendly conversation with him in a sort of final settlement of past differences preparatory to his stepping into his grave, where all distinctions are at an end."[16]

Others never found such amity. Buchanan retired from the presidency to Wheatland, his Lancaster, Pennsylvania, home, where he received throughout the war a steady stream of letters condemning his "treasonous" behavior. Pro-Union, he watched anxiously in the summer of 1863 as Lee's Army of Northern Virginia invaded the Keystone State. Urged by friends to vacate, he refused, though he sent his niece Harriet Lane, acting First Lady during her bachelor uncle's White House tenancy, to Philadelphia. A week after the Gettysburg campaign, during which Confederate forces under Jubal Early came within thirteen miles of his Federal-style mansion, Buchanan wrote a colleague with a firmness not always evident during his public career: "I felt no alarm at the approach of the rebels & with the help of God should not have removed from Wheatland had I been surrounded by a hundred thousand of them."[17] He died in 1868.

For Stephen Douglas, the twin setbacks of disunion and losing the presidency proved too much. Following a tempestuous secession winter, scarcely leavened by dancing the quadrille with Mrs. Lincoln at her husband's inaugural ball, he unexpectedly took ill, presuming "a severe attack of rheumatism" if not a "Torpor of the liver," though likely suffering a minor heart attack or stroke. Near the end his mind occasionally wavered, drawn back to the rough-and-tumble of congressional politics, as when telling an attendant physician, "Stop, there are twenty against me, the measure is defeated."[18] Always a young man on the make, he died on June 3, still in his forties.

There had been a time, of course, when Douglas's future seemed assured—and no one knew that better than his greatest rival. "Twenty-two years ago Judge Douglas and I first became acquainted," Lincoln reflected in the late 1850s, as though searching for an answer to a long-hanging question. "We were both young then. . . . Even then, we were both ambitious; I, perhaps quite as much so as he. With *me*, the race of ambition has been a failure—a flat failure; with *him* it has been a splendid success. His name fills the nation."[19] Neither man, linked by a common state, aspirations, and series of important debates on the future of the western territories, survived the war. Lincoln's shocking assassination occurred more than a year before his successor, the stocky Tennessean Andrew Johnson, in August 1866—following the defeat of Lee's army, the capture of Jefferson Davis, the end of hostilities in distant Texas, and the surrender of the iron-framed CSS *Shenandoah* to the British Royal Navy in Liverpool—signed a proclamation "Declaring that Peace, Order, Tranquility, and Civil Authority Now Exists in and Throughout the Whole of the United States of America."

But peace could only come with slavery's end, when the moral, economic, and juristic contradictions of bondage became too much to bear. As they did in 1854. From that point on the nation's shrinking political center ceased to hold. Americans were trading on borrowed time, living in soon-to-be kindled cities, farming in peach groves and wheat fields shortly to steep in the blood of fallen soldiers. "Through a shower of bullets and shells," wrote one wounded Pennsylvania private, caught, with the Union's collapse, in a hellish Maryland cornfield, "it was only the thoughts of home that brought me from that place."[20] Such is the ghostly verdict of one generation upon another. Ill served were the youth who came of age when a divided Congress passed the Kansas-Nebraska Act, in whose wake came a great reckoning, the measured resonance of an original sin that had long shaken the country—and stirs through it still.

Acknowledgments

A certain global pandemic imposed itself upon this project, and I am grateful for the revolution in recent years of digital libraries, particularly Internet Archive, HathiTrust, and Google Books. These sources were supplemented by the vital, improbably stocked, if winnowing world of secondhand bookstores—including Ann Arbor's Dawn Treader, Washburne's Chequamegon Books, Cincinnati's Ohio Book Store, and Yellow Springs's splendid Dark Star Books—as well as more conventionally kept materials at Elizabethtown College's High Library, to whose supportive staff I am yet again indebted.

My understanding of Transcendentalism, the book's true root, is informed by illuminating discussions led by Megan Marshall, John Matteson, the late Joel Myerson, Robert A. Gross, Laura Dassow Walls, and the late Sterling F. Delano at the National Endowment for the Humanities Summer Institute, "Transcendentalism and Social Action in the Age of Emerson, Thoreau, and Fuller." As the man (Henry David) once said, "The universe is wider than our views of it."

Thanks to my agent Chris Calhoun for the benefit of his expertise, to the matchless Scribner team—particularly my editor, Colin Harrison, and Emily Polson—for tremendous support, and to Mark LaFlaur for a careful combing of the manuscript.

Notes

Introduction: *Right from Wrong*

1   Henry Villard, *Memoirs of Henry Villard, Journalist and Financier*, vol. 1 (Boston: Houghton, Mifflin, 1904), 55; David M. Potter, *The Impending Crisis: America before the Civil War, 1848–1861* (New York: Harper & Row, 1976), 160. The germane language in the Missouri Compromise promising freedom in the greater part of Jefferson's Louisiana Purchase is in section 8 of the bill: "And it be further enacted. That in all that territory ceded by France to the United States, under the name of Louisiana, which lies north of thirty-six degrees and thirty minutes north latitude, not included within the limits of the state, contemplated by this act, slavery and involuntary servitude, otherwise than in the punishment of crimes, whereof the parties shall have been duly convicted, shall be, and is hereby, forever prohibited." https://www.ourdocuments.gov/doc.php?flash=false&doc=22&page= transcript.

2   Allan Nevins, *Ordeal of the Union: A House Dividing, 1852–1857*, vol. 2 (New York: Charles Scribner's Sons, 1947), 316; James M. McPherson, *Battle Cry of Freedom: The Civil War Era* (New York: Oxford University Press, 1988), 121; Allen C. Guelzo, review of John R. Wunder and Joann M. Ross, eds., *The Nebraska-Kansas Act of 1854* in *American Historical Review*, October 2009, 1084.

3   Larry Gara, *The Presidency of Franklin Pierce* (Lawrence: University Press of Kansas, 1991), 34, 29–32, 48.

4   Brown was typically clean-shaven but for two years wore a robust beard as a disguise following his violent incursion into Kansas, which had resulted in numerous federal and state (Missouri) arrest warrants. In John Steuart Curry's 1942 portrait, *Tragic Prelude*, housed in the Kansas State Capitol building, a hirsute Brown stands, arms extended, clutching a Bible and a rifle, between free-soil and proslavery forces as a tornado and raging prairie fire (the Civil War) approach. In 1974 the rock band Kansas popularized the image, putting it on the cover of their eponymously titled first album.

5   Don E. Fehrenbacher, *Slavery, Law, & Politics: The Dred Scott Case in Historical Perspective* (New York: Oxford University Press, 1981), 287. For a superb study on the *Dred Scott* decision's impact on American politics see Kenneth M. Stampp's *America in 1857: A Nation on the Brink* (New York: Oxford University Press, 1990).

6   Roy P. Basler, ed., *The Collected Works of Abraham Lincoln*, vol. 2 (New Brunswick, NJ: Rutgers University Press, 1953), 274.

7   Merrill D. Peterson, ed., *The Portable Thomas Jefferson* (New York: Penguin Books, 1975), 217.

8   Mary S. Lovell, *The Churchills: In Love and War* (New York: W. W. Norton, 2011), 65.

9   It was the English social theorist Harriet Martineau, known in this country for traveling through much of America in the 1830s, who described Calhoun, referencing his tendency to traffic in a mental world of abstractions, as "the cast-iron man, who looks as if he had never been born, and never could be extinguished." She wrote further of Calhoun and his cohort: "Because it was necessary to obtain new territory for the support of the destructive institution [of slavery], a process of aggression and annexation was entered upon. . . . It destroyed the career and broke the hearts of the most eminent of them—of Calhoun, of Clay, and of Webster." Marie Weston Chapman, ed., *Harriet Martineau's Autobiography*, vol. 1 (Boston: James R. Osgood, 1877), 372.

10 Abraham Lincoln, *Selected Speeches and Writings* (New York: Library of America, 1992), 131.

11 Wendell Phillips Garrison and Francis Jackson Garrison, *William Lloyd Garrison, 1805–1879: The Story of His Life Told by His Children*, vol. 1 (New York: Century, 1885), 123.

12 Authored by "A leading Democrat Living in 'Egypt' or Southern Illinois," "Where Will It End?" *Atlantic Monthly*, December 1857, 239–249; Henry Wilson, *History of the Rise and Fall of the Slave Power in America*, vol. 2 (Boston: Houghton, Mifflin, 1874), 406, 463.

13 Dwight Lowell Dumond, ed., *Southern Editorials on Secession* (New York: Century, 1931), 13–14.

14 Jefferson Davis, *The Rise and Fall of the Confederate Government*, vol. 1 (New York: D. Appleton, 1881), 83.

1: *Original Sin*

1   William E. Gienapp, ed., *This Fiery Trial: The Speeches and Writings of Abraham Lincoln* (New York: Oxford University Press, 2002), 220.

2   Fisher Ames, "To the Editor of the Mirror," *New-York Mirror, and Ladies Literary Gazette*, April 16, 1825, 303.

3   Harold C. Syrett, ed., *The Papers of Alexander Hamilton*, vol. 2 (New York: Columbia University Press, 1961), 401–2.

4   Richard B. Morris, *The Forging of the Union, 1781–1789* (New York: Harper & Row, 1987), 43; James Thomas Flexner, *Washington: The Indispensable Man* (New York: Signet, 1984), 174, 178.

5   William M. E. Rachal, ed., *The Papers of James Madison*, vol. 9 (Chicago: University of Chicago Press, 1975), 174; Jonathan Elliot, ed., *The Debates, Resolutions, and Other Proceedings, in Convention, on the Adoption of the Federal Constitution*, vol. 2 (Washington, DC: Printed and Sold by the Editor, 1828), 92.

6   Merrill D. Peterson, ed., *The Portable Thomas Jefferson* (New York: Penguin Books, 1975), 215; Edmund Clarence Stedman and Ellen Mackay Hutchinson, eds., *A Library of American Literature: From the Earliest Settlement to the Present Time*, vol. 3 (New York: Charles L. Webster, 1888), 329. As the New Jersey law of 1804

freed only those born after July 4, 1804, slavery persisted in the state until the December 1865 ratification of the Thirteenth Amendment. At that point, perhaps some one dozen enslaved people were released from their bondage.

7   Max Farrand, ed., *The Records of the Federal Convention of 1787*, vol. 1 (New Haven, CT: Yale University Press, 1911), 486.

8   Linda Grant DePauw et al., eds., *Documentary History of the First Federal Congress, 1789–1791*, vol. 1 (Baltimore: Johns Hopkins University Press, 1972), 162.

9   Max Farrand, ed., *The Records of the Federal Convention of 1787*, vol. 2 (New Haven, CT: Yale University Press, 1911), 373, 371.

10 (Northampton) *Hampshire Gazette*, June 4, 1788, in Sean Wilentz, *No Property in Man: Slavery and Antislavery at the Nation's Founding* (Cambridge, MA: Harvard University Press, 2018), 14.

11 For statistics on slave population and distribution in 1790 see Peter Kolchin, *American Slavery, 1619–1877* (New York: Hill and Wang, 1993), 242.

12 Farrand, *Records of the Federal Convention*, vol. 2, 364.

13 Ralph Ketcham, ed., *The Anti-Federalist Papers and the Constitutional Convention Debates* (New York: Mentor, 1986), 175; Henry D. Gilpin, *The Papers of James Madison*, vol. 3 (Washington, DC: Langtree & O'Sullivan, 1840), 1427.

14 Farrand, *Records of the Federal Convention*, vol. 2, 371.

15 Walter Edgar, *Partisans & Redcoats: The Southern Conflict That Turned the Tide of the American Revolution* (New York: HarperPerennial, 2001), xiv.

16 Charles F. Hobson, ed., *The Papers of James Madison*, vol. 10 (Chicago: University of Chicago Press, 1977), 214.

17 Isaac Kramnick, ed., *The Federalist Papers* (New York: Penguin Books, 1987), 275.

18 Garry Wills, *"Negro President": Jefferson and the Slave Power* (Boston: Houghton Mifflin, 2003), 51; Julian P. Boyd, ed., *The Papers of Thomas Jefferson*, vol. 1 (Princeton, NJ: Princeton University Press, 1950), 320–21. For a provocative study on the relationship between slavery and taxation see Robin L. Einhorn's *American Taxation, American Slavery* (Chicago: University of Chicago Press, 2006).

19 Farrand, *Records of the Federal Convention*, vol. 1, 580–81.

20 Ibid., 201; Kramnick, *The Federalist Papers*, 332.

21 Akhil Reed Amar, *America's Constitution: A Biography* (New York: Random House, 2005), 91.

22 Andrew Delbanco, *The War before the War: Fugitive Slaves and the Struggle for America's Soul from the Revolution to the Civil War* (New York: Penguin Press, 2018), 72–77; Gary B. Nash, *The Unknown American Revolution: The Unruly Birth of Democracy and the Struggle to Create America* (New York: Penguin Books, 2005), 339. On the long-term impact of Britain's mobilization of former slaves in the Chesapeake during the Revolutionary War see Alan Taylor's *The Internal Enemy: Slavery and War in Virginia, 1772–1832* (New York: W. W. Norton, 2013).

23 John P. Kaminski, ed., *A Necessary Evil?: Slavery and the Debate over the Constitution* (Madison, WI: Madison House, 1995), 170.

2: Of Crises and Compromises

1   John C. Miller, *The Federalist Era, 1789–1801* (New York: Harper & Brothers, 1960), 110; John C. Miller, *Crisis in Freedom: The Alien and Sedition Acts* (Boston:

Little, Brown, 1951), 132; Barbara B. Oberg, ed., *The Papers of Thomas Jefferson*, vol. 30 (Princeton, NJ: Princeton University Press, 2003), 388.

2 Oberg, *Papers of Thomas Jefferson*, vol. 30, 550–55.

3 Albert J. Beveridge, *The Life of John Marshall*, vol. 2 (Boston: Houghton Mifflin, 1916), 577; Miller, *Crisis in Freedom*, 171, 173.

4 Harold C. Syrett, ed., *The Papers of Alexander Hamilton*, vol. 22 (New York: Columbia University Press, 1975), 452–53; James Grant, *John Adams: Party of One* (New York: Farrar, Straus and Giroux, 2005), 395.

5 Miller, *Federalist Era,* 241; Miller, *Crisis in Freedom*, 172.

6 Miller, *Federalist Era*, 276.

7 *Works of Fisher Ames* (Boston: T. B. Wait, 1809), 277; Elisha P. Douglass, "Fisher Ames, Spokesman for New England Federalism," *Proceedings of the American Philosophical Society*, October 1959, 695.

8 Garry Wills, *"Negro President": Jefferson and the Slave Power* (Boston: Houghton Mifflin, 2003), 2.

9 Henry Adams, ed., *Documents Relating to New-England Federalism: 1800 to 1815* (Boston: Little, Brown, 1877), 341.

10 Ibid., 341, 345.

11 Ibid., 355; Stanley Elkins and Eric McKitrick, *The Age of Federalism: The Early American Republic, 1788–1800* (New York: Oxford University Press, 1993), 623.

12 Irving Brant, *James Madison: Commander in Chief, 1812–1836* (Indianapolis: Bobbs-Merrill, 1961), 342.

13 Ibid., 343–44.

14 Ibid., 360.

15 William McDonald, ed., *Select Documents: Illustrative History of the United States, 1776–1861* (New York: Macmillan, 1901), 200.

16 Daniel Walker Howe, *What Hath God Wrought: The Transformation of America, 1815–1848* (New York: Oxford University Press, 2007), 148.

17 *The Declaration of Independence & The Constitution of the United States*, introduction by Pauline Maier (New York: Bantam Books, 1998), 74; Glover Moore, *The Missouri Controversy 1819–1821* (Lexington: University Press of Kentucky, 1953), 90; Stanislaus Murray Hamilton, ed., *The Writings of James Monroe*, vol. 6 (New York: G. P. Putnam's Sons, 1902), 116; Lester J. Cappon, ed., *The Adams-Jefferson Letters: The Complete Correspondence between Thomas Jefferson & Abigail & John Adams* (Chapel Hill: University of North Carolina Press, 1959), 548–49.

18 Charles Francis Adams, ed., *Memoirs of John Quincy Adams*, vol. 5 (Philadelphia: J. B. Lippincott, 1875), 12.

19 H. A. Washington, ed., *The Writings of Thomas Jefferson*, vol. 7 (New York: J. C. Riker, 1855), 160–61; Joseph Ellis, *American Sphinx: The Character of Thomas Jefferson* (New York: Alfred A. Knopf, 1997), 306.

20 William W. Freehling, *Prelude to Civil War: The Nullification Controversy in South Carolina, 1816–1836* (New York: Harper & Row, 1965), 11.

21 Daniel Feller, Thomas Coens, and Laura-Eve Moss, eds., *The Papers of Andrew Jackson*, vol. 10 (Knoxville: University of Tennessee Press, 2016), 506.

22 *State Papers on Nullification* (Boston: Dutton and Wentworth, 1834), 219, 201; William J. Cooper Jr., *The South and the Politics of Slavery, 1828–1856* (Baton Rouge: Louisiana State University Press, 1978), 45.

23 Avery Craven, *The Coming of the Civil War* (Chicago: University of Chicago Press, 1942), 222.

24 Ibid., 220.

25 Ibid., 227.

26 Stephen E. Maizlish, *A Strife of Tongues: The Compromise of 1850 and the Ideological Foundations of the American Civil War* (Charlottesville: University of Virginia Press, 2018), 16.

27 David Donald, *Charles Sumner and the Coming of the Civil War* (New York: Alfred A. Knopf, 1960), 184.

28 Maizlish, *A Strife of Tongues*, 45, 44.

29 Ibid., 35; Robert J. Scarry, *Millard Fillmore* (Jefferson, NC: McFarland, 2001), 172.

30 Melba Porter Hay, ed., *The Papers of Henry Clay*, vol. 10 (Lexington: University Press of Kentucky, 1991), 816–17; C. H. Van Tyne, *The Letters of Daniel Webster: From Documents Owned Principally by the New Hampshire Historical Society* (New York: McClure, Phillips, 1902), 433.

3: Nebraska in the New Year

1 "Local," *Daily National Era*, January 2, 1854; "Speech of Mr. Calhoun, of South Carolina, on the Slavery Question" (Washington, DC: Buell & Blanchard, 1850), 1.

2 Linda K. Kerber, "Abolitionists and Amalgamators: The New York City Race Riots of 1834," *New York History*, January 1967, 28–39; Robert W. Johannsen, *Stephen A. Douglas* (New York: Oxford University Press, 1973), 21.

3 Alexis de Tocqueville, *Democracy in America*, ed. J. P. Mayer, trans. George Lawrence (New York: Harper Perennial, 1988), 499.

4 F. G. De Fontaine, *The Fireside Dickens: A Cyclopedia of the Best Thoughts of Charles Dickens* (New York: G. W. Dillingham, 1888), 505; Harriet Martineau, *Retrospect of Western Travel*, vol. 1 (London: Saunders and Otley, 1838), 144.

5 Johannsen, *Stephen A. Douglas*, 207.

6 Ibid., 208; Elizabeth Fries Ellet, *Court Circles of the Republic, or the Beauties and Celebrities of the Nation: Illustrating Life and Society under Eighteen Presidents; Describing the Social Features of the Successive Administrations from Washington to Grant,* (Hartford, CT: Hartford, 1869), 475.

7 Charles Francis Adams, ed., *Memoirs of John Quincy Adams*, vol. 12 (Philadelphia: J. B. Lippincott, 1877), 121.

8 Johannsen, *Stephen A. Douglas*, 236; Allen C. Guelzo, *Lincoln and Douglas: The Debates That Defined America* (New York: Simon & Schuster, 2008), 11–12.

9 John Rives, ed., *The Congressional Globe: Containing Sketches of the Debates and Proceedings of the Second Session of the Thirty-First Congress*, vol. 23 (Washington, DC: Printed at the Office of John C. Rives, 1851), 312.

10 Johannsen, *Stephen A. Douglas*, 398.

11 Robert W. Johannsen, ed., *The Letters of Stephen A. Douglas* (Urbana: University of Illinois Press, 1961), 268.

12 Johannsen, *Stephen A. Douglas*, 334.

13 Ibid., 407.

14 Alice Elizabeth Malavasic, *The F Street Mess: How Southern Senators Rewrote the Kansas-Nebraska Act* (Chapel Hill: University of North Carolina Press, 2017), 92;

Mrs. Archibald Dixon (Susan Bullitt Dixon), *The True History of the Missouri Compromise and Its Repeal* (Cincinnati: Robert Clarke, 1889), 445.

15 Leonard L. Richards, *The Slave Power: The Free North and Southern Domination, 1780–1860* (Baton Rouge: Louisiana State University Press, 2000), 85–86.

16 Nathaniel Hawthorne, *Life of Franklin Pierce* (Boston: Ticknor, Reed, and Fields, 1852), 27.

17 Jefferson Davis, *The Rise and Fall of the Confederate Government*, vol. 1 (New York: D. Appleton, 1881), 28.

18 Ibid; Larry Gara, *The Presidency of Franklin Pierce* (Lawrence: University Press of Kansas, 1991), 91.

19 "Nebraska—Slavery Overriding the Compromise," (Chicago) *Free West*, January 19, 1854; Avery Craven, *The Coming of the Civil War* (Chicago: University of Chicago Press, 1942), 333.

20 "Slavery Militant," *New-York Tribune*, January 11, 1854; Craven, *Coming of the Civil War*, 332.

21 *Charles Francis Adams, 1835–1915: An Autobiography* (Boston: Houghton Mifflin, 1916), 59. On Seward and higher law-ism, see Walter Stahr's *Seward: Lincoln's Indispensable Man* (New York: Simon & Schuster, 2012), 116–43.

22 George E. Baker, ed., *The Life of William H. Seward with Selections from His Works* (New York: J. S. Redfield, 1855), 164–66.

23 John Niven, ed., *The Salmon P. Chase Papers*, vol. 2 (Kent, OH: Kent State University Press, 1994), 382n1.

4: The Battle Begins

1 John Niven, ed., *The Salmon P. Chase Papers*, vol. 2 (Kent, OH: Kent State University Press, 1994), 381.

2 Carl Schurz, *The Reminiscences of Carl Schurz*, vol. 2 (London: John Murray, 1909), 34.

3 William E. Gienapp, *The Origins of the Republican Party, 1852–1856* (New York: Oxford University Press, 1987), 72.

4 Frederick J. Blue, *Salmon P. Chase: A Life in Politics* (Kent, OH: Kent State University Press, 1987), 2, 5. The British novelist Frances Trollope lived briefly in Cincinnati in the early 1830s as part of an extended sojourn in the United States, which she then wrote up in a two-volume travel book. "I never saw any people who appeared to live so much without amusement as the Cincinnatians," she sniffed. "They have no public balls, excepting, I think, six during the Christmas holydays. They have no concerts, they have no dinner-parties. They have a theatre, which is, in fact, the only public amusement of this triste little town; but they seem to care little about it, and either from economy or distaste it is poorly attended." Mrs. [Frances] Trollope, *Domestic Manners of The Americans* (London: Whittaker, Treacher, 1832), 74.

5 Blue, *Salmon P. Chase*, 15.

6 Albert Bushnell Hart, *Salmon Portland Chase* (Boston: Houghton, Mifflin, 1899), 50.

7 Blue, *Salmon P. Chase*, 31–32. While it is true that the Northwest Ordinance generally prohibited slavery, it also left room for planters to claim their fugitive property. Article 6 of the Ordinance reads: "There shall be neither slavery nor involuntary servitude in the said territory, otherwise than in the punishment of crimes whereof the party shall have been duly convicted: Provided, always, That any person escaping into the same, from whom labor or service is lawfully claimed in

any one of the original States, such fugitive may be lawfully reclaimed and conveyed to the person claiming his or her labor or service as aforesaid." https://www
.digitalhistory.uh.edu/disp_textbook.cfm?smtID=3&psid=255.

8   Joan D. Hedrick, *Harriet Beecher Stowe: A Life* (New York: Oxford University Press,
    1994), 82–83. For a study on southern migration into early Ohio, Indiana, and
    Illinois, see Nicole Etcheson's *The Emerging Midwest: Upland Southerners and the
    Political Culture of the Old Northwest, 1787–1861* (Bloomington: Indiana University Press, 1996).

9   Blue, *Salmon P. Chase*, 45–46.

10 Ibid., 91.

11 Ibid., 26.

12 Robert C. Winthrop, *Addresses and Speeches on Various Occasions*, vol. 2 (Boston:
    Little, Brown, 1867), 233–34.

13 Frederick W. Seward, *Seward at Washington, as Senator and Secretary of State: A
    Memoir of His Life, with Selections from His Letters, 1846–1861* (New York: Derby
    and Miller, 1891), 222.

14 "Appeal of the Independent Democrats in Congress to the People of the United
    States" (Washington, DC: Towers' Printers, 1854), 1, 2.

15 Ibid., 2, 3.

16 Ibid., 4.

17 Jacob P. Merriman, "The Climax of the Bank War: Biddle's Contraction, 1833–34,"
    Journal of Political Economy, August 1963, 384n19. For an older, absorbing study
    on the idea of intrigue in the antebellum era, see David Brion Davis's *The Slave
    Power Conspiracy and the Paranoid Style* (Baton Rouge: Louisiana State University
    Press, 1969).

18 "Appeal of the Independent Democrats in Congress," 6, 7.

19 Ibid., 7.

20 Ibid.

21 Schurz, *The Reminiscences of Carl Schurz*, 34.

22 Kenneth M. Stampp, ed., *The Causes of the Civil War* (New York: Simon & Schuster, 1991), 25, 27; Roy P. Basler, ed., *The Collected Works of Abraham Lincoln*, vol. 2
    (New Brunswick, NJ: Rutgers University Press, 1953), 548.

5: *About a Book*

1   Washington's February 28, 1776, letter expressing admiration for Wheatley's poetry is
    at the Library of Congress. https://www.loc.gov/resource/mgw3h.001/?q=wheatley
    &sp=13&st=text.

2   "To Mrs. Harriet Beecher Stowe," *Frederick Douglass's Paper*, February 3, 1854. This
    poem was actually Watkins's second ode to Stowe. The previous year she had published, first in William Lloyd Garrison's *Liberator* and subsequently in *Frederick
    Douglass's Paper*, a verse titled "Eliza Harris," in honor of a central character in
    Uncle Tom's Cabin.

3   Donald Yacovone, "Sacred Land Regained: Frances Ellen Watkins Harper and 'The
    Massachusetts Fifty-Fourth,' A Lost Poem," *Pennsylvania History*, Winter 1995, 91;
    William Still, *The Underground Rail Road* (Philadelphia: Porter & Coates, 1872),
    755–58; Melba Joyce Boyd, *Discarded Legacy: Politics in the Life of Frances E. W.
    Harper, 1825–1911* (Detroit: Wayne State University Press, 1994), 43.

4 Still, *Underground Rail Road*, 755, 757–58.

5 "To Mrs. Harriet Beecher Stowe," 4.

6 Joan D. Hedrick, *Harriet Beecher Stowe: A Life* (New York: Oxford University Press, 1994), 29–30.

7 Ibid., xi.

8 Barbara A. White, *The Beecher Sisters* (New Haven, CT: Yale University Press, 2003), 15; *A Statement of the Reasons Which Induced the Students of Lane Seminary, to Dissolve Their Connection with That Institution* (Cincinnati: no publisher identified, 1834), 3. Over thirty of these men resumed their studies at the Oberlin Collegiate Institute some thirty-five miles west of Cleveland, all but saving that nearly insolvent school.

9 Hedrick, *Harriet Beecher Stowe*, 108.

10 David S. Reynolds, *Mightier Than the Sword: Uncle Tom's Cabin and the Battle for America* (New York: W. W. Norton, 2011), 18–19; Charles Edward Stowe, ed., *Life of Harriet Beecher Stowe: Compiled from Her Letters and Journals* (Boston: Houghton, Mifflin, 1889), 198.

11 Harriet Beecher Stowe, *Uncle Tom's Cabin: or, Life among the Lowly*, vol. 2 (Boston: John P. Jewett, 1852), 314; Hedrick, *Harriet Beecher Stowe*, 204; Stowe, *Life of Harriet Beecher Stowe*, 146.

12 Harriet Beecher Stowe, *Uncle Tom's Cabin: or, Life among the Lowly* (Boston: Houghton, Mifflin, 1889), vii.

13 Joseph P. Roppolo, "Harriet Beecher Stowe and New Orleans: A Study in Hate," *New England Quarterly*, September 1957, 352.

14 Stowe, *Life of Harriet Beecher Stowe*, 149–50.

15 Roppolo, "Harriet Beecher Stowe and New Orleans," 355–56.

16 E. Bruce Kirkham, *The Building of Uncle Tom's Cabin* (Knoxville: University of Tennessee Press, 1977), 66.

17 Michael Winship, "Uncle Tom's Cabin: History of the Book in the 19th-Century United States," can be accessed at http://utc.iath.virginia.edu/interpret/exhibits/winship/winship.html.

18 Harriet Beecher Stowe, *Uncle Tom's Cabin: or, Life Among the Lowly*, vol. 1 (Boston: John P. Jewett, 1852), 34, 37, 221; Stowe, *Uncle Tom's Cabin*, vol. 2, 273.

19 Stowe, *Uncle Tom's Cabin*, vol. 1, 94.

20 Ibid., 95.

21 Ibid., 109.

22 Ibid., 257; Stowe, *Uncle Tom's Cabin*, vol. 2, 317; Charles Edward Stowe and Lyman Beecher Stowe, *Harriet Beecher Stowe: The Story of Her Life* (Boston: Houghton Mifflin, 1911), 141.

23 Thomas F. Gossett, *Uncle Tom's Cabin and American Culture* (Dallas: Southern Methodist University Press, 1985), 165; Stowe, *Life of Harriet Beecher Stowe*, 161, 162; Frederick Douglass, *Autobiographies*, ed. Henry Louis Gates (New York: Library of America, 1994), 726.

24 Henry James, *A Small Boy and Others* (New York: Charles Scribner's Sons, 1913), 158–59.

25 Sally Pook, "Palace Provides a Memory of US Picnic in the Park" *The Telegraph*, November 18, 2003. On a visit to Great Britain, then-president George W. Bush was shown the queen's 1853 copy of *Uncle Tom's Cabin*. Annie Fields, *Life and Letters of Harriet Beecher Stowe* (Boston: Houghton, Mifflin, 1898), 156; Harriet Beecher

Stowe, *Uncle Tom's Cabin: Or Life Among the Lowly* (New York: Modern Library, 2001), vi; Karen R. Smith, *"Resurrection, Uncle Tom's Cabin, and the Reader in Crisis,"* *Comparative Literature Studies* 33, no. 4 (1996): 350.

26 Reynolds, *Mightier Than the Sword*, 132.

27 Stowe, *Life of Harriet Beecher Stowe*, 226.

28 Hedrick, *Harriet Beecher Stowe*, 250.

29 Wendell Phillips Garrison and Francis Jackson Garrison, *William Lloyd Garrison, 1805–1879: The Story of His Life Told by His Children*, vol. 3 (Boston: Houghton, Mifflin, 1885), 396.

30 Gossett, *Uncle Tom's Cabin and American Culture*, 31; Stowe and Stowe, *Harriet Beecher Stowe*, 140.

31 Gossett, *Uncle Tom's Cabin and American Culture*, 189, 191, 53; Edgar Allan Poe quip in "Critical Notices," *Broadway Journal*, September 20, 1845.

32 John L. Brooke, *"There Is a North": Fugitive Slaves, Political Crisis, and Cultural Transformation in the Coming of the Civil War* (Amherst: University of Massachusetts Press, 2019), 170; Mrs. Mary H. Eastman, *Aunt Phillis's Cabin: or, Southern Life as It Is* (Philadelphia: Lippincott, Grambo, 1852), 24.

33 Gossett, *Uncle Tom's Cabin and American Culture*, 210.

34 Frederick Law Olmsted, *A Journey in the Seaboard Slave States* (New York: Dix and Edwards, 1856), 606.

35 Reynolds, *Mightier Than the Sword*, 142; Gossett, *Uncle Tom's Cabin and American Culture*, 211; Stowe, *Life of Harriet Beecher Stowe*, 163.

36 Stowe, *Uncle Tom's Cabin: or, Life Among the Lowly*, vol. 2, 300; Hedrick, *Harriet Beecher Stowe*, 235; Garrison and Garrison, *William Lloyd Garrison*, vol. 3, 362.

37 Hedrick, *Harriet Beecher Stowe*, 256.

6: Emerson in the Arena

1 A. W. Plumstead and Harrison Hayford, *The Journals and Miscellaneous Notebooks of Ralph Waldo Emerson*, vol. 7 (Cambridge, MA: Belknap Press of Harvard University Press, 1969), 342; Lawrence Buell, ed., *The American Transcendentalists: Essential Writings* (New York: Modern Library, 2006), 206.

2 Quoting from a letter in which Emerson writes of having "no symptoms that any physician extant can recognize or understand," biographer Gay Wilson Allen proposes that Waldo's fear of illness "does sound psychosomatic." Allen's *Waldo Emerson: A Biography* (New York: Viking Press, 1981), 94. William H. Gilman and Alfred R. Ferguson, eds., *The Journals and Miscellaneous Notebooks of Ralph Waldo Emerson*, vol. 3 (Cambridge, MA: Belknap Press of Harvard University Press, 1963), 60, 117.

3 Robert D. Richardson Jr., *Emerson: The Mind on Fire* (Berkeley: University of California Press, 1995), 3; Alfred R. Ferguson, ed., *The Journals and Miscellaneous Notebooks of Ralph Waldo Emerson*, vol. 4 (Cambridge, MA: Belknap Press of Harvard University Press, 1964), 27.

4 John Matteson, *The Lives of Margaret Fuller* (New York: W. W. Norton, 2012), 113.

5 Brooks Atkinson, ed., *The Essential Writings of Ralph Waldo Emerson* (New York: Modern Library, 2000), 133, 134, 138.

6 Julian Hawthorne, *Hawthorne and His Circle* (New York: Harper & Brothers, 1903), 65.

7 Joel Myerson, ed., *Transcendentalism: A Reader* (New York: Oxford University Press, 2000), 227–29.

8 Merton M. Sealts Jr., *The Journals and Miscellaneous Notebooks of Ralph Waldo Emerson*, vol. 5 (Cambridge, MA: Belknap Press of Harvard University Press, 1965), 505; Joel Myerson, ed., *A Historical Guide to Ralph Waldo Emerson* (New York: Oxford University Press, 2000), 183–84; Ralph H. Orth and Alfred R. Ferguson, eds., *The Journals and Miscellaneous Notebooks of Ralph Waldo Emerson*, vol. 13 (Cambridge, MA: Belknap Press of Harvard University Press, 1977), 281, 282.

9 Linda Allardt, ed., *The Journals and Miscellaneous Notebooks of Ralph Waldo Emerson*, vol. 12 (Cambridge, MA: Belknap Press of Harvard University Press, 1976), 152; Orth and Ferguson, *Journals and Miscellaneous Notebooks*, 13:35, 13:286; Len Gougeon, *Virtue's Hero: Emerson, Antislavery, and Reform* (Athens: University of Georgia Press, 1990), 66.

10 Lawrence Buell, *Emerson* (Cambridge, MA: Belknap Press of Harvard University Press, 2003), 259; Thomas Wentworth Higginson, *Cheerful Yesterdays* (Boston: Houghton, Mifflin, 1898), 174.

11 Hawthorne, *Hawthorne and His Circle*, 68.

12 Sandra Harbert Petrulionis, *To Set This World Right: The Antislavery Movement in Thoreau's Concord* (Ithaca, NY: Cornell University Press, 2006), 19. For a summary view of Transcendentalism's relationship to abolitionism see Manisha Sinha's *The Slave's Cause: A History of Abolition* (New Haven, CT: Yale University Press, 2016), 488–90, as well as Robert A. Gross's *The Transcendentalists and Their World* (New York: Farrar, Straus and Giroux, 2021), particularly chapter 15, "The Spirt of Reform." On Transcendentalism's populistic approach to antislavery (contra the image of Emerson, Thoreau, and company as dreamy philosophers) see Peter Wirzbicki's *Fighting for the Higher Law: Black and White Transcendentalists against Slavery* (Philadelphia: University of Pennsylvania Press, 2021), especially 67–83.

13 Edward Waldo Emerson and Waldo Emerson Forbes, eds., *Journals of Ralph Waldo Emerson*, vol. 7 (Boston: Houghton Mifflin, 1913), 26; Richardson, *Emerson*, 396.

14 Atkinson, *Essential Writings of Ralph Waldo Emerson*, 766, 770, 765.

15 Ralph Waldo Emerson, *Essays*, Second Series (Boston: Houghton, Mifflin, 1876), 291.

16 Edmund Clarence Stedman and Ellen Mackay Hutchinson, *A Library of American Literature: From the Earliest Settlement to the Present Time*, vol. 5 (New York: William Evarts Benjamin, 1894), 296.

17 *Speech of Hon. Daniel Webster on Mr. Clay's Resolutions in the Senate of the United States* (Washington, DC: Gideon, 1850), 42, 24, 47, 48–49.

18 Mary Tyler Peabody Mann, *Life of Horace Mann* (Boston: Walker, Fuller, 1865), 293; Linck C. Johnson, "'Liberty Is Never Cheap': Emerson, 'The Fugitive Slave Law,' and the Antislavery Lecture Series at the Broadway Tabernacle," *New England Quarterly*, December, 2003, 579; Robert V. Remini, *Daniel Webster: The Man and His Time* (New York: W. W. Norton, 1997), 675; Irving H. Bartlett, *Daniel Webster* (New York: W. W. Norton, 1978), 255; Orth and Ferguson, *Journals and Miscellaneous Notebooks of Ralph Waldo Emerson*, 13:111–12.

19 Daniel Webster, *Discourse, Delivered at Plymouth, in Commemoration of the First Settlement of New England* (Boston: Wells and Lilly, 1821), 7; *The Writings and Speeches of Daniel Webster*, vol. 6 (Boston: Little, Brown, 1903), 75; William H. Gilman, ed., *The Journals and Miscellaneous Notebooks of Ralph Waldo Emerson*, vol. 8 (Cambridge, MA: Belknap Press of Harvard University Press, 1970), 360.

20 Petrulionis, *To Set This World Right*, 76; William H. Gilman, ed., *The Journals and Miscellaneous Notebooks of Ralph Waldo Emerson*, vol. 11 (Cambridge, MA: Belknap Press of Harvard University Press, 1975), 344.

21 Richardson, *Emerson*, 496; Len Gougeon and Joel Myerson, eds., *Emerson's Antislavery Writings* (New Haven, CT: Yale University Press, 1995), 53, 56, 57, 64.

22 Johnson, "'Liberty Is Never Cheap,'" 557, 551.

23 Ibid., 577; Horace Henry Furness, ed., *Records of a Lifelong Friendship: Ralph Waldo Emerson and William Henry Furness* (Boston: Houghton Mifflin, 1910), 92–93; Orth and Ferguson, *Journals and Miscellaneous Notebooks of Ralph Waldo Emerson*, 13:283.

24 Susan Hayes Ward, *The History of the Broadway Tabernacle Church, from Its Organization in 1840 to the Close of 1900, Including Factors Influencing Its Formation* (New York: Broadway Tabernacle Church, 1901), 79, 29.

25 Hawthorne, *Hawthorne and His Circle*, 66.

26 Atkinson, *Essential Writings of Ralph Waldo Emerson*, 783, 784; Remini, *Daniel Webster*, 757–69.

27 Atkinson, *Essential Writings of Ralph Waldo Emerson*, 784–85.

28 Ibid., 786–87, 792.

29 Gougeon and Myerson, *Emerson's Antislavery Writings*, xlii; Johnson, "'Liberty Is Never Cheap,'" 585.

30 Joseph Slater, ed., *The Correspondence of Emerson and Carlyle* (New York: Columbia University Press, 1964), 499.

7: Republican Rubicon

1 For Van Buren's communication to Ritchie see, http://vanburenpapers.org/document-mvb00528; and for a broader overview of the New Yorker's politics at this time see *The Autobiography of Martin Van Buren*, ed., John C. Fitzpatrick, in *Annual Report of the American Historical Association for the Year 1918*, vol. 2 (Washington, DC: Government Printing Office, 1920), 139–40.

2 William E. Gienapp, *The Origins of the Republican Party, 1852–1856* (New York: Oxford University Press, 1987), 35.

3 Susan Sutton Smith and Harrison Hayford, eds., *The Journals and Miscellaneous Notebooks of Ralph Waldo Emerson*, vol. 14 (Cambridge, MA: Belknap Press of Harvard University Press, 1978), 380.

4 John Niven, ed., *The Salmon P. Chase Papers*, vol. 2 (Kent, OH: Kent State University Press, 1994), 384.

5 A. F. Gilman, "The Origin of the Republican Party" (Wisconsin: no publisher identified, 1914), 3; Irvin W. Near, "A Native of Jefferson County, New York, First Organized and Named the Republican Party," *Proceedings of the New York State Historical Association*, vol. 9 (Glen Falls, NY: New York State Historical Association, 1910), 100.

6 On the National Reform Association see Mark A. Lause, *Young America: Land, Labor, and the Republican Community* (Urbana: University of Illinois Press, 2005); David McLellan, ed., *Karl Marx: Selected Writings* (New York: Oxford University Press, 1977), 245.

7 Lause, *Young America*, 29, 36, 73.

8 Ibid., 113.

9 Gilman, *Origin of the Republican Party*, 3.

10 Frank A. Flower, *History of the Republican Party* (Springfield, IL: Union, 1884), 152.

11 Ibid., 160.

12 Ibid., 150; Jeter Allen Isley, *Horace Greeley and the Republican Party, 1853–1861: A Study of the New York Tribune* (Princeton, NJ: Princeton University Press, 1947), 13.

13 Gilman, *Origin of the Republican Party*, 5; Henry Wilson, *History of the Rise and Fall of the Slave Power in America*, vol. 2 (Boston: Houghton, Mifflin, 1874), 393.

14 Flower, *History of the Republican Party*, 163.

15 National Register of Historic Places Inventory, "Little White Schoolhouse; 'Birthplace of the Republican Party,'" United States Department of the Interior (July 1969), 136–38; Gilman, *Origin of the Republican Party*, 8.

16 Flower, *History of the Republican Party*, 164.

17 Ibid.; Tim Lyke, "No Dispute: Bovay Gave GOP Its Name," *Ripon Press*, April 27, 2011.

18 *The Correspondence of Thomas Carlyle and Ralph Waldo Emerson*, vol. 2 (London: Chatto & Windus, Piccadilly, 1883), 234.

19 Flower, *History of the Republican Party*, 153.

20 Ibid., 163.

21 Richard H. Sewell, *Ballots for Freedom: Antislavery Politics in the United States, 1837–1869* (New York: W. W. Norton, 1976), 264; Eric Foner, *Free Soil, Free Labor, Free Men: The Ideology of the Republican Party before the Civil War* (New York: Oxford University Press, 1970), 126; Allan Nevins, *Ordeal of the Union: A House Dividing, 1852–1857*, vol. 2 (New York: Charles Scribner's Sons, 1947), 322.

22 Gordon S. P. Kleeberg, *The Formation of the Republican Party* (New York: R. Sichel, 1906), 1.

23 David M. Potter, *The Impending Crisis: America before the Civil War, 1848–1861* (New York: Harper & Row, 1976), 247; Sewell, *Ballots for Freedom*, 265.

24 David Herbert Donald, *Lincoln* (New York: Simon & Schuster, 1995), 169.

8: *Forging a North*

1 https://www.aoc.gov/capitol-buildings/old-senate-chamber. A young, sojourning Sam Clemens, only eighteen and not yet Mark Twain, scored a seat in the Senate's visitors' balcony in February 1854 while the Kansas-Nebraska debate raged. Honing his skill for description and deflating commentary, he wrote of the upper chamber: "Its glory hath departed. Its halls no longer echo the words of a Clay, or Webster, or Calhoun . . . the void is felt. . . . Mr. Douglas . . . looks like a lawyer's clerk, and Mr. Seward is a slim, dark, bony individual, and looks like a respectable wind would blow him out of the country." Edgar Marquess Branch, ed., *Mark Twain's Letters*, vol. 1 (Berkeley: University of California Press, 1988), 41.

2 Robert W. Johannsen, *Stephen A. Douglas* (New York: Oxford University Press, 1973), 419, 420, 421.

3 David Donald, *Charles Sumner and the Coming of the Civil War* (New York: Alfred A. Knopf, 1960), 252; Johannsen, *Stephen A. Douglas*, 421.

4 *The Nebraska Question: Compromising Speeches in the United States Senate* (New York: Redfield, 1854), 54, 60. Chase's bravura performance ends with a near verbatim quotation (he says "great" rather than "noble") from John Milton's 1644 discourse, *Areopagitica*, page 34.

5 Paul Revere Frothingham, *Edward Everett: Orator and Statesman* (Boston:

Houghton Mifflin, 1925), 347, 348, 349; Allan Nevins, *Ordeal of the Union: A House Dividing, 1852–1857*, vol. 2 (New York: Charles Scribner's Sons, 1947), 141.

6 *The Nebraska Question*, 78.

7 William E. Gienapp, *The Origins of the Republican Party, 1852–1856* (New York: Oxford University Press, 1987), 87.

8 Frederick W. Seward, *Seward at Washington, as Senator and Secretary of State: A Memoir of His Life, with Selections from His Letters, 1846–1861* (New York: Derby and Miller, 1891), 221.

9 Ibid., 223; *The Nebraska Question*, 105.

10 Donald, *Charles Sumner and the Coming of the Civil War*, 254, 255; *The Nebraska Question*, 107, 116, 119.

11 Donald, *Charles Sumner and the Coming of the Civil War*, 256.

12 Allan Nevins and Milton Halsey Thomas, eds., *The Diary of George Templeton Strong*, vol. 2 (New York: Macmillan, 1952), 160; Johannsen, *Stephen A. Douglas*, 429; Donald, *Charles Sumner and the Coming of the Civil War*, 258.

13 Seward, *Seward at Washington, as Senator and Secretary of State*, 224; Donald, *Charles Sumner and the Coming of the Civil War*, 259.

14 Roy F. Nichols, *Blueprints for Leviathan: American Style* (New York: Atheneum, 1963), 104, 105; Joan D. Hedrick, *Harriet Beecher Stowe: A Life* (New York: Oxford University Press, 1994), 257.

15 Nichols, *Blueprints for Leviathan*, 106, 107.

16 Ibid., 108; Annie Powers, "'An Altercation Full of Meaning': The Duel between Francis B. Cutting and John C. Breckinridge," *Gettysburg College Journal of the Civil War Era* 1, article 5, (2010): 32–41.

17 Joanne B. Freeman, *The Field of Blood: Violence in Congress and the Road to the Civil War* (New York: Farrar, Straus and Giroux, 2018), 197–99; the *Richmond Examiner*'s concerns were printed in "Messrs. Cutting and Breckinridge," *New York Times* April 6, 1854.

18 Nichols, *Blueprints for Leviathan* 108; Johannsen, *Stephen A. Douglas*, 433; David M. Potter, *The Impending Crisis: America before the Civil War, 1848–1861* (New York: Harper and Row, 1976), 165.

19 Nichols, *Blueprints for Leviathan*, 115; Freeman, *Field of Blood*, 193.

20 http://history.furman.edu/benson/docs/knmenu.htm.

21 Ibid.

22 Nevins, *Ordeal of the Union*, 156, 157.

23 Larry Gara, *The Presidency of Franklin Pierce* (Lawrence: University Press of Kansas, 1991), 95.

24 Frederick J. Blue, *Salmon P. Chase: A Life in Politics* (Kent, OH: Kent State University Press, 1987), 95; *New York Times*, May 19, 1859; Nevins and Halsey, *Diary of George Templeton Strong*, 174.

25 Robert W. Johannsen, ed., *The Letters of Stephen A. Douglas* (Urbana: University of Illinois Press, 1961), 300; *Charles Sumner: His Complete Works*, vol. 4 (Boston: Lee and Shepard, 1900), 147.

9: Bibles and Guns

1 Samuel A. Johnson, *The Battle Cry of Freedom: The New England Emigrant Aid Company in the Kansas Crusade* (Lawrence: University of Kansas Press, 1954),

16–17; Eli Thayer, *A History of the Kansas Crusade: Its Friends and Its Foes* (New York: Harper & Brothers, 1889), 82; Allan Nevins, *Ordeal of the Union: A House Dividing, 1852–1857*, vol. 2 (New York: Charles Scribner's Sons, 1947), 309. In February 1855 the original charter was set aside due to concerns about liability and the Massachusetts legislature incorporated a new charter called the New England Emigrant Aid Company.

2 Eli Thayer, *The New England Emigrant Aid Company: And Its Influence, through the Kansas Contest, upon National History* (Worcester, MA: Franklin P. Rice, 1887), 13; Nevins, *Ordeal of the Union*, 307; *Frederick Douglass's Paper*, May 26, 1854.

3 Charles Nutt, *History of Worcester and Its People*, vol. 4 (New York: Lewis Historical Publishing Company, 1929), 577–80; Johnson, *The Battle Cry of Freedom*, 8, 9.

4 Jean Holloway, "Edward Everett Hale on 'How to Conquer Texas,'" *University of Texas Studies in English*, 1952, 69–70; Thayer, *The New England Emigrant Aid Company*, 18.

5 Thayer, *The New England Emigrant Aid Company*, 13.

6 Ibid., 14.

7 Ibid., 19.

8 Ibid.

9 Thayer, *History of the Kansas Crusade*, 36.

10 Thayer, *The New England Emigrant Aid Company*, 21. When Kansas erupted in a series of violent confrontations between northern and southern settlers, Greeley wrote an editorial suggesting the Free-Soilers might consider making their stand elsewhere. "In any moral controversy there was no limit to Mr. Greeley's persistency and endurance," Thayer later wrote, "but when it came to blood, he was apparently unreliable." Thayer, *History of the Kansas Crusade*, 182, 183; Jeter Allen Isley, *Horace Greeley and the Republican Party, 1853–1861: A Study of the New York Tribune* (Princeton, NJ: Princeton University Press, 1947), 132.

11 Gunja SenGupta, *For God & Mammon: Evangelicals and Entrepreneurs, Masters and Slaves in Territorial Kansas, 1854–1860* (Athens: University of Georgia Press, 1996), 14–15; Johnson, *The Battle Cry of Freedom*, 15.

12 *Miscellanies: The Complete Works of Ralph Waldo Emerson*, vol. 11 (Boston: Houghton, Mifflin, 1878), 257.

13 *The Complete Poetical Works of John Greenleaf Whittier* (Boston: Houghton, Mifflin, 1884), 146.

14 Nicole Etcheson, *Bleeding Kansas: Contested Liberty in the Civil War Era* (Lawrence: University Press of Kansas, 2004), 41.

15 Johnson, *The Battle Cry of Freedom*, 51, 53.

16 Thayer, *History of the Kansas Crusade*, 64, 185, 65.

17 Louise Barry, "The New England Emigrant Aid Company Parties of 1855," *Kansas Historical Quarterly*, August 1943, 227, 236, 246, 253.

18 Ibid., 260, 242; SenGupta, *For God & Mammon*, 47; Johnson, *The Battle Cry of Freedom*, 34.

19 Nevins, *Ordeal of the Union*, 310.

20 William E. Parrish, *David Rice Atchison of Missouri: Border Politician* (Columbia: University of Missouri Press, 1961), 161.

21 James C. Malin, "Emergency Housing at Lawrence, 1854," *Kansas History: A Journal of the Central Plains*, Spring 1954, 34–49; Lynda Lasswell Crist, ed., *The Papers*

of Jefferson Davis, vol. 5 (Baton Rouge: Louisiana State University Press, 1985), 85n2.

22 Crist, *Papers of Jefferson Davis*, 84; Thomas Goodrich, *War to the Knife: Bleeding Kansas, 1854–1861* (Mechanicsburg, PA: Stackpole Books, 1998), 28.

23 Johnson, *The Battle Cry of Freedom*, 97; Larry Gara, *The Presidency of Franklin Pierce* (Lawrence: University Press of Kansas, 1991), 117; Thayer, *The New England Emigrant Aid Company*, 32, 30.

24 David Donald, *Charles Sumner and the Coming of the Civil War* (New York: Alfred A. Knopf, 1960), 279, 278.

25 Oliver Johnson, *The Abolitionists Vindicated in a Review of Eli Thayer's Paper on the New England Emigrant Aid Company* (Worcester, MA: Franklin P. Rice, 1887), 13; Thayer, *The New England Emigrant Aid Company*, 35; Thayer, *History of the Kansas Crusade*, 82.

26 Avery Craven, *The Coming of the Civil War* (Chicago: University of Chicago Press, 1942), 357; Nevins, *Ordeal of the Union*, 381, 384, 382; Etcheson, *Bleeding Kansas*, 37; Barry, "The New England Emigrant Aid Company Parties of 1855," 228.

27 Johnson, *The Battle Cry of Freedom*, 65; David S. Reynolds, *John Brown, Abolitionist: The Man Who Killed Slavery, Sparked the Civil War, and Seeded Civil Rights* (New York: Vintage Books, 2005), 331.

28 W. H. Isely, "The Sharps Rifle Episode in Kansas History," *American Historical Review*, April 1907, 548, 551, 552; Nevins, *Ordeal of the Union*, 428.

10: *Empires to the South*

1 T. Robinson Warren, *Dust and Foam; or, Three Oceans and Two Continents* (New York: Charles Scribner, 1859), 213.

2 Henry Adams, *History of the United States of America during the Administrations of Thomas Jefferson* (New York: Library of America, 1986), 576.

3 Matthew Karp, *This Vast Southern Empire: Slaveholders at the Helm of American Foreign Policy* (Cambridge, MA: Harvard University Press, 2016), 183.

4 Warren, *Dust and Foam*, 212; Walter Johnson, *River of Dark Dreams: Slavery and Empire in the Cotton Kingdom* (Cambridge, MA: Belknap Press of Harvard University Press, 2013), 381.

5 James Carson Jamison, *With Walker in Nicaragua* (Columbia, MO: E. W. Stephens, 1909), 11–12. To some extent Jamison is ruminating on the evolving meaning of masculinity in the mid-nineteenth-century United States. This subject is gracefully covered in Amy S. Greenberg's *Manifest Manhood and the Antebellum American Empire* (New York: Cambridge University Press, 2005), which assays the relationship between filibustering and domestic change. For her treatment of Walker, see pages 135–69. Also note Greenberg's "The Grey-Eyed Man of Destiny: Character, Appearance, and Filibustering," *Journal of the Early Republic*, Winter 2000, 673–99.

6 Jamison, *With Walker in Nicaragua*, 19; Albert Z. Carr, *The World and William Walker* (New York: Harper & Row, 1963), 7; Charles H. Brown, *Agents of Manifest Destiny: The Lives and Times of the Filibusters* (Chapel Hill: University of North Carolina Press, 1980), 175.

7 Brown, *Agents of Manifest Destiny*, 176.

8   Jay Grossman, *Reconstituting the American Renaissance: Emerson, Whitman, and the Politics of Representation* (Durham, NC: Duke University Press, 2003), 184; Robert E. May, *The Southern Dream of a Caribbean Empire, 1854–1861* (Baton Rouge: Louisiana State University Press, 1973), 79.

9   William O. Scroggs, *Filibusters and Financiers: The Story of William Walker and His Associates* (New York: Macmillan, 1916), 18.

10 Ibid., 32. In his 1985 novel, *Blood Meridian or the Evening Redness in the West*, Cormac McCarthy evoked a Walkeresque character in "Captain White," who says to one recruit, "Right now they are forming in Washington a commission to come out here and draw up the boundary lines between our country and Mexico. I don't think there's any question that ultimately Sonora will become a United States territory. Guaymas a US port." McCarthy, *Blood Meridian or the Evening Redness in the West* (New York: Random House, 1985), 36–37.

11 William Walker, *The War in Nicaragua* (Mobile, AL: S. H. Goetzel, 1860), 21; Robert C. Stevens, "The Apache Menace in Sonora, 1831–1849," *Arizona and the West*, Autumn, 1964, 211.

12 James D. Richardson, *A Compilation of the Messages and Papers of the Presidents*, vol. 6 (New York: Bureau of National Literature, 1897), 2731; Brown, *Agents of Manifest Destiny*, 190.

13 Brown, *Agents of Manifest Destiny*, 192–93.

14 Ibid., 194.

15 Scroggs, *Filibusters and Financiers*, 38; Brown, *Agents of Manifest Destiny*, 192–93.

16 *New York Times*, January 10, 1854.

17 Brown, *Agents of Manifest Destiny*, 199–200.

18 Walker, *The War in Nicaragua*, 19.

19 Brown, *Agents of Manifest Destiny*, 207; Scroggs, *Filibusters and Financiers*, 46–47.

20 Brown, *Agents of Manifest Destiny*, 209, 211.

21 Ibid., 217.

22 William R. Manning, ed., *Diplomatic Correspondence of the United States: Inter-American Affairs, 1831–1860*, vol. 9 (Washington, DC: Carnegie Endowment for International Peace, 1937), 736–37.

23 James M. McPherson, *Battle Cry of Freedom: The Civil War Era* (New York: Oxford University Press, 1988), 112–15; Regis A. Courtemanche, "The Royal Navy and the End of William Walker," *The Historian*, May 1968, 350, 356, 363.

24 Walker, *The War in Nicaragua*, 271, 272.

11: *Boston Besieged*

1   Andrew Delbanco, *The War before the War: Fugitive Slaves and the Struggle for America's Soul from the Revolution to the Civil War* (New York: Penguin Press, 2018), 8.

2   Len Gougeon and Joel Myerson, eds., *Emerson's Antislavery Writings* (New Haven, CT: Yale University Press, 1995), 120.

3   Charles Emery Stevens, *Anthony Burns: A History* (Boston: John P. Jewett, 1856), 153, 172; Albert J. Von Frank, *The Trials of Anthony Burns: Freedom and Slavery in Emerson's Boston* (Cambridge, MA: Harvard University Press, 1998), 181. My approach to the Burns case is informed by Von Frank's astute study.

4   Stevens, *Anthony Burns*, 176–78.

5 Von Frank, *The Trials of Anthony Burns*, 84; Samuel Shapiro, "The Rendition of Anthony Burns," *Journal of Negro History*, January 1959, 36.
6 *The Liberator*, March 9, 1855; *The Boston Slave Riot, and Trial of Anthony Burns* (Boston: William V. Spencer, 1854), 5, 15.
7 Shapiro, "The Rendition of Anthony Burns," 37.
8 Nevins, *Ordeal of the Union*, 151; Von Frank, *The Trials of Anthony Burns*, 17.
9 *The Boston Slave Riot*, 7, 8; Samuel Sewall, *The Selling of Joseph* (Boston: Bartholomew Green and John Allen, 1700), 1; Von Frank, *The Trials of Anthony Burns*, 10, 54.
10 Stevens, *Anthony Burns*, 37, 38; *The Boston Slave Riot*, 9.
11 James Grant Wilson and John Fiske, eds., *Appleton's Cyclopædia of American Biography*, vol 4 (New York: D. Appleton, 1988), 655; James Brewer Stewart, *Holy Warriors: The Abolitionists and American Slavery* (New York: Hill and Wang, 1996), 162; Von Frank, *The Trials of Anthony Burns*, 59.
12 Von Frank, *The Trials of Anthony Burns*, 61.
13 *The Boston Slave Riot*, 10, 11; Thomas Wentworth Higginson, *Cheerful Yesterdays* (Boston: Houghton, Mifflin, 1898), 157.
14 Larry Gara, *The Presidency of Franklin Pierce* (Lawrence: University Press of Kansas, 1991), 107; Nevins, *Ordeal of the Union*, 151.
15 Von Frank, *The Trials of Anthony Burns*, 75.
16 *The Boston Slave Riot*, 16; Shapiro, "The Rendition of Anthony Burns," 40.
17 Von Frank, *The Trials of Anthony Burns*, 119; *The Boston Slave Riot*, 30.
18 *The Boston Slave Riot*, 41; Von Frank, *The Trials of Anthony Burns*, 130; Shapiro, "The Rendition of Anthony Burns," 41.
19 Shapiro, "The Rendition of Anthony Burns," 42.
20 Von Frank, *The Trials of Anthony Burns*, 195–96.
21 Ibid., 197; *The Boston Slave Riot*, 76, 82, 78.
22 Shapiro, "The Rendition of Anthony Burns," 45; Nevins, *Ordeal of the Union*, 150–51.
23 Stevens, *Anthony Burns*, 144; Von Frank, *The Trials of Anthony Burns*, 215; Shapiro, "The Rendition of Anthony Burns," 45.
24 Stevens, *Anthony Burns*, 149; Von Frank, *The Trials of Anthony Burns*, 213, 215; Stewart, *Holy Warriors*, 161.
25 Henry Adams, *The Education of Henry Adams* (Boston: Riverside Press, 1918), 42.
26 Stevens, *Anthony Burns*, 76.
27 Ibid., 77.
28 Shapiro, "The Rendition of Anthony Burns," 49.
29 Von Frank, *The Trials of Anthony Burns*, 234, 288–90.
30 Gara, *Presidency of Franklin Pierce*, 108; Ralph L. Rusk, ed., *The Letters of Ralph Waldo Emerson*, vol. 4 (New York: Columbia University Press, 1939), 448; Don E. Fehrenbacher, *The Slaveholding Republic: An Account of the United States Government's Relations to Slavery* (New York: Oxford University Press, 2001), 237.
31 Shapiro, "The Rendition of Anthony Burns," 49; Gara, *Presidency of Franklin Pierce*, 108.

12: Independence Day

1 Elaine Brooks, "Massachusetts Anti-Slavery Society," *Journal of Negro History*, July 1945, 311; *Walker's Appeal, in Four Articles; Together with a Preamble to the Coloured Citizens of the World, but in Particular, and Very Expressly, to Those of the*

United States of America (Boston: Printed and Published by David Walker, 1829), 2; William W. Freehling, *The Road to Disunion: Secessionists at Bay, 1776–1854* (New York: Oxford University Press, 1990), 182.

2 *The Declaration of Independence & The Constitution of the United States*, introduction by Pauline Maier (New York: Bantam Books, 1998), 79; William Lloyd Garrison, *No Compromise with Slavery: An Address* (New York: American Anti-Slavery Society, 1854), 5. Emphasis added.

3 Henry Mayer, *All on Fire: William Lloyd Garrison and the Abolition of Slavery* (New York: W. W. Norton, 1998), an image of the placard can be consulted in the photo insert section that faces page 456; "No Union with Slaveholders," *The Liberator*, July 7, 1854.

4 Mayer, *All on Fire*, 421; "No Union with Slaveholders," *The Liberator*, July 7, 1854.

5 "No Union with Slaveholders," *The Liberator*, July 7, 1854.

6 Ibid.

7 Ibid.

8 Ibid.

9 Ibid.

10 https://www.loc.gov/resource/rbpe.06100400/?st=text.

11 "No Union with Slaveholders," *The Liberator*, July 7, 1854.

12 Ibid.; Nell Irvin Painter, *Sojourner Truth: A Life, a Symbol* (New York: W. W. Norton, 1996), 137.

13 Von Frank, *The Trials of Anthony Burns*, 280; *The Liberator*, July 7, 1854.

14 Bradford Torrey, ed., *The Writings of Henry David Thoreau*, vol. 6 (Boston: Houghton Mifflin, 1906), 340, 370, 384; Ralph H. Orth and Alfred R. Ferguson, eds., *Journals and Miscellaneous Notebooks of Ralph Waldo Emerson*, vol. 9 (Cambridge, MA: Belknap Press of Harvard University Press, 1971), 445–47; Wendell Glick, ed., *Henry D. Thoreau: Reform Papers* (Princeton, NJ: Princeton University Press, 1973), 103.

15 Brooks Atkinson, ed., *The Essential Writings of Ralph Waldo Emerson* (New York: Modern Library, 2000), 809; Glick, *Henry D. Thoreau*, 91, 94, 96.

16 Glick, *Henry David Thoreau*, 98, 106, 102, 108.

17 Walter Harding, *The Days of Henry Thoreau: A Biography* (New York: Alfred A. Knopf, 1965), 318–19.

18 The second oration—"The Last Days of John Brown"—was read (though not by its author) at a memorial service in North Elba, New York, Brown's home and burial place. Thoreau closed stressing Brown's growing reputation: "He is not confined to North Elba nor to Kansas. He is no longer working in secret. He works in public, and in the clearest light that shines on this land." Glick, *Henry David Thoreau*, 153.

19 Sally G. McMillen, *Lucy Stone: An Unapologetic Life* (New York: Oxford University Press, 2015), 75, 76, 77. Stone's ubiquity extended beyond the 1850s and the antislavery crusade. In a January 1868 address at the second annual banquet of the Washington Newspaper Correspondents' Club, Mark Twain, speaking on "Woman: The Pride of the Professions," identified Stone among a number of history's "noble names." Harriet Elinor Smith and Richard Bucci, eds., *Mark Twain's Letters*, vol. 2 (Berkeley: University of California Press, 1990), 156.

20 "No Union with Slaveholders," *The Liberator*, July 7, 1854.

21 Ibid.

13: *No Roads Home*

1 Dorothy Sterling, *The Making of an Afro-American: Martin Robison Delany, 1812–1885* (Garden City, NY: Doubleday, 1971), 125, 130.

2 Ibid., 81; Frank A. Rollin, *Life and Public Service of Martin R. Delany* (Boston: Lee and Shepard, 1883), 14.

3 Howard H. Bell, "The Negro Emigration Movement, 1849–1854: A Phase of Negro Nationalism," *Phylon Quarterly*, 2nd Qtr., 1959, 132.

4 The American Colonization Society was the commonly used shorthand for the Society for the Colonization of Free People of Color of America.

5 Bell, "The Negro Emigration Movement," 137.

6 Ibid., 135; *African Repository and Colonial Journal*, January 1852, 4–8.

7 Robert S. Levine, ed., *Martin R. Delany: A Documentary Reader* (Chapel Hill: University of North Carolina Press, 2003), 189; Martin Robison Delany, *The Condition, Elevation, Emigration, and Destiny of the Colored People of the United States* (Philadelphia: Privately Printed, 1852), 31, 10.

8 Delany, *The Condition, Elevation, Emigration, and Destiny of the Colored People*, 14, 160, 169.

9 Ibid., 177, 176, 178, 180.

10 Ibid., 188, 181.

11 Levine, *Martin R. Delany*, 219, 232, 224.

12 Ibid., 226.

13 Bell, "The Negro Emigration Movement," 137, 139, 140.

14 *Proceedings of the Colored National Convention, Held in Rochester, July 6th, 7th, and 8th 1853* (Rochester, NY: Printed at the office of *Frederick Douglass's Paper*, 1853), 7, 8, 15.

15 Robert S. Levine and Ivy G. Wilson, eds., *The Works of James M. Whitfield: America and Other Writings by a Nineteenth-Century African American Poet* (Chapel Hill: University of North Carolina Press, 2011), 120–22; M. T. Newsome, ed., *Arguments, Pro and Con, on the Call for a National Emigration Convention, to Be Held in Cleveland, Ohio, August, 1854* (Detroit: George E. Pomeroy, 1854), 140.

16 Levine and Wilson, eds., *Works of James M. Whitfield*, 124.

17 Ibid., 127, 160.

18 *Proceedings of the National Emigration Convention of Colored People; Held at Cleveland, Ohio, on Thursday, Friday and Saturday, the 24th 25th, and 26th of August 1854* (Pittsburgh: A. A. Anderson, 1854), 7, 14.

19 Rollin, *Life and Public Service of Martin R. Delany*, 22; *Proceedings of the National Emigration Convention of Colored People*, 40.

20 *Proceedings of the National Emigration Convention of Colored People*, 40.

21 Ibid., 57, 63.

22 Ibid., 19, 27, 25; Newsome, *Arguments, Pro and Con*, 141; *Proceedings of the National Emigration Convention of Colored People*, 14.

23 Rollin, *Life and Public Service of Martin R. Delany*, 83–84; Martin R. Delany, *Blake; or, The Huts of America: A Corrected Edition*, ed. Jerome McGann (Cambridge, MA: Harvard University Press, 2017), 21; Eric Foner, *The Fiery Trial: Abraham Lincoln and American Slavery* (New York: W. W. Norton, 2010), 257.

14: *Freedom Defined: Thoreau's* Walden

1   Henry D. Thoreau, *Walden*, ed. J. Lyndon Shanley (Princeton, NJ: Princeton University Press, 1971), 366–67; Bradford Torrey, ed., *The Writings of Henry David Thoreau*, vol. 6 (Boston: Houghton Mifflin, 1906), 146–47; Milton Meltzer and Walter Harding, *A Thoreau Profile* (Lincoln, MA: Thoreau Society, 1998), 231.
2   Sandra Harbert Petrulionis, "Slavery and Abolition," in James S. Finley, ed., *Henry David Thoreau in Context* (New York: Cambridge University Press, 2017), 185–87.
3   Bradford Torrey, ed., *The Writings of Henry David Thoreau*, vol. 3 (Boston: Houghton, Mifflin, 1906), 37–38.
4   Moncure Daniel Conway, *Autobiography: Memories and Experiences of Moncure Daniel Conway*, vol. 1 (Boston: Houghton, Mifflin, 1904), 141.
5   Ibid., 140, 141; Brooks Atkinson, ed., *The Essential Writings of Ralph Waldo Emerson* (New York: Modern Library, 2000), 814; Walter Harding, *The Days of Henry Thoreau: A Biography* (New York: Alfred A. Knopf, 1965), 194.
6   Wendell Glick, ed., *Henry David Thoreau: Reform Papers* (Princeton, NJ: Princeton University Press, 1973), 83; Laura Dassow Walls, *Henry David Thoreau: A Life* (Chicago: University of Chicago Press, 2017), 209.
7   Glick, *Henry David Thoreau*, 82, 83.
8   Walls, *Henry David Thoreau*, 213.
9   *The Collected Works of Mahatma Gandhi*, vol. 7 (Delhi: Publications Division, Ministry of Information and Broadcasting, Government of India, 1962), 304; *The Autobiography of Martin Luther King, Jr.*, ed. Clayborne Carson (New York: Warner Books, 1998), 54; *The Complete Works of Count Tolstoy*, vol. 22, ed. and trans. Leo Wiener (Boston: Dana Estes, 1904), 525.
10 Glick, *Henry David Thoreau*, 64, 65, 66, 67.
11 Ibid., 76, 75.
12 Bradford Torrey, ed., *The Writings of Henry David Thoreau*, vol. 1 (Boston: Houghton, Mifflin, 1906), 299.
13 Richard J. Schneider, "Walden," in Joel Myerson, ed., *The Cambridge Companion to Henry David Thoreau* (New York: Cambridge University Press, 1995), 92.
14 J. Hector St. John de Crèvecœur, *Letters from an American Farmer* (New York: Fox, Duffield, 1904), 56.
15 Stanley Cavell, *The Senses of Walden* (Chicago: University of Chicago Press, 1992), 7, 10.
16 Henry S. Salt, *Life of Henry David Thoreau* (London: Richard Bentley & Son, 1890), 66–67.
17 Thoreau, *Walden*, 140.
18 Harding, *The Days of Henry Thoreau*, 182; Walls, *Henry David Thoreau*, 197; Bradford Torrey, ed., *The Writings of Henry David Thoreau*, vol. 9 (Boston: Houghton, Mifflin, 1906), 359; Salt, *Life of Henry David Thoreau*, 72.
19 Walls, *Henry David Thoreau*, 194; Thoreau, *Walden*, 7, 205.
20 Elise Lemire, *Black Walden: Slavery and Its Aftermath in Concord, Massachusetts* (Philadelphia: University of Pennsylvania Press, 2009), 129–35; Thoreau, *Walden*, 264.
21 Thoreau, *Walden*, 257.
22 Lemire, *Black Walden*, 135.
23 Elise C. Lemire, "Repeopling the Woods: Thoreau, Memory, and Concord's Black History," in Kristen Case and K. P. Van Anglen, eds., *Thoreau at Two Hundred:*

Essays and Reassessments (New York: Cambridge University Press, 2016), 64; Thoreau, *Walden*, 257–58.

24 Ibid., 257.
25 Thoreau, *Walden*, 264.
26 Harding, *The Days of Henry Thoreau*, 187; Ralph L. Rusk, ed., *The Letters of Ralph Waldo Emerson*, vol. 3 (New York: Columbia University Press, 1939), 377–78.
27 Robert D. Richardson Jr., *Henry Thoreau: A Life of the Mind* (Berkeley: University of California Press, 1986), 306.
28 Harding, *The Days of Henry Thoreau*, 335, 336.
29 Ibid., 337, 340; Richardson, *Henry Thoreau*, 67.
30 Robert N. Hudspeth, ed., *The Correspondence of Henry D. Thoreau*, vol. 2 (Princeton, NJ: Princeton University Press, 2018), 221, 226, 230. The poet is William Wordsworth; Thoreau is referencing "The World Is Too Much with Us," a sonnet first published in 1807.

15: *Freedom Denied: Fitzhugh's* Sociology for the South

1 Harvey Wish, *George Fitzhugh: Propagandist of the Old South* (Baton Rouge: Louisiana State University Press, 1943), 114; George Fitzhugh, *Sociology for the South; or, The Failure of Free Society* (Richmond: A Morris, 1854), 235.
2 Eugene D. Genovese, *The World the Slaveholders Made: Two Essays in Interpretation* (Hanover, NH: Wesleyan University Press, 1988), 230. Along with Thoreau, there are some passages in Henry James's 1907 travel book, *The American Scene*, that condemn dollar-chasing. Referring to Manhattan's "flaring streets," James wrote, "the blaze of the shops" ministered to "the wants, the gratifications, the aspirations of the 'poor' [which] . . . denoted a new style of poverty." Henry James, *The American Scene* (London: Chapman and Hall, 1907), 135–36.
3 Wish, *George Fitzhugh*, 3; C. Vann Woodward, "George Fitzhugh, Sui Generis," in *George Fitzhugh, Cannibals All!: Or Slaves Without Masters* (Cambridge MA: Belknap Press of Harvard University Press, 1960), xii, xiii; Michael O'Brien, *Conjectures of Order: Intellectual Life and the American South, 1810–1860*, vol. 1 (Chapel Hill: University of North Carolina Press, 2004), 972; Moncure D. Conway, *Addresses and Reprints, 1850–1907* (Boston: Houghton Mifflin, 1909), 112.
4 David Donald, "The Proslavery Argument Reconsidered," *Journal of Southern History*, February 1971, 10; Fitzhugh, *Sociology for the South*, iv.
5 John Immerwahr, "Hume's Revised Racism," *Journal of the History of Ideas*, July–September 1992, 481; Somogy Varga, *Naturalism, Interpretation, and Mental Disorder* (Oxford, UK: Oxford University Press, 2015), 219.
6 William Sumner Jenkins, *Pro-slavery Thought in the Old South* (Chapel Hill: University of North Carolina Press, 1935), 4; George H. Moore, ed., *Notes on the History of Slavery in Massachusetts* (New York: D. Appleton, 1866); Cotton Mather, *Essays to Do Good: Addressed to All Christians, Whether in Public or Private Capacities* (Portsmouth, NH: T. H. Miller and H. Gray, 1824), 57.
7 James Otis, *The Rights of the British Colonies Asserted and Proved* (Boston, 1764), 43; Maurice Jackson, *Let This Voice Be Heard: Anthony Benezet, Father of Atlantic Abolitionism* (Philadelphia: University of Pennsylvania Press, 2009), 127; Merrill D. Peterson, ed., *The Portable Thomas Jefferson* (New York: Penguin Books, 1975), 238.
8 Jenkins, *Pro-slavery Thought in the Old South*, 60; Adam L. Tate, *Conservatism and*

Southern Intellectuals, 1789–1861: Liberty, Tradition, and the Good Society (Columbia: University of Missouri Press, 2005), 91.

9   Daniel Walker Howe, *What Hath God Wrought: The Transformation of America, 1815–1848* (New York: Oxford University Press, 2007), 480; Edward Brown, *Notes on the Origins and Necessity of Slavery* (Charleston, SC: A. E. Miller, 1826), 6; J. W. Randolph, ed., *Early History of the University of Virginia: As Contained in the Letters of Thomas Jefferson and Joseph C. Cabell* (Richmond: C. H. Wynne, 1856), 1.

10 Donald, "Proslavery Argument Reconsidered," 4; Peterson, *The Portable Thomas Jefferson*, 187. For a survey of Jefferson's scientific thought see Keith Thomson's *Jefferson's Shadow: The Story of His Science* (New Haven, CT: Yale University Press, 2012).

11 Jenkins, *Pro-slavery Thought in the Old South*, 248; Samuel George Morton, *Crania Americana: Or, A Comparative View of the Skulls of Various Aboriginal Nations of North and South America* (Philadelphia: J. Dobson, 1839), 88. The commonness of the inferiority argument in America struck an English traveler, who wrote in the 1850s: "There seems . . . to be a fixed notion throughout the whole of the States, whether slave or free, *that the colored is by nature a subordinate race*; and that, in no circumstances, can it be considered equal to the white. . . . This opinion lies at the root of American slavery." E. N. Elliott, ed., *Cotton Is King: And Pro-slavery Arguments* (Augusta, GA: Prichard, Abbott & Loomis, 1860), 169.

12 Fitzhugh, *Sociology for the South*, 7, 11.

13 John J. Grayson, *The Hireling and the Slave* (Charleston, SC: John Russell, 1855), 20, 42, 44, 29.

14 Fitzhugh, *Sociology for the South*, 10.

15 Theodore Roosevelt, *Theodore Roosevelt: An Autobiography* (New York: Macmillan, 1913), 525; Fitzhugh, *Sociology for the South*, 27.

16 Fitzhugh, *Sociology for the South*, v, 226–27, 235. Franklin published *Poor Richard's Almanack* from 1732 to 1758; it enjoyed an enormously successful circulation in the colonies, as many as ten thousand copies a year. Filled with practical items, including weather forecasts, puzzles, and math exercises, it further offered instruction on how to accrue wealth.

17 Fitzhugh, *Sociology for the South*, 246, 253, 233.

18 Ibid., 8, 11, 12.

19 Ibid., 23, 163.

20 Ibid., 83, 86; Edmund Wilson, *Patriotic Gore: Studies in the Literature of the American Civil War* (New York: Oxford University Press, 1962), 342.

21 Thomas E. Schneider, *Lincoln's Defense of Politics: The Public Man and His Opponents in the Crisis over Slavery* (Columbia: University of Missouri Press, 2006), 64; Fitzhugh, *Sociology for the South*, 56.

22 Wish, *George Fitzhugh*, 128–42.

23 Ibid.

24 Emanuel Hertz, ed., *The Hidden Lincoln: From the Letters and Papers of William H. Herndon* (New York: Viking Press, 1938), 96; Fitzhugh, *Sociology for the South*, 222.

16: The Ostend Fiasco

1   Jefferson to Monroe, October 24, 1823, at https://founders.archives.gov/documents/Jefferson/98-01-02-3827; Robert Granville Caldwell, *The López Expeditions to Cuba, 1848–1851* (Princeton, NJ: Princeton University Press, 1915), 15.

2 Caldwell, *The López Expeditions to Cuba*, 43; Amy S. Greenberg, *Manifest Mission and the Antebellum American Empire* (New York: Cambridge University Press, 2005), 183.

3 Tom Chaffin, *Fatal Glory: Narciso López and the First Clandestine U.S. War against Cuba* (Charlottesville: University Press of Virginia, 1996), 69; Caldwell, *The López Expeditions to Cuba*, 50, 48–49.

4 Caldwell, *The López Expeditions to Cuba*, 92; Chaffin, *Fatal Glory*, 215–16; Greenberg, *Manifest Mission*, 269.

5 James M. McPherson, *Battle Cry of Freedom: The Civil War Era* (New York: Oxford University Press, 1988), 106.

6 Ibid.

7 May, *The Southern Dream of a Caribbean Empire*, 46.

8 Ibid., 47, 48.

9 Ibid., 49, 50; "A Letter of Alexander H. Stephens, 1854," *The American Historical Review* (October 1902), 97.

10 May, *The Southern Dream of a Caribbean Empire*, 51.

11 C. Stanley Urban, "The Africanization of Cuba Scare, 1853–1855," *Hispanic American Review* (February 1957), 29–45.

12 David M. Potter, *The Impending Crisis: America before the Civil War, 1848–1861* (New York: Harper & Row, 1976), 187; Gara, *Presidency of Franklin Pierce*, 151.

13 May, *The Southern Dream of a Caribbean Empire*, 54.

14 Richardson, *Compilation of the Messages and Papers of the Presidents*, vol. 6, 2741–42; William R. Manning, ed., *Diplomatic Correspondence of the United States: Inter-American Affairs, 1831–1860*, vol. 11 (Washington, DC: Carnegie Endowment for International Peace, 1939), 171.

15 May, *The Southern Dream of a Caribbean Empire*, 53.

16 Brown, *Agents of Manifest Destiny*, 131–32.

17 Potter, *Impending Crisis*, 184; Manning, ed., *Diplomatic Correspondence of the United States*, vol. 11, 169; John Slidell, "Suspension of the Neutrality Laws," *The Congressional Globe*, May 1, 1854, 1024.

18 Manning, *Diplomatic Correspondence of the United States*, vol. 11, 174.

19 Ibid., 175.

20 Robert E. May, *The Southern Dream of a Caribbean Empire, 1854–1861* (Baton Rouge: Louisiana State University Press, 1973), 59–61; James D. Richardson, *A Compilation of the Messages and Papers of the Presidents*, vol. 7 (New York: Bureau of National Literature, 1897), 2805–06.

21 May, *The Southern Dream of a Caribbean Empire*, 67; Brown, *Agents of Manifest Destiny*, 138–39.

22 Brown, *Agents of Manifest Destiny*, 139, 140.

23 William R. Manning, ed., *Diplomatic Correspondence of the United States: Inter-American Affairs, 1831–1860*, vol. 7 (Washington, DC: Carnegie Endowment for International Peace, 1936), 581–84.

24 Ibid., 582–83.

25 Manning, *Diplomatic Correspondence of the United States*, vol. 11, 826; Potter, *Impending Crisis*, 191-92.

17: *Lincoln Arrives*

1 Roy P. Basler, ed., *The Collected Works of Abraham Lincoln*, vol. 4 (New Brunswick, NJ: Rutgers University Press, 1953), 61; Benjamin P. Thomas, *Abraham Lincoln* (New York: Alfred A. Knopf, 1952), 67.

2 Emily Todd Helm, "Reminiscences and Letters of the Wife of President Lincoln," *McClure's*, September 1898, 477.

3 Ibid., 478.

4 Eric Foner, *The Fiery Trial: Abraham Lincoln and American Slavery* (New York: W. W. Norton, 2010), 52; Abraham Lincoln, *Selected Speeches and Writings* (New York: Library of America, 1992), 65.

5 Lincoln, *Selected Speeches and Writings*, 62–63, 70; Foner, *Fiery Trial*, 53; David Herbert Donald, *Lincoln* (New York: Simon & Schuster, 1995), 131.

6 John G. Nicolay and John Hay, eds., *Abraham Lincoln: Complete Works*, vol. 1 (New York: Century, 1920), 178.

7 Charles Dickens, *American Notes* (London: Chapman and Hall, 1842), 109–10; Don E. Fehrenbacher, *Prelude to Greatness: Lincoln in the 1850s* (Stanford, CA: Stanford University Press, 1962), 5–8.

8 *The Autobiography of Abraham Lincoln* (New York: Francis D. Tandy, 1905), 35; John G. Nicolay and John Hay, *Abraham Lincoln: A History*, vol. 1 (New York: Century, 1890), 370.

9 Robert W. Johannsen, *Stephen A. Douglas* (New York: Oxford University Press, 1973), 453, 454; Nicolay and Hay, *Abraham Lincoln: A History*, 370.

10 Donald, *Lincoln*, 171.

11 Nicolay and Hay, *Abraham Lincoln: A History*, 373–74.

12 Donald, *Lincoln*, 146; William H. Herndon and Jesse William Weik, *Herndon's Lincoln: The True Story of a Great Life: The History and Personal Recollections of Abraham Lincoln*, vol. 3 (Chicago: Belford, Clarke, 1889), 588, 586, 587; *The Uncollected Poetry and Prose of Walt Whitman*, vol. 2, ed. Emory Holloway (Garden City, NY: Doubleday, Page, 1921), 23. Whitman first sighted Lincoln in February 1861 as the president-elect stopped briefly in New York during a twelve-day journey from Springfield to the nation's capital. Sitting atop an omnibus on Broadway, Whitman watched as Lincoln passed by with a small party, making for the Astor House. He later wrote: "I had, I say, a capital view of it all, and especially of Mr. Lincoln, his look and gait—his perfect composure and coolness—his unusual and uncouth height, his dress of complete black, stovepipe hat push'd back on the head, dark-brown complexion, seam'd and wrinkled yet canny-looking face, black, bushy head of hair, disproportionately long neck, and his hands held behind him as he stood observing the people." Justin Kaplan, *Walt Whitman: A Life* (New York: Simon & Schuster, 1980), 260.

13 Roy P. Basler, ed., *Collected Works of Abraham Lincoln*, vol. 2 (New Brunswick, NJ: Rutgers University Press, 1953), 226, 228.

14 Ibid., 230; Thomas, *Abraham Lincoln*, 147.

15 Lewis E. Lehrman, *Lincoln at Peoria: The Turning Point* (Mechanicsburg, PA: Stackpole Books, 2008), 52; Donald, *Lincoln*, 178.

16 *Abraham Lincoln's Speech at Peoria, Illinois* (Peoria: Logan, 1952), 7; Lehrman, *Lincoln at Peoria*, 53, 54; Nicolay and Hay, *Abraham Lincoln: Complete Works*, vol. 1, 180.

17 William H. Herndon, *Herndon's Lincoln: The True Story of a Great Life*, vol. 2 (Springfield, IL: Herndon's Lincoln, 1921), 405.

18   Nicolay and Hay, *Abraham Lincoln: Complete Works*, vol. 1, 181–82.

19   Ibid., 183, 186, 187.

20   Ibid., 192, 197.

21   Ibid., 195.

22   Ibid., 203.

23   Lincoln, *Selected Speeches and Writings*, 364.

24   Horace White, *The Life of Lyman Trumbull* (Boston: Houghton Mifflin, 1913), 39; Donald, *Lincoln*, 178.

25   Lincoln, *Selected Speeches and Writings*, 152. The "beau ideal" line comes from Lincoln's August 21, 1858, debate with Douglas in Ottawa, Illinois, in which Lincoln further described Clay as "the man for whom I fought all my humble life." Ibid. Clay helped to affect a series of sectional compromises in 1820 (bringing Missouri into the Union as a slave state and Maine as a free state), 1833 (reducing the federal tariff and thus appeasing South Carolina's nullifiers), and 1850 (responding to the question of slavery's place in the western territories).

26   Fehrenbacher, *Prelude to Greatness*, 33; Basler, *Collected Works of Abraham Lincoln*, vol. 2, 288. In November 1856, following the defeat of Republican presidential candidate John C. Frémont, Mary Todd Lincoln wrote to her half sister Emily Todd Helm: "Although Mr. Lincoln is, or was, a Frémont man, you must not include him with so many of those who belong to that party, an abolitionist. In principle his is far from it. All he desires is that slavery shall not be extended, let it remain where it is." Helm, "Reminiscences and Letters of the Wife of President Lincoln," 479.

27   Thomas, *Abraham Lincoln*, 152; Basler, *Collected Works of Abraham Lincoln*, vol. 2, 288.

28   Donald, *Lincoln*, 90–91; Ronald C. White Jr., *Lincoln: A Biography* (New York: Random House, 2009), 114.

29   Will Carlton, H. W. Clendenin, and William Jayne, "Dr. William Jayne," *Journal of the Illinois State Historical Society*, April 1916, 93; Donald, *Lincoln*, 91, 92; Jean H. Baker, *Mary Todd Lincoln: A Biography* (New York: W. W. Norton, 1987), 95–96.

30   White, *The Life of Lyman Trumbull*, 42.

31   Basler, *Collected Works of Abraham Lincoln*, vol. 2, 306.

18: *Electoral Upheaval*

1   Lincoln (twice), Ulysses Grant (twice), Rutherford B. Hayes, and James Garfield were the Republicans who claimed Electoral College majorities between 1860 and 1880.

2   Eric Foner, *Free Soil, Free Labor, Free Men: The Ideology of the Republican Party before the Civil War* (New York: Oxford University Press, 1970), 115.

3   Edward L. Pierce, ed., *Memoir and Letters of Charles Sumner*, vol. 3 (London: Sampson Low, Marston, 1893), 395; David Donald, *Charles Sumner and the Coming of the Civil War* (New York: Alfred A. Knopf, 1960), 267.

4   Donald, *Charles Sumner and the Coming of the Civil War*, 267. When Whiggery died, Eliot became a Republican and served five terms in the House of Representatives.

5   Tyler Anbinder, *Nativism and Slavery: The Northern Know Nothings and the Politics of the 1850s* (New York: Oxford University Press, 1992), 3.

6   On the Hungry Forties in Europe, see Richard J. Evans, *The Pursuit of Power: Europe 1815–1914* (New York: Penguin Books, 2016), 113–32; Anbinder, *Nativism and Slavery*, 8.

7   Ray Allen Billington, *The Protestant Crusade: A Study of the Origins of American Nativism* (New York: Rinehart, 1938), 2–8.

8   "Transcript: JFK's Speech on His Religion," https://www.npr.org/templates/story /story.php?storyId=16920600.

9   Historian Michael Holt writes: "Although the secrecy and fluctuating membership of the [Know-Nothings] makes exact calculation of its total strength impossible, contemporary estimates ranged from 800,000 to 1,500,000 nationally." Michael Holt, *The Political Crisis of the 1850s* (New York: John Wiley & Sons, 1978), 157; Elizabeth R. Varon, *Disunion!: The Coming of the American Civil War, 1789–1859* (Chapel Hill: University of North Carolina Press, 2008), 257; David J. Endres, "Know-Nothings, Nationhood, and the Nuncio: Reassessing the Visit of Archbishop Bedini," *U.S. Catholic Historian*, Fall 2003, 1.

10 Foner, *Free Soil, Free Labor, Free Men*, 196.

11 William E. Gienapp, *The Origins of the Republican Party, 1852–1856* (New York: Oxford University Press, 1987), 138, 181, 99.

12 Allen C. Guelzo, *Lincoln and Douglas: The Debates That Defined America* (New York: Simon & Schuster, 2008), 19; David M. Potter, *The Impending Crisis: America before the Civil War, 1846–1861* (New York: Harper & Row, 1976), 239; https://history .house.gov/Institution/Party-Divisions/Party-Divisions/.

13 Donald, *Lincoln*, 178.

14 Foner, *Free Soil, Free Labor, Free Men*, 231; Gienapp, *Origins of the Republican Party*, 136–37; Allan Nevins, *Ordeal of the Union: A House Dividing, 1852–1857*, vol. 2 (New York: Charles Scribner's Sons, 1947), 342.

15 Sewell, *Ballots for Freedom*, 272.

16 Nevins, *Ordeal of the Union*, 344; Johannsen, *Stephen A. Douglas*, 461; Foner, *Free Soil, Free Labor, Free Men*, 238.

17 Nevins, *Ordeal of the Union*, 345.

18 Gara, *Presidency of Franklin Pierce*, 99; Gienapp, *The Origins of the Republican Party*, 161; John Niven, ed., *The Salmon P. Chase Papers*, vol. 2 (Kent, OH: Kent State University Press, 1994), 393.

19 Varon, *Disunion!*, 261; Foner, *Free Soil, Free Labor, Free Men*, 239; Potter, *Impending Crisis*, 256.

20 Potter, *Impending Crisis*, 252.

21 Anbinder, *Nativism and Slavery*, 50; General Roeliff Brinkerhoff, *Recollections of a Lifetime* (Cincinnati: Robert Clarke, 1900), 91–92.

22 Gara, *Presidency of Franklin Pierce*, 99. On Whiggery's passing see chapters 22–26 in Michael Holt's *The Rise and Fall of the American Whig Party: Jacksonian Politics and the Onset of the Civil War* (New York: Oxford University Press, 1999).

23 On the role of antislavery Democrats in the emerging Republican coalition, see the Conclusion of Jonathan H. Earle's *Jacksonian Antislavery and the Politics of Free Soil, 1824–1854* (Chapel Hill: University of North Carolina Press, 2004).

19: *Endings and Beginnings*

1   Allan McLane Hamilton, *The Intimate Life of Alexander Hamilton* (New York: Charles Scribner's Sons, 1910), 98, 96. Tench Tilghman, a secretary to Washington, reported of Eliza at the age of eighteen: "I called at Genl Schulyer's seat to pay my compliments to the Genl his Lady & Daughter. I found none of them at home but

Miss Betsy Schuyler, the General's 2^{d} daughter. . . . I was prepossessed in fav^{r} of this young lady the moment I saw her. A Brunette with the most good natured lively dark eyes that I ever saw, which threw a beam of good temper and benevolence over her whole Countenance." *Memoir of Lieut. Col. Tench Tilghman* (Albany: J. Munsell, 1876), 90.

2 Ron Chernow, *Alexander Hamilton* (New York: Penguin Books, 2004), 725; Jenny L. Presnell, "Elizabeth Schuyler Hamilton," *American National Biography*, http://exhibitions.nysm.nysed.gov//albany/bios/s/elschuyleranb.html.

3 Hamilton, *Intimate Life of Alexander Hamilton*, 220–21.

4 Ibid., 110,115; *Washington's Farewell Address* (New York: D. Appleton, 1861), 13, 21, 9.

5 Ibid., 115; Chernow, *Alexander Hamilton*, 2; Wendy Kail, "Tudor Place: America's Story Lives Here," 1, http://www.tudorplace.org/wp-content/uploads/2019/02/HStreet-NW-11.28.2018-jw.pdf.

6 "Reminiscences of Mrs. Alexander Hamilton," *The Atlantic Monthly*, vol. 78 (Boston: Houghton, Mifflin, 1896), 282–83.

7 Milo Milton Quaife, ed., *The Diary of James K. Polk*, vol. 1 (Chicago: A. C. McClurg, 1910), 226. Over the succeeding decades interest in the Hamilton clan remained strong among presidents. In 1906 Theodore Roosevelt promised a correspondent an invitation that would allow "you [to] meet one of Hamilton's many descendants, Miss Louisa Lee Schuyler of whom I am very fond; she is a dear—almost an elderly lady now; whenever she comes to dine at the White House she wears a brooch with Hamilton's hair." Elting E. Morison, ed., *The Letters of Theodore Roosevelt*, vol. 5 (Cambridge, MA: Harvard University Press, 1952), 352.

8 Anne Hollingsworth Wharton, *Social Life in the Early Republic* (Philadelphia and London: J. B. Lippincott, 1902), 306; Allen C. Clark, *Life and Letters of Dolley Madison*, (Washington, DC: Press of W. F. Roberts, 1914), 429.

9 J. Courtney Sullivan, "After the Broadway Show, a Trip to Hamilton's Grave," *New York Times*, March 5, 2016, https://www.nytimes.com/2016/03/06/fashion/hamilton-fans-grave-broadway.html.

10 Edwin G. Burrows, *The Finest Building in America: The New York Crystal Palace, 1853–1858* (New York: Oxford University Press, 2018), 6.

11 Ibid., 7, 18, 19; https://www.bl.uk/victorian-britain/articles/the-great-exhibition.

12 Edwin G. Burrows and Mike Wallace, *Gotham: A History of New York City to 1898* (New York: Oxford University Press, 1999), 669; George J. Lankevich, *New York City: A Short History* (New York: New York University Press, 2002), 93.

13 Burrows, *The Finest Building in America*, 68; Lee E. Gay, *From Ascending Rooms to Express Elevators: A History of the Passenger Elevator in the 19th Century* (Mobile, AL: Elevator World, 2002), 24–26; "The New York 'Eiffel' Tower of 1853," *Engineering News and American Railway Journal*, vol. 22 July–December 1889 (New York: Engineering News, 1889), 482.

14 William C. Richards, *A Day in the New York Crystal Palace, and How to Make the Most of It* (New York: G. P. Putnam, 1853), 27.

15 Burrows, *The Finest Building in America*, 144; Justin Kaplan, *Walt Whitman: A Life* (New York: Simon & Schuster, 1980), 180; Richards, *A Day in the New York Crystal Palace*, 111–68.

16 Albert Bigelow Paine, *Mark Twain: A Biography*, vol. 1 (New York: Harper & Brothers, 1912), 94–95.

17 Kaplan, *Walt Whitman*, 183; Walt Whitman, *Leaves of Grass* (New York: Barnes & Noble, 1992), 168.

18 Bradford Torrey, ed., *The Writings of Henry David Thoreau: Journal*, vol. 7 (Boston: Houghton Mifflin, 1906), 76; Burrows, *The Finest Building in America*, 144, 147.

19 Burrows, *The Finest Building in America*, 147, 155; P. T. Barnum, *Life of P. T. Barnum* (Buffalo: Courier, 1888), 140.

20 Burrows, *The Finest Building in America*, 32.

20: The Ship of Zion

1 Sarah H. Bradford, *Scenes in the Life of Harriet Tubman* (Auburn, NY: W. J. Moses, 1869), 5, 65.

2 Ibid., 7.

3 Kate Clifford Larson, *Bound for the Promised Land: Harriet Tubman, Portrait of an American Hero* (New York: Ballantine Books, 2004), 24.

4 Ibid., 32, 10; Catherine Clinton, *Harriet Tubman: The Road to Freedom* (New York: Little, Brown, 2004), 12.

5 Bradford, *Scenes in the Life of Harriet Tubman*, 73; Clinton, *Harriet Tubman*, 13.

6 Larson, *Bound for the Promised Land*, 56.

7 Emma Telford, "Harriet: The Modern Moses of Heroism and Visions," as dictated to Emma Telford, 1911, Cayuga County Historical Society, Auburn, New York, as quoted in Clinton, *Harriet Tubman*, 22; Bradford, *Scenes in the Life of Harriet Tubman*, 74.

8 Clinton, *Harriet Tubman*, 24.

9 https://www.census.gov/history/www/through_the_decades/index_of_questions/1850_1.html; Larson, *Bound for the Promised Land*, 85.

10 Sarah H. Bradford, *Harriet: The Moses of Her People* (New York: Geo. R. Lockwood & Son, 1886), 24; Larson, *Bound for the Promised Land*, 73.

11 Bradford, *Harriet: The Moses of Her People*, 29.

12 Larson, *Bound for the Promised Land*, 78.

13 Bradford, *Scenes in the Life of Harriet Tubman*, 16.

14 Ibid., 19.

15 Clinton, *Harriet Tubman*, 81; Larson, *Bound for the Promised Land*, 90.

16 Clinton, *Harriet Tubman*, 83; Milton C. Sernett, *Harriet Tubman: Myth, Memory, and History* (Durham, NC: Duke University Press, 2007), 357.

17 Bradford, *Harriet: The Moses of Her People*, 39; Bradford, *Scenes in the Life of Harriet Tubman*, 79.

18 Bradford, *Scenes in the Life of Harriet Tubman*, 20; Bradford, *Harriet: The Moses of Her People*, 90.

19 Larson, *Bound for the Promised Land*, 102; R. C. Smedley, *History of the Underground Railroad: In Chester and the Neighboring Counties of Pennsylvania* (Lancaster, PA: John A. Hiestand, 1883), 251.

20 Bradford, *Scenes in the Life of Harriet Tubman*, 57.

21 Ibid., 60; Larson, *Bound for the Promised Land*, 339n40; William Still, *The Underground Rail Road* (Philadelphia: Porter & Coates, 1872), 296.

22 Sernett, *Harriet Tubman*, 323.

23 Larson, *Bound for the Promised Land*, 203–24.

Coda: *Meanings*

1 John Niven, ed., *The Salmon P. Chase Papers*, vol. 2 (Kent, OH: Kent State University Press, 1994), 391; Robert W. Johannsen, ed., *The Letters of Stephen A. Douglas* (Urbana: University of Illinois Press, 1961), 331.

2 Larry Gara, *The Presidency of Franklin Pierce* (Lawrence: University Press of Kansas, 1991), 161.

3 Ibid., 168; Jean H. Baker, *James Buchanan* (New York: Times Books, 2004), 102.

4 David M. Potter, *The Impending Crisis: America before the Civil War, 1848–1861* (New York: Harper & Row, 1976), 316.

5 In contrast, the Democratic Party's various opponents—Federalists, National Republicans, and Whigs—almost entirely failed over the sixty-year period of their shared existences (1796–1856) to elect consecutive presidential candidates. This happened only once, when George Washington, retiring after a second term, gave way to fellow Federalist John Adams in 1796.

6 Kenneth M. Stampp, ed., *The Causes of the Civil War* (New York: Simon & Schuster, 1991), 25–26.

7 Henry Adams, ed., *Documents Relating to New England Federalism: 1800 to 1815* (Boston: Little, Brown, 1877), 352.

8 Charles Francis Adams, ed., *Memoirs of John Quincy Adams*, vol. 5 (Philadelphia: J. B. Lippincott, 1875), 4; "Remarks of the Hon. Daniel Webster, of Massachusetts on the Three Million Bill" (Washington, DC: J. & G. S. Gideon, 1847), 4.

9 Frederick Douglass, *Autobiographies*, ed. Henry Louis Gates (New York: Library of America, 1994), 742; Roy P. Basler, ed., *Collected Works of Abraham Lincoln*, vol. 2 (New Brunswick, NJ: Rutgers University Press, 1953), 268; Lord Charnwood, *Abraham Lincoln* (New York: Henry Holt, 1917), 117.

10 R. W. Emerson, *An Address Delivered in the Court-House in Concord, Massachusetts* (Boston: James Munroe, 1844), 34.

11 David Donald, *Charles Sumner and the Coming of the Civil War* (New York: Alfred A. Knopf, 1960), 285, 294.

12 Ronald Takaki, "The Movement to Reopen the African Slave Trade in South Carolina," *South Carolina Historical Magazine*, January 1965, 39.

13 Wendell Glick, ed., *Henry David Thoreau: Reform Papers* (Princeton, NJ: Princeton University Press, 1973), 112.

14 Joan D. Hedrick, *Harriet Beecher Stowe: A Life* (New York: Oxford University Press, 1994), 306; Charles Edward Stowe and Lyman Beecher Stowe, *Harriet Beecher Stowe: The Story of Her Life* (Boston: Houghton Mifflin, 1911), 203.

15 Mark Twain, *Merry Tales* (New York: Charles L. Webster, 1892), 18, 21, 24.

16 David W. Blight, *Frederick Douglass: Prophet of Freedom* (New York: Simon & Schuster, 2018), 592–94; Frederick Douglass, *The Life and Times of Frederick Douglass* (Hartford, CT: Park Publishing Co. 1881), 477, 534.

17 Philip Shriver Klein, *President James Buchanan: A Biography* (University Park: Penn State University Press, 1962), 423.

18 Allen C. Guelzo, *Lincoln and Douglas: The Debates That Defined America* (New York: Simon & Schuster, 2008), 308; Johannsen, *Stephen A. Douglas*, 871–72.

19 Basler, *Collected Works of Abraham Lincoln*, vol. 2, 382–83.

20 https://www.nps.gov/anti/learn/photosmultimedia/tour-stop-4.htm.

Illustration Credits

18. Library of Congress, Prints and Photographs Division
19. Library of Congress, Prints and Photographs Division
20. National Portrait Gallery, Smithsonian Institution
21. Library of Congress, Geography and Map Division
22. Library of Congress, Prints and Photographs Division

Index

Page references in italics indicate illustrations.